IMI
Information Centre

Corporate Entrepreneurship

Corporate Entrepreneurship

Building the Entrepreneurial Organization

Second Edition

Paul Burns

palgrave
macmillan

First edition 2005
Second edition 2008

Published by
PALGRAVE MACMILLAN
Houndmills, Basingstoke, Hampshire RG21 2XS and
175 Fifth Avenue, New York, N.Y. 10010
Companies and representatives throughout the world

PALGRAVE MACMILLAN is the global academic imprint of the Palgrave
Macmillan division of St. Martin's Press, LLC and of Palgrave Macmillan Ltd.
Macmillan is a registered trademark in the United States, United Kingdom
and other countries. Palgrave is a registered trademark in the European
Union and other countries.

ISBN-13: 978–0–230–54263–1
ISBN-10: 0–230–54263–8

This book is printed on paper suitable for recycling and made from
fully managed and sustained forest sources. Logging, pulping and
manufacturing processes are expected to conform to the environmental
regulatons of the country of origin.

A catalogue record for this book is available from the British Library.

A catalog record for this book is available from the Library of Congress.

10   9   8   7   6   5   4   3   2   1
17   16   15   14   13   12   11   10   09   08

Printed and bound in China

To my wife, Jean,
who brings me happiness every day
and the boys: Oliver, Alex and Ben,
who remind me not to take it for granted

Contents Overview

Preface to the Second Edition   xviii
Guided Tour of the Book and Website   xxvi

PART 1 THE ENTREPRENEURIAL DNA
  1 The Entrepreneurial Revolution   3
  2 Entrepreneur Super-hero   22
  3 Entrepreneurial Spiderman   42
  4 Entrepreneurial Architecture   64

PART 2 LEADING AND MANAGING THE ENTREPRENEURIAL
          ORGANIZATION
  5 Entrepreneurial Leadership   85
  6 Creating the Entrepreneurial Culture   110
  7 Building the Entrepreneurial Structure   136
  8 Intrapreneurship and Corporate Venturing   158
  9 Managing the Entrepreneurial Organization   174

PART 3 STRATEGIES FOR THE ENTREPRENEURIAL ORGANIZATION
  10 Entrepreneurial Strategies   201
  11 Life Cycle and Portfolio Strategies   232
  12 Developing Strategies for Growth   252

PART 4 CREATIVITY AND INNOVATION
  13 Encouraging Entrepreneurial Innovation   281
  14 Encouraging Creativity   315
  15 Encouraging Marketing and Product Innovation   343
  The Profile of an Entrepreneurial Organization   363

Corporate Entrepreneurship Exercise   362
Learning Resources   372
Subject Index   379
Author Index   383

Contents

Case Insights: The Businesses/Personalities   xv

Quotes: The Personalities   xvi

List of Figures   xvii

List of Tables   xix

Preface to the Second Edition   xx

Guided Tour of the Book and Website   xxviii

PART 1   THE ENTREPRENEURIAL DNA

1   The Entrepreneurial Revolution   3
The revolution   4
Factors behind the revolution   5
Entrepreneurs   7
Large companies   10
Corporate entrepreneurship   12
Entrepreneurial management   14
Summary   17

2   Entrepreneur Super-hero   22
Personal character traits   23
The survival instinct   25
The growth instinct   28
Antecedent influences   34
Implications for entrepreneurial management   36
Summary   37
  Measuring Entrepreneurial Personality: The General Enterprise Tendency Test   39

3   Entrepreneurial Spiderman   42
Decision making   43
Strategy development   44
Relationships and networks   47
  Case with questions: Stephen Waring and Green Thumb   49
The entrepreneurial spider's web   50
The changing entrepreneur   52
Implications for corporate entrepreneurship   57
  Case with questions: Richard Branson and Virgin   59
Summary   61

4   Entrepreneurial Architecture   **64**
    Dominant logic   65
    Entrepreneurial intensity   65
    Architecture   67
    The learning organization   69
    Creating an entrepreneurial architecture   73
    Environment   75
       Case with questions: 3M   76
    Summary   79

PART 2 LEADING AND MANAGING THE ENTREPRENEURIAL
        ORGANIZATION

5   Entrepreneurial Leadership   **85**
    Management and leadership   86
    Entrepreneurial leadership   87
    Vision and mission   90
    Values   93
    Leadership style   95
    Building the management team   100
    Entrepreneurial leadership skills   103
    Summary   104
       Leadership Style Questionnaire   106

6   Creating an Entrepreneurial Culture   **110**
    Culture   111
    Constructing culture   112
    Dimensions of culture   115
    Mapping the dimensions of entrepreneurial culture   120
    International influences on culture   121
    Culture in the entrepreneurial organization   123
    Culture and leadership style   127
    Reconstructing culture   128
       Case with questions: HFL Ltd   130
    Summary   132

7   Building an Entrepreneurial Structure   **136**
    Size   137
    Traditional large firm structures   139
    Environmental change and task complexity   141
    Organic structures   142
       Case with questions: Virgin   144
    Networks and other new forms of organizing   146
       Case with questions: Dell   150
    Strategic alliances   151
    Summary   153

8 **Intrapreneurship and Corporate Venturing**   **158**
Intrapreneurship   159
Encouraging intrapreneurship   161
Venture teams and new venture divisions   163
Organizing new venture developments   165
Corporate venturing   167
   Case with questions: Pret A Manger   169
   Case with questions: Nokia   170
Summary   171

9 **Managing the Entrepreneurial Organization**   **174**
Barriers to corporate entrepreneurship   175
Change   178
Managing change   179
Freedom and control   183
Balance   184
Management and structure   187
Managing risk   189
   Case with questions: M&S   191
Summary   195

PART 3 STRATEGIES FOR THE ENTREPRENEURIAL ORGANIZATION

10 **Entrepreneurial Strategies**   **201**
The strategic process   202
Strategic planning   203
Strategic analysis   204
Strategy misfit   208
Strategic vision   209
Generic marketing strategies   211
   Case with questions: Stellios Haji-Ioannou and easyJet 213
Value drivers   217
Successful entrepreneurial strategies   220
Differentiation   221
   Case with questions: Anita and Gordon Roddick and Body Shop 224
Summary   227
Financial analysis checklist   231

11 **Life Cycle and Portfolio Strategies**   **232**
Life cycles   233
Product portfolios   236
   Case with questions: Heineken   237
Portfolio strategies   238
Managing the product life cycle   239
   Case with questions: Barbie®: Mattel Corporation 241
Financial implications of the product portfolio   242
Implications for management   244
Corporate and industry life cycles   246
   Case with questions: Cadbury   247
Summary   250

12 Developing Strategies for Growth 252
Opportunities for growth 253
Market penetration 254
Market development 256
    Case with questions: Royal Bank of Scotland 259
Product/service development 261
Diversification 262
Mergers and acquisitions 264
    Case with questions: Ineos Group 267
Sustainability and corporate social responsibility 268
    Case with questions: M&S 270
Sustaining growth 272
    Case with questions: BAE Systems 273
Summary 274

PART 4 ENCOURAGING CREATIVITY AND INNOVATION

13 Encouraging Entrepreneurial Innovation 281
Innovation and invention 282
Innovation and entrepreneurship 286
Creativity and entrepreneurship 288
Innovation and risk 290
The process of innovation and risk 293
    Case with question: Glaxo Smith Kline 295
Innovation and size 296
Discontinuous innovation 298
    Case with questions: Lastminute 302
Strategic innovation 303
Successful innovation 306
    Case with questions: Dangdang 308
Summary 309
    Innovative thinker test 311

14 Encouraging Creativity 315
Understanding creativity 316
The creative process 318
Blocks to individual creativity 322
Techniques for generating new ideas 322
Finding opportunity 326
Blocks to organizational creativity 331
Encouraging organizational creativity 332
    Case with questions: Hallmark 333
Developing national creativity 334
    Case with questions: Nintendo and the Wii 338
Summary 339
    Creativity test 340

15	**Encouraging Marketing and Product Innovation**	**343**
	Relationship marketing	344
	Value-driven marketing	345
	Marketing innovation	346
	Product innovation	349
	Case with questions: LG Electronics	353
	Structures to support product development	354
	Case with questions: LEGO®	355
	Summary	357

The Profile of an Entrepreneurial Organization **360**
Case with questions: 3M 361

Corporate Entrepreneurship Exercise 362
Learning Resources 372
   Selected case studies 372
   Selected further reading 374
   Selected journals 376
   Selected journal articles 376
   Selected websites 377

Subject Index 379
Author Index 383

Case Insights:
The Businesses/Personalities

Apple iPod	328	McDonald's	285
Babbage, Charles	283	Microsoft/Bill Gates	17
Bayer	167	Monorail Corporation	318
BBC	153	MYCFO/Jim Clark	59
Body Shop/Anita and		NCsoft	328
Gordon Roddick	11, 91, 94	Netscape/Marc Andreesen/	
Boeing	160	Jim Clark	69, 321
Carphone Warehouse/		Nike+iPod Sports Kit	351
Charles Dunstone	219	Oxford Asymmetry	
Daewoo	348	International/Stephen Davies	331
DangDang/Peggy Yu	153	PayPal	264
Dell Computers/Michael Dell	8, 91, 95	Quanta Computer/Barry Lam	217
Dyson, James	298	RadioScape/Peter Florence	289
easyJet/Stelios Haji Ioannou	56, 91	Reliance Group/	
eBay	264	Dhirubhai Ambani	266
Enron	187	Silicon Graphics/Jim Clark	69
Friendsreunited.co.uk	328	Smartwater Europe/Phil Cleary	330
Great Ormond Street Hospital		SouFun	153
for Children	320	Standard Chartered/	
Healtheon/Jim Clark	59	Mervyn Davies	255
IBM/Louis Gerstner	129, 153	Sun Microsystems	153
Intel	153	Swatch	209
J D Wetherspoon/Tim Martin	177	Telemedicine Clinic/	
John Lewis Partnership/		David Bäckström	305
John Spedan Lewis	111	Wilkin & Sons	114
Jordans	224	World Wide Web	321
KongZhong	153	Xeikon	167
Levi	352	Xerox	91, 165
Liberty Life/Trevor Baylis/		Xerox Technology Ventures	165
Christopher Staines	287	Yahoo	328

➡ at the end of a case or quote indicates that it continues.

● at the end of a case or quote indicates that it does not continue.

Quotes:
The Personalities

Adizes, I.   86

Arculus, David   87

Barrell, Geoff   100

Bennis, Warren   15

Branson, Richard   8, 29, 33, 45, 102

Cadbury, Sir Adrian   222

Collin, Derrick   32, 92

Collins, James   13

Darling, David   45

Dell, Michael   7, 27, 29, 43, 47, 54, 70, 73, 92, 100, 113, 139, 143, 175, 191, 219, 220, 222, 322, 327

Deshpande, Gururaj   28, 92, 126

Drucker, Peter   10

Elnaugh, Rachel   316

Elvidge, Jonathan   26, 27, 28, 34, 48, 96, 327

Farmer, Tom   31, 102

Hamel, Gary   6

Hisrich, Robert   10

Hoberman, Brent   26

Ingram, Chris   31

Jordan, Bill

Kelly, Neil   30

Lane Fox, Martha   32

Mathewson, Sir George

Muirhead, Charles   25

Naisbitt, John   4

Nanus, Burt   15

Notley, Anne   27

Peters, Michael   10

Porras, Jerry   13

Roddick, Anita   216

Rose, Stuart   90

Saddler, Terry   33

Shah, Eddy   25

Speakman, David   43

Thompson, Diane   14

Thompson, Richard   30

Timmons Jeffrey   5

Worcester, Bob   32

Yip, Wing   33

➡ at the end of a case or quote indicates that it continues.

● at the end of a case or quote indicates that it does not continue.

List of Figures

1.1	Entrepreneurs can come from small and large firms	7
1.2	Disciplines influencing entrepreneurial management	16
2.1	Influences on owner-managers and entrepreneurs	23
2.2	Character traits of entrepreneurs	24
2.3	Entrepreneurial culture	36
3.1	The strategy formulation cycle	46
3.2A	The entrepreneurial spider's web	50
3.2B	The entrepreneurial spider's web grows	51
3.3	Greiner growth model	53
3.4	The cultural web of an entrepreneurial organization	58
4.1	The entrepreneurial grid	66
4.2	The wheel of learning	71
4.3	The wheel of learning and our mental models	72
4.4	Influences on organizational architecture	74
5.1	Values, vision, strategy and tactics	94
5.2	Leadership style	96
5.3	Leader and task	97
5.4	Leader and group	97
6.1	Influences on culture	112
6.2	Hofstede's dimensions of culture	116
6.3	The entrepreneurial culture mapped onto Hofstede's dimensions	118
6.4	Entrepreneurial culture summarized by Hofstede's dimensions	121
6.5	Success and failure in the entrepreneurial organization	124
6.6	The cultural web hierarchy in an entrepreneurial organization	126
7.1A	The hierarchical structure	140
7.1B	The matrix structure	141
7.2	Organization structure based upon task complexity and environment	142
7.3	An organic structure	143
8.1	Dealing with new venture developments	165
9.1	Work effectiveness through change	178
9.2	The change cube	182
9.3	Freedom vs control	185
9.4	Organizational structure and management style	188
9.5	Organization structure, management style and the concept of cycling	189
9.6	Risk classification	189
10.1	The strategic planning process	203
10.2	Generic marketing strategies	212
10.3	Economies of scale and economies of small scale	213
10.4	The value chain	218
10.5	Dimensions of differentiation	222

10.6	The customer loyalty ladder	223
11.1	The product/service life cycle	234
11.2	The Boston matrix	237
11.3	The Boston matrix – strategy implications	238
11.4	Boston matrix for a hypothetical company	239
11.5	Product life cycle management	240
11.6	Cash flow implications of the Boston matrix	243
11.7	ABC analysis contribution chart	244
11.8	Industry life cycles and acquisitions and mergers	247
12.1	The product/market matrix	254
12.2	Porter's five forces	257
12.3	Entry and exit barriers, profitability and risk	258
13.1	The spectrum of product/service and process development	283
13.2	Frequency and degree of innovation	284
13.3	Invention, opportunity and entrepreneurship	288
13.4	Invention and entrepreneurship	289
13.5	Growth and risk	291
13.6	Risk and the process of innovation	294
13.7	Risk and innovation process time	294
13.8	Innovation networks	300
13.9	From information to knowledge	301
13.10	A specimen risk portfolio	305
14.1	Dimensions of creative (lateral) vs logical (vertical) thinking	317
14.2	The creative process	319
14.3	Sources of awareness and ideas	319
14.4	Why? Why? diagram	329
14.5	Technology, talent, tolerance and economic growth	335
14.6	The creativity matrix	337
15.1	From transactions, brands and relationships to value	345
15.2	Entrepreneurial vs non-entrepreneurial planning pathways	346
15.3	The entrepreneurial marketing planning process	347
15.4	The product development process	350
15.5	Parallel development of new products	352

List of Tables

1.1	The antecedence of modern entrepreneurship	9
1.2	Traditional vs entrepreneurial management	15
3.1	Relationship vs transactional marketing	48
3.2	Churchill and Lewis growth model	54
3.3	Burns growth model	55
3.4	Management characteristics of the entrepreneurial organization	58
3.5	Structural characteristics of the entrepreneurial organization	59
4.1	The learning organization: major concepts	73
5.1	Entrepreneurial leadership skills	104
6.1	Entrepreneurial vs administrative cultures	124
6.2	Cultures that enhance vs cultures that inhibit learning	125
8.1	Factors encouraging intrapreneurship	162
10.1	Tools of the SWOT analysis	206
10.2	The influence of life cycle on organizational culture	208
11.1	New products: average time to take-off in Europe	235
13.1	Two approaches to problem solving	285
13.2	Characteristics of innovation and marketing strategy	306
15.1	Relationship vs transactional marketing	344

Preface to the Second Edition

Purpose of the book

Over the last twenty years the business world has fallen in love with the idea of entrepreneurship. Entrepreneurs have evolved to become super-heroes who valiantly and single-handedly battle to make the most of business opportunities, pulling together resources they do not own, finding willing suppliers and eager customers and, just sometimes, against all the odds, winning out to become millionaires. It is the stuff of dreams. Entrepreneurs are held up as role models. They are said to embody ephemeral qualities that we ought to emulate – freedom of spirit, creativity, vision, zeal. Above all, they have the courage and self-belief to turn their dreams into reality. Is it any wonder that we envy them?

But most of the literature on entrepreneurs focuses on start-ups. Some go further and look at growth and development, noting in passing how many entrepreneurs cannot make the transition to managing a larger firm. And often, in passing, it is assumed that large organization equals bureaucratic organization. But does it always have to be so? Can the DNA of the entrepreneur be transplanted into a larger organization? Can you go about systematically developing corporate entrepreneurship?

The opportunities created by a successful transplant are enormous. Large organizations have more resources than small ones – more cash to invest, more people to make things happen, more organizational knowledge to harness. It is easier for them to invest in and develop new technologies. It is easier for them to market on a global basis. And today's market is indeed global, bringing together competitors from around the world. So developing sustainable competitive advantage is vital. And what better to base this on than corporate entrepreneurship.

Corporate entrepreneurship is about the ability of a large organization – not an individual – to make the most of commercial opportunities, to innovate, to do things differently. It is about developing an organizational and strategic capability not just to manage change, but to embrace it, create it and shape it – quickly. It is about developing an organizational and strategic willingness to take measured risks – sometimes failing, but learning by those mistakes – and putting in place the processes and procedures to monitor those risks and take early corrective action if required. It is about bringing back personality into management, so that relationships are important in shaping what employees do, rather than rule books. It is about getting rid of the grey suits. It is about creating a balance so that some control is given back to employees whilst they are still held to account for their actions. It is about creating 'space' to be creative and innovative.

In *Entrepreneurship and Small Business* I observed that the major challenge facing business schools today is how to encourage and develop the entrepreneurial skills of students. That challenge still remains. The problem is that most of their students will start their working lives in larger organizations – where entrepreneurship might be positively discouraged. But the danger is that if the business schools are successful they will breed a generation of disgruntled managers, unhappy at work, who yearn to go out and set up their own business, and often reinventing the wheel as they do so. 98% of start-ups never grow to any size. What if these managers could change the large organizations they are in, from within, so that they become more entrepreneurial? Think of the opportunities that could be pursued. Think of the wealth that could be generated – for the individual, for other stakeholders and for society as a whole. And think of the fun they would have in doing it!

Changes to the second edition

The popular features of the first edition remain in the second: the blend of theoretical and practical; the informal style that makes the book so accessible; the quotes from entrepreneurs reinforcing the theory; and the case insights linking theory with practice. These have been updated. The most noticeable change to the second edition is the inclusion of 25 longer cases with questions covering the manufacturing, service and retail sectors and companies based in the UK, USA, Denmark, Holland, China, Japan and Korea.

There is a greater focus on organizational structures, particularly networking, strategic alliances and other new forms of organizing and, in particular how they can facilitate knowledge transfer and innovation. At the same time more space has been devoted to intrapreneurship and corporate venturing. These are reinforced by cases on *Dell*, *Virgin*, *Pret A Manger* and *Nokia*.

The section on creativity and innovation has been generally strengthened by the inclusion of issues like national creativity, where Richard Florida's interesting research is now addressed, and how companies can prepare themselves for the increasingly frequent phenomena of discontinuous innovation. The section is reinforced by new cases on *LEGO®*, *LG Electronics*, *Nintendo and the Wii*, *GlaxoSmithKline* and *Hallmark* and the more familiar dot.com cases on *Lastminute* and *Dangdang*.

The strategy section has been strengthened by the coverage of sustainability and corporate social responsibility – probably the most important issue facing any business today – and how it might be integrated into the overall business strategy. This is reinforced by a new two-part case on *M&S* – the store with probably the most ambitious plans in this area in the UK. Other cases in this section include familiar ones like *easyJet* and *Body Shop* along with less familiar ones like *Barbie®*, *Heineken*, *Cadbury*, *Royal Bank of Scotland*, *Ineos Group* and *BAE Systems*.

The section on culture has been extended to include international influences and reinforced by a new case on *HFL Ltd*. Finally there are cases on entrepreneurial companies and their personalities: the well known *Richard Branson and Virgin*, the less well known *Stephen Waring and Green Thumb*, and the classic case on corporate entrepreneurship, *3M*.

Finally, the book now has an accompanying website with resources for students and staff, including two electronic tests with automatic analysis:

- The *General Enterprise Tendency (GET) Test* (produced by Durham University Business School), to enable students to better understand whether they have the characteristics required to be entrepreneurial.
- The *Corporate Entrepreneurship (CE) Audit*, that provides a check on the potential for an organization to be entrepreneurial.

Courses using this book

This book is intended for third year undergraduate or postgraduate students. Because the focus is on larger, existing organizations rather than start-ups, it is ideal for a part-time MBA course on entrepreneurship because many of the exercises and assignments can be applied directly to the larger firms in which the students are likely to be working.

Organization of the book

Part 1 sets the scene by trying to isolate the characteristics of entrepreneurship as we see them in small, fast growing organizations – based upon the characteristics of the individual entrepreneur – and then distilling what this means for the larger organization. It sets out the case for why large organizations need to become more entrepreneurial and charts the rapid growth of the literature associated with corporate entrepreneurship. Chapter 1 introduces the concept of corporate entrepreneurship – why it is important and how it has evolved. It examines the global commercial revolution that has happened over the last two decades – and make no mistake, it has been a revolution. It defines the newly emerging discipline and charts its antecedence. Chapters 2 and 3 unpick the DNA of entrepreneurs – the personal character traits that contribute to their strengths as well as their weaknesses and their approach to managing an organization and doing business. They catalogue the implications and challenges for corporate entrepreneurship. Chapter 4 sets out how the DNA can be replicated – through an entrepreneurial architecture that itself creates sustainable competitive advantage. It links this with the literature on learning organizations and considers the importance of context. It outlines the tools for creating the architecture – leadership, strategy, structure and culture.

Part 2 has been expanded. Chapter 5 goes into more detail about how this DNA can be created through appropriate leadership and management – dealing with important issues like vision and values, leadership styles and team building. Chapter 6 addresses the importance of organizational culture and how it can be influenced. Chapter 7 looks at structures that both encourage and discourage entrepreneurship as well as the issue of size. It looks at networks, strategic alliances and other new forms of organizing that can be more effective in today's rapidly changing environment. Chapter 8 looks at organizational mechanisms that encourage entrepreneurship like intrapreneurship, venture teams, new venture divisions and corporate venturing.

Part 3 considers strategy – how it is developed in an entrepreneurial organization as well as which strategies are most likely to lead to successful growth. Chapter 10 looks at successful entrepreneurial strategies, focusing particularly on creating sustainable competitive advantage through differentiation. Chapter 11 looks at issues around the product portfolio and in particular how products at the end of their life cycle can still benefit from innovation. Chapter 12 looks at how growth can be achieved systematically. It looks at mergers and acquisitions and sustainability and corporate social responsibility.

Part 4 deals with that quality which most distinguishes entrepreneurs – their ability to be creative and innovate in terms of product/service or marketing and how this might be encouraged within an organization. Chapter 13 looks at general innovation, how to manage it and the risks associated with it. It also looks at the problem of discontinuous innovation and how an organization might prepare for it. Chapter 14 looks at individual, organizational and national creativity and how it might be encouraged. Finally Chapter 15 looks specifically at market and product innovation and the organizational structures that might facilitate it.

Learning styles and the learning resources

Daniel Kim (1993) suggests *effective* learning can be considered to be a revolving wheel (Figure A). During half the cycle, you test and experiment with concepts and observe what happens through concrete experience – learning 'know-how'. In the second half of the cycle, you reflect on the observations and form concepts or theories – learning 'know-why'. This is often called 'double-loop learning' – the best sort of

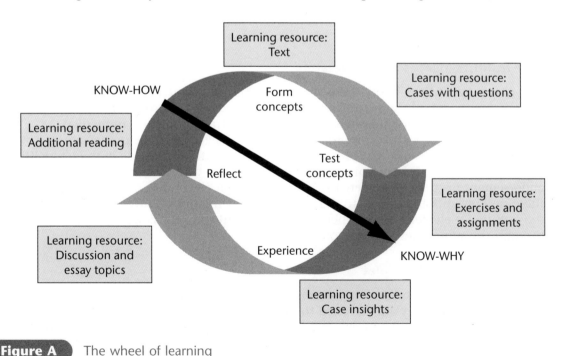

Figure A   The wheel of learning

learning which links knowing how with knowing why, linking theory with practice. So effective learning involves forming concepts, testing concepts, experience and reflection. Traditionally education has focused too much on the second half of the cycle – forming concepts or theories and reflection – and it is difficult to break away from this in a textbook which, inevitably, focuses on the concepts and theories. However, I have tried to do so by including a number of learning resources. Each learning resource is designed to influence a particular learning style. Taken together, they should complete the wheel of learning.

Cases with questions

Embedded in the chapters are 25 real company cases with questions, designed to make students think about and apply the concepts being discussed in that chapter. The book's website (www.palgrave.com/business/burns) also provides printable versions of the cases for classroom use. These cases have web references so that company information can be updated (except for one, where the website is in Chinese). This provides the basis for the testing stage of the wheel of learning. Recommended longer, more complex cases are given in the Learning Resources at the end of the book.

Exercises and assignments

For use in the testing and experimenting phase of the cycle there are exercises and assignments, which additionally involve doing something, in the main further research. This research is often desk-based – including visits to websites – but some of the most popular assignments, in my experience, involve students going out to do things – such as interviewing entrepreneurs. This is very much the 'testing concepts' part of the wheel of learning.

Case insights, quotes and summaries

Spread throughout the book, there are some 100 case insights and quotes from entrepreneurs around the world. There are numerous quotes from Michael Dell and Richard Branson – individuals who have made the transition from individual entrepreneur to corporate entrepreneur. The case insights and the quotes are designed to illustrate and reinforce the theoretical points being made in the text with practical examples and opinions from the real world – there is nothing like an endorsement from an entrepreneur. The summary at the end of each chapter links these case insights and quotes to the main points being made in that chapter. This is the experience element of the wheel of learning, linked to the concepts and theories through the summaries and case questions.

Discussion and essay topics

Each chapter has topics for group discussion or essay writing. These can be used as a basis for tutorials. They are designed to make students think about the text material and develop their critical and reflective understanding of it and what it means in the real world. The summary and discussion topics help students discriminate between main and supporting points and provide mechanisms for self-teaching.

The discussion and essay topics also form the reflective element of the wheel of learning, forcing students to think through the theories and concepts, often linking them to the real world.

There are also three web-based tests that allow students to assess the extent to which they are:

- Entrepreneurial (Chapter 2);
- Innovative (Chapter 13);
- Creative (Chapter 14).

In my experience students love these tests. Coupled with the writing of an evaluative report about their personal qualities, they can form the basis of part of the student assessment.

Other learning resources in the book

At the end of the book there selected international case studies that are linked to the themes in various chapters. Some of the cases have related videos or DVDs. All these can be obtained from the European Case Clearing House. These are particularly valuable for postgraduate teaching. Use of these case studies forces students to test concepts, and reflect on them in the face of the real-world experience they provide. The shorter cases are more suitable for undergraduate teaching.

Each chapter has full journal and book references. There are also selected further textbooks, organized by topic, and selected journals at the end of the book. Finally there are selected websites where further learning resources can be accessed.

Visiting speakers

Courses on entrepreneurship are greatly enriched by visiting speakers, particularly the entrepreneurs themselves. As well as entrepreneurs who have succeeded in growing their own business, 'big company' managers can be insightful, particularly on topics like turnaround situations, managing change and encouraging innovation. They can tell students what it is really like trying to make organizations more entrepreneurial. My experience is that these talks are normally the highlight of the course. No matter how good the teacher there is no substitute for the real thing – somebody who did it.

Corporate entrepreneurship exercise

At the end of the book there is a four-part exercise, designed to help assess the entrepreneurial orientation of an organization and the opportunities it faces. It comprises:

1. A mapping of the frequency (volume) and scale (quality) of innovation within the organization to arrive at an assessment of the extent of innovative activity currently taking place in the organization.
2. A review of the strategies the organization is currently employing to achieve its growth objectives and the risks that it faces.
3. A Corporate Entrepreneurship (CE) Audit. This provides a check on the potential for the organization to be entrepreneurial, as well as the appropriateness of this orientation in terms of the environment.

A web-based version of the CE Audit tool, with automatic mapping, can be found on the website accompanying this book (www.palgrave.com/business/burns). This exercise is a vital part of the wheel of learning. It forces students to integrate all four aspects of learning and helps ensure that they not only know 'why' but also 'how'. Coupled with the writing of an evaluative report about the organization, this can form the basis of part of the student assessment.

Undertaking all learning activities in this book should indeed ensure that the student can 'build an entrepreneurial organization', both in theory and in practice.

Website (www.palgrave.com/business/burns)

The website accompanying this book contains additional resources. The student site has:

- Printable versions of the Cases with questions;
- A web-based version of the General Enterprise Tendency (GET) Test, together with automatic analysis, so that students can better understand whether they have the characteristics required to be entrepreneurial;
- A web-based version of the Corporate Entrepreneurship (CE) Audit, with automatic mapping, so that students can assess the entrepreneurial orientation of an organization and the opportunities it faces;
- Any updates or revisions.

The lecturer site contains:

- A PowerPoint presentation to support each chapter
- Notes to the case studies
- Specimen assessment strategy

Learning outcomes

Each chapter has clear learning outcomes that identify the key concepts to be covered. These assume that students will undertake the essays and discussion topics as well as assignments and exercises, at the end of each chapter.

On completing the course based on this book a student should be able to:

1. Evaluate the entrepreneurial orientation of an organization and the opportunities it faces.
2. Analyze how any deficiencies might be remedied and explain how they might be addressed.
3. Describe the nature of entrepreneurship in individuals – character traits and approaches to business and management – and be able to evaluate their own entrepreneurial qualities.
4. Describe the process of creativity and innovation, being able to evaluate their own creative and innovative aptitude, and explain how creativity and innovation might be encouraged within an organization.

5. Explain what is required to become a leader of an entrepreneurial organization and how this can be achieved in a larger organization.
6. Analyze and evaluate leadership styles.
7. Describe how strategies are developed in an entrepreneurial organization and explain which strategies are most likely to lead to success.
8. Analyze, evaluate and decide upon strategic options.
9. Explain which structures facilitate corporate entrepreneurship and which inhibit it.
10. Describe the culture that encourages corporate entrepreneurship and explain how it might be achieved.

Key and cognitive skills for the course

Having completed a course in corporate entrepreneurship using this book, with the seminar discussion topics, exercises and activities designed around it, a student should have developed a number of important skills:

- Information interpretation, critical analysis and evaluation skills.
- Data analysis and interpretation skills.
- Problem identification and solving skills.
- ICT skills, in particular the use of the internet.
- Independent and/or team working skills.
- Writing and presentation skills.

Students should also have developed a range of applied business and management skills in a holistic way that can be applied to help a developing or existing organization become more entrepreneurial.

Acknowledgements

Every effort has been made to trace all the copyright holders, but if any have been inadvertently overlooked the publishers will be pleased to make the necessary arrangements at the first opportunity.

I would particularly like to thank Durham University Business school for permission to reproduce a web-based version of their GET test on the website accompanying this book.

I would also like to thank my editor, Ann Edmondson, for her diligence and hard work on this and my other books

Reference

Kim, D.H. (1993) 'The Link between Individual and Organizational Learning', *Sloan Management Review*, Fall.

Guided Tour of the Book ...

Cases with questions encourage students to apply theory to real-world situations.

The embedded sample page (top right) reads:

Case with questions

Stephen Waring and Green Thumb

The motivation to set up your own business can come from deep inside and wait a long time to find the best opportunity. The process is not linear or necessarily sequential – and many might say luck is involved. Stephen Waring's entrepreneurial instinct kicked in at the age of 14 when he started framing old prints and selling them at local fetes around his home town in North Wales in his spare time. Stephen's father was the sales director for a loft insulation firm and by the age of 16 he was helping canvass potential customers by knocking on doors. He was good at selling, and so when he left school at 17 he set up his own loft insulation firm – it came naturally. He was so successful he even persuaded his older brother to come and help him. So when his brother married an American girl in 1985, Stephen went to the USA for the wedding. There he met her uncle who owned a lawn-treatment company. He also found out that 24% of homes in the USA hired someone to treat their lawns in some way.

Despite sceptical parents, Stephen researched the idea. First he set out to find competitors by looking through the Yellow Pages telephone directories, but he could not find anybody offering the same service in the UK. The question was whether nobody else had thought about this idea or whether there was no demand for this sort of service. Stephen could not believe that a service that sold to millions of people in the USA would not sell in the UK so he decided to persevere. Next he set out to find the best mix of fertilizer ingredients for the UK. He experimented on his parents' lawn, turning it orange and black in the process. Having perfected a suitable mix, Stephen next spent £64 on printing 1000 leaflets and hand delivered them around housing estates near his home. Then he went around doing what he did best – knocking on doors and selling. In this way he secured 70 customers.

In this way Green Thumb was born. Stephen quickly developed a routine of visiting customers four or five times a year to treat their lawns, like in the USA. The treatment worked and word-of-mouth attracted more customers, so Stephen brought in his younger brother to help him. By 1995, Green Thumb had several thousand regular customers and that was when the next stage in the business's development came about. A customer asked him to sell him a Green Thumb franchise. In 1996 Stephen started selling franchises around the UK. By 2005 there were some 113 franchises servicing over seven million customers, each spending about £26 per year on lawn treatment. Franchisees had sales of £25 million a year, giving the company royalties of £5 million. Green Thumb is growing at 5% per year.

'When people ask me if I ever imagined that my business would be as successful as it has turned out to be, I have to say yes. And we are still embryonic in our growth ... The challenge was developing an industry from scratch as opposed to jumping on the bandwagon of somebody else who was already doing it ... It helps to have a strong belief in your abilities and not to feel insecure.'
Sunday Times, 2 October 2005

Up-to-date information on Green Thumb can be found on the website: www.greenthumb.co.uk

Questions
1. In what ways did Stephen minimize his start-up and growth costs?
2. How did he use relationships?
3. How much of Stephen's success was down to luck?
4. Would Stephen have succeeded in any business?

Case insights and **quotes** illustrate theoretical points with practical examples and opinions from the real world.

The embedded sample page (bottom) reads:

15
Encouraging Marketing and Product Innovation

Contents
- Relationship marketing
- Value-driven marketing
- Marketing innovation
- Product innovation
- Structures to support product development
- Summary

LEARNING OUTCOMES

By the end of this chapter you should be able to:

- Explain the difference between transactional and relationship marketing;
- Describe what is involved in relationship selling;
- Explain what is meant by value-driven marketing and how this can be used very effectively by an entrepreneurial organization;
- Explain how to go about the process of marketing innovation;
- Explain the entrepreneurial marketing planning process;
- Explain how to go about the process of new product development;
- Describe the structures that might support this process and have a basis for deciding which might be most appropriate;
- Analyze how organizations innovate successfully.

'I am often asked what it is to be an entrepreneur and there is no simple answer. It is clear that successful entrepreneurs are vital for a healthy, vibrant and competitive economy. If you look around you, most of the largest companies have their foundations in one or two individuals who have the determination to turn a vision into reality.'
Richard Branson
from Anderson, 1995

creates opportunities that they can exploit. Sometimes they initiate the change themselves – they innovate in some way and do things differently. At other times they exploit change created by the external environment. Often in doing so they destroy the established order and complacency of existing social and economic systems. How entrepreneurs manage and deal with change is central to their character and essential if they are to be successful. Most 'ordinary' people find change threatening. Entrepreneurs welcome it because it creates opportunities that can be exploited and often create it through innovation.

Another key feature of entrepreneurs is their willingness to accept risk and uncertainty. In part this is simply the consequence of their eagerness to exploit change. However, the scale of uncertainty they are willing to accept is altogether different from that of other managers. This high degree of

Case insight

Born in 1965, **Michael Dell** is the ninth richest man in the world with a fortune in excess of £12.5 billion. Michael started **Dell Computers** in 1984 with just £620. Since then the company has grown at five times the industry average growth rate to become one of the biggest manufacturers and marketers of PCs in the world. Its share price has increased 36,000 per cent in the last decade. Today Michael is CEO of a company that is worth over $18 billion and employs some 37,000 people, globally.

'We built the company around a systematic process: give customers the high-quality computers they want at a competitive price as quickly as possible, backed by great service.'

Michael Dell's entrepreneurial career started early. At the age of 12 he made £1200 by selling his stamp collection. At the age of 14 he devised a marketing scheme to sell newspapers which earned him over £11,000. From the age of 15 his interest in calculators and then computers started to grow. He purchased his first computer – an Apple II – in 1980 and immediately took it apart to see how it was built. Within a couple of years he had started buying microchips and other bits of computer hardware in order to build systems because he realised that he could buy, say, a disk drive for £500 which would sell in the shops for £1800. In 1983 he began a pre-med degree at the University of Texas but continued his lucrative business selling upgraded PCs and add-on components out of his dormitory room.

Michael Dell started life as an entrepreneur, but to grow a successful international organisation of this size in such a short time demonstrates that he has become a truly excellent and exceptional entrepreneurial manager.

unless otherwise indicated, all quotes by Michael Dell are taken from his book, Direct from Dell: Strategies that Revolutionized an Industry, 1999

Learning outcomes identify the key concepts to be covered within the chapter and the key knowledge and skills that students will obtain by reading it.

Summaries link the in-chapter case insights and quotes to the main points discussed in the chapter.

Exercises and assignments involve students in additional research activities in order to develop their knowledge and skills much further.

Essays and discussion topics encourage students to critically reflect on the material within the text and to link theory to real-world scenarios. They can be used as a basis for tutorials.

---

250 ○ Strategies for the Entrepreneurial Organization

Summary

Products and services face a predictable life cycle that has implications for marketing strategy at different phases. Most firms, like **Heineken** and **Cadbury Schweppes**, have a range of products and services at different stages of their life cycle. These can be represented in a Boston matrix – a loose conceptual framework that helps clarify the complexity of the portfolio. The two axes of the matrix represent market attractiveness and market strength. Products at different points in the matrix have different strategic imperatives and different marketing strategies.

You can manage the product life cycle through product modification, expansion and extension. By using these strategies, the **Barbie** doll has been around for over 40 years.

The Boston matrix has cash-flow implications; problem children use cash, stars are cash-neutral, generating but also using large amounts, and cash cows generate cash. Only when the portfolio is balanced will cash flow be stable. However, cash flow is not the same as profitability. The ABC analysis allows you to analyse product in terms of sales and contribution – those with high levels of both are very attractive (class A products). But equally it can be used to adjust other elements of the marketing mix, such as price, so as to maximize sales.

Problem children are best managed by entrepreneurs – or entrepreneurial firms – cash cows by accountants – or administrative firms. Where a business has a balanced portfolio of product, the challenge is to find a form of organization that allows both to flourish. There are many different approaches to this.

Companies and industries also have life cycles. Companies do not last forever and they must plan for their own replacement. Similarly industries grow, mature and decline, and by the maturity phase a company should have become a dominant player in the market – perhaps through mergers, acquisitions and alliances – so that it can maximize its returns.

Cadbury Schweppes have been past masters of this strategy which, together with expansion into emergent markets where their mature products were new, has yielded them good financial results. However, by 2007 realizing that they were failing to dominate the drinks market, they have decided to focus on confectionery.

Essays and discussion topics

1. Some products – basic necessities such as food and water – do not have a life cycle. Discuss.
2. How useful are the labels of 'innovators', 'early adopters', late adopters' and 'laggards' to customers at different stages of the life cycle?
3. In practical terms it is impossible to find out where a product is at in its life cycle. Discuss.
4. What is the relationship between marketing mix and the product life cycle?
5. How useful is the Boston matrix?
6. How would you go about creating a scale for each axis of the Boston matrix that reflects a range of factors? Give a practical example.
7. In what circumstances might you not want to 'shoot a dog'?
8. Give some examples of product expansions and extensions.
9. Cash flow is not the same as profit. Discuss.
10. Contribution is not the same as profit. Discuss.
11. Can a problem child be profitable? Why?
12. Is a star always likely to a 'class A' product? Explain.

---

228 ○ Strategies for the Entrepreneurial Organization

imperatives emerge from the analysis of life cycles and product portfolios.. However, as **Michael Dell** underlines, these strategies must essentially add value for the customer in a way that competitors find difficult to replicate. **Carphone Warehouse** added value by offering independent personal advice on the purchase of mobile phones. But can this be copied?

The key theme that comes out from theorists and empirical research in strategy formulation is that strategy should emphasize something that makes the firm as *unique* as possible and delivers as much *value* to the customer as possible today and, more importantly, tomorrow. As **Michael Dell** emphasizes, it is important to differentiate your product/market offering. He believes building a business *solely* on cost or price will not lead to sustainable advantage.

Research tells us that the strategy with the best chance of generating the highest profits is to differentiate with the aim of dominating that market and do this effectively and quickly, and continue to innovate based on your differential advantage.

Whilst the entrepreneurial architecture itself is a key differentiating factor that gives competitive advantage, other more tangible aspects include a focus on quality, innovation, use of different channels of distribution and so on. However, unless patented or copyrighted, these can often be copied. Aesthetics and emotions generated by the product or service are more difficult to copy.

As **Adrian Cadbury** emphasizes, branding helps differentiation and promotes customer loyalty. In a highly competitive market, the specialist cereals producer, **Jordans**, is trying to do just this.

Essays and discussion topics

1. Which comes first, strategy or action?
2. What are the differences between the 'Positional' and 'Process' Schools of strategy?
3. What is the 'Entrepreneurial School' of strategy?
4. 'Entrepreneurs are incapable of developing strategy.' Discuss.
5. What exactly is strategising?
6. How would you go about undertaking a SWOT analysis on an established small firm?
7. How useful is a strategic tool-kit?
8. What is a core competency? How can it be identified?
9. 'If you thought knowledge was expensive you should try ignorance.' Discuss.
10. You cannot determine profit in a small firm because there are too many ways for the entrepreneur to manipulate it. Any form of financial analysis will therefore not work. Discuss.
11. How might you go about determining the profitability of a small firm so that financial analysis can be undertaken?
12. 'Entrepreneurial strategy is simple. Find out what others are doing and do the opposite.' Discuss.
13. Was Swatch really innovative?
14. Can you really develop strategic vision?
15. We can only guess what the future might hold, so there is no point in trying to predict it. Discuss.
16. How do you think music will be sold in the future? How can firms make a profit?
17. What did Porter actually say about generic marketing strategies? Is it really 'a glimpse of the blindingly obvious'?

Entrepreneurial Strategies ○ 229

18. Porter wants you to select cost leadership, differentiation or focus, Hamel and Prahalad want you to focus on core competencies and Treacy and Wiersema want you to select operational excellence, product leadership or customer intimacy. All these strategies are just fad and fancy. Nobody really knows how to generate competitive advantage. Discuss.
19. Value chains are an elegant concept but cannot be operationalized. Discuss.
20. How can you differentiate a product or service and ensure that competitors do not copy it?
21. How important is the brand? Can it be valued?
22. What constitutes the 'ideal' brand?
23. How can you safeguard your competitive advantage?
24. Is there really such a thing as strategy or is it something that academics dreamed up?

Exercises and assignments

1. Select a successful entrepreneur, like Michael Dell or Richard Branson, and research his or her background. Show how the business developed and analyse why has he or she been so successful.
2. Select a well-known product that is now in the mature phase of its life cycle and chart how the marketing strategy has changed over that life cycle.
3. For your University, College or Department:
   – Undertake a SLEPT analysis. Based upon this, try scenario planning on one major trend that you identify.
   – Undertake a SWOT analysis.
   – Undertake a comprehensive SWOT analysis on your course.

   Draw up a list of Action Points that follow from your analysis.
4. For a selected company, undertake a SLEPT analysis. Based upon this, try scenario planning on one major trend that you identify.
5. Consider the case of Jordans, undertaking more research as necessary. Where does its competitive advantage lie and how can it secure it?
6. Consider the case of Dell Computers, undertaking more research as necessary. Where does its competitive advantage lie and how can it secure it?

References

3i European Enterprise Centre (1991) *High Performance SMEs: A Two Country Study*, Report 1, September.
3i European Enterprise Centre (1993) *Britain's Superleague Companies*, Report 9, August.
Bagozzi, R. P. (ed.) (1994) *Principles of Market Research*, Oxford: Blackwell.
Birley, S. and Westhead, P. (1990) 'Growth and Performance Contrasts between Types of Small Firms', *Strategic Management Journal*, vol. II.
Biro, R. (1999) *The Effective Use of Market Research*, London: Kogan Page.
Boston Consulting Group (1968) *Perspectives on Experience*, Boston, Mass: Boston Consulting Group.
Boston Consulting Group (1972) *Perspectives on Experience*, Boston, Mass: Boston Consulting Group.
Burns, P. (1994) *Winners and Losers in the 1990s*, 3i European Enterprise Centre, Report 12, April.
Burns, P. (2007) *Entrepreneurship and Small Business*, 2nd edn, Basingstoke: Palgrave Macmillan.
Buzzell, R. D. and Gale, B. T. (1987) *The PIMS Principles – Linking Strategy to Performance*, New York: Free Press.
Buzzell, R. D. Heany, D. F. and Schoeffer, S. (1974) 'Impact of Strategic Planning on Profit Performance', *Harvard Business Review*, 52/2.

Additional resources . . .

Additional exercises and learning resources – cases, further readings, journals and websites help learning

Corporate Entrepreneurship Exercise

This exercise is to help assess the entrepreneurial orientation of an organization and the opportunities it faces. It has three parts.

1. A mapping of the frequency (volume) and scale (quality) of innovation within the organization to arrive at an assessment of the extent of innovative activity currently taking place in the organization. This is a subjective assessment but it does get you to think about the degree and nature of the innovation.
2. A review of the strategies the organization is currently employing to achieve its growth objectives and the risks that it faces. This uses the Ansoff matrix as its base.
3. Completion of a Corporate Entrepreneurship Audit (the CE Audit tool online at www.edtocomplete.com). This provides a check on the potential for the organization to be entrepreneurial, as well as the appropriateness of this orientation in terms of the environment.

The CE Audit looks at entrepreneurial characteristics in the four dimensions of architecture outlined in the book: leadership, culture, structure and strategy. However, these must be placed in the context of the environment within which the organization operates. Only if the environment is suitable will an entrepreneurial response be appropriate. These factors are mapped onto a CE Audit Grid that measure both entrepreneurial potential and the appropriateness of corporate entrepreneurship for the competitive environment facing the organization. The environmental footprint, ideally, should map onto the entrepreneurial potential, otherwise there is a mismatch. This diagnostic tool can be applied to any level of organization – the organization overall,

3 Corporate entrepreneurship audit

The web-based version is available on www.edtocomplete.com.

Circle the number that best describes your opinion about the characteristic, as it applies to the organization being audited.

Leadership		Low	Average		High
1	Clarity of vision	0 1 2 3 4
2	Definition of values	0 1 2 3 4
3	Grasp of reality	0 1 2 3 4
4	Effectiveness of communication	0 1 2 3 4
5	Willingness to 'walk the talk'	0 1 2 3 4
6	Level of trust generated	0 1 2 3 4
7	Care and respect shown for individuals	0 1 2 3 4
8	Consistency of behaviour	0 1 2 3 4
9	Ability to influence individuals and outcomes informally	0 1 2 3 4
10	Ability to think strategically	0 1 2 3 4
11	Ability to motivate	0 1 2 3 4
12	Ability to manage change	0 1 2 3 4
13	Ability to resolve or reconcile conflict	0 1 2 3 4
14	Ability to build confidence in the organization	0 1 2 3 4
15	Appropriateness of leadership style	0 1 2 3 4

Total score

Justification for scores

Learning Resources

Selected case studies

Chapters 2–3: The individuals
Richard Branson/Herb Kelleher – Leaders Extraordinaire.
Case 803-005–1. Teaching note: 803-005–8.
Written by V. Sarvai, under the direction of A. Mukund, ICFA Center for Management Research (ICMR), Hyderabad, India.

Michael Dell – The Man Behind Dell.
Case 402-015–1. Teaching note: 402-015–8.
Written by K Subhadra, under the direction of A. Mukund, ICFA Center for Management Research (ICMR), Hyderabad, India.

Larry Ellison: A Samurai Warrior in Silicon Valley.
Case 402-038–1. No teaching note.
Written by M. Kets de Vries and E. Florent-Treacy, INSEAD, Fontainebleau, France.

Chapters 4–8: Management, leadership, culture and structure
The 3M Company: (A) Building the Entrepreneurial Corporation (1902–1950).
Case 802-001–1. No teaching note.

The 3M Company: (B) Defining Strategy (1950–1990).
Case 802-002–1. No teaching note.

The 3M Company: (C) Dynamic Balance for the 90s.
Case 802-003–1. No teaching note.
Written by M. Ackenhusen, N. Churchill and D. Muzyka, INSEAD, Fontainebleau, France.

3M's Organisational Culture.
Case 403-041–1. Teaching note: 403-041–8.
Written by S. Dutta, K. Subhadra, ICFAI Center for Management Research (ICMR), Hyderabad, India.

3M Optical Systems: Managing Corporate Entrepreneurship.
Case: 9–395–017. Video: 9–395–513. Teaching note: 9–395–017.
Written by C.A. Bartlett and A. Mohammed, Harvard Business School, Boston, USA.

British Petroleum: Transformational Leadership in a Transnational Organisation.
Case: 497-013–1. Interviews: 497-013–4. Video: 497-013–3. Teaching note: 497-013–8.
Written by M. Kets de Vries, INSEAD, Fontainebleau, France.

Branson's Virgin: The Coming of Age of a Counter-Cultural Enterprise.
Case: 495-014–1. Supplement: 495-014–4. Interview: 495-014–5. Video: 495-015–3. Teaching note: 495-014–8.
Written by M. Kets de Vries, INSEAD, Fontainebleau, France.

The House that Branson Built: Virgin's Entry into the New Millenium.
Case 400-002–1. Teaching note: 400-002–8.
Written by M. Kets de Vries, INSEAD, Fontainebleau, France.

372

. . . Website

Additional teaching and learning resources on www.palgrave.com/business/burns including the General Enterprise Tendency Test

Part 1

The Entrepreneurial DNA

1   The Entrepreneurial Revolution

2   Entrepreneur Super-hero

3   Entrepreneur Spiderman

4   Entrepreneurial Architecture

1

The Entrepreneurial Revolution

Contents

- The revolution
- Factors behind the revolution
- Entrepreneurs
- Large companies
- Corporate entrepreneurship
- Entrepreneurial management
- Summary

LEARNING OUTCOMES

By the end of this chapter you should be able to:

- Explain why entrepreneurs and small firms are so important to the economies of modern countries and the particular importance of the small number of rapidly growing firms;

- Describe the influences that have contributed to their increasing importance;

- Explain the problems large firms have in coping with the new, rapidly changing environment;

- Describe what an entrepreneur is, what they do and why they are so important;

- Explain what is meant by the term 'corporate entrepreneurship' and the schools of literature that have delineated the emerging discipline;

- Explain what is meant by the term 'entrepreneurial management' and how it is different from traditional management;

- List the range of different disciplines that contribute to this emerging, new discipline.

The revolution

We are in the middle of a business revolution. In the last twenty years entrepreneurs establishing new firms have done more to create wealth than firms at any time before them – ever! Ninety-five per cent of the wealth of the USA has been created since 1980. When Michael Dell set up Dell Computer Corporation in 1984 IBM still dominated the computer market with over 70% of the market and more cash on its balance sheet than the sales of all the rest of the industry put together. Since then its share price has plummeted and its workforce has been slashed as it struggled to stay alive, whilst Dell has prospered to become one of the biggest manufacturers and marketers of PCs in the world. By the start of the twenty-first century, one in every three households in the USA – 37% or 35 million households – had at least one person who was involved in a primary role in a new or emerging business (*Economic News*, 1997). Small firms, virtually no matter how they are defined, now make up at least 95% of enterprises in the European Community.

'In the years ahead all big companies will find it increasingly difficult to compete with – and in general will perform more poorly than – smaller, speedier, more innovative companies. The mindset that in a huge global economy the multinationals dominate world business couldn't have been more wrong. The bigger and more open the world economy becomes, the more small and middle-sized companies will dominate. In one of the major turnarounds of my lifetime, we have moved from economies of scale to "diseconomies of scale"; from bigger is better to bigger is inefficient, costly, wastefully bureaucratic, inflexible, and, now, disastrous. And the paradox is that that has occurred as we move to a global context: The smaller and speedier players will prevail on a much expanded field.'

John Naisbitt
entrepreneur and author, 1994

Over the last twenty years people have also begun to appreciate the contribution these firms make to the economies of their countries. It was David Birch (1979) who, arguably, started this process with his seminal research which showed that 81.5% of new jobs in the USA, between 1969 and 1976, were created by small firms (under 500 employees). The general pattern has been repeated yearly. Small, growing firms have outstripped large ones in terms of job generation, year after year. At times when larger companies retrenched, smaller firms continued to offer job opportunities. It has been estimated that in the USA small firms now generate 50% of GDP and over 50% of exports now come from firms employing less than 20 people. In 1996 there were some 3.5 million start-ups.

Europe lags a little behind the USA. Overall in the EU small firms generate 66% of employment. In Italy the proportion is 79%, in France it is 63% and in Germany it is 60%. In the UK they generate 62% of employment and over 25% of GDP. With some 4 million small firms, the UK now has one of the highest business start-up rates in Europe. By just about any measure the contribution small firms make to the economy of any country is increasing and their importance is now fully recognized.

But the focus is not just on small firms. It is also on high-growth firms. Despite being few in number, high-growth businesses are disproportionately important to national economies. Harrison and Taylor (1996) claim that in the USA it has been estimated that, whilst 15,000 medium-sized businesses represent just 1% of all businesses, they generate a quarter of all sales and they employ a fifth of all private sector labour. In the UK, Storey *et al.* (1987) asserted that 'out of every 100 small firms, the fastest growing four firms will create half the jobs in the group over a decade' – an assertion that has stood the test of time.

'The Entrepreneurial Revolution is here to stay, having set the genetic code of the US and global economy for the 21st century, and having sounded the death knell for Brontosaurus Capitalism of yesteryear. Entrepreneurs are the creators, the innovators, and the leaders who give back to society, as philanthropists, directors and trustees, and who, more than any others, change the way people live, work, learn, play, and lead. Entrepreneurs create new technologies, products, processes, and services that become the next wave of new industries. Entrepreneurs create value with high potential, high growth companies which are the job creation engines of the US economy.'

Jeffrey Timmons
author, 1999
●

As the pace of change in just about every aspect of our life accelerates, small firms seem more able to cope than large. Start-ups are on the increase across the world. Whilst the number of small firms is increasing, big firms are struggling to survive. In the UK there are just 7000 firms employing over 250 employees. Many are slimming down or deconstructing – becoming many small firms – because this is the only way they can cope with the pace of change and remain responsive to changes in the market. The entrepreneur has been recognized as a vital part of the process of economic wealth generation. But large organizations are desperate to learn from the entrepreneur and become more entrepreneurial themselves. After all, increasing size is a natural consequence of businesses being set up by entrepreneurs and being successful. The trick is to learn the lessons of that success and not allow the organization to fossilize and die.

However, according to Arie de Geus (1997) large organizations have proved amazingly inept at survival. He quoted a Dutch survey showing the average corporate life expectancy in Japan and Europe was 12.5 years. 'The average life expectancy of a multinational corporation – the Fortune 500 or equivalent – is between 40 and 50 years.' The reality is that large companies die young, or at least their ownership changes fairly quickly. But the other side of the coin is that most small firms remain very small and do not grow. In the UK 63% are sole traders or partnerships with no employees and 95% have fewer than 10 employees. What is more, 50% of businesses will cease trading within the first three years of their existence.

Factors behind the revolution

The major factor causing this revolution is change. The pace of change has accelerated. Change itself has changed to become discontinuous, abrupt but all pervasive. And small, entrepreneurial firms are better able to cope. Their flexibility and speed of response to changing market circumstances is well documented. In a turbulent world, full of uncertainties, they seem better able to survive and prosper.

This is the essence of their success – their ability to spot an opportunity arising out of change or even create it and then focus resources on delivering what the market wants quickly. In essence they are expert in innovation. And that often means taking risks that larger businesses are unwilling or unable to take. This all boils down to one word – entrepreneurship. It is the entrepreneurial small firms that have been able to capitalize most on the turbulent world we face today. These are the entrepreneurial firms led by their founders like Michael Dell, Richard Branson, Anita Roddick, Bill Gates, all of whom we shall examine in some detail in this book.

> 'We now stand on the threshold of a new age – the age of revolution. In our minds, we know the new age has already arrived: in our bellies, we're not sure we like it. For we know it is going to be an age of upheaval, of tumult, of fortunes made and unmade at head-snapping speed. For change has changed. No longer is it additive. No longer does it move in a straight line. In the twenty first century, change is discontinuous, abrupt, seditious.'
>
> **Gary Hamel**
> author, 2000

But a number of other influences have accelerated this trend towards smaller firms. Firstly there has been the shift in most economies away from manufacturing towards the service sectors where small firms often flourish because of their ability to deliver a personalized, flexible, tailor-made service at a local level. The 'deconstruction' of larger firms into smaller, more responsive units concentrating on their core activities, often sub-contracting many of their other activities to smaller firms has also contributed to the trend. Large firms and even the public sector became leaner and fitter in the 1980s in a bid to reduce fixed costs and reduce risks. Small firms have benefited, although they may be seen as dependent on large ones.

Technology has played its part. It has influenced the trend in three ways. Firstly, the new technologies that swept the late twentieth century business world have been pioneered by new, rapidly growing firms. Small firms have pioneered innovation in computers and the internet, although only time will tell whether these markets will start to consolidate and amalgamate into larger units as they mature. Secondly, these technologies have actually facilitated the growth of self-employment and small business by easing communication, encouraging working from home and allowing smaller and smaller market segments to be serviced. Indeed information has become a product in its own right and one that can be generated anywhere around the world and transported at the touch of a button. Finally, many new technologies, for example digital printing, have reduced fixed costs so that production can be profitable in smaller, more flexible units.

Social and market trends have also accelerated the growth of small firms. Firstly, customers increasingly expect firms to address their particular needs. Market niches are becoming slimmer and markets more competitive – better served by smaller firms. Secondly, people are wanting to control their own destiny more. After periods of high unemployment, they now see self-employment as more attractive and more secure than employment. Redundancy pushed many people into self-employment at the same time as the new 'enterprise culture' gave it political and social respectability. The growth of 'new age' culture and 'alternative' life styles have also encouraged the development of a whole new range of self-employment opportunities.

Entrepreneurs

Most owner-managers of small firms are, in fact, not at all entrepreneuial. They prefer to manage businesses that will not grow but rather deliver a life style that they enjoy. The real driving force behind this revolution are those 'super-heroes' called entrepreneurs. They have become the stuff of legends, increasingly held in high esteem and held up as role models to be emulated. They are often held out as embodying many ephemeral qualities – freedom of spirit, creativity, vision, zeal. Like Michael Dell, they have the courage, self-belief and commitment to turn their dreams into realities. They are the catalysts for economic change. They see an opportunity, commercialize it and in the process create jobs from which the rest of society benefits. Entrepreneurs can be described in terms of their characteristics and defined by their actions and one of the major differentiating factors is the degree of innovation they practise. But, as shown in Figure 1.1, entrepreneurs are not confined to small firms.

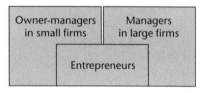

Figure 1.1 Entrepreneurs can come from small and large firms

Interestingly for something so popular, there is no universally accepted definition of the term 'entrepreneur'. The Oxford English Dictionary defines an entrepreneur as 'a person who attempts to profit by risk and initiative'. This definition emphasizes that entrepreneurs exercise a high degree of initiative and are willing to take a high degree of risk. But it covers a wide range of occupations, including that of a paid assassin. No wonder there is an old adage that if you scratch an entrepreneur you will find a 'spiv'. The difference is more than just one of legality. Therefore a question you might ask is 'How do they do it?'.

Back in 1800, Jean-Baptiste Say, the French economist usually credited with inventing the word, said: 'entrepreneurs shift economic resources from an area of lower productivity into an area of higher productivity and greater yield'. In other words entrepreneurs create value by exploiting some form of change, for example in technology, materials, prices or demographics. We call this process innovation and this is an essential tool for entrepreneurs. Entrepreneurs, therefore, create new demand or find new ways of exploiting existing markets. They identify a commercial opportunity and then exploit it.

Central to all of this is change. Change causes disequilibrium in markets out of which come the commercial opportunities that entrepreneurs thrive upon. To them change

> 'We learned the importance of ignoring conventional wisdom and doing things our way … It's fun to do things that people don't think are possible or likely. Its also exciting to achieve the unexpected.'
>
> **Michael Dell**
> ➡

'I am often asked what it is to be an entrepreneur and there is no simple answer. It is clear that successful entrepreneurs are vital for a healthy, vibrant and competitive economy. If you look around you, most of the largest companies have their foundations in one or two individuals who have the determination to turn a vision into reality.'

Richard Branson
from Anderson, 1995
➡

creates opportunities that they can exploit. Sometimes they initiate the change themselves – they innovate in some way and do things differently. At other times they exploit change created by the external environment. Often in doing so they destroy the established order and complacency of existing social and economic systems. How entrepreneurs manage and deal with change is central to their character and essential if they are to be successful. Most 'ordinary people' find change threatening. Entrepreneurs welcome it because it creates opportunities that can be exploited and often create it through innovation.

Another key feature of entrepreneurs is their willingness to accept risk and uncertainty. In part this is simply the consequence of their eagerness to exploit change. However, the scale of uncertainty they are willing to accept is altogether different from that of other managers. This high degree of

Case insight

Born in 1965, **Michael Dell** is the ninth richest man in the world with a fortune in excess of £12.5 billion. Michael started **Dell Computers** in 1984 with just £620. Since then the company has grown at five times the industry average growth rate to become one of the biggest manufacturers and marketers of PCs in the world. Its share price has increased 36,000 per cent in the last decade. Today Michael is CEO of a company that is worth over £36 billion and employs some 37,000 people, globally.

'We built the company around a systematic process: give customers the high-quality computers they want at a competitive price as quickly as possible, backed by great service.'

Michael Dell's entrepreneurial career started early. At the age of 12 he made £1200 by selling his stamp collection. At the age of 14 he devised a marketing scheme to sell newspapers which earned him over £11,000. From the age of 15 his interest in calculators and then computers started to grow. He purchased his first computer – an Apple II – in 1980 and immediately took it apart to see how it was built. Within a couple of years he had started buying microchips and other bits of computer hardware in order to build systems because he realised that he could buy, say, a disk drive for £500 which would sell in the shops for £1800. In 1983 he began a pre-med degree at the University of Texas but continued his lucrative business selling upgraded PCs and add-on components out of his dormitory room.

Michael Dell started life as an entrepreneur, but to grow a successful international organization of this size in such a short time demonstrates that he has become a truly excellent and exceptional entrepreneurial manager.

➡

unless otherwise indicated, all quotes by Michael Dell are taken from his book,
Direct from Dell: Strategies that Revolutionized an Industry, 1999

uncertainty reflects itself in the risks they take for the business and for themselves. And for some this can become so addictive that they become 'serial entrepreneurs', best suited to going on starting up businesses and unwilling to face the tedium of day-to-day management.

It is no wonder that entrepreneurship has been described as 'a slippery concept ... not easy to work into a formal analysis because it is so closely associated with the temperament or personal qualities of individuals' (Penrose, 1959). But notice in these definitions that there is no mention of small firms. The point is that *entrepreneurs are defined by their actions, not by the size of organization they happen to work within.* Any

Table 1.1 The antecedence of modern entrepreneurship

Date	Author	Concept
1755	Cantillon	Introduced the concept of entrepreneur from 'entreprendre' (ability to take charge).
1803, 1815	Jean-Baptiste Say	Emphasized the ability of the entrepreneur to 'marshal' resources in order to respond to unfulfilled opportunities.
1871/1981	Carl Menger	Noted the ability of entrepreneurs to distinguish between 'economic goods' – those with a market or exchange value – and all others.
1893	Ely and Hess	Attributed to entrepreneurs the ability to take integrated action in the enterprise as a whole, combining roles in capital, labour, enterprise and entrepreneur.
1911/1934, 1928	Schumpeter	Envisioned that entrepreneurs proactively 'created' opportunity using 'innovative combinations' which often included 'creative destruction' of passive or lethargic economic markets.
1921	Knight	Suggested that entrepreneurs were concerned with the 'efficiency' in economic factors by continually reducing waste, increasing savings and thereby creating value, implicitly understanding the opportunity–risk–reward relationship.
1948, 1952, 1967	Hayek	Continued the Austrian tradition of analytical entrepreneurs giving them capabilities of discovery and action, recognizing the existence of information asymmetry which they could exploit.
1975, 1984, 1985	Shapero	Attributed a 'judgement' ability to entrepreneurs to identify 'credible opportunities' depending on two critical antecedents – perceptions of 'desirability' and 'feasibility' from both personal and social viewpoints.
1974	Drucker	Attributed to entrepreneurs a sense to 'foresee' market trends and make a timely response.
1973, 1979, 1997, 1999	Kirzner	Attributed to entrepreneurs a sense of 'alertness' to identify opportunities and exploit them accordingly.

Source: Adapted from Etemad, H (2004): 'International Entrepreneurship as a Dynamic Adaptive System: Towards a Grounded Theory', *Journal of International Entrepreneurship*, 2.

manager can be entrepreneurial. The manager of a small firm may not be an entrepreneur – an important distinction that is often missed in the literature. Equally entrepreneurs can exist within large firms, even ones that they did not set up themselves, and how large firms encourage and deal with this is an important issue for them.

The way our notion of entrepreneur has been crafted has a long history, dating back to Cantillon in 1755. These concepts have shifted and developed. Table 1.1 summarizes some of the major developments in the concept. Combining these concepts and definitions together with elements of character, I would propose the following definition for this elusive term:

Entrepreneurs use innovation to exploit or create change and opportunity for the purpose of making profit. They do this by shifting economic resources from an area of lower productivity into an area of higher productivity and greater yield, accepting a high degree of risk and uncertainty in doing so.

Large companies

'The guiding principles in a traditional corporate culture are: follow the instructions given; do not make any mistakes; do not fail; do not take initiatives but wait for instructions; stay within your turf; and protect your backside. The restrictive environment is of course not conducive to creativity, flexibility, independence, and risk taking – the jargon of intrapreneurs.'
Robert Hisrich and Michael Peters
authors, 1992

Large companies are struggling with these challenges – and seem not to be winning. They cut budgets, close plants, downsize, rightsize, deconstruct – and go out of business. Traditional management practices focus on efficiency and effectiveness rather than creativity and innovation – control rather than empowerment. They look for cost savings through scale efficiencies rather than differentiation through economies of small scale. They look for uniformity rather than diversity and stress discipline rather than motivation.

And yet big business comes with significant advantages – financial resources, credibility with stakeholders, established routes to market, trusted brands and, most valuable of all, large work-forces. If only they can continue to be entrepreneurial as they grow and, just perhaps, turn from being bureaucratic to become entrepreneurial. The holy grail they seek is sustainable competitive advantage through the ability to change and adapt to suit a constantly changing environment where continuous

'Today's businesses, especially the large ones, simply will not survive in this period of rapid change and innovation unless they acquire entrepreneurial competence.'
Peter Drucker
author, 1985

innovation yields substantial rewards – and increases longevity. But big business remains typically risk averse. Whether this comes from size or age is difficult to discern. And this creates the culture of bureaucracy which in turn stifles entrepreneurship and all it represents – particularly innovation.

And with this, entrepreneurship has become something that society, governments and organizations of all sizes and forms wish to encourage and promote. Whether it be creating a new venture or breathing life into an old one, whether it is creating new products or finding new ways to market old ones, whether it is doing new things or finding new ways of doing old things, entrepreneurial management has become a highly valued skill to be nurtured, developed and encouraged. Fostering entrepreneurship in all aspects of their teaching is probably one of the major challenges facing Business Schools in the twenty-first century.

However, whilst the boards of larger companies are often criticized for the marked absence of entrepreneurs, there is a pervading suspicion that, whilst entrepreneurs might be good at that 'vision thing' and launching new ventures, they can become a dangerous liability once a company is established. And too many in one organization

Case insight

Anita Lucia Roddick, née Perilla, was born in Littlehampton, England in 1942, one of four children of Italian immigrants. Her parents settled in Littlehampton to run the Clifton Cafe. Her father died when she was ten and the children then helped to run the cafe. From school she went to Bath College of Education where she took a Teacher Training course. She started teaching, but wanted to live abroad so she got a job with the United Nations in Geneva. Anita had never had a holiday as a child and so, with the tax-free money she earned in Geneva, she decided to spend a year travelling around the world. She visited Polynesia, New Caledonia, Australia and Africa where her interest in the use of natural ingredients for cosmetic purposes was aroused. In Tahiti she saw local women plastering themselves with cocoa butter. Half the bean was used for chocolate and the other half was used as a cosmetic. In Morocco she saw women washing their hair in mud.

Returning to England, she met Gordon Roddick, a graduate of the Royal Agricultural College at Cirencester. He had farmed overseas and in the UK before settling in Littlehampton. They married in 1970. Originally they planned to travel overland to Australia and buy a pineapple plantation, but the arrival of first one and then two children made them change their plans. Instead they bought and ran a restaurant and later a small hotel in Littlehampton.

In 1976 Anita opened the first **Body Shop** in a back street in Brighton. The roof leaked and the ugly unpainted walls were covered with green garden lattice primarily because it was cheap. The shop sold only about a dozen inexpensive 'natural' cosmetics, herbal creams and shampoos, all in simple packaging. Pot plants were placed between the products to fill the space. Anita thought these products would only appeal to a small number of customers that shared her values. Her husband, Gordon, even went off to ride a horse across the Americas about a month after it opened.

The Roddicks started a business that became a multinational enterprise with a life of its own. At the time of Anita's death in 2007, the Roddicks were ranked among the top 100 richest people in the UK. They had come a long way from the first small shop in Littlehampton.

➡

is bound to lead to conflict, disagreement and disaster as they move off, often at speed, in different directions. There is some truth in this as it is a real danger. But it is a predictable danger and one, therefore, that can be avoided with proper management. What is more, to be effective within an organization, entrepreneurial behaviour needs to be encouraged at all levels within it, not just at the top. It needs to be institutionalized, ingrained in the culture of the organization. But equally it needs to be focused and directed. Finally it needs to be the appropriate response to the environment the organization faces. Not all industrial sectors face turbulence and change – these were broad generalizations. Not all firms need to encourage innovation. Out of an appropriate context, entrepreneurship is an inappropriate response – an issue to which we return in Chapter 4. However, at the risk of generalizing, entrepreneurial management is a response that has proved more successful in the latter half of the twentieth century than traditional management.

By looking at both successful and unsuccessful entrepreneurs and their businesses we can start to understand what it takes to build and sustain a truly entrepreneurial organization. And the lessons are valuable to organizations of any size that need to make the most of the opportunities created by rapid change. The challenge, then, is to isolate the very DNA of entrepreneurship and, through genetic engineering, replicate it within and throughout a larger organization using all the skills of systematic management. The challenge is called 'corporate entrepreneurship'.

Corporate entrepreneurship

'Corporate entrepreneurship' is the term used to describe entrepreneurial behaviour in an established, larger organization. The objective of this is simple – to gain competitive advantage by encouraging innovation at all levels in the organization – corporate, division, business unit, functional or project team levels. Even as late as the 1980s some academics still believed it was difficult, if not impossible, for entrepreneurial activity to take place in larger, bureaucratic organizations (Morse, 1986). Nevertheless there is a large literature on the general phenomenon stretching back over 30 years. Despite this there is no real consensus on what the term means. Vesper (1984) suggested it was characterized by three activities:

- the creation of new business units by an established firm;
- the development and implementation of entrepreneurial strategic thrusts;
- the emergence of new ideas from various levels in the organization.

Notwithstanding this, Zahra (1991) still defined corporate entrepreneurship as 'activities aimed at creating new businesses in established companies'. Guth and Ginsberg (1990) expanded the definition to include 'transformation of organizations through strategic renewal'. More recently Zahra *et al.* (1999) suggested that there are many facets to entrepreneurship at firm level which reflect different combinations of:

- the content of entrepreneurship – corporate venturing, innovation, proactivity;
- the sources of entrepreneurship – both internal and external;
- the focus of entrepreneurship – formal or informal.

'Imagine you met a remarkable person who could look at the sun or stars at any time of day or night and state the exact time and date: "It's April 23, 1401, 2:36 am, and 12 seconds." This person would be an amazing time teller, and we'd probably revere that person for the ability to tell the time. But wouldn't that person be even more amazing if, instead of telling the time, he or she built a clock that could tell time forever, even after he or she was dead and gone.

Having a great idea or being a charismatic, visionary leader is time telling; building a company that can prosper far beyond the presence of any single leader and through multiple product life cycles is clock building. The builders of visionary companies tend to be clock builders, not time tellers. They concentrate primarily on building an organisation – building a ticking clock – rather than on hitting a target market just right with a visionary product ... And instead of concentrating on acquiring the individual personality traits of visionary leadership, they take an architectural approach and concentrate on building the organizational traits of visionary companies. The primary output of their efforts is not the tangible implementation of a great idea, the expression of a charismatic personality, the gratification of their ego, or the accumulation of personal wealth. Their greatest creation is the company itself and what it stands for.'

James Collins and **Jerry Porras**
authors, 1994

These views cover a wide range. Trying to pull together these different strands, Birkinshaw (2003) identifies four strands of the literature that he calls 'basic schools of thought'.

1. **Corporate venturing**   This is concerned with larger businesses needing to manage new, entrepreneurial businesses separately from the mainstream activity. It is concerned with investment by larger firms in strategically important smaller firms and different forms of corporate venturing units (Chesbrough, 2002). It is concerned with the organizational structures needed to encourage new businesses whilst aligning them to the company's existing activities (Burgelman, 1983; Drucker, 1985; Galbraith, 1982). It also deals with how companies can manage disruptive technologies (Christensen, 1997).

2. **Intrapreneurship**   This is concerned with individual employees and how they might be encouraged to act in an entrepreneurial way within a larger organization. It looks at the systems, structures and cultures that inhibit this activity and how they might be circumvented or even challenged. It is concerned with the character and personality of this strange hybrid of entrepreneur and 'company-man'. The term was introduced and popularized by Gifford Pinchot (1985) building on the earlier work of Ross Kanter (1982). In many ways it was this school that launched the idea that large organizations could change and be something different from what, all too often, they had become.

3. **Bring the market inside**   This focuses mainly on the structural changes needed to encourage entrepreneurial behaviour and argues for a market approach to resource allocation and people management systems using market-based techniques such as spin-offs and venture capital operations (Foster and Kaplan, 2001; Hamel, 1999).

4. **Entrepreneurial transformation**   The premise behind this strand of literature is that large firms need to adapt to an ever-changing environment if they are to survive and to do so they need to adapt their structures and cultures so as to encourage entrepreneurial activity in individual employees (Ghoshal and Bartlett, 1997; Kanter, 1989; Peters and Waterman, 1982; Tushman and O'Reilly, 1996). According to this school individual behaviour is fashioned by the leadership, strategy, systems, structures and culture in the organization.

This book is written very much from the perspective of the fourth school. Corporate venturing and intrapreneurship are seen simply as techniques that can help bring about the entrepreneurial transformation. They are dealt with in Chapter 8. Techniques that bring the market inside the organization are similarly useful and are covered, where relevant, throughout the book. However, the book is written from the viewpoint that, in order to be entrepreneurial, the whole organization must be transformed. The very DNA of the entrepreneur must, somehow, be replicated in the larger corporate entity. This we call 'entrepreneurial architecture' – a strategic architecture that is sufficiently detailed to provide guidance about how it can be achieved, but not so prescriptive as to become constraining. Indeed one of the paradoxes of this architecture is that it cannot be prescriptive but it must evolve and develop – and yet the architecture needs to be such as to ensure this can happen.

What is more, the book is written from the viewpoint that this can be achieved, indeed certain elements may be easier to achieve because they are less reliant on one individual – the entrepreneur. Size can be good because it can bring more resources to bear on the problem. And central to the process of transformation is the concept of entrepreneurial management.

Entrepreneurial management

The emerging discipline of entrepreneurial management – the ability to lead and manage this larger entrepreneurial organization – is about encouraging opportunity seeking and innovation in a systematic manner throughout the organization, always

'There is a real need for corporate entrepreneurs at the moment. For too long the prevailing consensus has been if it ain't broke, don't fix it but entrepreneurs recognise that action and change are crucial for maximising potential and taking advantage of opportunities. You have to be tough and outgoing and not afraid of leaving calm waters to ride the waves of a storm. I consider myself to be a corporate entrepreneur. I have not created the company I am in charge of, but I have changed the way it is run and have made a real difference. I think times have changed and entrepreneurs don't have to be totally out on a limb. There are plenty of opportunities for entrepreneurialism in large companies too.'

Diane Thompson
Chief Executive, **Camelot** (also founder of an advertising agency)
Sunday Times, 17 March 2002

'If there is a spark of genius in the leadership function at all, it must lie in the transcending ability, a kind of magic, to assemble ... out of a variety of images, signals, forecasts and alternatives ... a clearly articulated vision of the future that is at once simple, easily understood, clearly desirable, and energizing.'

Warren Bennis and Burt Nanus
authors, 1985

questioning the established order, seeking ways to improve and create competitive advantage. It is about encouraging the qualities enjoyed by successful entrepreneurs such as vision and drive. It is about learning new ways to manage organizations involving relationships and culture rather than discipline and control. It is about new ways of dealing with risk, uncertainty and ambiguity so as to maintain flexibility – and allowing failure. It is about institutionalizing a process of continuous strategizing, learning from customers, competitors and the environment. It is about encouraging change and managing rapid growth. And it is about doing these things throughout an organization so that it reflects the entrepreneurial characteristics of its managers – responding quickly and effectively to opportunities or changes in the market place. Entrepreneurial management is therefore about a different set of imperatives to traditional management. These are summarized in Table 1.2.

In short entrepreneurial management is about creating and managing an entrepreneurial architecture – the network of relational contracts within, or around, an organization, its employees, suppliers, customers and networks. Drucker (*op. cit.*)

Table 1.2 Traditional vs entrepreneurial management

Traditional management	Entrepreneurial management
• Encouraging control	• Encouraging opportunity seeking
• Encouraging discipline	• Encouraging innovation
• Encouraging uniformity	• Encouraging questioning of the status quo
• Encouraging conformity	• Encouraging vision
• Encouraging efficiency	• Encouraging drive
• Encouraging effectiveness	• Encouraging relationships within and outside the organization
• Encouraging contractual relationships only	• Encouraging strategizing at all levels in the organization
• Encouraging long-term planning	• Encouraging learning
• Encouraging 'training'	• Encouraging the rapid transfer of knowledge and information
• Encouraging functional management	• Encouraging co-operation
• Compartmentalizing knowledge and information	• Tolerating uncertainty and ambiguity
• Trying to create certainty and clarify ambiguity	• Taking risks
• Avoiding risk	• Allowing failure
• Discouraging failure	• Accepting and embracing change
• Seeing change as a threat	• Not controlling too strongly

delineated the discipline as follows: 'Entrepreneurship is based upon the same principles, whether the entrepreneur is an existing large institution or an individual starting his or her new venture single-handed. It makes little or no difference whether the entrepreneur is a business or a non-business public-service organization, nor even whether the entrepreneur is a government or non-government institution. The rules are pretty much the same, and so are the kinds of innovation and where to look for them. In every case there is a discipline we might call Entrepreneurial Management.'

This entrepreneurial architecture creates within the organization the knowledge and routines that allow it to respond flexibly to change and opportunity in the way the entrepreneur does. It is a very real and valuable asset. It creates competitive advantage and can be sustained. In reality the discipline of entrepreneurial management draws on and brings together many different business disciplines, some established and others emerging in their own right, and themes from them. These strands are shown in Figure 1.2.

So, entrepreneurial management is something altogether different from being an entrepreneur. It is a group not an individual activity. It is about systems, processes and structures more than being wrapped up in the behaviour of a single individual. It is systematic rather than capricious. When Mintzberg *et al.* (1998) say that the entrepreneurial school of strategy (yes, there is one) 'presents strategy formation as all wrapped up in the behaviour of a single individual, yet never really says much about what the process is', the challenge is to start to delineate what those processes are and the principles on which they are based.

Nevertheless, at this stage, little progress has been made in developing a coherent theory of corporate entrepreneurship or entrepreneurial management although progress has been made in the individual areas that contribute to it. This book attempts to pull these strands together. However the interaction of so many different variables makes the outcomes difficult to predict. The complexity of the entrepreneurial process demands a multidimensional approach, but the best we can do is to examine the influences on the process one by one. But we must start the process by examining the entrepreneurs themselves – their character and their approach to business and management.

Figure 1.2 Disciplines influencing entrepreneurial management

Case insight

Bill Gates and **Microsoft** is probably the outstanding business success story of a generation. Born in 1955 in Seattle, he and his friend Paul Allen, 'begged, borrowed and bootlegged' time on their school's computer to undertake software commissions. The two went to Harvard University together, using the University's computer to start their own business. Bill's big break came when he approached Altair, a computer company in Albuquerque, New Mexico, trying to sell it a customized version of the BASIC programming language for the PC it produced. The only problem was that, at the time, he and his partner, Paul Allen, had not finished writing it. He had a vision of what it would look like and how it would operate, but no software. That was not finished until some weeks later and with it Microsoft came about. The package was later licensed to Apple, Commodore and IBM. IBM later commissioned Microsoft to develop its own operating system and that was how Microsoft Disk Operating System (MS DOS) was born. Founded in the late 1970s, by 1980 Microsoft was seen as a successful start-up with turnover of £8 million from just 38 employees.

Since then Microsoft's growth has been amazing. Microsoft is now the world's largest software company producing a range of products and services, including the Windows operating systems and Office software suite. By 2005 Microsoft employed some 61,000 people and made profits of over $12 billion on turnover of just under $40 billion – not bad for a business that was only 30 years old. And its ambitions are still anything but small. The company has expanded into markets such as video game consoles, interactive television, and internet access. With its core markets maturing, it is targeting services for growth, looking to transform its software applications into web-based services. Microsoft has also reached a settlement to end an ongoing antitrust investigation, agreeing to uniformly license its operating systems and allow manufacturers to include competing software with Windows.

➜

Summary

Entrepreneurial, small firms are a vital part of the economies of most Western countries. In the USA they generate 50% of GDP. In the UK they generate over 25%. In the EU small firms generate 66% of employment. In the UK they generate 62%. But the UK is catching up and now has the highest rate of business start-ups in Europe. Whilst big firms are struggling to survive, small firms are increasing in number.

Over the last twenty years many start-ups, like **Dell Computer Corporation**, have overtaken the market leaders of their time. So much so that it is estimated that 95% of the wealth of the USA has been created since 1980. High-growth firms set up by entrepreneurs like **Michael Dell** have been the real drivers of economic growth.

The increasing number of small firms is a result of many trends – the move from manufacturing to the service sectors, the 'deconstruction' of many large firms and trend towards sub-contracting, the influence of new technologies and social and market changes. However, a vital ingredient in their success is the entrepreneur.

Entrepreneurs, like **Bill Gates**, **Michael Dell** and **Anita Roddick**, are defined primarily by their actions, although, as we shall see in the next chapter, they can have certain identifiable characteristics. They use innovation to exploit or create change and opportunity for the purpose of making profit. They do this by shifting economic resources from an area of lower productivity into an area of higher productivity and greater yield, accepting a high degree of risk and uncertainty in doing so. They make 'the stuff of dreams' come true.

Not all owner-managers are entrepreneurs, indeed most are not entrepreneurial at all. What is more, like **Diane Thompson**, Chief Executive of Camelot, the firm running the National Lottery, managers in large organizations can be entrepreneurial.

Corporate entrepreneurship is the term used to describe entrepreneurial behaviour in an established, larger organization. It is an emerging discipline. A more precise definition is difficult but there are four identifiable strands of literature:

1. Corporate venturing.
2. Intrapreneurship.
3. Bring the market inside.
4. Entrepreneurial transformation.

Entrepreneurial transformation is about adapting large firms through their leadership, strategies, systems, structures and cultures so that they are better able to cope with change and innovation.

Entrepreneurial management is about the ability to lead and manage this larger entrepreneurial organization. It involves the development of an entrepreneurial architecture – the network of relational contracts within, or around, an organization, its employees, suppliers, customers and networks – that encourages:

- opportunity seeking and innovation;
- vision and drive;
- relationships and culture;
- new ways of dealing with risk and uncertainty;
- institutionalizing a process of continuous learning and strategizing.

This entrepreneurial architecture creates within the organization the knowledge and routines that allow it to respond flexibly to change and opportunity in the very way the entrepreneur does. To develop it we need to draw on many existing management disciplines.

Essays and discussion topics

1. Why have small firms prospered rather than large firms over the last 50 years?
2. In a turbulent, changing environment what advantages do small firms have?
3. In a turbulent, changing environment what advantages do large firms have?
4. Why is there more entrepreneurial activity in the USA than anywhere else?
5. Why is innovation so important in today's economic environment?
6. Why are owner-managers not all entrepreneurs?
7. Was Enron an entrepreneurial organization?
8. What is the relationship between entrepreneurship and legality?
9. Can large firms also be entrepreneurial? Is it in their interests to be so? What pressures are there for them not to be entrepreneurial?
10. What is corporate entrepreneurship?
11. What do you think of the four 'schools' of literature identified by Birkinshaw?
12. What is entrepreneurial management? How does it differ from traditional management?

13. Can a traditional manager become an entrepreneurial manager?
14. What do you understand by the term 'entrepreneurial architecture'? Why are relationships rather than legal contracts important?
15. Do you consider entrepreneurial management to be a discipline in its own right, or just a conglomerate of real disciplines?

Exercises and assignments

1. Identify two large organizations that you would describe as entrepreneurial and explain why you would describe them this way. Are they commercially successful? Can you identify any clues as to why they might be successful?

References

Anderson, J. (1995) *Local Heroes*, Scottish Enterprise, Glasgow.

Bennis, W. and Nanus, B. (1985) *Leaders: The Strategies for Taking Charge*, New York: Harper & Row.

Birch, D. L. (1979) 'The Job Creation Process', unpublished report, *MIT Program on Neighbourhood and Regional Change*, prepared for the Economic Development Administration, US Department of Commerce, Washington, DC.

Birkinshaw, J. M. (2003) 'The Paradox of Corporate Entrepreneurship', *Strategy and Business*, 30, Spring.

Branson, R. (1998) *Losing my Virginity*, London: Virgin.

Burgelman, R. A. (1983) 'A Process Model of Internal Corporate Venturing in the Diversified Major Firm', *Administrative Science Quarterly*, 28.

Cantillon, R. (1755) *Essai sur la Nature du Commerce en General*, London and Paris: R. Gyles; translated (1931) by Henry Higgs, London: Macmillan; see also Resources on Cantillon available at cepa.newschool.edu/het/profiles/cantillon.htm.

Chesbrough, H. W. (2002) 'Making Sense of Corporate Venture Capital', *Harvard Business Review*, March.

Christensen, C. M. (1997) *The Innovator's Dilemma: When New Technologies Cause Great Firms to Fail*, Boston: Harvard Business School Press.

Collins, J. C. and Porras, J. I. (1994) *Built to Last: Successful Habits of Visionary Companies*, New York: Harper Business.

de Geus, A. (1997) *The Living Company*, Boston: Harvard Business Press.

Dell, M. (1999) *Direct from Dell: Strategies that Revolutionized an Industry*, New York: Harper Business.

Drucker, P.F. (1974) *Management Tasks, Responsibilities, Practices*, New York: Harper & Row.

Drucker, P. F. (1985) *Innovation and Entrepreneurship: Practice and Principles*, London: Heinemann.

Ely, R.T. and Hess, R.H. (1893) *Outline of Economics*, New York: Macmillan.

Economic News, *The Small Business Advocate*, February 1997, Washington, DC, Office of Advocacy, SEA.

Foster, R. N. and Kaplan, S. (2001) *Creative Destruction: Why Companies that are Built to Last Underperform the Market – and How to Successfully Transform Them*, New York: Currency Doubleday.

Galbraith, J. (1982) 'Designing the Innovating Organisation', *Organisational Dynamics*, Winter.

Ghoshal, S. and Bartlett, C. A. (1997) *The Individualized Corporation: A Fundamentally New Approach to Management*, New York: Harper Business.

Guth, W. D. and Ginsberg, A. (1990) 'Corporate Entrepreneurship', *Strategic Management Journal* (Special Issue) 11.

Hamel, G. (1999) 'Bringing Silicon Valley Inside', *Harvard Business Review*, September.

Hamel, G. (2000) *Leading the Revolution*, Boston: Harvard Business School Press.

Harrison, J. and Taylor, B. (1996) *Supergrowth Companies: Entrepreneurs in Action*, Oxford: Butterworth-Heinemann.

Hayek, F. A. (1948) 'The Use of Knowledge in Society', in *Studies in Philosophy, Politics and Economics*, Chicago: University of Chicago Press.

Hayek, F. A. (1952) *The Sensory Order*, Chicago: University of Chicago Press.

Hayek, F. A. (1967a) 'Competition as a Discovery Procedure', in F. A. Hayek, *New Studies in Philosophy, Politics, Economics and History of Ideas*, Chicago: Chicago University Press.

Hayek, F. A. (1967b) 'The Results of Human Action, but not Human Design', in F.A. Hayek, *New Studies in Philosophy, Politics, Economics and History of Ideas*, Chicago: Chicago University Press.

Hisrich, R. D. and Peters, M. P. (1992) *Entrepreneurship: Starting, Developing and Managing a New Enterprise*, Homewood, IL: Irwin.

Kanter, R. M. (1982) 'The Middle Manager as Innovator', *Harvard Business Review*, July.

Kanter, R. M. (1989) *When Giants Learn to Dance: Mastering the Challenge of Strategy, Management and Careers in the 1990s*, New York: Simon & Schuster.

Kirzner, I. M. (1973) *Competition and Entrepreneurship*, Chicago: University of Chicago Press.

Kirzner, I. M. (1979) *Perception, Opportunity and Profit: Studies in the Theory of Entrepreneurship*, Chicago: University of Chicago Press.

Kirzner, I. M. (1997) 'Entrepreneurial Discovery and Competitive Market Processes: An Austrian Approach', *Journal of Economic Literature*, 35.

Kirzner, I. M. (1999) 'Creativity and/or Alertness: A Reconsideration of the Schumpeterian Entrepreneur', *Review of Austrian Economics*,11.

Knight, F. (1921) *Risk, Uncertainty and Profit*, Chicago: University of Chicago Press.

Menger, C. (1871/1981) *Principles of Economics*, New York: New York University Press.

Mintzberg, H., Ahlstrand, B. and Lampel, J. (1998) *Strategy Safari*, New York: The Free Press.

Morse, C. W. (1986) 'The Delusion of Intrapreneurship', *Long Range Planning*, 19(2).

Naisbitt, J. (1994) *Global Paradox: The Bigger the World Economy, the more Powerful its Smallest Players*, London: BCA.

Penrose, E. T. (1959) *The Theory of the Growth of Firms*, Oxford: Basil Blackwell.

Peters, T. and Waterman, R. (1982) *In Search of Excellence: Lessons from America's Best-Run Companies*, New York: Harper Row.

Pinchot III, G. (1985) *Intrapreneuring: Why You Don't Have to Leave the Company to Become an Entrepreneur*, New York: Harper Row.

Say, J.-B. (1803) *Trait d'economie politique ou simple exposition de la maniere dont se forment, se distribuent, et se consomment les riches*; revised (1819); translated (1830) by R. Prinsep, *A Treatise on Political Economy: On Familiar Conversations On the Manner in Which Wealth is Produced, Distributed and Consumed by Society*, Philadelphia: John Grigg and Elliot. See also Resources for Say at cepa.newschool.edu/het/profiles/say.htm.

Say, J.-B. (1815) *Catechisme d'Economie Politique*, translated (1921) by John Richter, *Catechism of Political Economy*

Shapero, A. (1975) 'The Displaced, Uncomfortable Entrepreneur', *Psychology Today*, 8.

Shapero, A. (1984) 'The Entrepreneurial Event', in C. Kent (ed.) *The Environment for Entrepreneurship*, Lexington, Mass: DC Health.

Shapero, A. (1985) 'Why Entrepreneurship?', *Journal of Small Business Management*, 23(4).

Schumpeter, J.A. (1911) *Theorie der wirtschaftlichen Entwicklung*, Munich and Leipzig: Dunker und Humblat; translated (1934) by R. Opie, *The Theory of Economic Development*, Cambridge, Mass: Harvard University Press.

Schumpeter J.A. (1928) 'The Instability of Capitalism', *Economic Journal*, 38.

Storey, D., Keasey, K., Watson, R. and Wynarczyk, P. (1987) *The Performance of Small Firms: Profits Jobs and Failure*, London: Croom Helm.

Timmons, J. A. (1999) *New Venture Creation: Entrepreurship for the 21st Century*, Boston: Irwin/ McGraw-Hill.

Tushman, M. L. and O'Reilly, C. A. (1996) 'Ambidextrous Organizations: Managing Evolutionary and Revolutionary Change', *California Management Review*, 38(4).

Vesper, K. H. (1984) 'The Three Faces of Corporate Entrepreneurship: A Pilot Study', in J. A. Hornaday *et al.* (eds), *Frontiers of Entrepreneurial Research*, Wellesley, Mass: Babson College.

Zahra, S. A. (1991) 'Predictors and Financial Outcomes of Corporate Entrepreneurship: An Exploratory Study', *Journal of Business Venturing*, 6(4), July.

Zahra, S. A., Jennings, D. F. and Kuratko, D. F. (1999) 'The Antecedents and Consequences of Firm Level Entrepreneurship: The State of the Field', *Entrepreneurship: Theory and Practice*, 24.

2

Entrepreneur Super-hero

Contents

- Personal character traits
- The survival instinct
- The growth instinct
- Antecedent influences
- Implications for entrepreneurial management
- Summary

LEARNING OUTCOMES

By the end of this chapter you should be able to:

- Describe the character traits of owner-managers and entrepreneurs and explain how they affect their approach to management;

- Explain the methodological problems associated with trying to measure character traits and, in particular, the linkages with growth businesses;

- Explain the influence of cognitive theory;

- Describe and give examples of the antecedent influences on successful entrepreneurs;

- Assess the implications of all these factors for corporate entrepreneurship.

Personal character traits

In order to understand the nature of corporate entrepreneurship we need to understand the entrepreneurs themselves – their personal characteristics, their personality and how they go about business. They shape the organization they start up. They dominate it to the extent that it takes on many of their characteristics. They are its strengths and can be its weaknesses.

Entrepreneurs are both born and made. They have certain personal character traits that they are born with, but they also shaped by their background, history and experience of life – called antecedent influences – as well as the culture of the different groups of society in which they operate. Some cultures encourage entrepreneurial activity, others discourage it. Figure 2.1 summarizes the effects of these influences.

Despite the limitations of this research, a focus on research into the character traits of owner-managers of growth businesses – who should mainly be entrepreneurs – does allow us to come to some broad conclusions and to paint a picture of the different character traits of both owner-managers and entrepreneurs. Figure 2.2 summarizes these traits. Of course, by definition, owner-manager entrepreneurs share the character traits of owner-managers, since these influenced their decision to start their own business in the first place. The character traits of owner-manager entrepreneurs therefore comprise two parts perhaps generating two instincts. The first relates to survival and its traits are found in the owner-manager. The second relates to growth and its traits are found in the entrepreneur.

The problem of linking the personal character traits of any individual to the success of a business needs to be approached with caution and can be an academic minefield. As we have seen, success or failure in business, comes from a mix of many different things and the character of the entrepreneur is just one factor in the equation. We

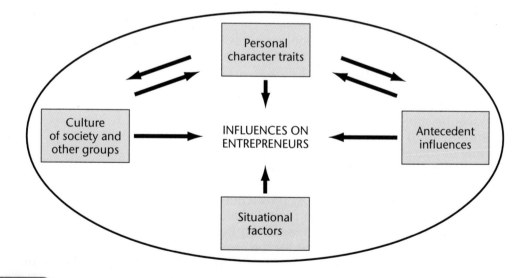

Figure 2.1 Influences on entrepreneurs

Sources: Based on Aldrich and Martinez, 2003; Andersson et al., 2004; Baty, 1990; Bell et al., 1992; Blanchflower and Meyer, 1991; Brockhaus and Horwitz, 1986; Brush, 1992; Buttner and More, 1997; Caird, 1990; Chell, Haworth and Brearley, 1991; Cuba et al., 1983; de Bono, 1985; Hirsch and Brush, 1987; Kanter, 1983; Kirzner, 1973, 1979, 1997, 1999; McClelland, 1961; Pinchot, 1985; Rosa et al., 1994; Schein et al., 1996; Schumpeter, 1996; Schwartz, 1997; Shapero, 1985; Shaver and Scott, 1992; Storey and Sykes, 1996.

Figure 2.2 Character traits of owner-managers and entrepreneurs

have no way of knowing how important the different ingredients are at any point of time. What is more, it takes time for the owner-manager entrepreneur to prove that the business he or she manages is in fact a successful growth business. So, do you measure aspirations or reality, and over what time scale? We have held up Michael Dell and Richard Branson as successful entrepreneurs, but will their companies eventually fail and their reputations become tarnished? And, if so, what part will their personalities play in this? Furthermore, many of the character traits that have been found significant in entrepreneurs are similar to those found in other successful people such as politicians or athletes (Chell, Haworth and Brearley, 1991). Perhaps, the argument goes, it just happens that the individual has chosen an entrepreneurial activity as a means of self-satisfaction.

There are also a number of methodological problems associated with attempting to measure personality characteristics which are worth bearing in mind when interpreting these results (Deakins, 1996):

- The traits are not stable and change over time.
- They require subjective judgements.
- Measures tend to ignore cultural and environmental influences.
- The role of education, learning, training is often overlooked.
- Issues such as age, sex, race, social class and education may also be ignored.

Notwithstanding these issues, most researchers believe that, collectively, owner-manager entrepreneurs have certain typical character traits, although the mix and emphasis of these characteristics will inevitably be different for each individual. These character traits and their implications for the entrepreneurial organization need to be explored in more detail. We shall characterize those of the owner-manager as an instinct for survival – since most owner-managed businesses never grow to any size – and those of the entrepreneur as an instinct for growth.

The survival instinct

Need for independence

> 'Entrepreneurs don't like working for other people ... I was once made redundant by the Manchester Evening News. I had a wife who had given up a promising career for me, and a baby. I stood on Deansgate with £5 in my pocket and I swore I would never work for anyone else again.'
>
> **Eddy Shah**
> founder of Messenger Group
> *The Times*, 16 March 2002

Owner-managers and entrepreneurs have a high need for independence. This is most often seen as the need to 'be your own boss' and is the trait that is most often cited, and supported, by researchers and advisors alike. However, independence means different things to different people, such as controlling your own destiny, doing things differently or being in a situation where you can fulfil your potential. It has often been said that, once you run your own firm, you cannot work for anybody else.

Implications for the entrepreneurial organization:

- *Issues for management style.* If individual members of the organization are entrepreneurial they will need to be managed with a 'light touch' and given independence of decision making.
- *Issues for culture.* Will entrepreneurial members of the organization naturally want to leave, often to set up in competition? If so, can they be tied into the organization by sharing in its success through share ownership etc.? Can other psychological needs be met so as to compensate for this need for independence? They need to feel they belong to and even 'own' the organization.
- *Issues for structure* Staff will need to feel independent to some extent but will an entrepreneurial unit or division have to be separate from the rest of the organization in order to satisfy the aspirations of its members? Can the separate identity be recognized in any way other than by structure?

Need for achievement

> 'Most of the pleasure is not the cash. It is the sense of achievement at having taken something from nothing to where it is now.'
>
> **Charles Muirhead**
> founder of **Orchestream**
> *Sunday Times*, 17 September 1999

Owner-managers and entrepreneurs typically have a high need for achievement, a driving force that is particularly strong for entrepreneurs. Achievement for individuals means different things depending on the type of person they are: for example, the satisfaction of producing a beautiful work of art, employing their hundredth person, or making the magic one million pounds. Often money is just a badge of achievement to the successful entrepreneur. It is not an end in itself.

> 'We don't feel like millionaires at all. Money doesn't come into it. It's not really why you do it, it really isn't.'
>
> **Brent Hoberman**
> co-founder of **Lastminute.com**
> *Sunday Times,*
> 17 September 1999
> ➡

Public recognition of achievement can be important to some owner-managers and entrepreneurs. And this can lead to certain negative behaviours or unwise decisions: for example, overspending on the trappings of corporate life – the office, the company car and so on (often called the corporate flag-pole syndrome) – or the 'big project' that is very risky but the entrepreneur 'knows' it is achievable. These can lead to cash flow problems that put at risk the very existence of the business.

Implications for the entrepreneurial organization:

● *Issues for culture.* An achievement-orientated culture needs to be created. Goals need to be set and achievement encouraged, publicly acknowledged and rewarded.

Internal locus of control

If you believe that you can exercise control over your environment and ultimately your destiny, you have an internal locus of control. If, however, you believe in fate, you have an external locus of control and you are less likely to take the risk of starting a business. Owner-managers typically have a strong internal locus of control, which is the same for many senior managers in large firms.

> 'I want to take control of my life and achieve something.'
>
> **Jonathan Elvidge**
> founder of **Gadget Shop**
> *Sunday Times,* 17 March 2002
> ➡

In extreme cases this trait can also lead to certain negative behaviours. In particular, it can show itself as a desire to maintain personal control over every aspect of the business. That can lead to a preoccupation with detail, over-work and stress. It also leads to an inability or unwillingness to delegate as the business grows. Again, in extreme cases it might show itself as a mistrust of subordinates. Kets de Vries (1985) thinks these behaviours can lead to the danger of subordinates becoming 'infantilized'. They are expected to behave as incompetent idiots, and that is the way they behave. They tend to do very little, make no decisions and circulate very little information. The better ones do not stay long. For an entrepreneurial manager this needs to be avoided.

This need for control can also show itself in the unwillingness of many owner-managers to part with shares in their company. They just do not want to lose control, at any price. This also needs to be avoided because, as we shall see later, sharing ownership can be a very positive motivation for staff that encourages an entrepreneurial culture.

Implications for the entrepreneurial organization:

- *Issues for culture.*   Create a 'can-do' culture.
- *Issues for management style.*   If individual members of the organization are entrepreneurial they need to be managed with a 'light touch' so that they believe they can control their own destiny. There is therefore likely to be a high degree of delegation.

Ability to live with uncertainty and take measured risks

Whilst all owner-managers are willing to take risks and live with uncertainty, true entrepreneurs are willing to take far greater risks and live with far greater uncertainty. Often they are willing to put their own home on the line and risk all, so strong is their belief in their business idea, despite the uncertainties surrounding it.

'You have to be prepared to lose everything and remember that the biggest risk is not taking any risk at all.'
Jonathan Elvidge
founder of **Gadget Shop**
Sunday Times, 17 March 2002
➡

'You have to have nerves of steel and be prepared to take risks. You have to be able to put it all on the line knowing you could lose everything.'
Anne Notley
co-founder of **The Iron Bed Company**
Sunday Times, 28 January 2001
●

'People ask me now, "Were you scared?" Sure. Nearly everyone's motivated by fear in some form. I was afraid that I wouldn't do a good enough job, that the business would be a complete failure. However, in my case the downside was limited.'
Michael Dell
➡

Human beings, typically, do not like uncertainty and one of the biggest uncertainties of all is not having a regular pay cheque coming in – particularly when you have a family to support. That is not to say owner-managers or entrepreneurs like this aspect of risk and uncertainty. Uncertainty about income can be a major cause of stress. The possibility of missing out on some piece of business that might affect their income is one reason why they are so loath to take holidays. However, true entrepreneurs thrive on uncertainty and risk. They love pitching their judgement against the odds, although they believe they will win. This is one reason why so many grow tired of a business after a while and sell it on or bring in professional managers to free them from day-to-day involvement.

There are other commercial aspects of uncertainty that owner-managers or entrepreneurs have to cope with. Often they cannot influence many aspects of the market in which they operate, for example, price. They must therefore react to changes in the market that others might bring about. If a local supermarket has a special price promotion on certain goods it may well affect sales of similar goods in a local corner shop. A business with a high level of borrowing must find a way of paying

'Taking a chance, a risk or a gamble is what unites entrepreneurs. Without risk there is no reward. You won't discover America if you never set sail.'

Jonathan Elvidge
founder of **Gadget Shop**
The Times, 6 July 2002
→

'Don't worry about failure: if you lose because of market conditions then another time someone will say "Hey, this guy can make things happen. I'll back him".'

Gururaj Deshpande
serial entrepreneur and founder of
Sycamore Networks
The Financial Times, 21 February 2000
→

interest charges but has no direct influence over changes in interest rates. Many small firms also have a limited customer or product base and this can bring further uncertainty. If, for whatever reason, one large customer ceases buying, it can have an enormous impact on a small firm.

Hand in hand with the ability to live with uncertainty is the willingness to take measured risks. Most people are risk averse. They try to avoid risks and insure against them. Setting up your own business is risky and owner-managers are willing to take more risks with their own resources than most people.

Owner-managers and entrepreneurs might risk their reputation and personal standing if they fail. However, they do not like this risk and try always to minimize their exposure; hence their preference to risk other people's money and borrow, sometimes too heavily, from the bank. Another example of this is the way they often 'compartmentalize' various aspects of their business. For example, an entrepreneur might open a second and third restaurant but set each one up as a separate limited company just in case any should fail and endanger the others. In this way they sometimes develop a portfolio of individually small businesses and their growth and success is measured not just in the performance of a single one but rather by the growth of the portfolio.

Implications for the entrepreneurial organization:

- *Issues for management style.* If the organization faces uncertainty, management need to engender a 'positive' attitude, one that builds self-confidence and self-efficacy.
- *Issues for culture.* Measured risk taking needs to be encouraged rather than penalized.

The growth instinct

Opportunistic

This is the first of the two prime distinguishing features of entrepreneurs. By definition, entrepreneurs exploit change for profit. In other words they seek out opportunities to make money. Often entrepreneurs see opportunities where others see problems. Whereas ordinary mortals dislike the uncertainty brought about by change, entrepreneurs love it because they see opportunity and they do not mind the uncertainty.

'I have always lived my life by thriving on opportunity and adventure. Some of the best ideas come out of the blue, and you have to keep an open mind to see their virtue.'

Richard Branson
➡

'Hundreds of computer stores were popping up in Houston. And dealers would pay $2000 for an IBM PC and sell it for $3000, making $1000 profit. They also offered little or no support to the customer. Yet they were making lots of money because people really wanted computers. At this point, I was already buying the exact same components that were used in these machines, and I was upgrading my machines selling them to people I knew. I realized that if I could sell even more of them, I could actually compete with the computer stores – and not just on price but on quality. I could also earn a nice little profit and get all the things your typical high school kid would want. But beyond that, I thought, "Wow, there's a lot of opportunity here."'

Michael Dell
➡

For many entrepreneurs the problem is focusing on just one opportunity, or at least one opportunity at a time, and then exploiting it systematically. They see opportunity everywhere and have problems following through on any one before becoming distracted by another. This is one reason why some entrepreneurs are not able to grow their business beyond a certain size. They get bored by the routines and controls, they see other market opportunities and yearn for the excitement of another start-up. Many would probably be well advised to sell up and do just that, but go on to try to manage a company they have really lost interest in. And the result can be disastrous.

However, some entrepreneurs do appreciate this element of their character and play to it, becoming serial entrepreneurs, moving to set up and sell on one business after another. You see this very often in the restaurant business where entrepreneurial restaurateurs launch one new restaurant and make it successful, then sell it on so as to move onto another new venture. They make money by creating a business with capital value, not necessarily income for themselves.

Implications for the entrepreneurial organization:

- *Issues for culture.* Change should be endemic, seen as the norm and not something to be avoided. Opportunity perception, through closeness to customers, needs to be encouraged.
- *Issues for structure.* Systems for sharing information and knowledge – including opportunity perception – need to be in place. However, the challenge is to pursue only those opportunities where the organization has distinctive capabilities upon which it can capitalize.

Innovative

The ability to innovate is the second most important distinguishing feature of entrepreneurs. Innovation is the prime tool they use to create or exploit opportunity.

> 'True innovation is rarely about creating something new. Its pretty hard to recreate the wheel or discover gravity; innovation is more often about seeing new opportunities for old designs.'
> **Neil Kelly**
> owner and managing director of **PAV**
> *Sunday Times*, 9 December 2001
> ●

Entrepreneurs link innovation to the market place so as to exploit an opportunity and make their business grow. Although innovation is difficult to define and can take many forms, entrepreneurs are always, in some way, innovative. We shall explore how spotting opportunities and developing innovation can be institutionalized in a subsequent chapter.

> **Implications for the entrepreneurial organization:**
>
> - *Issues for culture.* Innovation needs to be encouraged, never penalized. The process of innovation needs to be understood. Continuous improvement is seen as the regular part of the innovation process.
> - *Issues for structure.* Systems and structures that encourage creativity and innovation need to be in place.

Self-confident

> 'My mother gave me a massive self-belief. I will always try things – there is nothing to lose.'
> **Richard Thompson**
> founder and chairman of **EMS**
> Rupert Steiner; *My First Break: How Entrepreneurs Get Started*,
> Sunday Times Books, 1999
> ●

Facing uncertainty, you have to be confident in your own judgement and ability to start up your own business. Many training programmes for start-ups recognize this by trying to build personal self-confidence through developing a business plan that addresses the issue of future uncertainty. As well as being a useful management tool, the plan can become a symbol of certainty for the owner-manager in an otherwise uncertain world. Some can keep it with them at all times, using it almost like a bible, to reassure them of what the future will hold when the business eventually becomes successful. Entrepreneurs, therefore, need self-confidence aplenty to grow their business, given the extreme uncertainty they face. If they do not believe in the future of the business, how can they expect others to do so? However, the self-confidence can be overdone and turn to an exaggerated opinion of their own competence and even arrogance.

Some researchers believe entrepreneurs are actually 'delusional'. In an interesting piece of research, two American academics tested the decision-making process of 124 entrepreneurs (defined as people who started their own firm) and 95 managers of big companies in two ways (Busenitz and Barney, 1997). Firstly, they asked five factual questions each of which had two possible answers. They asked respondents to rate their confidence in their answer (50%, a guess; 100%, perfect confidence). Entrepreneurs turned out to be much more confident about their answers than

> 'An entrepreneur is unfailingly enthusiastic, never pessimistic, usually brave, and certainly stubborn. Vision and timing are crucial. You have to be something of a workaholic, too. You have to be convinced that what you are doing is right. If not you have to recognise this and be able to change direction swiftly – sometimes leaving your staff breathless – and start off again with equal enthusiasm.'
>
> **Chris Ingram**
> founder of **Tempus**
> *Sunday Times*, 17 March 2002

managers, especially those who gave wrong answers. Secondly, they were given a business decision. They were told they must replace a broken foreign-made machine and they had two alternatives. The first was an American-made machine, which a friend had recently bought and had not yet broken down, and the second a foreign-built machine, which was statistically less likely to break down than the other. 50% of the entrepreneurs opted for the American machine whilst only 10% of the managers opted for it. The researchers concluded that the entrepreneurs were more prone to both delusion and opportunism than normal managers, who were seen as more rational. So the question is raised, is entrepreneurial self-confidence so strong as to make them delusional, blinding them to the reality of a situation?

Implications for the entrepreneurial organization:

- *Issues for culture.*   Need to build a self-confident organization by celebrating achievement in the face of uncertainty. However, this self-confidence needs to be grounded in reality – a realistic understanding of the organization's capabilities and achievements.

Proactive and decisive with high energy

> 'Neither my grandfather nor my father would be surprised if they could see me now. My success didn't just happen As a young boy, I was always working. My parents and my brothers and sisters all had high energy.'
>
> **Tom Farmer**
> founder of **Kwik-Fit**
> *Daily Mail*, 11 May 1999

Entrepreneurs tend to be proactive rather than reactive and more decisive than other people. They are proactive in the sense that they seek out opportunities, they do not just rely on luck – this is part of their nature. They act quickly and decisively to make the most of the opportunity before somebody else does – this is the only way to achieve success.

Entrepreneurs are often seen as restless and easily bored. They can easily be diverted by the most recent market opportunity and often seem to do things at twice the pace of others, unwilling or unable to wait for others to complete tasks. Patience is certainly not a virtue many possess. Many entrepreneurs seem to work twenty-four hours a day and their work becomes their life with little separating the two. It is little wonder that it places family relationships under strain.

> 'Enthusiasm is my strength. And good health, and energy and endeavour. I love what I do. It's just so interesting, it is new every day, exciting every day. I work 364 days a year. The only day I don't work is Christmas Day, because its my wife's birthday.'
>
> **Bob Worcester**
> founder of **MORI**
> *The Financial Times*, 7 April 2002

> 'Never sit back and admire what you've achieved, never think you have a divine right to succeed. What you have already done is just the starting point – it's all about the future, about the ability to push the boundaries out as far as they will go and create concepts and answers that don't yet exist.'
>
> **Derrick Collin**
> founder of **Brulines Ltd**
> *The Times*, 10 October 2002

One important result of this characteristic is that entrepreneurs act first and then learn from the outcomes of the action. They tend to learn by doing. This is logical since time is important in pursuing opportunity. Extensive analysis of a market opportunity is likely to mean that the entrepreneur will not be first to market. It is part of their incremental approach to decision making, each small action and its outcomes take them closer to the market opportunity and contribute to the learning process which mitigates the risks they face.

> **Implications for the entrepreneurial organization:**
>
> - *Issues for culture.* Need to develop a 'can-do', achievement-orientated culture which generates enthusiasm, commitment and a willingness and ability to act quickly. Need to build learning into the culture – 'learn' from all aspects of the business and disseminate knowledge.

Self-motivated

Entrepreneurs are highly self-motivated, amounting almost to a driving urge to succeed in their economic goals. This is driven by their exceptionally strong inner need for achievement, far stronger than with the average owner-manager. Running your own business is a lonely affair, without anyone to motivate and encourage you. You work long hours, sometimes for little reward. You therefore need to be self-motivated, committed and determined to succeed.

This strong inner drive – what psychologists call type 'A' behaviour – is quite unique and can be seen as almost compulsive behaviour. This is not to say that entrepreneurs are not motivated by other things as well, such as money. But often

> 'I have never had anything to do in my life that provides so many challenges – and there are so many things I still want to do.'
>
> **Martha Lane Fox**
> co-founder of **Lastminute.com**
> *Sunday Times*, 17 September 1999

> 'I am motivated by my success not money. But success is partly measured by money.'
>
> **Wing Yip**
> founder of **W Wing Yip & Brothers**
> *Sunday Times*, 2 January 2000
> ●

money is just a badge of their success that allows them to measure their achievement. What drives them is their exceptionally high need to achieve. 'A' types tend to be goal-focused, wanting to get the job done quickly. However, they also focus mainly on the future and are often not in control of the present, appearing highly reactive – entrepreneurs are notorious for their unwillingness to focus on issues of detailed financial control.

> 'Fun is at the core of the way I like to do business and has informed everything I've done from the outset. More than any other element fun is the secret of Virgin's success.'
>
> **Richard Branson**
> ➔

An important aspect of this self-motivation is the enjoyment of doing it – enjoyment in the challenges of being entrepreneurial. They do what they do because they enjoy doing it, not because they are forced to in any way. Entrepreneurs actually enjoy their work – often to the exclusion of other things in more ordinary people's lives such as spouse and family. The long hours worked by entrepreneurs have often been known to break marriages. But ultimately entrepreneurs will always regard their business as 'fun', and this is one reason they can be so passionate about it. This provides for them an intrinsic motivation and generally people with an intrinsic motivation outperform those who undertake tasks because of extrinsic motivation – doing something because of an external influence or simply because they 'have to'.

Implications for the entrepreneurial organization:

- *Issues for culture.* Need to develop a 'can-do', achievement-orientated culture which generates enthusiasm and commitment. Need to build 'fun' and learning into the culture – 'learn' from all aspects of the business and disseminate knowledge.

Vision and flair

To succeed, entrepreneurs need to have a clear vision of what they want to achieve – a vision that stays with them giving them direction when all around is uncertainty.

> 'You must have a vision of what you want to achieve and be very single minded in achieving it. Do not be deflected. Never say die.'
>
> **Terry Saddler**
> founder of **Bioglan Pharma**
> *The Times*, 10 October 2001
> ●

That is part of the fabric of their motivation. It motivates them and also helps bring others with them, both employees and customers. It is the cornerstone of their motivation and self-confidence.

The flair comes with the ability to be in the right place at the right time. Timing is everything. Innovation that is before its time can lead to business

> 'You have to have passion, a clear goal and the drive to see it through.'
> **Jonathan Elvidge**
> founder of **Gadget Shop**
> *Sunday Times*, 17 March 2002
> ➡

failure. Innovation that is late results in copy-cat products or services that are unlikely to be outstanding successes. A question constantly asked about successful entrepreneurs is whether their success was due to good luck or good judgement? The honest answer in most cases is probably a bit of both.

Implications for the entrepreneurial organization:

- *Issues for management.* Vision is vital. It also needs to be communicated effectively. Timing is crucial, but only easily judged with the benefit of hindsight.

Antecedent influences

Whilst inherent character traits are important, there are other influences at work and there are other approaches to trying to explain the complicated process of entrepreneurship. Cognitive theory shifts the emphasis from the individual towards the situations that lead to entrepreneurial behaviour. Research has started to distinguish a certain 'antecedent influence' – the entrepreneur's history and experience of life (Carter and Cachon, 1988). However, whilst these may be interesting observations – part of the literature on picking entrepreneurial 'winners' – they are of little use in constructing an entrepreneurial organization as they cannot be influenced *ex-post*. The most important of these is education which is an important antecedent influence for start-up but more particularly for entrepreneurial growth (Evans and Leighton, 1990; Storey, 1994). Success seems to be associated with a better education – particularly in the USA. This perhaps mirrors the generally accepted importance of education and training as an important strategic tool in the development of the organization. As we shall see in a later chapter, continual learning is an important characteristic of the entrepreneurial organization.

Burns' (2007) summary of the important antecedent influences on the owner-manager of a growth business – an entrepreneur – does have implications for an entrepreneurial organization. He concludes that the true entrepreneur is more likely to be:

- Better educated.
- Leaving a managerial job to start the business.
- Middle-aged and experienced. (There are, however, a small but significant and growing number of very young entrepreneurs with little or no business experience, who are usually successful because of their innovative business ideas.)
- Starting the business because of positive motivations such as a need for independence, achievement or recognition, personal development or simply a desire to make money.
- Willing to share ownership of the business.

Implications for the entrepreneurial organization:

- *Issues for structure and culture.* Continual learning from experience is important.
- *Issues for culture.* Positive motivation – rather than compulsion – is the most important motivation for staff.

One further strand of cognitive theory is worthy of note because it reinforces at least two elements of trait theory. Chen *et al.* (1998) set out the idea that successful entrepreneurs possess high levels of 'self-efficacy'. Self-efficacy is 'the strength of an individual's belief that he or she is capable of successfully performing the roles and tasks of an entrepreneur'. Clearly this is part of the self-confidence of entrepreneurs referred to in the last section, but it is also created by their internal locus of control and rooted firmly in their need for achievement and therefore more than just self-confidence. Chen *et al.* argue that it is self-efficacy that motivates entrepreneurs and gives them the dogged determination to persist in the face of adversity when others just give in. With this characteristic entrepreneurs become more objective and analytical and attribute failure to insufficient effort or poor knowledge. They argue that self-efficacy is affected by a person's previous experiences – success breeds success.

Implications for the entrepreneurial organization:

- *Issues for culture.* Building organizational self-confidence and creating organizational self-efficacy is important. Celebrate achievement. Nothing breeds success like previous success.

There are other influences, most of which have few implications for the entrepreneurial organization. Self-employment normally needs a trigger. Unemployment is a strong push into self-employment but entrepreneurial growth businesses are more likely to set up for more positive motives such as the need for independence, achievement etc. (Abdesselam, Bonnet and Le Pape, 1999; Storey, 1994). It is possible that having a parent who was previously self-employed is more likely to lead a person to set up his or her own firm (Stanworth *et al.*, 1989) and observation tells us that immigration to a foreign country is another influence (Harper, 1985).

Cognitive theory underlines the fact that entrepreneurs are both born (with character traits) and, more importantly, made – shaped by their environment and experiences. In other words, it acknowledges that an entrepreneurial organization *can* be created, with individuals within it shaped by the environment it creates and the experiences it faces – part culture, part structure. However, it also implies that the organization itself must deal with the environmental context in which it is placed – commercial, political, national and economic. It also underlines the complexity of the influences on individuals, many of which are outside the control of the organization – family, race, religion, nationality. Developing the entrepreneurial organization is an imprecise science.

> **Implications for the entrepreneurial organization:**
>
> • Entrepreneurial organizations can be constructed through culture and structure, but this is a complex process and there are many influences outside the control of the organization.

Implications for entrepreneurial management

This chapter has looked at the personal characteristics of entrepreneurs. Most of these characteristics need to be replicated either in the management, structure or, most importantly, through the culture of the entrepreneurial organization – entrepreneurship is primarily a frame of mind, a set of beliefs, a way of thinking and approaching life. Figure 2.3 summarizes many of the words that would be used to describe this entrepreneurial culture, insofar as they are derived from the character of the entrepreneur.

The two most important personal characteristics of the entrepreneur that any organization must ensure are replicated are, of course, the ability to spot opportunities and innovate. However, there are others. The entrepreneurial culture must:

• Spot opportunities;
• Value creativity and innovation;
• Recognize the importance of balanced risk taking and not unnecessarily penalize failure;
• Recognize change as endemic, the norm, not something to be avoided;
• Motivate people to achieve – goals set, achievement encouraged, publicly acknowledged and rewarded.
• Be a 'can-do' and 'work-is-fun' culture;
• Encourage organizational self-confidence and self-efficacy by celebrating achievement and success, but not at the expense of recognizing reality;
• Share information, knowledge and learning;
• Encourage people to belong to and 'own' the organization.

Figure 2.3 Entrepreneurial culture

As we shall see in the next chapter, many of these cultural characteristics are reinforced by the way entrepreneurs do business and manage the organization. There are also further implications for entrepreneurial culture that derive from how they do business and manage people as the firm grows as well as some pitfalls to be avoided.

There are additional implications for organizational structure that derive from the personal characteristics of entrepreneurs. These are also reinforced and further developed in the next chapter as we look at how entrepreneurs do business. Structures must facilitate by:

- Encouraging opportunity spotting, creativity and innovation;
- Sharing information, knowledge and learning, so as to react quickly to environmental changes and capitalize on opportunities;
- Encouraging a sense of belonging and 'ownership', ensuring remuneration is adequate and other psychological needs met, so that staff are motivated not to leave the organization;
- Delegating and decentralizing. Does the entrepreneurial unit or division have to be small and separate from the rest of the organization? Is size a limiting factor?

Finally, there are some direct implications for management of the entrepreneurial organization:

- Strong vision is essential;
- Effective communication is vital;
- Timing is crucial, but difficult to manage;
- Management with a 'light touch' and a high degree of autonomy and delegation required;
- 'Positive' attitude required to encourage organizational self-confidence and self-efficacy.

The next chapter develops these implications further as we look at how the entrepreneur does business and manages the organization as it grows.

Summary

Entrepreneurs are both born and made. They have certain personal character traits that they are born with and are shaped by their history and experience of life – their background – as well as the culture of the society they are born into.

The issue of linking the character traits of an individual to the success of a business needs to be approached with caution because it is not always possible to link the individual and his or her traits solely to the success or failure of the venture. The character of the manager is just one factor in the equation. Success or failure in business comes from a mix of many different things including the history and experience of the entrepreneur – entrepreneurs are both born and made. However it also comes out of the commercial decisions the business makes in relation to its strengths and weaknesses and the environment it faces.

Notwithstanding these issues, researchers generally agree that entrepreneurs have the following 'survival' character traits:

- A need for independence; evidenced by the comments of **Eddy Shah**.
- A need for achievement; evidenced by the comments of **Brent Hoberman** and **Charles Muirhead**.
- An internal locus of control, that is a belief that they can control their own destiny; evidenced by the comments of **Jonathan Elvidge**. In extremes this can lead to a desire to maintain personal control over every aspect of the business.
- Ability to live with uncertainty and take measured risks; evidenced by the comments of **Jonathan Elvidge** and **Anne Notley**. However, uncertainty is a major cause of stress and entrepreneurs will always try to minimize their own downside risk; evidenced by the comments of **Michael Dell**.

In addition, entrepreneurs have the following 'growth' character traits:

- Opportunistic, creating or exploiting change for profit; evidenced by the comments of **Richard Branson** and **Michael Dell**.
- Innovative, using innovation as their prime tool to create or exploit opportunity; evidenced by the comments of **Neil Kelly**.
- Self-confident; evidenced by the comments of **Richard Thompson** and **Chris Ingram**.
- Proactive and decisive with high energy; evidenced by the comments of **Tom Farmer** and **Derrick Collin**.
- Self-motivated, enjoying what they do; evidenced by the comments of **Martha Lane Fox**, **Wing Yip** and **Richard Branson**. Self-efficacy is a stronger, deeper version of this and is built on previous experience.
- Vision and flair; evidenced by the comments of **Terry Saddler** and **Jonathan Elvidge**.

Growth companies are more likely to be set up by groups of better educated, middle-aged managers with previous experience, often sharing ownership to attract other experienced managers, rather than individuals. They leave their jobs for positive motivations, such as the need for independence, achievement or recognition. There are, however, a small but significant number of very young entrepreneurs with little or no business experience, who are usually successful because of their innovative business ideas.

Entrepreneurship is also influenced by its environment. In other words, entrepreneurial organizations can be constructed but they and the individuals that work in them are in turn influenced by the complex environment they find themselves in.

Deriving from the entrepreneurs' character are certain words and phrases that describe their beliefs and the way they think. These start to describe the entrepreneurial culture. They include: change is normal, achievement, creative, innovative, opportunistic, continual learning, self-confident but realistic, 'can-do', sharing information and knowledge, belonging, ownership, 'work is fun', celebrating success, measured risk taking. These are further developed in the next chapter.

There are also implications for the appropriate organizational structure and the style and approach to management in an entrepreneurial organization. These are also developed in the next chapter.

Measuring Entrepreneurial Personality

The **General Enterprising Tendency (GET)** test has been developed by staff at Durham University Business School over a number of years. It is a 54-question instrument that measures entrepreneurial personality traits in five dimensions:

- Need for achievement – 12 questions.
- Autonomy – 6 questions.
- Drive and determination – 12 questions.
- Risk taking – 12 questions.
- Creativity and potential to innovate – 6 questions.

It is relatively quick and simple to administer – with either agree or disagree questions – and score. Each dimension receives a score of up to 12 points (Autonomy 6 points) and the final composite score measures inherent entrepreneurial character traits on a scale of 0–54. The test is available free of charge from Durham University Business School.

Stormer *et al.* (1999) applied the test to 128 owners of new (75) and successful (53) small firms. They concluded that the test was acceptable for research purposes, particularly for identifying owner-managers, it was poor at predicting small business success. They concluded that either the test scales need to be refined for this purpose or that the test did not include sufficient indicators of success such as situational influences on the individual (see next section) or other factors related to the business rather than the individual setting it up. It would seem that, while entrepreneurs are both born and made, success requires more than an ounce of commercial expertise ... oh yes ... and a little luck!

An electronic version of the tool is available online at the website accompanying this book (www.palgrave.com/business/burns). Why not answer the questions and see if you are entrepreneurial? It will take about 10 minutes.

Essays and discussion topics

1. Are entrepreneurs born or made? Which factors are most important and why?
2. Do you think you have what it takes to be an owner-manager or entrepreneur, or both?
3. How do you think a manager of an entrepreneurial organization might differ from an entrepreneur?
4. What are the defining characteristics of an entrepreneur?
5. What character traits do you think affect the success or otherwise of a business venture?
6. What are the possible negative consequences of the entrepreneur's strong internal locus of control?
7. Do you think it is possible to 'pick winners'?
8. Is entrepreneurship really just for the middle-aged?
9. Why might so many e-commerce entrepreneurs be young and well educated?
10. Does previous business failure mean that you are more likely to succeed in the future?
11. Is entrepreneurship just a set of beliefs, a way of thinking and an approach to life?
12. How much control does the CEO or MD of an organisation have over its culture?
13. Can training help develop entrepreneurship?
14. Has your education, so far, encouraged you to be entrepreneurial? If so, how? If not, how could it be changed?
15. Does this course encourage entrepreneurship?

Exercises and assignments

1. Answer the GET test and write a report analyzing whether or not you are entrepreneurial. When agreeing or disagreeing with the results of the test, be sure to give concrete examples of your past behaviour that support your analysis.
2. List any additional questions you would ask an owner-manager or entrepreneur in trying to assess their character traits.
3. Use the GET test and exercise 2 to conduct an interview with an owner-manager of a local firm. Analyze their responses and write a report supporting your view as to whether they are entrepreneurial or not. Make sure you justify your conclusions with evidence from the interview or other objective information.

References

Abdesselam, R., Bonnet, J. and Le Pape, N. (1999) 'An Explanation of the Life Span of New Firms: An Empirical Analysis of French Data', *Entrepreneurship: Building for the Future*, Euro PME 2nd International Conference, Rennes.

Aldrich, H. E. and Martinez, M. (2003) 'Entrepreneurship as a Social Construction: A Multi-Level Evolutionary Approach', in Z. J. Acs and D. B. Audretsch (eds), *Handbook of Entrepreneurship Research: A Multidisciplinary Survey and Introduction*, Boston, Mass: Kluwer Academic Publishers.

Andersson, S., Gabrielsson, J. and Wictor, I. (2004) 'International Activities in Small Firms – Examining Factors Influencing the Internationalisation and Export Growth of Small Firms', *Canadian Journal of Administrative Science*, 21(1).

Baty, G. (1990) *Entrepreneurship for the Nineties*, New Jersey: Prentice Hall.

Bell, J., Murray, M. and Madden, K. (1992) 'Developing Expertise: An Irish Perspective', *International Small Business Journal*, 10(2).

Blanchflower, D. G. and Meyer, B. D. (1991) 'Longitudinal Analysis of Young Entrepreneurs in Australia and the United States', *National Bureau of Economic Research*, Working Paper 3746, Cambridge, MA.

Brockhaus, R. and Horwitz, P. (1986) 'The Psychology of the Entrepreneur' in Sexton, D. and Smilor, R. (eds), *The Art and Science of Entrepreneurship*, Cambridge: Ballinger Publishing Company.

Brush, C. G. (1992) 'Research on Women Business Owners: Past Trends, A New Perspective and Future Directions', *Entrepreneurship: Theory and Practice*, 16(4).

Burns, P. (2007) *Entrepreneurship and Small Business*, 2nd edn, Basingstoke: Palgrave Macmillan.

Busenitz, L. and Barney, J. (1997) 'Differences between Entrepreneurs and Managers in Large Organisations: Biases and Heuristics in Strategic Decision Making', *Journal of Business Venturing*, 12.

Buttner, E. and More, D. (1997) 'Women's Organisational Exodus to Entrepreneurship: Self-Reported Motivations and Correlates with Success', *Journal of Small Business Management*, 35(1).

Caird, S. (1990) 'What does it Mean to be Enterprising?', *British Journal of Management*, 1(3).

Carter, S. and Cachon, J. (1988) *The Sociology of Entrepreneurship*, Stirling: University of Stirling.

Chell, E., Haworth, J. and Brearley, S. (1991) *The Entrepreneurial Personality*, London: Routledge.

Chen, P. C., Greene, P. G. and Crick, A. (1998) 'Does Entrepreneurial Self Efficacy Distinguish Entrepreneurs from Managers?', *Journal of Business Venturing*, 13.

Cuba, R., Decenzo, D. and Anish, A. (1983) 'Management Practises of Successful Female Business Owners', *American Journal of Small Business*, 8(2).

Deakins, D. (1996) *Entrepreneurs and Small Firms*, London: McGraw-Hill.

de Bono, E. (1985) *Six Thinking Hats*, Boston: Little Brown & Company.

Evans, D. S. and Leighton, L. S. (1990) 'Small Business Formation by Unemployed and Employed Workers', *Small Business Economics*, 2(4).

Harper, M. (1985) 'Hardship, Discipline and Entrepreneurship', *Cranfield School of Management*, Working Paper 85(1).

Hirsch, R. D. and Brush, C. G. (1987) 'Women Entrepreneurs: A Longitudinal Study', *Frontiers in Entrepreneurship Research*, Wellesley, Mass: Babson College.

Kanter, R. M. (1983) *The Change Masters*, New York: Simon & Schuster.

Kets de Vries, M. F. R. (1985) 'The Dark Side of Entrepreneurship', *Harvard Business Review*, November/December.

Kirzner, I. M. (1973) *Competition and Entrepreneurship*, Chicago: University of Chicago.

Kirzner, I. M. (1979) *Perception, Opportunity and Profit: Studies in the Theory of Entrepreneurship*, Chicago: University of Chicago.

Kirzner, I. M. (1997) 'Entrepreneurial Discovery and Competitive Market Processes: An Austrian Approach', *Journal of Economic Literature*, 35.

Kirzner, I. M. (1999) 'Creativity and/or Alertness: A Reconsideration of the Schumpeterian Entrepreneur', *Review of Austrian Economics*, 11.

McClelland, D. C. (1961) *The Achieving Society*, Princeton, NJ: Van Nostrand.

Pinchot, G. (1985) *Intrapreneuring*, New York: Harper & Row.

Rosa, P., Hamilton, S., Carter, S. and Burns, H. (1994) 'The Impact of Gender on Small Business Management: Preliminary Findings of a British Study', *International Small Business Journal*, 12(3).

Schein, V., Mueller, R., Lituchy, T. and Liu, J. (1996) 'Thinking Manager – Think Male: A Global Phenomenon?', *Journal of Organisational Behaviour*, 17.

Schumpeter, J. A. ([1983] 1996) *The Theory of Economic Development*, New Jersey: Transaction Publishers.

Schwartz, E. B. (1997) 'Entrepreneurship: A New Female Frontier', *Journal of Contemporary Business*, Winter.

Shapero, A. (1985) *Managing Professional People – Understanding Creative Performance*, New York: Free Press.

Shaver, K. and Scott, L. (1992) 'Person, Processes and Choice: The Psychology of New Venture Creation', *Entrepreneurship Theory and Practice*, 16(2).

Stanworth, J., Blythe, S., Granger, B. and Stanworth, C. (1989) 'Who Becomes an Entrepreneur?', *International Small Business Journal*, 8(1).

Storey, D. J. (1994) *Understanding the Small Business Sector*, London: International Thomson Business Press.

Storey, D. and Sykes, N. (1996) 'Uncertainty, Innovation and Management' in P. Burns and J. Dewhurst (eds), *Small Business and Entrepreneurship*, Basingstoke: Macmillan – now Palgrave Macmillan.

Stormer, R., Kline, T. and Goldberg, S. (1999) 'Measuring Entrepreneurship with the General Enterprise Tendency (GET) Test: Criterion-related Validity and Reliability', *Human Systems Management*, 18(1).

3

Entrepreneur Spiderman

Contents

- Decision making
- Strategy development
- Relationships and networks
- The entrepreneurial spider's web
- The changing entrepreneur
- Implications for corporate entrepreneurship
- Summary

LEARNING OUTCOMES

By the end of this chapter you should be able to:

- Describe how entrepreneurs approach decision making and the formulation of strategy and explain how this affects their approach to management;

- Describe how entrepreneurs form personal relationships and networks with all the stakeholders in the business and explain how this affects their approach to management;

- Explain how the entrepreneur must change as the business grows;

- Assess the implications of growth models for entrepreneurs, their style of management and the organization of the firm;

- Assess the implications of all these factors for corporate entrepreneurship.

Decision making

Entrepreneurs have a particular and characteristic approach to doing business and managing the organization. What is more, this must change and adapt as the organization grows – size does matter. They approach decision making and strategy formulation differently and they rely heavily on informal relationships and influences for many aspects of business and management, whereas large organizations rely far more on formal, often contractual, relationships.

> 'In leadership, it's important to be intuitive, but not at the expense of facts. Without the right data to back it up, emotion-based decision making during difficult times will inevitably lead a company into greater danger.'
> **Michael Dell**
> ➡

Entrepreneurs are often seen as being intuitive, almost whimsical, in their decision making. True, economists find it difficult to understand and to model their approach to decision making. It certainly does not fit well into 'logical' economic models such as discounted cash flow. The reason lies at the heart of any entrepreneurial venture – the greater degree of risk and uncertainty it faces. The result is a different approach to developing strategy and making decisions that is just as logical but little understood.

One important result of the approach of owner-managers and entrepreneurs, particularly in Britain, to dealing with uncertainty and risk is their short-term approach to most business decisions, especially those involving investment and financing (Burns and Whitehouse, 1995a and 1995b). It really is a case of not being certain that the business will survive until tomorrow and not having the resources to commit in the first place. Therefore decision making is often short-term and incremental and investment minimal, using any resources available. However, as the business grows, decision making needs to be more long-term whilst maintaining maximum flexibility – not always an easy task. Short-term financing decisions can increase the business risk. Short-term investment decisions can mean that opportunities are not pursued sufficiently rapidly.

> 'The ideal business has no fixed overheads, commission only sales, large volume and low overheads.'
> **David Speakman**
> founder of **Travel Counsellors**
> *Sunday Times*, 6 December 1998
> ●

This aspect of entrepreneurial behaviour needs to be corrected, but in a way that maintains flexibility and responsiveness to changing market conditions. This is not easy because there is another, more positive aspect of this behaviour and another, more logical, way of regarding it. Entrepreneurs seek to keep their fixed costs as low as possible because they are trying to minimize the risk they face. They tend to commit costs only after the opportunity has proved to be real, which may be prudent and reflect their resource limits but then they run the risk of losing first mover advantage in the market place – a difficult judgement call.

Entrepreneurs also see an asset as a liability rather than just an asset in the balance-sheet sense – limiting the flexibility that they need and committing them to a course of action that may prove unsound. In many respects this is again just prudent financial control, which is just as well since finding the resources for a new business is usually a problem. Indeed one of the well documented routes to disaster is financial profligacy – a factor ignored by many companies in the days of the dot.com boom.

Implications for the entrepreneurial organization:

- *Issues for management style.* Avoid any over-tendency towards short-termism in decision making and at the same time any tendency towards profligacy. This is a question of judgement.

Strategy development

An important aspect of this behaviour is the different approach entrepreneurs have to developing strategy. Strategies often evolve on a step-by-step basis. If one step works then the second is taken. At the same time entrepreneurs will keep as many options open as possible, because they realize the outcome of any action is very uncertain.

Whilst strategy can be developed in a systematic, almost mechanistic, manner many entrepreneurs develop strategy instinctively and intuitively – often they call it 'gut feel'. They do not know the jargon, do not use the frameworks we have developed – and justified with empirical evidence – but instinctively they arrive at the right decision. There is nothing wrong with this. The words and frameworks we might use give meaning and logic to what they do. Many excellent musicians or athletes were not taught. They picked up the skills instinctively. Explaining why they do what they do can give them confidence to replicate their successes and even improve.

Strategic frameworks replicate what is good practice. They ought to be logical, common sense. They are not in the nature of a scientific discovery. They are, to quote a colleague, 'a glimpse of the blindingly obvious', something you knew all along but were never quite able to express in that simple way. As John Kay (1998) explains:

'An organizational framework can never be right, or wrong, only helpful or unhelpful. A good organizational framework is minimalist – it is as simple as is consistent with illuminating the issues under discussion – and is memorable ... The organizational framework provides the link from judgement through experience to learning. A valid framework is one which focuses sharply on what the skilled manager, at least instinctively, already knows. He is constantly alive to strengths, weaknesses, opportunities, threats which confront him ... A successful framework formalizes and extends their existing knowledge. For the less practised, an effective framework is one which organizes and develops what would otherwise be disjointed experience.'

Some entrepreneurs may claim to have achieved their success through luck. Never underestimate luck. We all need it, but remember that entrepreneurs have a strong internal locus of control which means that they may believe in luck but they do not believe in fate. They believe they can, and will, shape their own destinies and that may mean working to create more opportunities than most people. By creating more strategic options and opportunities they improve their chances of successfully pursuing at least one. Make no mistake, entrepreneurs to a large extent create their own luck.

And yet there is always the nagging doubt that perhaps entrepreneurs are more opportunistic and adaptive, rather than calculating and planning in the way strategy is laid out in books. In fact this view is as old as strategy itself and was called by Lindblom (1959) 'the science of muddling through'. The implications of this for strategy were developed by Mintzberg (1978) who contrasted deliberate with emergent strategy. As he put it:

> 'The strategy-making process is characterized by reactive solutions to existing problems ... The adaptive organization makes its decisions in incremental, serial steps.'

And here we do catch reflections of how the entrepreneur approaches decision making in a risky, uncertain and rapidly changing environment. There is nothing wrong with strategy that is incremental and adaptive but that does not say that strategy cannot be analyzed, managed and controlled. The strategic frameworks are just as useful. And successful entrepreneurs are constantly strategizing – thinking about the future and analyzing their options. Indeed, Sir George Mathewson, Executive Deputy Chairman of the very entrepreneurial Royal Bank of Scotland Group (which includes NatWest, Direct Line and even Coutts Bank) has gone so far as to propose that formalized strategic planning is inappropriate in today's changing environment and what is needed instead is more strategizing and the development of strategic options – options that lead the firm in the general direction it wants to go – but decisions on which option to select depend upon market conditions and opportunities. The greater the number of strategic options open to the firm, the safer it is in an uncertain environment (Mathewson, 2000).

So for some firms strategy development may be systematic and deliberate but for many entrepreneurial firms it is likely to be emergent. It is likely to be incremental and adaptive. 'Strategic intent' is still needed to give the firm clear direction, only the path to achieve these goals is not always clear. In these circumstances the process of strategizing or strategy development is vital. The development of multiple strategic options is the key to success, with decision making based upon opportunistic circumstances at the time.

What holds this all together is a strong vision of where the organization is going. Thus entrepreneurs need to know the goal they are ultimately seeking and need to have the frameworks to make those incremental, adaptive decisions. There is nothing wrong with having a map with a planned route, but it makes sense to find a way around any road blocks you encounter rather than going headlong into them. And, as we shall see in the next section,

> 'You just need to look at where Virgin is now to see that business is a fluid, changing substance. As far as I'm concerned, the company will never stand still. It has always been a mutating, indefinable thing and the past few years have demonstrated that.'
>
> **Richard Branson**
> ➡

> 'If you set yourself goals that are really high and keep working to achieve them, then success should be possible. Just look back and say I gave it my best shot.'
>
> **David Darling**
> founder **Codemaster**
> *The Times*, 10 October 2002
> ●

some of these road blocks are the crises that a firm will inevitably encounter as it passes through the predictable phases of growth. These phases suggest that the entrepreneur's natural style of management needs to change as the organization grows.

One interesting research study indicates that these stages might lead, not only to changes in strategy, but also to changes in the strategy development process itself, causing shifts from the emergent to the deliberate style, at least for a period (McCarthy and Leavy, 2000). The study suggests that the strategy development process in small firms is *both* deliberate and emergent in nature and the degree of deliberateness in the early phase of development is influenced most by the personality of the entrepreneur and the nature of the business context. Over time strategy formation follows a phase pattern, moving from an early fluid phase to a more defined phase, usually triggered by a crisis or defining episode, so that the degree of deliberateness is also a function of history, with firms oscillating between emergent strategy development, when learning is taking place, and deliberate planning modes over time. Rather than entrepreneurs having only one style, they would seem to adopt both, depending on circumstances. In this way the well-documented process of growth to crisis to consolidation parallels a process of emergent to deliberate to emergent strategy formulation, represented in Figure 3.1.

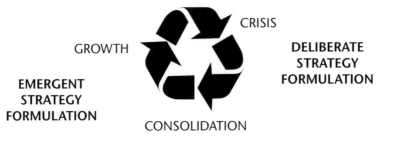

Figure 3.1   The strategy formulation cycle

Implications for management of the entrepreneurial organization:

- Continuous strategizing needs to be encouraged at all levels with good information flows encouraging objectivity and opportunity perception.
- The process of strategy formulation should not only be 'top-down'. It must be flexible, iterative, coming both from the top and from the bottom. Strategizing should lead to the creation of strategic options. Options need to be evaluated in the light of the most up-to-date information so as to react quickly to changes in market opportunities or threats.
- An incremental and adaptive approach to decision making is to be encouraged. This is designed to maintain maximum flexibility for as long as possible. The free flow of accurate, realistic information is essential to inform this process and ensure the best decisions possible are made at each stage.
- Strategizing is to be underpinned by a strong vision that sets the general direction of the organization and motivates staff to make the best decisions for the organization.

Relationships and networks

At the core of the entrepreneurial approach to doing business is the development of relationships – with customers, staff, suppliers and all the stakeholders in the business. It is the personal touch that distinguishes them from the faceless, grey-suited managers in large companies. These relationships build into an invaluable network of contacts and goodwill – based essentially on trust and respect – that can be used whenever the firm needs to change or do something just a little more risky than the average firm.

It is at the start-up phase of business when entrepreneurs start to develop these skills. They need the resources to start up but often have to work hard to gain the credibility to obtain money from a banker or venture capitalist. And there are other less obvious resource needs. The business needs customers, suppliers, perhaps employees and a landlord. The process of assembling these resources is a difficult one and is crucially dependent on one factor – credibility. As a start-up, if you go to a banker with an ill thought-through proposal, not knowing how much money you need, your credibility in terms of whether you are likely to manage the start-up effectively will be very low. Bankers are looking to have you persuade them that your start-up will succeed. They might suggest you go out and get your first customer. But if you go to potential customers and ask them to place an order for your product or service they might ask about reliability or after-sales service. They might also reasonably expect to see the product. They might even ask for evidence of previous satisfied customers. The same problem happens when you approach suppliers or a landlord. They will ask for a bank reference, or look to a trading track record – none of which you have. So how does the entrepreneur establish credibility?

Credibility can be established in a number of ways at start-up. Education and track record are important. If you can demonstrate achievements, particularly in the industry in which you want to start up, it counts for a lot. But personal contact is the key to any relationship and networks of friends and commercial contacts can be important. A strong personal relationship can bring credibility with it. A network of contacts can provide your first customer, or low-cost or free office space. These

> 'Dell is very much a relationship orientated company . . . how we communicate and partner with our employees and customers. But our commitment doesn't stop there. Our willingness and ability to partner to achieve our common goals is perhaps seen in its purest form in how we forge strong alliances with our suppliers.
>
> As a small start-up, we didn't have the money to build the components ourselves . . . but we actually had an option: to buy components from the specialists, leveraging the investment they had made and allowing us to focus on what we did best – designing and delivering solutions and systems directly to customers. In forging these early alliances with suppliers, we created exactly the right strategy for a fast-growing company.'
>
> **Michael Dell**
>
> ➡

'Contacts are important but you have to get out there and meet people. It can be difficult when you are absorbed in running a business. But there is always something to learn from meeting someone new and a lot to learn from meeting someone old. The right contacts can become an invaluable source of learning as well as an inspiration and support.'

Jonathan Elvidge
founder of **Gadget Shop**
The Times, 6 July 2002
➡

contacts might even provide the cash that the banker is so reluctant to provide. Networks can also provide professional advice and opinion, often without charge.

Another area in which the entrepreneur places a heavy reliance upon relationships and networks – at least in the start-up phase of the business – is marketing. Again this is born out of necessity, because of problems of credibility and lack of cash to spend on the more conventional tools of the marketing mix such as advertising and promotion. More recently this has been recognized and christened 'relationship marketing', which can be contrasted to the more traditional transaction marketing mainly practised by larger companies. Supporters of this 'new' approach – in fact, long used by small firms – believe that

it can deliver sustainable customer loyalty (Webster, 1992). The two approaches are contrasted in Table 3.1. Nevertheless, as we shall explore later, whilst a reliance on relationships may be a characteristic of smaller firms, it is not in itself sufficient to mark out the true entrepreneurial firm – that relies more on an entrepreneurial approach to the whole area of marketing.

Table 3.1　Relationship vs transactional marketing

Relationship marketing	Transactional marketing
• Encourages close, frequent customer contact	• Limited contact
• Encourages repeat sales	• Orientated towards single purchase
• Focus on customer service	• Limited customer service
• Focus on value to the customer	• Focus on product/service benefits
• Focus on quality of total offering	• Focus on quality of product
• Focus on long-term performance	• Focus on short-term performance

Implications for the culture of the entrepreneurial organization:

- *Close relationships with customers* can generate extra sales and improve loyalty. They can also lead to improved opportunity perception.
- *Close relationships with suppliers* can reduce lead times, improve quality and efficiency and lead to competitive advantage. They may lead to close partnerships, joint ventures or other approaches to reducing or spreading risk, particularly when it comes to new product or market opportunities.

Stephen Waring and Green Thumb

The motivation to set up your own business can come from deep inside and wait a long time to find the best opportunity. The process is not linear or necessarily sequential – and many might say luck is involved. Stephen Waring's entrepreneurial instinct kicked in at the age of 14 when he started framing old prints and selling them at local fetes around his home town in North Wales in his spare time. Stephen's father was the sales director for a loft insulation firm and by the age of 16 he was helping canvass potential customers by knocking on doors. He was good at selling, and so when he left school at 17 he set up his own loft insulation firm – it came naturally. He was so successful he even persuaded his older brother to come and help him. When his brother married an American girl in 1985, Stephen went to the USA for the wedding. There he met her uncle who owned a lawn-treatment company. He also found out that 24% of homes in the USA hired someone to treat their lawns in some way.

Despite sceptical parents, Stephen researched the idea. First he set out to find competitors by looking through the Yellow Pages telephone directories, but he could not find anybody offering the same service in the UK. The question was whether nobody else had thought about this idea or whether there was no demand for this sort of service. Stephen could not believe that a service that sold to millions of people in the USA would not sell in the UK so he decided to persevere. Next he set out to find the best mix of fertilizer ingredients for the UK. He experimented on his parents' lawn, turning it orange and black in the process. Having perfected a suitable mix, Stephen next spent £64 on printing 1000 leaflets and hand delivered them around housing estates near his home. Then he went around doing what he did best – knocking on doors and selling. In this way he secured 70 customers and Green Thumb was born.

Stephen quickly developed a routine of visiting customers four or five times a year to treat their lawns, like in the USA. The treatment worked and word-of-mouth attracted more customers, so Stephen brought in his younger brother to help him. By 1995, Green Thumb had several thousand regular customers and that was when the next stage in the business's development came about. A customer asked Stephen to sell him a Green Thumb franchise. In 1996 Stephen started selling franchises around the UK. By 2005 there were some 113 franchises servicing over seven million customers, each spending about £26 per year on lawn treatment. Franchisees had sales of £25 million a year, giving the company royalties of £5 million. Green Thumb is growing at 5% per year.

'When people ask me if I ever imagined that my business would be as successful as it has turned out to be, I have to say yes. And we are still embryonic in our growth ... The challenge was developing an industry from scratch as opposed to jumping on the bandwagon of somebody else who was already doing it ... It helps to have a strong belief in your abilities and not to feel insecure.' *Sunday Times*, 2 October 2005

Up-to-date information on Green Thumb can be found on the website: www.greenthumb.co.uk

Questions
1. In what ways did Stephen minimize his start-up and growth costs?
2. How did he use relationships?
3. How much of Stephen's success was down to luck?
4. Would Stephen have succeeded in any business?

The entrepreneurial spider's web

The final, and probably most important, area where the entrepreneur makes use of relationships and networks is in the management of staff. Entrepreneurial organization structures, seen most clearly at the start-up phase, have been likened to the spider's web shown in Figure 3.2A. The entrepreneur sits at the centre of the web with each new member of staff reporting to him or her. The management style tends to be informal, one of direct supervision. Just as entrepreneurs prefer informal marketing techniques, building on relationships, they prefer informal organization structures and influences rather than rigid rules and job definitions. They persuade and cajole employees, showing them how to do things on a one-to-one basis, rather than having prescribed tasks. They rely on building personal relationships. After all, the business is growing rapidly and there are no precedents to go by. The future is uncertain, so flexibility is the key. The pace of change probably means that rigid structures would be out of date quickly. What is more, in a small firm everybody has to be prepared to do other people's jobs because there is no cover, no slack in the system if, for example, someone goes off sick. It is also perfectly flat and therefore efficient – overheads are reduced – and it is responsive – communication times are minimized. This is the typical small, entrepreneurial structure with the entrepreneur leading by example and communicating directly. It is motivating and works – up to a certain size – with the right person as leader.

The entrepreneurial structure works quite well up to a couple of dozen employees. However, around this point it starts creaking at the seams as the entrepreneur tries to do everything personally. Even when he or she tries to delegate and introduce new staff who report to existing members of staff, the entrepreneur tends to meddle and the new employees soon find an informal reporting line to the entrepreneur, short-circuiting the manager or supervisor they are supposed to report to, as in Figure 3.2B. It is no wonder that this creates frustration, resentment and an unwillingness to accept responsibility in the managers. Why should they take responsibility when

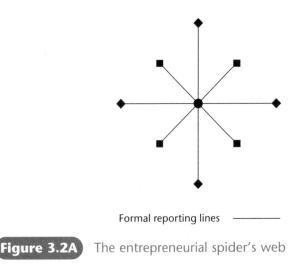

Formal reporting lines   ———

Figure 3.2A   The entrepreneurial spider's web

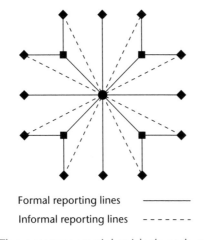

Formal reporting lines ————
Informal reporting lines - - - - - - -

Figure 3.2B The entrepreneurial spider's web grows

their decisions are likely to be questioned or reversed, or when staff supposedly reporting to them are constantly being supervised by the entrepreneur?

The root cause of these problems lies in the entrepreneurial character and in particular the strong need for control that can exhibit itself in some entrepreneurs. Derek du Toit (1980), an entrepreneur himself, said that 'an entrepreneur who starts his own business generally does so because he is a difficult employee.' He probably finds it difficult to be in the alternating dominant and then submissive role so often asked of middle management. He hates being told what to do and wants to tell everybody what to do. He also believes he can do the job better than others, which may be true, but he must find a way of working through others if the business is to grow successfully.

Kets de Vries (1985) was probably the first to argue that these traits can lead to entrepreneurs wanting to over-control their business – becoming 'control freaks'. This is not such a problem in micro businesses, where the owner-managers do everything themselves anyway, where their business is their life and their life is the business. Indeed it can be a virtue – making certain everything gets done properly. However, as the business grows this characteristic starts to be a problem. For example, in a fruit-juice bottling plant with about 200 employees the owner-manager could not bear to relinquish any control to senior managers and insisted that copies of all external correspondence came to him. In this way he believed he still had some control. The problem was that his senior managers felt they could not be trusted even to write a letter and the best left quickly.

The entrepreneurial firm faces the challenge of maintaining close personal relationships with staff and flexible job structures – which are motivating and effective in an uncertain environment – without the dangers this can present. And this is just the tip of the iceberg of problems facing entrepreneurs as the business grows. As it does so, they have to change and adapt – or face the prospect of their business failing, often because of the prevalence of the very qualities that led to success at start-up.

> **Implications for the entrepreneurial organization:**
>
> - *Issues for culture.* Relationships are more important than formal structures. A culture that encourages the development of relationships with all the stakeholders of the organization, at all levels, underpins the entrepreneurial organization. It also encourages entrepreneurial networks. Close relationships with staff at all levels of the organization can improve motivation, speed of response and information flows. Culture is infectious and is communicated through close relationships.
> - *Issues for structure.* Avoid over-control. Are smaller structures required to maintain closeness of relationships?

The changing entrepreneur

As the business grows entrepreneurs face challenges and problems as the nature of the organization changes. As it changes, they too need to change and adapt. The more rapid the growth, the more difficult this is. Entrepreneur super-heroes need to metamorphosize into entrepreneurial leaders. They need to change the way they operate – recruit reliable managers, delegate to them and control and monitor their performance. The organization must become more formal, but, if it wishes to retain its entrepreneurial character, without becoming more bureaucratic. And all of these changes need to be properly managed if the firm is to grow successfully. It is little wonder that so few firms grow to any size. Some entrepreneurs even decide not to grow their business because they realize they cannot manage these changes or because they do not want to change the way they do business. And from those who successfully make the metamorphosis, we learn a lot about how the entrepreneurial organization needs to be structured, about its culture, but most about the style of management and leadership needed.

There are a number of well-known growth models that seek to describe the changes that the entrepreneur faces and, by inference, how the changes need to be managed. One of the most widely used models was developed by Greiner (1972). This is shown in Figure 3.3. It offers a five-stage framework for considering the development of a business, but more particularly the managerial changes facing the founder. Each phase of growth is followed by a crisis that necessitates a change in the way the founder manages the business if it is to move on and continue to grow. If the crisis cannot be overcome then it is possible that the business might fail. The length of time it takes to go through each phase depends on the industry in which the company operates. In fast-growing industries, growth periods are relatively short; in slower-growth industries they tend to be longer. Each evolutionary phase requires a particular management style or emphasis to achieve growth. Each revolutionary period presents a management problem to overcome. Only phases 1 to 4 really apply to smaller firms.

- **Phase 1:** Growth comes through entrepreneurial creativity. However, this constant seeking out of new opportunities and the development of innovative ways of doing things leads to a crisis of leadership. Staff, financiers and even customers increasingly fail to understand the focus of the business – where it is going, what it

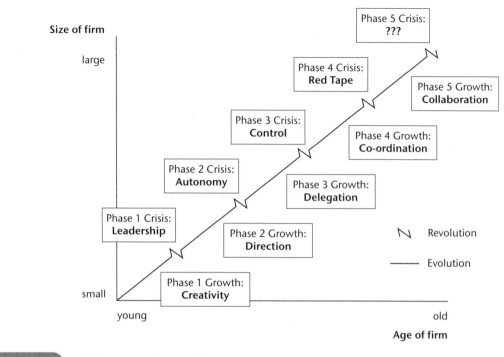

Size of firm

large

small

young   old

Age of firm

Phase 5 Crisis:
???

Phase 4 Crisis:
Red Tape

Phase 5 Growth:
Collaboration

Phase 3 Crisis:
Control

Phase 4 Growth:
Co-ordination

Phase 2 Crisis:
Autonomy

Phase 3 Growth:
Delegation

Phase 1 Crisis:
Leadership

Phase 2 Growth:
Direction

Revolution

Evolution

Phase 1 Growth:
Creativity

Figure 3.3 Greiner growth model

is selling – and resources become spread too thinly to follow through effectively on any single commercial opportunity.

- **Phase 2:** Growth comes from the direction given by effective leadership in this phase. The entrepreneur must become more of a leader and give the business the direction it needs. However, entrepreneurs have a strong internal locus of control, which means that there is a danger that they will be unable or unwilling to delegate responsibility to their management team. The leader then faces a crisis of autonomy that will only be addressed by putting that management team in place and delegating work to it.
- **Phase 3:** Growth in this phase comes because the team is in place and effective delegation is taking place. The business is no longer a one-man-band. However, there is always the danger that delegation becomes abdication of responsibility and, as the firm continues to grow, there is a loss of proper control. Entrepreneurs are notorious for not being interested in the detail of controlling a business. The next crisis, inevitably, is one of control.
- **Phase 4:** Growth now comes from effective co-ordination of management and its work force. Controls are in place and are working effectively. By this stage the firm will have ceased to have many of the characteristics of an owner-managed firm because there are set procedures and policies for doing things. The danger now is that it might lose its entrepreneurial drive and the next crisis it might face is one of red tape or bureaucracy. Greiner says this can only be overcome by collaboration – making people work together through a sense of mission or purpose rather than by reference to a rule book – an important point for the entrepreneurial organization.

'We had to learn the basic steps that most companies, which grow and mature more slowly, learn when they are much smaller in size. We were moving in the right direction with our emphasis on liquidity, profitability and growth. But we were also challenged by a cultural issue. We had created an atmosphere in which we focused on growth ... We had to shift to focus away from an external orientation to one that strengthened our company internally.

For us growing up meant figuring out a way to combine our signature informal, entrepreneurial style and want-to attitude with the can-do capabilities that would allow us to develop as a company. It meant incorporating into our everyday structures the valuable lessons we'd begun to learn using P&Ls [profit and loss accounts]. It meant focusing our employees to think in terms of shareholder value. It meant respecting the three golden rules at Dell:

1. Disdain inventory.
2. Always listen to the customer.
3. Never sell indirect.'

Michael Dell
➡

To address each of these crises entrepreneurs need to adapt and change. In particular, they need to develop into leaders. They need to put in place a management team and work as part of this team – difficult when you consider many of the strong personal characteristics exhibited by entrepreneurs, particularly the extreme behaviour that can result from their internal locus of control. Alongside this the organizational structure of the firm will need to adapt and change and an appropriate culture created in the business.

Other models, such as the one developed by Churchill and Lewis (1983) and summarized in Table 3.2, also emphasize the shift in the personal skills required of entrepreneurs as the business grows away from their operational abilities towards their strategic and management abilities. The model seeks to describe factors as a business develops and, in that context, the entrepreneurial firm that interests us is

Table 3.2 Churchill and Lewis growth model

Growth phase	Owner's attributes				Management style	Organization structure
	Own goals	Operational ability	Management ability	Strategic ability		
Existence	☆☆☆	☆☆☆	☆	☆	Direct supervision	Simple
Survival	☆	☆☆☆	☆☆	☆☆	Supervised supervision	Growing
Growth	☆☆☆	☆☆	☆☆	☆☆☆	Functional	Growing
Take-off	☆☆☆	☆☆	☆☆☆	☆☆☆	Divisional	Growing
Maturity	☆☆	☆	☆☆	☆☆☆	Line and staff	Sophisticated

Critical ☆☆☆   Important but manageable ☆☆   Not very important ☆

likely to be constantly in the growth or take-off phase. At these stages development of strategy becomes vital. Entrepreneurs' personal goals – their motivation, determination and, most importantly, their vision – are critical both at the start-up and growth phases, arguably when uncertainty is greatest. The model also underlines the changing management style needed as the organization grows, with the growing importance of developing a management team and more conventional or formal structures, although the model tells us little about the most appropriate structure.

Another model proposed by Burns (1996) also emphasizes the drift from informal to more formal structures as the firm grows. In this model life-style businesses – ones that are set up because the owner-manager enjoys some functional aspect of the business and never grow beyond a level that generates a sufficient income to satisfy him or her – can survive using an informal, tactical orientation, on a day-to-day basis. On the other hand growth businesses, having proved that their business model works, go into the success and take-off phases, when rapid growth can be expected. In this phase they need to take a far more strategic orientation, with more formalized procedures and structures. They recruit new managers to the business and must learn to delegate to and control a management team. The recruitment of managers from other, often larger, firms is a characteristic associated with successful growth companies. Perhaps this is related to the changes in culture that are taking place in the firm at this stage. This model goes further, summarizing the main business imperatives and describing the changes in the main functional disciplines of management, marketing, accounting and finance as the firm grows. Table 3.3 summarizes only the management changes highlighted in the model.

Table 3.3 Burns growth model

Growth phase	Orientation	Management
Existence	Tactical	• Owner is the business and is 'jack of all trades' • Spider's web organization • Informal, flexible systems • Opportunity driven
Survival	Tactical	• Owner is still the business • Still spider's web organization • Some delegation, supervision and control
Success	Strategic	• Staff start to be recruited • Organization starts to become formalized • Staff encouraged and motivated to grow into job • Delegation, supervision and control • Strategic planning
Take-off	Strategic	• Staff roles clearly defined • Decentralization starts • Greater co-ordination and control of staff • Emergence of professional management • Operational and strategic planning

These models are probably best used as checklists of the imperatives that entrepreneurs and firms ought to face up to if they wish to grow through the different stages of development. The models should not be applied mechanistically, but rather with judgement and discretion, particularly in relation to sequence and timing. However, they provide an invaluable description of the changing role of entrepreneurs and the skills they need. And the cycle of growth followed by crisis, usually then followed by a period of consolidation, highlighted in Figure 3.1, is well documented.

Entrepreneurs therefore face two challenges if the organization is to grow successfully. The first is the personal challenge to develop and change their management style and skills in an appropriate way as the organization grows, in particular, to develop their skills of leadership, delegation and team working. The second is the organizational challenge to ensure that, as the organization grows, it retains its entrepreneurial characteristics and does not become overly bureaucratic,

---

Case insight

Stelios Haji-Ioannou, a graduate of London Business School, founded the low-cost airline **easyJet** in 1995 with £5 million borrowed from his father, a Greek shipping tycoon. The first route was from Luton to Scotland. He then launched similar low-cost, no-frills services to continental Europe. The company has transformed the European air travel market and has outdone many rival imitators. easyJet was floated on the Stock Market in 2000 at 310p a share, making Stelios £280 million profit.

'You start the business as a dream, you make it your passion for a while and then you get experienced managers to run it because it's not as much fun as starting. I think there's a lot to be said about starting a business and a lot to be said about running a business when it's mature.'
Sunday Times, 29 October 2000

Only seven years later, in 2002, and still owning 29 per cent of easyJet Stelios realized that he was not suited to managing an established public company and was better suited to being a serial entrepreneur so he resigned as Chairman, aged only 35. He was to be replaced by Sir Colin Chandler, aged 62, part of London's financial establishment as chairman of Vickers Defence Systems, deputy chairman of Smiths Group and director of Thales. Soon after easyJet took over Go, the low-cost airline set up by British Airways and sold off to its management. Newspaper comment at the time suggested Stelios had been blocking such a deal and this might have been one reason for his departure.

'Running a company that is listed on the Stock Exchange is different from building up and running a private company. The history of the City is littered with entrepreneurs who hold onto their creations for too long, failing to recognise the changing needs of the company. I am a serial entrepreneur ... It is all part of growing up. I've built something and now it is time to move on.'
The Times, 19 April 2002

Stelios still had many other 'easy' ventures to grow. These include **easyRental** – a car rental business, **easyEverything** – a chain of internet cafes and cinemas and **easyValue** – which provides impartial comparisons for online shopping. He still has everything to play for doing something he enjoys more and possibly does better.

thus avoiding Greiner's crisis of red tape. This means putting in place an appropriate organizational structure, but most important of all, an appropriate organizational culture. What is more they need to manage these changes and deal with the conflicts that inevitably will arise.

Implications of growth models for the entrepreneurial organization:

- *Issues for structure.* Entrepreneurs find difficulty in 'letting go' of their business, but they cannot control it in the same way as they do as a start-up. The entrepreneurial organization must find ways of delegating authority, whilst giving strong direction and ensuring co-ordination. Without this it is likely to go from one crisis to another. Along with delegation, decentralization will probably be needed so as to allow good managers the space to manage. Team working becomes increasingly important. Is size a limiting factor? The organization must become more formal as it grows but must also avoid bureaucracy at all costs through collaboration – making people work together through a sense of purpose or mission, rather than by reference to the rule book.
- *Issues for management.* Strategic capability is vital in a period of growth. If it is not just the entrepreneur who is to be entrepreneurial then all staff must have it. Not all entrepreneurs can run large organizations – even entrepreneurial ones.

Implications for corporate entrepreneurship

This chapter has looked at entrepreneurs' approach to decision making, strategy and business development and management in general. It has looked at how this approach must change as the organization increases in size. In particular it has emphasized the importance of relationships in developing business and approaching management, characterizing the entrepreneur as a spider in the middle of a web of relationships.

The most important – and different – approach to management is the reliance entrepreneurs place upon relationships rather than formal structures or contracts. The development of relationships with all stakeholders in the organization is the cornerstone of the entrepreneurial approach to management. The organization can try to replicate these characteristics through processes, structures, incentives and – most important of all – culture. This important aspect of entrepreneurial culture is superimposed on the other elements, highlighted in the previous chapter, to form the spider's web of culture for an entrepreneurial organization (Figure 3.4). How this might be developed is discussed in subsequent chapters.

The most important – and different – approach to decision making is the entrepreneur's ability to strategize and develop strategic options. This maintains flexibility and allows the organization to react quickly to changes in the market place. It is the entrepreneur's way of dealing with uncertainty. Effective strategizing is fed by good information flows and good feedback or learning from experience – including mistakes. Information from the environment, but customers in particular, helps identify opportunities. The more strategic options that exist, the more the entrepreneurial organization is to succeed.

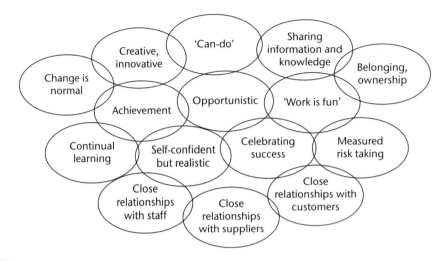

Figure 3.4   The cultural web of an entrepreneurial organisation

Some of the personal characteristics of entrepreneurs are unwelcome as the organization grows. In particular, entrepreneurs are reluctant to delegate and this can inhibit growth. The successful start-ups are those that have grown through a process of the entrepreneur giving direction and being able to delegate whilst still maintaining control. As it grows, the organization must become more formal but must avoid becoming too bureaucratic – through collaboration – making people work together through a sense of purpose or mission, rather than by reference to the rule book. Combining these with the implications for management developed in the last chapter allows us to highlight the essential characteristics of management of the entrepreneurial organization. These are shown in Table 3.4. Many successful start-up entrepreneurs are not good large organization entrepreneurs and may need to be replaced.

Table 3.4   Management characteristics of the entrepreneurial organization

- Strong vision
- Effective communication
- Timing is crucial, but difficult to manage
- Management with a 'light touch' – a high degree of autonomy without need to revert to a 'rule book'
- Delegation
- Effective team working and collaboration
- 'Positive' attitude required to encourage organizational self-confidence and self-efficacy
- Continuous strategizing with the development of strategic options to maintain maximum flexibility in the face of an uncertain, changing environment
- Incremental, adaptive approach to decision making
- Openness that encourages accurate and speedy information flows and learning
- Avoidance of short-termism, bureaucracy and over-control

Table 3.5 Structural characteristics of the entrepreneurial organization

- Reliance on relationships rather than formal structures for authority
- Encourages opportunity spotting, creativity and innovation
- Shares information, knowledge and learning, so as to react quickly to environmental changes and capitalise on opportunities
- Encourages a sense of belonging and 'ownership', ensuring remuneration is adequate and other psychological needs met, so that staff are motivated not to leave the organization
- Encourages and facilitates delegation and decentralization. Does the entrepreneurial unit or division have to be small and separate from the rest of the organization? Is size a limiting factor?

Finally, Table 3.5 summarizes the likely structural characteristics of an entrepreneurial organization, replicated from the previous chapter. The question raised is whether size is a limiting factor. The next chapter will demonstrate ways in which larger firms have successfully addressed this issue.

I call the combination of these characteristics the entrepreneurial architecture of the organization – a system of processes, structures underpinned by a style of management, reinforced by a particular culture and given direction in an uncertain world by a strong vision. It is the architecture that creates the entrepreneurial organization. Having explained what it is, the next chapter starts to explain how it can be developed.

Case with questions

Richard Branson and Virgin

Richard Branson is probably the best known entrepreneur in Britain today and his name is closely associated with all the many businesses that carry the Virgin brand name. He is outward-going and an excellent self-publicist. He has been called an 'adventurer', taking risks that few others would contemplate. This shows itself in his personal life with his transatlantic power boating and round-the-world ballooning exploits, as well as in his business life where he has challenged established firms like British Airways and Coca-Cola.

Born in 1950, Richard comes from a well-off background. His father was a barrister and he went to school at Stowe, a leading private school (called 'public' in Britain, just to confuse). However, he was never academic and suffered from dyslexia. Nevertheless this did not dent his self-confidence. His mother encouraged this. She commented: 'bringing him up was like riding a thoroughbred horse. He needed guiding but you were afraid to pull the reins too hard in case you stamped out the adventure and wildness.'

He left Stowe at the age of 16 to launch his first business – Connaught Publications – and publish Student magazine. This was based in his parents' house in Bayswater, London. He wrote to well known personalities and celebrities – pop and film stars and politicians – and persuaded many to contribute articles or agree to interviews. He persuaded a designer to work for no fee, negotiated a printing contract for 50,000 copies and got Peter Blake, the designer of The Beatles' Sgt Pepper album cover, to draw the cover picture of a student. The magazine made money by selling advertising space.

➡

Case with questions continued

Richard Branson and Virgin

The venture was not a success, so in 1970 he set up Virgin Records, originally selling records by mail order, at discount prices so as to undercut the competition. But this was also beset by problems, not least some allegedly 'dubious' dealings with the tax authorities. He decided he needed to move to a retail site and persuaded the owners of his first store, above a shoe shop in London's Oxford Street, to let him have it rent-free because it would generate more customers for the shoe shop.

It was a great success and Richard next branched into the music business with Virgin Records. Mike Oldfield's enormous hit Tubular Bells was recorded in Virgin's first recording studio – an Oxfordshire barn – and released in 1973. Other star names signed by Virgin Records included The Rolling Stones, Genesis, Phil Collins, Peter Gabriel, Bryan Ferry, Janet Jackson, Culture Club, Simple Minds and The Sex Pistols. In 1992 he sold Virgin Records to Thorn-EMI for almost £500 million.

Since those early days the Virgin brand has found its way onto aircraft, trains, cola, vodka, mobile phones, cinemas, a radio station, financial services and most recently the internet. In 1986 Virgin was floated but later reprivatized because Richard did not like to be accountable for his actions to institutional shareholders. Richard may have been lucky to find someone willing to let him have the premises for his first Oxford Street record shop rent-free in those early days, but good luck does not just keep happening. His endurance and eye for a business opportunity have been proved again and again, as well as his knack of minimizing his personal risk. When he launched Virgin Atlantic he showed that he understood that high capital costs lead to high risks. He minimized these risks by leasing everything and then being able to offer a good quality service at attractive prices. In 1999 a 49 per cent stake in the airline was sold to Singapore Airlines for £600 million. Today Virgin describes itself as a 'branded venture capital company', having created over 270 businesses. Many of these are joint ventures with other companies. They bring the operating capability and Virgin brings the brand. The Virgin Group itself is estimated to have a value of some £2 billion.

Richard Branson's main skills are said to be networking, finding opportunities and securing the resources necessary for their exploitation. His network of personal influence and contacts is legendary. Equally important is his ability to bring out the best and motivate people. He does this with an informal style and system of communication, facilitated by the way the company is structured into so many relatively independent smaller companies, although all under the Virgin umbrella. He hates formal meetings and has no central headquarters, not even a board room as the company does not hold regular board meetings. Instead he prefers to make decisions on a face-to-face basis, albeit sometimes over the phone, but always developing and testing his personal relationships.

Up-to-date information on Virgin and Richard Branson can be found on their website: www.virgin.com

Questions
1. How many of the entrepreneurial characteristics outlined in Chapters 2 and 3 does Richard Branson exhibit?
2. Has Richard Branson just been lucky with his business ventures? How does he handle risk?

Summary

The approach entrepreneurs take to decision making is often thought to be intuitive, even whimsical, and if unstructured this can lead to problems; evidenced by the comments of **Michael Dell**. At its worst it is extremely short-term. In fact it is shaped by the greater risk and uncertainty they face.

The positive aspect of their approach is their incremental and adaptive approach to strategy development with continual strategizing and the development of strategic options. The more strategic options that are generated, the more likely the entrepreneurial organization is to succeed. Strategy can be both emergent and deliberate; illustrated by the comments of **Richard Branson**. Underpinning the strategy is a strong vision of where the organization is going; evidenced by the comments of **David Darling**.

Entrepreneurs can also be very careful at conserving resources – money in particular – and keeping fixed costs as low as possible; evidenced by the comments of **David Speakman** and the actions of **Stephen Waring**.

As the comments of **Richard Branson** and the case of **Stephen Waring** illustrate, at the core of the entrepreneur's approach to doing business is the development of relationships and networks with all the stakeholders of the business – customers, staff and suppliers. As **Michael Dell** comments, relationships and networks are used to generate resources at start-up, and often for growth. Entrepreneurs frequently place a heavy reliance on relationship marketing, which, it is believed, delivers sustainable customer loyalty. Relationships also open the door to opportunity and, as **Jonathan Elvidge** comments, they bring learning and inspiration to the organization.

Entrepreneurs manage informally, using influence and direct supervision, building on personal relationships to motivate staff. Since flexibility is the key, job descriptions are often minimal. Entrepreneurial organization structures have been likened to a spider's web with the entrepreneur at the centre and every member of staff reporting to him or her, either formally or informally. However, these informal structures only work up to a certain size and then start to break down.

As firms grow the role of founders needs to change. Like **Michael Dell**, they need to metamorphosize into leaders. This change is not easy. As they develop, firms typically go through a period of growth, followed by crisis and then a period of consolidation. This is interposed with periods of deliberate strategy development – typically after a crisis – and emergent strategy development, which is the natural preference of the entrepreneur. Greiner's growth model predicts the crises a firm will face as it grows and the associated causes of growth. These are:

Growth through creativity

⇩

Crisis of leadership

⇩

Growth through direction

⇩

Crisis of autonomy

Growth through delegation

⇩

Crisis of control

⇩

Growth through co-ordination

⇩

Crisis of red tape

To succeed, the entrepreneur therefore needs to develop skills of leadership, delegation and team working. Other models stress the need for continuous strategy development and the growth of more formalized structures. To avoid bureaucracy the firm needs to be managed in a collaborative fashion – making people work together through a sense of mission, rather than by reference to the rule book.

The entrepreneurial organization needs to balance all these factors, maintaining the entrepreneurial characteristics and approaches to doing business, whilst avoiding the pitfalls associated with growth. The combination of these characteristics is called the entrepreneurial architecture of the organization – a system of processes, structures underpinned by a style of management, reinforced by a particular culture and given direction in an uncertain world by a strong vision. These are summarized in Figure 3.4 and Tables 3.4 and 3.5. It is the architecture that creates the entrepreneurial organization.

Essays and discussion topics

1. How do entrepreneurs approach decision making? Why?
2. Are entrepreneurs short-term in their decision making? Is this a bad thing?
3. What does emergent strategy really mean? Is it just *ex post* rationalization?
4. Are strategic tools really useful or are they just the fabrication of academic theorists?
5. Are formal, written business plans really necessary? Under what circumstances might an entrepreneur decide to prepare one?
6. How do entrepreneurs approach the task of management? How is this different from the approach in larger organizations? Is it better?
7. Discuss how the typical entrepreneur's preference for physical intervention and informal, personal control shows itself. Is this a good thing?
8. What does it take to develop a lasting relationship – with anybody?
9. What are the advantages of forming relationships with customers?
10. Can a spider's web organization work? What are the limits and how might they be overcome?
11. How does the role of the entrepreneur change as the organization grows?
12. Is the Greiner growth model an accurate predictor or descriptor of the growth process and the problems it creates? What is the difference between a descriptive model and a predictive model?
13. Critically evaluate the Burns growth model.
14. What are the possible negative consequences of the entrepreneur's strong internal locus of control?
15. Have attitudes to entrepreneurs changed in this country over the last twenty years?
16. Does this country have an enterprise culture, compared to others?

17. How can enterprise culture be encouraged?
18. How important is good luck in business? Can you make your own luck, or at least influence the odds of achieving a particular outcome?

Exercises and assignments

1. Write a mini case study about how an entrepreneur you know set up their own business and set about assembling the resources they needed.
2. List all the relatives, friends and business contacts you have and jot down how they might be useful to you if you were to set up your own business.

References

Burns, P. (1996) 'Growth', in P. Burns and J. Dewhurst (eds), *Small Business and Entrepreneurship*, Basingstoke: Macmillan – now Palgrave Macmillan.

Burns, P. and Whitehouse, O. (1995a) *Investment Criteria in Europe*, 3i European Enterprise Centre, Report no. 16, July.

Burns, P. and Whitehouse, O. (1995b) *Financing Enterprise in Europe 2*, 3i European Enterprise Centre, Report no. 17, October.

Churchill, N. C. and Lewis, V. L. (1983) 'The Five Stages of Small Business Growth', *Harvard Business Review*, May/June

du Toit, D. E. (1980) 'Confessions of a Successful Entrepreneur', *Harvard Business Review*, November/December.

Greiner, L. E. (1972) 'Evolution and Revolution as Organizations Grow', *Harvard Business Review*, July/August.

Kay, J. (1998) *Foundations of Corporate Success*, Oxford: Oxford University Press.

Kets de Vries, M. F. R. (1985) 'The Dark Side of Entrepreneurship', *Harvard Business Review*, November/December.

Lindblom, L. E. (1959) 'The Science of Muddling Through', *Public Administration Review*, 19, Spring.

Mathewson, Sir G. (2000) Keynote address, *British Academy of Management Annual Conference*, Edinburgh.

McCarthy, B. and Leavy, B. (2000) 'Strategy Formation in Irish SMEs: A Phase Model of Process', *British Academy of Management Annual Conference*, Edinburgh.

Mintzberg, H. (1978) 'Patterns in Strategy Formation', *Management Science*.

Webster, J. E. (1992) 'The Changing Role of Marketing in the Corporation', *Journal of Marketing*, 56, October.

4

Entrepreneurial Architecture

Contents

- Dominant logic
- Entrepreneurial intensity
- Architecture
- The learning organization
- Creating an entrepreneurial architecture
- Environment
- Summary

LEARNING OUTCOMES

By the end of this chapter you should be able to:

- Explain how 'dominant logic' influences the way managers see the world;

- Define the dimensions along which entrepreneurial activity can be measured;

- Explain the meaning of the term 'learning organization' and describe the key characteristics of such an organization;

- Demonstrate that an entrepreneurial organization is also a learning organization;

- Explain how the development of an entrepreneurial architecture can lead to sustainable competitive advantage in an appropriate context or environment;

- Describe the tools that are available to create this architecture;

- Show how an entrepreneurial architecture might have to adapt to suit different environmental contexts.

Dominant logic

The last two chapters have focused on the characteristics and qualities of the individual entrepreneur. The challenge for corporate entrepreneurship is to transplant this entrepreneurial DNA into a larger, established organization. 'Dominant logic' is the phrase coined by Bettis and Prahalad (1995) to describe the way managers in an organization conceptualize the business and make important resource allocation decisions. It is the mindset with which they see the organization, the world it inhabits and its position with customers, competitors and other stakeholders. It filters the information they receive, subconsciously interpreting environmental data in a certain way. In fact, managers may only consider information that they believe relevant to the prevailing dominant logic in the organization. Dominant logic influences behaviour, routines, strategies, structures, culture and systems – virtually everything the organization does and is.

Dominant logic takes time to build, but what may be appropriate for today's environment may not be appropriate for tomorrow's. Dominant logic must therefore constantly be learned and unlearned – a difficult thing to do. The dominant logic of the old way may inhibit the learning related to the new way. And the longer the logic has been in place the more difficult it is likely to be to unlearn. Most people resist change and it often takes a crisis to push them into changing their ways and changing their dominant logic. In that sense today's environment with its fierce competition, rapid changes in markets and technologies, uncertainties about the future and ever-increasing complexity is likely to throw up crises aplenty and act as a catalyst for change.

The challenge is to build into the dominant logic of the organization the concept of constant change so that it becomes a dynamic dominant logic. Entrepreneurship can be the basis for that dominant logic. Entrepreneurship embraces and welcomes change as creating new commercial opportunities. It promotes flexibility, creativity and innovation in pursuing those opportunities. And the implications for how the organization functions are enormous.

Entrepreneurial intensity

Entrepreneurship can be an imprecise term in so many different ways. So what constitutes an entrepreneurial firm? Morris and Kuratko (2002) make a useful distinction between the *frequency* of entrepreneurial acts and the *degree* of each entrepreneurial act. One firm might produce a small number of breakthrough developments (high on degree, low on frequency) whilst another might produce many small developments, none of which are breakthrough (low on degree, high on frequency). They argue that truly revolutionary firms combine high levels of degree with high levels of frequency. They describe these revolutionary firms as showing a high degree of entrepreneurial *intensity*. Intensity is therefore a combination of degree and frequency. These factors, together with example companies, are reflected in the entrepreneurial grid in Figure 4.1. Firms with a high degree of entrepreneurial intensity are forever pushing out the entrepreneurial frontier represented by the dashed line.

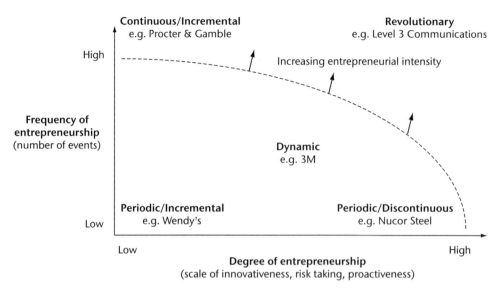

Source: Adapted from Morris, M. H. and Kuratko, D. F. (2002) *Corporate Entrepreneurship*, Fort Worth, Harcourt College Publishing.

Figure 4.1 The entrepreneurial grid

Locating firms on the grid requires a degree of judgement. However, by identifying where the firm falls on the grid, you are effectively describing the nature of its entrepreneurial strategy – entrepreneurial degree vs entrepreneurial frequency. The five examples used by the authors are all successful companies in their own right – the degree of entrepreneurial intensity does not necessarily guarantee success. Other factors, in particular an appropriate environment, need to be present. Wendy's, the US-based fast-food chain, rapidly captured third place in the industry by developing an innovative product delivery system and by targeting young adults who want higher-quality fast-food. Since then their innovations have been neither frequent nor dramatic (e.g. drive-by windows, new menus). Procter & Gamble remain at the top of the highly competitive consumer packaged goods industry by releasing a continuous stream of product improvements and the occasional new product. Nucor introduced a radically new technical process for producing sheet metal in small arc furnaces – mini-mills – transforming the competitive and economic structure of the steel industry. 3M (see the case with questions at the end of this chapter) seems to be able to continuously develop new commercial uses for new technologies. Level 3 Communications was the first company to build an end-to-end internet protocol international communications network for internet service providers and telecom carriers and is aggressively expanding its network in the USA and Europe where it is continuously offering more and more services.

Notwithstanding the examples above, some researchers claim a statistically significant linkage exists between entrepreneurial intensity and a number of measures of firm performance such as profitability, income/sales ratio, revenue growth, asset growth, employment growth (Covin and Slevin, 1989; Davis, Morris and Allen, 1991; Miller and Friesen, 1983; Morris and Sexton, 1996; Peters and

Waterman, 1982). This is particularly the case in changing, turbulent environments. Hence they would argue that the most successful firms are those that exhibit the greatest entrepreneurial intensity. However, one factor to be borne in mind is risk. All entrepreneurial activity is inherently risky. However, it can be argued that a strategy involving *both* large scale *and* high frequency is extremely risky. And any finance expert will tell you that risk and return go hand in hand.

This useful distinction, then, helps you focus on what it is the firm (or a competitor) does or needs to do in the way of entrepreneurial activity and how it fits into the 'dominant logic' of the firm. It articulates a core dilemma in describing entrepreneurship – whether to focus on the size or scale of the change involved or the frequency of the changes undertaken. However, the question still remains. How can you embed this into an organization?

Architecture

Architecture is the term used by John Kay (1993) to describe the relational contracts within and around the organization – with customers, suppliers and staff. These are long-term relationships, although not necessarily just legal contracts, which are only partly specified and only really enforced by the need of the parties to work together. Like all relationships, architecture is based upon mutual trust, although underpinned by mutual self-interest. This self-interest discourages one party from acting in some way at the expense of the other because it is important that they continue to work together. We have already stressed the importance of relationships in the way the entrepreneur does business.

Just as entrepreneurs use networks of relationships to help them operate in a way that allows them to seize opportunities quickly, architecture allows the entrepreneurial firm to respond quickly and effectively to change and opportunity. Developing organizational architecture is a systematic exploitation of one of the main distinctive capabilities of entrepreneurs. It builds in dynamic capabilities that are difficult to copy. It does so by creating within the organization the knowledge and routines that enable this to happen smoothly and unhindered. Staff are somehow motivated in themselves to make this happen, knowing it is good for the organization – what has been called empowerment. Architecture can create barriers to entry and competitive advantage by institutionalizing these relationships. It is difficult to copy because it is not a legal contract and not written down anywhere, relying instead on the complex network of personal relationships throughout the organization. Architecture is created partly through appropriate strategies, partly through appropriate structures, but mainly through developing the appropriate culture in the organization.

Kay (*op. cit.*) emphasizes the advantages of architecture:

'The value of architecture lies in the capacity of organizations which establish it to create organizational knowledge and routines, to respond flexibly to changing circumstances, and to achieve easy and open exchanges of information. Each is capable of creating an asset for the firm – organizational knowledge which is more than the sum of individual knowledge, flexibility, and responsiveness which extends to the institution as well as to its members.'

Using examples of small and large organizations, Kay emphasizes that architecture comprises patterns of long-term relationships which are 'complex, subtle and hard to define precisely or to replicate' and he observes that it is easier to sustain than to create and even more difficult to create in an organization that does not have it in the first place. Individuals participate in these relationships voluntarily because of a strong personal feeling that it is in their interests because they are participating in a 'repeated game' in which they share the rewards of collective achievement. The relationships solve problems of co-operation, co-ordination and commitment. They set the rules of the game and if you cheat you would find it difficult to play the game again with the same players. These relationships are characterized as having a high but structured degree of informality, something that can be mistaken as haphazard, chaotic or just lucky. In this way the architecture is distinctive and difficult to copy because individuals only know or understand a small part of the overall structure.

Kay (*op. cit.*) continues:

'There is an expectation of long-term relationships both within the firm and between its members, a commitment to a sharing of the rewards of collective achievement, and a high but structured degree of informality. This informality is sometimes mistaken for disorganization – in popular discussion of chaos, *entrepreneurship*, or adhocracy as conditions of innovation – but truly chaotic organizations rarely perform well, and a system of relational contracts substitutes an extensive set of unwritten rules and expectations of behaviour for the formal obligations of the classical contract.'

With this description we start to glimpse reflections of the start-up entrepreneur in the middle of the spider's web of informal, personal relationships, recognizing opportunity everywhere, trying to innovate and trying to replicate success, using networks, relying on personal relationships with customers, staff and suppliers. Entrepreneurs prefer influence and informal relationships to formal contracts. They use these to secure repeat sales at the expense of competitors and to secure resources or competitive advantage that they might not otherwise have. Close partnerships with suppliers where information and knowledge is shared can lead to significant advantages in lowering costs, lead times and inventories. All these relationships are based on trust – 'my word is my bond' – and most involve a degree of self-interest. The challenge is to replicate these relationships across the organization and develop that entrepreneurial architecture.

Kay (*op. cit.*) sees no conflict in the need for stability and continuity in relationships and the equal need for change and flexibility in an entrepreneurial firm:

'If there is a single central lesson from the success ... of cases developed in this book, it is that the stability of relationships and the capacity to respond to change are mutually supportive, not mutually exclusive, requirements. It is within the context of long-term relationships, and often only within that context that the development of organizational knowledge, the free exchange of information, and a readiness to respond quickly and flexibly can be sustained.'

And here lies an important by-product of this architecture – it creates organizational learning and knowledge that can be used to create competitive advantage.

Jim Clark is worth about $3 billion. He is now a cross between a serial entrepreneur and a venture capitalist because he realized that he is better at start-ups than running the business in the longer term. He discovered this with his first company, **Silicon Graphics (SGI)** which he built around a graphic chip called the Geometry Engine that he invented in the 1970s. He spent 13, mainly unhappy, years at **SGI** where he found he just did not like the discipline of running a successful growing business.

He left in 1994 and invested $3 million of his own money in a primitive web browser called Mosaic and a 22-year-old who helped develop it called Marc Andreesen. **Netscape** went public 18 months later and made Jim Clark a billionaire.

In 1995 he moved on and founded another company called **Healtheon**, which uses the internet to share patient and administrative information between doctors, hospitals, insurance companies and the patients themselves. Again the business was run by somebody else, Mike Long.

Jim Clark has now started up another company, **MYCFO**, this time using the internet to help the wealthy manage their financial affairs. It also satisfies a necessary condition for success: Jim Clark is not planning to run it.

Entrepreneurs learn by doing, and they learn quickly not to repeat mistakes but to capitalize on success. Because they are one person, knowledge and learning is transferred continuously, quickly and without barriers. As the organization grows the challenge is for knowledge and learning to continue to be transferred in this way. But how do you translate what happens in the brain of one person into the operations of an entire organization? And what does learning really mean? The answer to this lies in the concept of the 'learning organization'.

The learning organization

The person most associated with the concept of the learning organization is Peter Senge. His book, *The Fifth Discipline: The Art and Science of the Learning Organization*, published in 1990, was a loose collection of ideas about change, learning and communication drawn from an eclectic variety of sources. However the central concept was inherently attractive:

'As the world becomes more interconnected and business becomes more complex and dynamic, work must become more "learningful" ... It is no longer sufficient to have one person learning for the organization ... It's just not possible any longer to "figure it out" from the top, and have everyone else following the orders of the "grand strategist". The organizations that will truly excel in the future will be the organizations that discover how to tap people's commitment and capacity to learn at all levels in the organization.'
(Senge, 1990)

If the grand strategist is the entrepreneur, then you can see that the challenge laid down is one of making the whole organization entrepreneurial. A learning organization has been defined as one that 'facilitates the learning of all its members

'There are countless successful companies that are thriving now despite the fact that they started with little more than passion and a good idea. There are also many that have failed, for the very same reason. The difference is that the thriving companies gathered the knowledge that gave them the substantial edge over their competition, which they then used to improve their execution, whatever their product or service ... The key is not so much one great idea or patent as it is the execution and implementation of a great strategy.'

Michael Dell
➡

and continuously transforms itself ... adapting, changing, developing and transforming themselves in response to the needs, wishes and aspirations of people, inside and outside' (Pedler *et al.*, 1991). Writings on the learning organization stress how it is flexible, adaptable and better equipped to thrive in a turbulent environment – the very environment that entrepreneurs and entrepreneurial firms inhabit. A learning organization facilitates learning for all its members and continually transforms itself:

- Encouraging systematic problem solving;
- Encouraging experimentation and new approaches;
- Learning from past experience and history;
- Learning from best practice and outside experience;
- Being skilled at transferring knowledge in the organization.

Peter Senge (1992) observes that learning organizations can only be built by leaders with fire and passion: 'Learning organizations can be built only by individuals who put their life spirit into the task.' The similarity to the entrepreneur is striking. Indeed the similarities can also be seen from the literature about entrepreneurs. Timmons (1999) says successful entrepreneurs are: 'patient leaders, capable of instilling tangible visions and managing for the long haul. *The entrepreneur is at once a learner and a teacher*, a doer and a visionary.' Being a learner and a teacher are two of the prime tasks for a leader in a learning organization. Stata (1992) even predicts that the rate at which individuals or organizations learn may become the only sustainable competitive advantage, and this perspective sees learning as a capability that can be nurtured and developed by organizations (e.g., Leonard-Barton, 1992, Teece, Pisano and Shuen, 1997).

Truly entrepreneurial organizations, therefore, are in fact learning organizations. This goes to the heart of the architecture that needs to be put in place to develop them and, as we shall develop in the next chapter, it also goes to the heart of the qualities demanded of a successful entrepreneurial leader.

A learning organization thrives in turbulent and changing environments. It is fast and responsive. It requires unitarism – a belief that the interests of the organization and the individual are the same. Shared values are at the core of this, as is being part of a team or an 'ingroup' (the terminology used by Hofstede in his analysis of culture, reviewed in Chapter 6). This results in staff feeling empowered to influence the direction of the organization and believing that continually developing, learning and acquiring new knowledge is the way to do this.

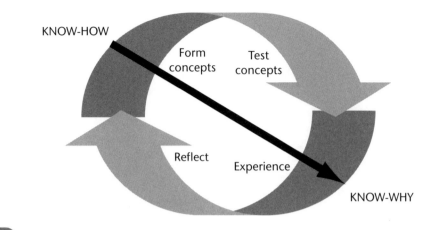

KNOW-HOW

Form concepts

Test concepts

Reflect

Experience

KNOW-WHY

Figure 4.2 The wheel of learning

Continually developing, learning and acquiring new knowledge is therefore at the heart of a learning organization. But knowledge is about more than just information sharing. It is about learning from each other and from outside the organization. It is about a better understanding of interrelationships, complexities and causalities. Daniel Kim (1993) suggests effective learning can be considered to be a revolving wheel (Figure 4.2). During half the cycle, you test concepts and observe what happens through experience – learning 'know-how'. In the second half of the cycle, you are reflecting on the observations and forming concepts – learning 'know-why'. This is often called 'double-loop learning'. It is this second sort of learning that is of particular value to the organization because it is at this point that root causes of problems are diagnosed and systematic solutions put in place.

So real learning is about application, continuous problem solving, understanding the root cause of problems rather than being distracted by the symptoms. It is about continually challenging the mental models we hold – deeply-held beliefs about how the world works that are shaped by our experiences and shape our experiences. It occurs when people within organizations share, explore and challenge their mental models. When this happens the wheel of learning both affects and is affected by our mental models, as shown in Figure 4.3. Once we start to share our knowledge of know-why and/or know-how with others, organizational learning takes place. The difficulties in doing this increase with the size of the organization. However, the constantly increasing amount of know-how and know-why, accumulated through years of turning of the wheel of learning and sharing of mental models becomes part of the collective memory of the organization. Although this accumulated knowledge is tacit, shadowy and fragile it is unique and can be part of the organizational architecture that underpins its competitive advantage.

Again, the similarities with the way entrepreneurs operate are pronounced. The learning organization literature stresses incrementalism and learning by doing on the job, rather than in the classroom. It stresses questioning of the status quo. What is more it explains why entrepreneurs are more comfortable continuously strategizing and why strategy tends frequently to emerge, based on the learning that is continuously taking place.

Figure 4.3   The wheel of learning and our mental models

The ability to adapt is what makes the difference between survival and growth in an uncertain, turbulent environment and an organization's ability to adapt is the direct result of its ability to learn collectively about the factors that influence it. Constant learning by organizations requires the acquisition of new knowledge and skill and the willingness to apply it to decision making (Miller, 1996). It includes the unlearning of old routines (Markoczy, 1994) so that the range of potential behaviour is altered (Wilpert, 1995).

Some academics however, such as Symon (2002), are cynical about the concept of a learning organization, arguing that the literature relies on 'metaphor, exaggeration and justification', observing that the concept was introduced when 'structural and political changes swung the balance of power in favour of the employer' and seeing it as a device to 'lure them (the workers) into their control'. Certainly Senge's 1990 book was a loose collection of ideas couched in mystical terminology and was light on practicality. But others have built on this in a more structured manner. Theoretical and empirical research does, however, show that many barriers exist to implementing the concept of a learning organization and many academics would say that, in its extreme form, the learning organization is indeed a utopian ideal and that it is a journey rather than a destination ever to be arrived at. Table 4.1 summarizes some of the major concepts about learning organizations.

Our mental models, those deeply-held images of how the world works, are both shaped by our experiences and help shape our experiences. And from school onwards, all too often, conformity is rewarded, mistakes punished and too much questioning discouraged. How can we possibly make the leap of faith required to convince us that things could be different? And how robust are our learning processes? Do we have the skill, let alone the time, to reflect in this modern world? Can these learning processes ever be sufficiently robust to get us to see how information, action and results form a

Table 4.1 The learning organization: major concepts

- True learning requires the acquisition of both know-how and know-why through the wheel of learning so that chains of causality can be identified
- Mental models are shaped by experience and help shape experience
- Learning occurs when individuals share, examine and challenge their mental models
- The most important learning occurs on the job
- The most effective learning is social and active, not individual and passive
- The most important things to learn are tacit things – intuition, judgement, expertise

chain of causality – the key to understanding the root cause of a problem? And how can an organization encourage all this to take place? This brings us back to the challenge of building an entrepreneurial architecture that encourages these qualities.

Creating an entrepreneurial architecture

> 'The best way I know to establish and maintain a healthy, competitive culture is to partner with your people – through shared objectives and common strategies.'
>
> **Michael Dell**
> ➔

Strong organizational architecture can be both internal and external. Internal focuses on the employees, generating a strong sense of collectivism rather than individuality and implying strong job security. This collectivism comes from shared objectives and commonly accepted strategies. And this brings with it potential weaknesses: 'Firms with strong *internal* architecture tend to restrict individuality and recruit employees of characteristic, and familiar type, inflexibility is a potential weakness' (Kay, *op. cit.*). This we also recognize as a familiar potential weakness for entrepreneurs in growing firms. From the literature on barriers to growth (see previous chapter), we know that the entrepreneur must change and adapt as the organization grows, moving towards a more managerial style (Miner, 1990). However, whilst adopting certain administrative traits is critical for successful growth (Cooper, 1993), both the entrepreneur and the organization must also remain essentially entrepreneurial. Retaining a balance is crucial, building on the distinctive traits, skills, capabilities and approach to business of the entrepreneur and institutionalizing elements of their approach – replicating their DNA within the organization's culture.

> 'Early in Dell's history we had more than 140 different suppliers providing us with component parts ... Today our rule is to keep it simple and have as few partners as possible. Fewer than 40 suppliers provide us with about 90 percent of our material needs. Closer partnerships with fewer suppliers is a great way to cut cost and further speed products to market.'
>
> **Michael Dell**
> ➔

External architecture is found where firms share knowledge with outsiders, which encourages flexibility and fast response times. It is based on deep relationships and is often found in networks or clusters of small firms in particular geographic areas where they depend on each other for various aspects of their commercial activity. For example, in the UK there is a cluster of small firms in South Wales which manufacture sofas. Around them is a skilled workforce and the infrastructure needed to support them. Italy has developed these clusters in numerous industries from knitwear and ties to tiles, all based in different geographic clusters. Some larger firms, such as Dell, have developed competitive advantage based upon the development of distinctive global supply networks – which are also based on effective external architecture.

Whether internal or external, architecture is based upon mutually supportive, long-term relationships. Any relationship is based upon trust and trust can take a long time to build but can be lost very quickly. It is also based on mutual self-interest – there must be something in it for both parties. It is based on knowledge and information and is essentially informal rather than formal. It can be planned and it can be engineered, but it is not easy to achieve. It needs cultivating and managing and its roots lie deep in the interpersonal relationships in the organization.

So how can architecture be shaped? The tools available are highlighted in Figure 4.4 and discussed in greater detail in subsequent chapters. Many are inter-related – each affects the other. The environment affects a number of the variables and, whilst strategy is the outcome, that clearly affects the architecture and therefore other variables. These tools are:

- Leadership and management of the company;
- The culture in the company;
- The structure, size and organization of the company.

What the company does with this architecture depends on the strategies it adopts. Entrepreneurial architecture can create competitive advantages on which the organization can build effective strategies for succeeding against competitors. However, how the organization approaches strategy development will also influence, and be influenced by, this architecture. The interplay of these factors helps determine strategy in an entrepreneurial organization and strategy development becomes part of its architecture – something difficult to copy because it is constantly evolving and adapting to the changing market place.

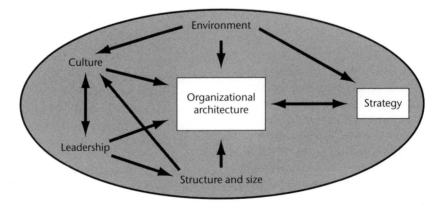

Figure 4.4   Influences on organizational architecture

The degree and direction of entrepreneurial intensity has implications for the entrepreneurial architecture – leadership, culture and structure. For example, infrequent major innovation is risky and requires a certain culture and structure that is different from that required for what might be described as continuous, incremental improvement, which is less risky. If Nucor's mini-steel mills had not been successful the company would have been in deep trouble. The way this was managed and then subsequently rolled out into the market is very different from the way Procter & Gamble manage their product innovations.

The leader's role in all of this is clearly crucial since he or she is responsible for the culture and structure of the organization and the strategies it develops. But, as we saw in the last chapter, effective leadership in a growing organization means changing with the organization and delegating downwards – and that means leaders can evolve at all levels within the entrepreneurial organization.

Environment

The environment in which these factors play upon each other is an important factor. It plays a profound role in influencing corporate entrepreneurship and research indicates it is an important antecedent of corporate entrepreneurship (Ferreira, 2002). Entrepreneurial intensity is environmentally dependent for its success. So, in what sort of environments are entrepreneurial organizations likely to thrive? The answer is that they thrive in changing, unstable or disruptive environments – even chaos. They thrive where there is complexity and fierce competition (Porter's Five Forces can be a useful tool in assessing this – see Chapter 12), low concentration of firms, a high degree of product or market heterogeneity and where technology is constantly changing. They thrive in environments where change is the norm and opportunities are constantly presenting themselves. These environments are characterized by high degrees of uncertainty – even contradiction – and difficulty in operating the firm. Entrepreneurial organizations are also likely to be most effective early in the product life cycle, with its emphasis on innovation, rather than later on, when the emphasis shifts to operations control (see Chapter 11).

When the environment is stable or hospitable, entrepreneurship is unlikely to flourish. There is simply no need to change. This happens when industries are highly concentrated and firms have little direct competition, when customers are locked into their supplier, margins are high and technologies rarely change. In these cases radical action is inappropriate, fine tuning the order of the day. Similarly products at the mature stage of their life cycle need to be managed to generate cash and there is little scope for entrepreneurial flair. In these circumstances a more conservative or bureaucratic approach to management is likely to be more effective. An entrepreneurial approach to management is unlikely to thrive in Wendy's.

However, the effect of environment is altogether more complex than these broad generalizations imply. It can affect the very architecture of the organization. The complex interplay of different market conditions, different countries, different local cultures make it very difficult to be prescriptive about how the successful entrepreneurial organization might look in different parts of the world – what leadership style is appropriate, what the culture might be and how the organization might be structured. Entrepreneurial architectures that might succeed in one geographic environment might fail in another without significant local variation.

Firms also face different environments as they grow and develop and their markets change. Growth itself creates turbulence but, if the firm follows the same path as a product life cycle, it may face maturity and stability at some stage. By this point the entrepreneurial organization would probably have re-invented itself by going into different product/market offerings. And this creates the problem of accommodating the need for different managerial approaches within one organizational structure.

So within these broad generalizations it is quite possible that the same company may have different degrees of entrepreneurship in different subsidiaries, divisions, units, departments and geographical areas – depending on the external factors they face. The more turbulent the environment, the more the need for an entrepreneurial organization. Structuring the organization so that each operating unit – whatever its basis – can be organized in such a way as to best deal with the environment it faces is quite a challenge. The result is structures within structures, sub-cultures within cultures and different approaches to leadership within an overall approach – a real portfolio approach to management.

This is particularly complex when the core business faces a stable environment and the core is large and needs to be maintained. In that case the overarching structures, culture and leadership, will struggle to accommodate entrepreneurship, even at the peripheries of the organization, seeing it as destabilizing and disruptive. At this point separate organizational structures need to be considered which is where spin-outs or corporate venturing may be relevant.

The point is that there cannot be a prescriptive blueprint for entrepreneurial architecture. The principles outlined in subsequent chapters must be adapted and modified to suit specific environments. But then we always knew that management was an art rather than a science.

Case with questions

3M

3M has been known for decades as an entrepreneurial company that pursues growth through innovation. It generates a quarter of its annual revenues from products less than five years old. 3M started life as the Minnesota Mining and Manufacturing Company back in 1902. Its most successful product – flexible sandpaper – still forms an important part of its product line but this now comprises over 60,000 products that range from adhesive tapes to office supplies, medical supplies and equipment to traffic and safety signs, magnetic tapes and CDs to electrical equipment. Originally innovation was encouraged informally by the founders, but over more than a century some of these rules have been formalized. But most important of all there has built up a culture which encourages innovation. And because this culture has built up a history of success, it perpetuates itself.

3M started life selling a somewhat inferior quality of sandpaper. The only way the company could promote this was by getting close to the customer – demonstrating it to the workmen that used it and persuading them to specify the product – an early form of relationship selling.

→

This was the first strategic thrust of the fledgeling business – get close to customers and understand their needs.

However, the company was desperate to move away from selling a commodity product and competing primarily on price, and its closeness to the customer led it to discover market opportunities that it had the expertise to capitalize on. The first such product was Three-M-Ite Abrasive – an abrasive cloth using aluminium oxide for durability in place of a natural abrasive. This was followed by waterproof sandpaper – an idea bought from an inventor who subsequently came to work for 3M. This was followed shortly by Wetordry – a product designed for use by the car industry in finishing bodywork. And with this the second strategic thrust of the company was developed – to seek out niche markets, no matter how small, which would allow it to charge a premium price for its products. The company began to realize that many small niche markets could prove to be more profitable than a few large ones.

In the 1990s this began to change somewhat, to the extent that some technologies became more sophisticated and the investment needed to develop new products increased. Therefore the return required became larger and markets needed to be correspondingly bigger. Luckily the world was increasingly becoming a global market place. At the same time, competition was becoming tougher and the rapidity of technological change and shortening of product life cycles made 3M recognize the need to dominate any market niche quickly. Speed of response was vital. By the 1990s, many of the market niches 3M was pioneering were turning out to be not that small at all, particularly in the global market place. So, the approach remained the same, but the speed of response and size of market niche, world-wide, increased.

The company really started to diversify when it entered the tape market in the 1920s, but even this built on its expertise in coatings, backings and adhesives. What is more the way the first product evolved demonstrates perfectly how an entrepreneurial architecture works. By being close to its customers 3M saw a problem that it was able to solve for them through its technical expertise. In selling Wetordry to car-body finishers, an employee realised how difficult it was for the painters to produce the latest fad in car painting – two tone paintwork. The result was the development of masking tape – imperfect at first, but developed over the years 'out-of-hours' by an employee to what we know it to be today and from that technology developed the Scotch range of branded tapes. So, the third strategic thrust was developed – having identified a market opportunity through closeness to the customer, diversify into these related areas. Once 3M found a niche product to offer in a new market, it soon developed other related products and developed a dominant position in the new market. In the 1990s 3M came to recognize that it did best when it introduced radically innovative products into a niche market in which it already had a toe hold.

This experience also taught 3M the value of research but in particular to value maverick inventors who were so attached to their ideas that they would push them through despite the bureaucracy of the company. In the late 1920s it developed the policy of allowing researchers to spend up to 15% of their time working on their own projects. To this day, it tries to make innovation part of the corporate culture by encouraging staff to spend 15% of their time working on pet ideas that may one day become new products for the company. Staff can also get money to buy equipment and hire extra help. To get an idea accepted, they must first get the personal backing of a member of the main board. Then an inter-disciplinary team of engineers, marketing specialists and accountants is set up to take the idea further. Failure is not punished, but success is well rewarded.

➡

Case with questions continued

3M

Perhaps the best known contemporary example of the success of this policy is the development of the Post-It Note by Art Frye in the 1980s. He was looking for a way to mark places in a hymn book – a paper marker that would stick, but not permanently. At the same time the company had developed a new glue which, unfortunately as it seemed at the time, would not dry. Art spotted a use for the product but what was different was the way he went about persuading his bosses to back the project. He produced the product, complete with its distinctive yellow colour, and distributed it to secretaries who started using it throughout 3M. Art then cut their supplies, insisting that there would be no more unless the company officially backed the product. The rest is history.

So the fourth strategic thrust of the company was developed – to pursue product development and innovation at every level in the organization through research. This was formalized when the Central Research Laboratory was set up in 1937, but maverick research continued to be encouraged. In 1940, a New Product Department was developed to explore the viability of new products or technologies unrelated to existing ones. In 1943, a Product Fabrications Laboratory was set up to develop manufacturing processes. In the 1980s four Sector Labs were created with a view to being more responsive to the market place and undertaking medium-term research (5–10 years): Industrial and Consumer, Life Sciences, Electronic and Information Technologies and Graphic Technologies. The Central Lab, renamed the Corporate Lab, was maintained to undertake more long-term research (over 10 years). In addition most of the Divisions had their own Labs undertaking short-term, developmental research (1–5 years).

3M has always been admired for its ability to share knowledge across the organization and link technologies to produce numerous products that could be sold in different markets. One example of this is Scotchlite Reflective Sheeting used for road signs, developed in the 1940s – in fact as a result of failed research to develop reflective road markings. This combined research from three different laboratories to produce signs with a waterproof base onto which a covering of an opaque, light-reflecting pigment was added followed by microscopic beads. This was all sealed with a thin coat of plastic to ensure weather durability. Strategy five had emerged – get different parts of the organization to communicate and work together and, most important of all, share knowledge.

This became formalized in the 1950s with the establishment of the Technical Forum, set up with the aim of sharing knowledge across the company. It held annual shows. Out of this came the Technical Council, made up of technical directors and technical personnel, which met several times a year to review research and address common problems. Alongside this the Manufacturing Council and then the Marketing Council were established. At the same time Technical Directors and researchers regularly moved around the different divisions. The fifth strategy was in place – share knowledge.

The culture in 3M evolved out of its place of origin and has been called 'Minnesota nice'. It has been described as non-political, low ego, egalitarian and non-hierarchical as well as hardworking and self critical. It has also, at least in its earlier days, been described as paternalistic in its approach to employees. Above all, 3M is achievement-orientated and achievement, particularly in research, was rewarded, often through promotion. For example successful new product teams were spun off to form new divisions. The leader of the team often

➜

became general manager of the new division and this was seen as a great motivator. Lesser achievements were also acknowledged. Researchers who consistently achieved 'high standards of originality, dedication and integrity in the technical field' – as judged by their peers, not management – were invited to join the exclusive 'Calton Society'. The 'Golden Step' and 'Pathfinder' awards were also given to those helping develop successful new products. Achievement was lauded at all levels. Strategy six was emerging – encourage achievement through reward.

Today 3M faces many challenges to maintaining its reputation for innovation. As it becomes larger and more complex, involved in different markets with different products and technologies, at different stages of their life cycle, it recognizes that different managerial approaches may be necessary. The 'maverick', high-risk approach to research and development may not be appropriate in certain sectors. The 25% rule – the proportion of new product sales – may not be achievable by all Divisions. 3M also faces stiffer competition which means that cost economies have had to be made to maintain profitability. As a result the 15% rule – slack time to research new products – is under severe pressure, to the point where it is described as more of an attitude than a reality. Nevertheless, 3M has for over a century successfully practised corporate entrepreneurship.

Up-to-date information on 3M can be found on their website: www.3M.com

Questions
1. Describe the organizational structures and devices 3M uses to encourage entrepreneurial activity. Why do they work?
2. How does 3M distinguish between incremental and fundamental innovations?
3. Describe, as best you can from the case, the culture of the organization. What does this depend upon?
4. Why has 3M been such a successful innovator for so long?
5. Can other companies just copy 3M's structures and culture and become successful innovators also?

A series of case studies on 3M, tracking its history and development since its inception in 1902, have been written by Research Associate Mary Ackenhusen, Professor Neil Churchill and Associate Professor Daniel Muzyka from INSEAD. They can be obtained from the Case Clearing House, England and USA.

Summary

Dominant logic is the mind set of managers that influences how they see the organization in its environment and how they interpret information. It influences everything they do. Entrepreneurship needs to be at the centre of the dominant logic of an organization coping with continuous change and facing fierce competition.

Entrepreneurial intensity can be measured in two dimensions: frequency (number of events) and degree (scale of innovativeness, risk taking or proactiveness). These can be combined to develop an entrepreneurial grid that describes the nature of the entrepreneurial strategy.

Some researchers claim a link between entrepreneurial intensity and firm performance but, equally, high entrepreneurial intensity is likely to mean high risk, which is normally associated with high returns, if successful.

Architecture is the term used to describe the long-term relational contracts within and around the organization – with customers, suppliers and staff. They are not necessarily legal contracts and often only partly specified, therefore not easy to copy. They are based upon trust and mutual self-interest. Because it is complex, architecture can be a major source of sustainable competitive advantage. **Michael Dell** endorses the need for 'partnering with people' – developing deep relationships (internal architecture) – and demonstrates the benefits to **Dell** from partnering with suppliers (external architecture).

Organizational learning and knowledge is an important by-product of architecture, and, as **Michael Dell** says, this can give you an edge over the competition. An entrepreneurial organization is a learning organization, one that facilitates learning for all its members and continuously transforms itself:

- Encouraging systematic problem solving;
- Encouraging experimentation and new approaches;
- Learning from past experience and history;
- Learning from best practice and outside experience;
- Being skilled at transferring knowledge in the organization.

Learning organizations thrive in turbulence. Real knowledge means using the wheel of learning (Figure 4.3) to understand the root cause of problems so as to put in place systematic solutions to problems – 'knowing-how', 'knowing-why' and doing something about it. It means linking this to our mental models so as to challenge how things are. The most important learning occurs on the job. It is social and active. It is about learning tacit knowledge – intuition, judgement and expertise.

The entrepreneurial organization must build an entrepreneurial architecture. The tools available to construct architecture are organizational culture, structure and the leadership of the organization. What it does with the architecture depends on its strategies, but how it develops strategies influences the architecture. Architecture is not easy to build and develop, and many entrepreneurs, like **Jim Clark**, decide it is not something they wish to do.

Entrepreneurial firms thrive in environments of change, chaos, complexity, competition, uncertainty and even contradiction.

The exact nature of effective entrepreneurial architecture depends on the environment. It can be sectorally and geographically dependent. It can vary with the nature of the entrepreneurial intensity. The point is that there can be no prescriptive blueprint for entrepreneurial architecture. However, generally entrepreneurial firms thrive in changing, unstable or disruptive environments.

Essays and discussion topics

1. Which is riskier, frequency of entrepreneurship or degree of entrepreneurship?
2. Why are organizations with a high degree of entrepreneurial intensity likely to show above-average performance?

3. What are the implications for a company that emphasizes frequency of entrepreneurship rather than degree of entrepreneurship?
4. What is architecture?
5. Why can the architecture of a firm give it sustainable competitive advantage?
6. Why should an entrepreneur find building this architecture easier than other people?
7. What is needed to build long-term relationships?
8. Is the learning organization a romantic dream?
9. How can you spot a learning organization?
10. How does an entrepreneur learn?
11. Is the entrepreneurial organization really a learning organization?
12. How do you really learn?
13. How do you spread learning and knowledge in an organization?
14. Do you have mental models? How do these ever change?
15. Is there such a thing as an organizational mental model?
16. Is Dell's competitive advantage based solely on its external architecture?
17. Why is the leader's role crucial in developing an entrepreneurial organization?
18. Will an entrepreneurial organization succeed in all circumstances?
19. In what circumstances might a bureaucratic organization be more successful than an entrepreneurial organization?
20. How might the geographic environment affect an effective entrepreneurial architecture?

Exercises and assignments

1. List the type of organizations and market sectors or environments that face high degrees of turbulence. Select a particularly turbulent sector and research how the organizations within it are organized and the success, or otherwise, they have in dealing with it.

References

Bettis, R. A. and Prahalad, C. K. (1995) 'The Dominant Logic: Retrospective and Extension', *Strategic Management Journal*, 16.

Cooper, A. C. (1993) 'Challenges in Predicting New Firm Performance', *Journal of Business Venturing*, May.

Covin, J. G. and Slevin, D. P. (1989) 'Strategic Management of Small Firms in Hostile Behaviour', *Entrepreneurship Theory and Practice*, 16.

Davis, D., Morris, M. and Allen, J. (1991) 'Perceived Environmental Turbulence and Its Effect on Selected Entrepreneurship, Marketing and Organisational Characteristics in Industrial Firms', *Journal of Academy of Marketing Science*, 19

Ferreira, J. (2002) 'Corporate Entrepreneurship: A Strategic and Structural Perspective', *47th International Council for Small Business World Conference*, Puerto Rico, June.

Kay, J. (1993) *Foundations of Corporate Success*, Oxford: Oxford University Press.

Kim, D. H. (1993) 'The Link between Individual and Organizational Learning', *Sloan Management Review*, Fall.

Leonard-Barton, D. (1992) 'Core Capabilities and Core Rigidities: A Paradox in Managing New Product Development', *Strategic Management Journal*, 13 (special issue).

Markoczy, L. (1994) 'Modes of Organisational Learning: Institutional Change and Hungarian Joint Ventures', *International Studies of Management and Organisations*, 24, December.

Miller, A. (1996) *Strategic Management*, Maidenhead: Irwin/McGraw-Hill.

Miller, D. and Friesen, P. H. (1983) 'Innovation in Conservative and Entrepreneurial Firms: Two Models of Strategic Momentum', *Strategic Management Journal*, 3(1).

Miner, J. B. (1990) 'Entrepreneurs, High Growth Entrepreneurs, and Managers: Contrasting and Overlapping Motivational Patterns', *Journal of Business Venturing*, July.

Morris, M. H. and Kuratko, D. F. (2002) *Corporate Entrepreneurship*, Fort Worth: Harcourt College Publishing.

Morris, M. H. and Sexton, D. L. (1996) 'The Concept of Entrepreneurial Intensity', *Journal of Business Research*, 36(1).

Pedler, M., Burgoyne, J. G. and Boydell, T. (1991) *The Learning Company: A Strategy for Sustainable Development*, London: McGraw-Hill.

Peters, T. and Waterman, R. (1982) *In Search of Excellence*, New York: Harper & Row.

Senge, P. (1990) *The Fifth Discipline: The Art and Science of the Learning Organization*, New York: Currency Doubleday.

Senge, P. (1992) 'Mental Models', *Planning Review*, March–April.

Stata, R. (1992) 'Management Innovation', *Executive Excellence*, 9, June.

Symon, G. (2002) 'The 'Reality' of Rhetoric and the Learning Organisation in the UK', *Human Resource Development International*, 5(2).

Teece, D.J., Pisano, G. and Schuen, A. (1997) 'Dynamic Capabilities and Strategic Management', *Strategic Management Journal*, 18(7).

Timmons, J. A. (1999) *New Venture Creation: Entrepreneurship for the 21st Century*, Singapore: Irwin/McGraw-Hill.

Wilpert, B. (1995) 'Organisational Behaviour', *Annual Review of Psychology*, 46, January.

Part 2

Leading and Managing the Entrepreneurial Organization

5 Entrepreneurial Leadership

6 Creating the Entrepreneurial Culture

7 Building the Entrepreneurial Structure

8 Intrapreneurship and Corporate Venturing

9 Managing the Entrepreneurial Organization

5

Entrepreneurial Leadership

Contents

- Management and leadership
- Entrepreneurial leadership
- Vision and mission
- Values
- Leadership style
- Building the management team
- Entrepreneurial leadership skills
- Summary
- Leadership style questionnaire

LEARNING OUTCOMES

By the end of this chapter you should be able to:

- Explain the difference between management and leadership and describe the qualities needed for entrepreneurial leadership;

- Explain what is meant by vision and values – what they entail and how they can be communicated effectively;

- Write a vision or mission statement;

- Describe the influences on leadership style and explain which styles are appropriate to different circumstances;

- Evaluate your preferred leadership style and that of other individuals;

- Evaluate how you and other people handle conflict;

- Evaluate your preferred team role;

- Explain why some teams work and others do not;

- Explain what is required to become an entrepreneurial leader and how this can be done in a larger organization.

Management and leadership

Leading and managing an entrepreneurial organization is a challenge that requires some distinctive skills and capabilities. Management and leadership are different and distinct terms, although the skills and competencies associated with each are complimentary. Management is concerned with handling complexity in organizational processes and the execution of work. It is linked to the authority required to manage, somehow given to managers, within some form of hierarchy. Back in the nineteenth century Max Fayol defined the five functions of management as planning, organizing, commanding, co-ordinating and controlling. Today, these sound very much like the skills needed to lead a communist-style command economy. Fayol's work outlined how these functions required certain skills which could be taught and developed systematically in people. Management is therefore about detail and logic. It is about efficiency and effectiveness.

> 'A well-managed organisation must produce the results for which it exists. It must be administered, that is, its decisions must be made in the right sequence and with the right timing and right intensity, In the long run, a well-managed organisation must adapt to its external environment. The entrepreneurial role focuses on the adaptive changes, which requires creativity and risk taking. And to ensure that the organisation can have a life span longer than that of any of its key managers, the fourth role – integration – is necessary to build a team effort. Effective and efficient management over the short and long term requires the use of all four roles.'
>
> **I. Adizes**
> author, 1978
> ●

Leadership on the other hand is concerned with setting direction, communicating and motivating. It is about broad principles and emotion and less detail. It is particularly concerned with change. It is therefore quite possible for an organization to be over-managed but under-led, or vice versa. In a start-up good leadership is essential while effective management quickly becomes increasingly important to get things done. A larger organization, therefore, needs to be both effectively led and managed.

The consensus of opinion is that leaders are not born. The idea that they may have traits or characteristics which typify them has largely been discredited. However, like entrepreneurs, they are shaped by their history and experience. The one characteristic that separates them from others is the obvious one that they have willing followers. Their characteristics and personality traits tell us very little. Leadership is about what you do with who you are – your relationships with followers – rather than just who you are. And as we have seen entrepreneurs are rather good at relationships.

Blank (1995) argues that leadership is an 'event' – a 'discrete interaction each time a leader and a follower join ... Leadership can appear continuous if a leader manifests multiple leadership events.' One consequence of this is that, like entrepreneurs, leaders can have roller-coaster careers as they exhibit leadership characteristics at certain discrete times and with different people, but not at others. Winston Churchill was widely acknowledged as a great war-time leader but a poor peace-time leader. Therefore entrepreneurs can be good leaders for the business at start-up but no good for either the growth or the maturity phase unless they adapt and change their style.

Our traditional view of leaders is that they are special people – often charismatic heroes like Churchill – who set direction, make key decisions and motivate staff, often prevailing against the odds at times of crisis. They have vision – something entrepreneurs certainly have. They are strategic thinkers and are effective communicators whilst still being able to monitor and control performance. Above all, they create the appropriate culture within the organization to reflect their priorities. If there were ever a job description for a leader, therefore, it would probably include five elements:

'Management is about communication and listening to people. I believe the people on the ground have the answer. If you can find what the answer is you'll get a much better solution for the business ... Leadership to me is picking good teams and putting them together. And also putting yourself out for those people in terms of helping them when they're stuck, finding out what their concerns are, navigating them through problems. That, to me, is what leadership is about – not doing it yourself, but putting in place people who can do it for you.'

David Arculus, former MD, Emap group, Chief Operating Officer, United News and Media and chairman, IPC

The Times, 3 May 2004

1. Having a vision for the organization.
2. Being able to communicate effectively – particularly the vision.
3. Being able to think strategically.
4. Creating an appropriate culture in the organization.
5. Controlling and monitoring performance.

Entrepreneurial leadership

Our image of a leader tends to propagate the myth of the individual focusing on short-term results, often overcoming some sort of crisis, rather than the systematic pursuit of long-term excellence. The image is often based on implicit assumptions of the general powerlessness, lack of personal vision and inability or unwillingness to change of other people. But in reality successful entrepreneurial leaders are different. We have already commented on Timmons' (1999) description of successful entrepreneurs as 'patient leaders, capable of instilling tangible visions and managing for the long haul. The entrepreneur is at once a learner and a teacher, a doer and a visionary.' And we have already observed that this is almost identical to the definition of the leader of a learning organization – all very different from the charismatic hero much loved by folklore.

Senge (1992) explains that leaders of learning organizations have three prime tasks:

- *Designing the organization and its architecture so as to encourage the learning process.* This involves 'integrating vision, values, and purpose, systems thinking, and mental models.' It also involves designing an organizational architecture that is continually able to learn, adapt and change – encouraging people to focus activity where change, with the minimum of effort, will lead to significant and lasting improvement for the organization.

- *Being the steward of a vision that inspires staff and is transmitted to others.* 'Building a shared vision is important early on because it fosters a long-term orientation and an imperative for learning ... Crafting a larger story is one of the oldest domains of leadership ... In a learning organization, leaders may start by pursuing their own vision, but as they learn to listen carefully to others' visions they begin to see that their own personal vision is part of something larger. This does not diminish any leader's sense of responsibility for the vision – if anything it deepens it.' The vision becomes the focus for the organization. The leader's job involves creating tension and even measured conflict by building a shared vision that is contrasted to a constantly updated view of current reality. Here entrepreneurs must avoid the danger of their self-confidence leading them into delusional behaviour. This creative tension motivates people to do 'the right thing' – whatever that might be – to resolve a problem or secure an opportunity for the good of the organization, even if it is not in their job description. There are parallels here with the concept of individual empowerment.
- *Teaching learning or how to develop systematic understanding of how to approach and exploit change.* 'Many visionary strategists have rich intuitions about the causes of change, intuitions that they cannot explain. They end up being authoritarian leaders, imposing their strategies and policies or continually intervening in decisions. They fall into this fate even if their values are contrary to authoritarian leadership – because *only* they see the decisions that need to be made. Leaders in learning organizations have the ability to conceptualize their strategic insights so that they become public knowledge, open to challenge and further improvement.' At the heart of this is their ability to teach the organization how to restructure views of reality in such a way as to understand the root causes of a problem and address them so as to produce an enduring solution rather than simply addressing the short-term symptoms. This involves seeing interrelationships, not static images. It involves moving beyond blame to understanding the causes of problems. It involves understanding 'dynamic complexity' – cause and effect over time – rather than detail complexity. Ultimately it involves putting in place systematic structures that address the generic problem or opportunity.

The cement binding this organization together is its culture. The essence of an organization's culture is the values and beliefs shared by the people in it. And it is this that effective leaders strive to construct, define and gain commitment to. To achieve this leaders need to:

- Define clearly what the vision is. This provides a clear focus on key issues and concerns for the organization.
- Get everyone in the organization to understand the vision through effective communication practices.
- Guide the development of policies and programmes that support the vision.
- Encourage the enactment of the vision through their own personal actions – 'walking the talk' – acting consistently over time to develop trust, showing that they are reliable and can be trusted to do what they promise. This reassures people who are concerned about change.
- Show concern and respect for the members of the organization, demonstrating through actions that they are important.

Therefore, along with vision, entrepreneurial leaders need to develop a style of management that creates an entrepreneurial culture which motivates individuals to achieve. They need to build an effective management team, to be able to operate in a turbulent environment and unblock barriers to change, dealing with the inevitable conflict that this causes. They need to be adept at managing knowledge and learning and handling risk, ambiguity and uncertainty.

Are you a Visionary Leader?

In *Becoming a Visionary Leader* (HRD Press, Amherst, Mass, 1996) Marshall Sashkin defines a visionary leader as one who:

- Provides *clear* leadership which focuses people on goals that are part of a vision and on key issues and concerns;
- Has good *interpersonal communication skills* that gets everyone to understand the focus and to work together towards common goals;
- Acts *consistently* over time to develop trust;
- *Cares* and respects others, making them self-confident, whilst having an inner self-confidence themselves;
- Provides *creative* opportunities that others can buy into and 'own' – empowering opportunities that involve people in making the right things their own priorities.

The booklet contains a series of questions designed to see whether you might be a visionary leader. These start with an 'Impact Focus Scale' which looks at your motivations for wanting to be a leader. These are measured in three dimensions or scores. Effective leaders score high in each area:

1. *Impact belief score* – which measures your belief that you can make a difference within the organization.
2. *Social power need* – which measures the value you place on power and influence for the good that you can do with it within the organization.
3. *Dominance avoidance* – which measures your need for dominance or vice versa. Effective leaders do not need to dominate.

The second part involves a 'Cultural Functions Inventory' which is designed to help decide whether an organization's culture is effective at facilitating certain crucial functions. The resulting scores measure the ability to adapt to change, attain goals, co-ordinate teamwork and systems stability.

Finally, Sashkin has produced the *Leader Behaviour Questionnaire* (available from HRD Press), which is a 360-degree assessment instrument that measures visionary leadership behaviours, characteristics and contextual effects. The behaviours measured are:

- How well you manage to focus people's attention on key issues;
- How effective you are at communication, including 'active listening';
- How consistent your views and actions are;
- Whether you demonstrate regard for others;
- Whether you come up with ideas and opportunities that others find attractive and wish to take part in.

'M&S is about three things – the product, the shops, the delivery of our service – and five words that describe what we do: quality, value, service, innovation and trust. Nothing else. There is no strategy. We're shopkeepers whose job is to satisfy customers ... We don't just trade on price alone but price times quality times styling. We don't want fleeces at knockdown prices – that's not what our customers want from us. We're about eight to 80 (age), Christian and Jew, fat and thin. We want to deliver to all of them.

We took out the whole board [when Stuart Rose joined in 2004] – we got rid of the stores chief, the personnel director and others. We had an exciting battle with Philip Green but, after it, we reduced the board to 12 non-executive directors and three executive directors ... We sit here and take decisions very fast. Compared to the old M&S, we've cut out the jaw-jaw. Everything goes straight down the line. We're supported by a strong team of divisional heads, but it's very different from the old M&S ... It's not about one person, it's about teams of people. We've got 85,000 in the organisation. They're responsible for our success.'

Stuart Rose, CEO **M&S**
Management Today, December 2006

Vision and mission

Vision is a key element of both entrepreneurship and leadership. A vision is a shared mental image of a desired future state – an ideal of what the enterprise can become – a new and better world. It must be a realistic, credible and attractive future and one that engages and energizes people (Nanus, 1992). It is usually *qualitative* rather than quantitative (that is the role of the objectives). Vision is seen as inspiring and motivating, transcending logic and contractual relationships. It is more emotional than analytic, something that touches the heart. It gives existence within an organization to that most fundamental of human cravings – a sense of meaning and purpose. As Bartlett and Ghoshal (1994) explain: 'Traditionally top-level managers have tried to engage employees intellectually through the persuasive logic of strategic analysis. But clinically framed and contractually based relationships do not inspire the extraordinary effort and sustained commitment required to deliver consistently superior performance ... Senior managers must convert the contractual employees of an economic entity into committed members of a purposeful organization.' In other words vision is the cornerstone of the entrepreneurial architecture we want to create.

Visions, then, are aspirational but they can take many forms. They can be intrinsic, directing the organization to do things better in some way such as improving customer satisfaction or increasing product innovation. They can be extrinsic, for example beating the competition. But what do you do when you have beaten the competition? Vision is formally communicated through the vision or mission statement. This often includes reference to the product or service (basis for competitive advantage, quality, innovation and so on), customer groups and the benefits they derive or competitors. Often it will encompass the *values* upheld by the company. Any vision or mission statement should be short, snappy and as memorable as possible. Some examples are given in the box below. Wickham (2001) suggests a generic format:

'The (*company*) aims to use its (*competitive advantage*) to achieve/maintain (*aspirations*) in providing (*product scope*) which offers (*benefits*) to satisfy the (*needs*) of (*customer scope*). In doing this the company will at all times strive to uphold (*values*).'

Having your own individual vision is relatively easy. Building a shared vision in an organization is no easy task – it is not about simply going off and writing a 'vision statement'. Visions are living things that evolve over time. Developing the vision is a continuous process. It involves continually checking with staff to ensure that the vision has a resonance with them – modifying it little by little, if appropriate. Entrepreneurs can find this difficult and frustrating as they are more used to setting goals and seeking compliance. But to survive in a larger organization they need to develop their political skills.

Good visions motivate. Two strong motivations for people are fear and aspiration. Fear is probably the strongest motivation that helps galvanize action and force people to change, but probably lasts only a short time. This motivation worked well for Winston Churchill in the Second World War. However, aspiration – what we might

Case insight

Dell Mission

Dell's mission is to be the most successful computer company in the world at delivering the best computer experience in markets we serve. In doing so, Dell will meet customer expectations of:
- Highest quality;
- Leading technology;
- Competitive pricing;
- Individual and company accountability;
- Best-in-class service and support;
- Flexible customization capability;
- Superior corporate citizenship;
- Financial stability.

easyJet Mission

To provide our customers with safe, good value, point-to-point air services. To effect and to offer a consistent and reliable product and fares appealing to leisure and business markets on a range of European routes. To achieve this we will develop our people and establish lasting relationships with our suppliers.

Xerox Mission

Our strategic intent is to help people find better ways to do great work by consistently leading in document technologies, products and services that improve our customers' work processes and business results.

→

'Entrepreneurs have to make their own decisions and follow their vision. They must motivate their team, get them to ignore shaky markets and a possible war and look positively to the future, to keep exploring uncharted territory. To do that they have to subscribe to the entrepreneur's vision – but they don't necessarily have to agree with it.'

Derrick Collin
founder and managing director
of **Brulines Ltd**
The Times, 10 October 2001
●

'Communicating is one of the most important tools in recovering from mistakes. When you tell someone, be it a designer, a customer, or the CEO of the company, "Look, we've got a problem. Here's how we're going to fix it," you diffuse the fear of the unknown and focus on the solution.'

Michael Dell
➡

'Where any three people within an organization will give the same answer to a question on the company's mission statement. That reflects total coherency and a focused workforce.'

Gururaj Deshpande
serial entrepreneur and
founder of **Sycamore Networks**
The Financial Times,
21 February 2000
➡

become – has a greater longevity and is altogether a more positive motivator. It is the one that underpins most entrepreneurial organizations. It emphasizes striving – a continuous journey of improvement.

It is not sufficient simply to have a vision, that vision must also be communicated. In this respect the leader is often held out as being a storyteller. Gardner (1995) maintains this is *the* key leadership skill. This storytelling skill can be either verbal or written, however, leaders must 'walk the talk' – practise what they preach – otherwise they have no credibility and are not believed. Gardner maintains that the most successful stories are simple ones that hit an emotional resonance with the audience, addressing questions of identity and providing answers to questions concerning personal, social and moral choices. Is it any wonder that entrepreneurs skilled at developing personal relationships can also become powerful leaders?

Senge (*op. cit.*) highlights the creative tension this storytelling must instil in a learning organization: 'The leader's story, sense of purpose, values and vision establish the direction and target. His relentless commitment to the truth and to inquiry into the forces underlying current reality continually highlight the gaps between reality and the vision. Leaders generate and manage this creative tension – not just themselves but in an entire organization. This is how they energize an organization. That is their basic job. That is why they exist.' He goes on to underline how this can create within an entire organization the sense of internal locus of control – emphasizing the belief in control over destiny – that is an essential part of the entrepreneurial character: 'Mastering creative tension throughout an organization leads to a profoundly different view of reality. People literally start to see more and more aspects of reality as something that they, collectively, can influence.' And this is one important psychological way that individuals within the entrepreneurial organization deal with the uncertainty they face. You might recognize it as one aspect of 'empowerment'. *An entrepreneurial organization is an empowered learning organization.*

Bennis and Nanus (1985) talk about a 'spark of genius' in the act of leadership which 'operates on the emotional and spiritual resources of the organization.' For them the genius of the leader lies in 'this transcending ability, a kind of magic, to assemble – out of a variety of images, signals, forecasts and alternatives – a clearly articulated vision of the future that is at once simple, easily understood, clearly desirable, and energizing'. But entrepreneurial leadership that is to perpetuate itself is more than just charismatic leadership. Charismatic leaders deal in visions and crises, but little in between. Entrepreneurial leadership is about systematic and purposeful development of leadership skills and techniques – which can take a long time. It is about developing relationships. It is about creating long-term sustainable competitive advantage based upon the architecture of entrepreneurial leadership.

John Kotter's Seven Principles for Successfully Communicating a Vision

1. *Keep it simple*: Focused and jargon-free.
2. *Use metaphors, analogies and examples*: Engage the imagination.
3. *Use many different forums*: The same message should come from as many different directions as possible.
4. *Repeat the message*: The same message should be repeated again, and again, and again.
5. *Lead by example*: Walk the talk.
6. *Address small inconsistencies*: Small changes can have big effects if their symbolism is important to staff.
7. *Listen and be listened to*: Work hard to listen, it pays dividends.

Adapted from Kotter, J. P. (1996) *Leading Change*, Boston: Harvard Business School Press.

Values

Values are the core beliefs upon which the organization is founded. They underpin vision and, as you can see with the case of Body Shop, they also underpin the mission of the organization. They set expectations regarding how the organization operates and how it treats people. The vision and mission must be consistent with the values of the organization. All three go hand in hand, one reinforcing the others. In a start-up they reflect the values of the founder, but as the organization grows they often reflect a wider community and face the risk of being diluted to the point where they are not clear. Organizations with strong values tend to recruit staff who are able to identify with those values and thus they become reinforced. Body Shop tends to recruit franchisees who identify with its moral and environmentally friendly values.

Values are important because they create a constant framework within which to operate in a turbulent, changing environment. As represented in Figure 5.1, whilst strategies and tactics might change rapidly in an entrepreneurial firm, vision and values are enduring. They form the 'road-map' that tells everyone in the organization

Figure 5.1 Values, vision, strategy and tactics

where it is going and how it will get there, even when one route is blocked. Values form part of the cognitive processes that help shape and develop the culture of the organization. They guide strategy and help delegate authority – telling people what is the 'right' thing to do. Shared values form a bond that binds the organization together – aligning and motivating people. They help develop a high-trust culture that cements long-term relationships.

Case insight

Body Shop

Values
- We consider testing products or ingredients on animals to be morally and scientifically indefensible;
- We support small producer communities around the world who supply us with accessories and natural ingredients;
- We know that you are unique, and we'll always treat you as individual. We like you just the way you are;
- We believe that it is the responsibility of every individual to actively support those who have human rights denied to them;
- We believe that a business has the responsibility to protect the environment in which it operates, locally and globally.

Mission
- To dedicate our business to the pursuit of social and environmental change;
- To creatively balance the financial and human needs of our stakeholders, employees, customers, franchisees and shareholders;
- To courageously ensure that our business is ecologically sustainable: meeting the needs of the present without compromising the future;
- To meaningfully contribute to local, national and international communities in which we trade, by adopting a code of conduct which ensures care, honesty, fairness and respect;
- To passionately campaign for the protection of the environment, human and civil rights, and against animal testing within the cosmetics and toiletries industry;
- To tirelessly work to narrow the gap between principle and practice, whilst making fun, passion and care part of our daily lives.

Values need to be articulated and taught by leaders by 'walking the talk' or practising what they preach. They are not negotiable and need to be reinforced through recognition and reward. They need to be embedded in the systems and procedures of the organization, so that everybody can see clearly that the organization means what it says. Nonaka (1991) recommends the use of language, metaphor and analogy in promoting values which are seen as promoting the special capabilities of the organization that enable resources to be leveraged internally, thereby creating competitive advantage.

Case insight

The Soul of Dell

Dell calls its corporate philosophy the 'Soul of Dell'. The core elements are:

Customers   We believe in creating loyal customers by providing a superior experience at a greater value. We are committed to direct relationships, providing the best products and services based on standards-based technology, and outperforming the competition with value and a superior customer experience.

The Dell Team   We believe our continued success lies in teamwork and the opportunity each team member has to learn, develop and grow. We are committed to being a meritocracy, and to developing, retaining and attracting the best people, reflective of our worldwide marketplace.

Direct Relationships   We believe in being direct in all we do. We are committed to behaving ethically: responding to customer needs in a timely and reasonable manner; fostering open communications and building effective relationships with customers, partners, suppliers and each other; and operating without inefficient hierarchy and bureaucracy.

Global Citizenship   We believe in participating responsibly in the global marketplace. We are committed to understanding and respecting laws, values and cultures wherever we do business; profitably growing in all markets; promoting a healthy business climate globally; and contributing positively in every community we call home, both personally and organizationally.

Winning   We have a passion for winning in everything we do. We are committed to operational excellence, superior customer experience, leading in the global markets we serve, being known as a great place to work, and providing superior shareholder value over time.

Leadership style

The role of leader is normally based on some sort of authority. Authority can derive from role or status, tradition, legal position, expert skills or charismatic personality. However, Timmons (*op. cit.*) believes that in successful entrepreneurial ventures leadership is based on expertise rather than authority and this then means there is no competition for leadership. Many of the best known, successful entrepreneurs clearly also have charisma.

As we have seen, like entrepreneurship, leadership is a skill that can be developed. However, it is a complex thing. As represented in Figure 5.2, it depends upon the interactions and interconnections between the leader, the task, the group being led

Figure 5.2   Leadership style

and the situation or context – called 'contingency theory'. The theory emphasizes that there is no one 'best' way of managing or leading. It depends on the interaction of all these factors. A leader may personally prefer an informal, non-directional style, but faced with a young apprentice working a dangerous lathe he might be forgiven for reverting to a fairly formal, directive style with heavy supervision. In that situation the change in style is appropriate. Try the same style with a group of senior creative marketing consultants and there would be problems. Many different styles may be effective, with different tasks, different groups and in different contexts. What is more, there is no evidence of any single leadership style characterizing successful businesses. Nevertheless, by picking off the individual elements of these four factors we can understand what style is best suited to different circumstances.

> 'Once you have a business up and running the best way to keep in touch is to employ great people and empower them. This brings with it trust, communication and team spirit. When you work as a team you are in touch. My business style is non-aggressive, non-confrontational – it's who I am. It's important to be yourself. It comes from a background where you have to get on with people to get on. I believe that if you treat people like dirt on the way up it will come to haunt you as you find yourself on the way down.'
>
> **Jonathan Elvidge**
> founder of **Gadget Shop**
> *The Times*, 6 July 2002
> ➜

Leader and task

The leadership grid shown in Figure 5.3 was developed by Blake and Mouton (1978). It shows style as dependent upon the leader's concern for task compared to the concern for people. Entrepreneurs are usually more concerned with completing the task but, as the firm grows, must become more concerned with people if the tasks are to be accomplished. Task leadership may be appropriate in certain situations, for example emergencies. However, concern for people must surface at some point if effective, trusting relationships are to develop. Low concern for both people and task is hardly leadership at all. High concern for people – the country club style – is rare in business but can be appropriate in community groups, small charities or social clubs where good relationships and high morale might be the dominant objectives.

Timmons (*op. cit.*) believes that the emphasis in successful entrepreneurial ventures is more on performing task-orientated roles although 'someone inevitably provides

Figure 5.3 Leader and task

for maintenance and group cohesion by good humour and wit'. If this is the case then it is even more important to ensure that there is an appropriate and effective management team in place. Entrepreneurs must realize that, as the number of people they employ increases, they must increase their 'concern for people' and move more towards a 'team leadership' style.

Leader and group

Leadership style also depends on the relationship of the leader with the group he or she is leading. Figure 5.4 shows this in relation to the leader's degree of authority and the group's autonomy in decision making. If a leader has high authority but the group has low autonomy, he will tend to adopt an autocratic style, simply instructing people what to do. If he has low authority, for whatever reason, he will tend to adopt a paternalistic style, cajoling the group into doing things, picking off individuals and offering grace and favour in exchange for performance. If the leader has low authority and the group has high autonomy, then he will tend to adopt a participative style, involving the whole group in decision making and moving forward with consensus. If the leader has high authority then he will seek opinions but make the decision himself using a consultative style.

A survey of small business managers in Britain, France, Germany, Spain and Italy showed that most used a consultative style (Burns and Whitehouse, 1996). However, 20–30% of managers in all countries other than Germany used an autocratic style. It has been said that growth-orientated companies are initially characterized by an autocratic or dictatorial style but as the company grows a more consultative style

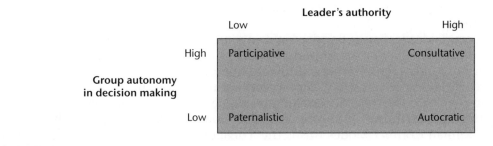

Figure 5.4 Leader and group

develops as the entrepreneur recruits managers and gives them more autonomy (Ray and Hutchinson, 1983). Burns and Whitehouse's survey (*op. cit.*) confirmed this. Leadership styles also seem to be influenced by national culture. The survey revealed that a significant proportion (35%) of German managers use a participative style, despite the fact that none of them thought their subordinates liked it. This probably reflects cultural differences at a national level, where consultative or participative decision making is the norm, particularly when unions are involved. However, this mismatch between actual style, dictated by cultural norms, and desired style must create tensions for German entrepreneurs.

Leader and situation

John Adair (1984) put forward the view that the weight the leader should put on these different influences depends on the situation or context. In an entrepreneurial firm that situation can be characterized as one of uncertainty, ambiguity and rapid change. What does that tell us about the context? Timmons (*op. cit.*) observed that: 'There is among successful entrepreneurs a well developed capacity to exert influence without formal power. These people are adept at conflict resolution. They know when to use logic and when to persuade, when to make a concession, and when to exact one. To run a successful venture, an entrepreneur learns to get along with different constituencies, often with conflicting aims – the customer, the supplier, the financial backer, the creditor, as well as the partners and others on the inside. Success comes when the entrepreneur is a mediator, a negotiator, rather than a dictator.'

How a good entrepreneurial leader approaches any task, with any group, therefore depends on the situation he faces. But entrepreneurial firms face an environment that is constantly changing, which can often lead to conflict as they try to get people to do different things or things differently. The Thomas-Kilman Conflict Modes instrument gives us an insight into how conflict might be handled. Whilst each style has its advantages in certain situations, compromise or better still collaboration is generally thought to be the best way for a team to work.

Entrepreneurial leaders face uncertainty and ambiguity, trying to manage people who often have unclear job definitions because they are having to cope with change. This can create conflict that has to be resolved on an every-day basis. The implications of the entrepreneurial situation are:

- Entrepreneurial leaders must move away from using an autocratic or dictatorial leadership style, especially with their senior management team, if they want staff to take more control over their actions and develop an entrepreneurial organization.
- Entrepreneurial leaders must be adept at using informal influence. Their powers of persuasion and motivation are important. They should meet and influence people. Relationships and organizational culture are important.
- Entrepreneurial leaders must be adept at conflict resolution. In these situations Timmons (*op. cit.*) observes: 'Successful entrepreneurs are interpersonally supporting and nurturing – not interpersonally competitive.' In terms of the Thomas-Kilman Conflict Modes this is the 'collaborating' or 'compromising' mode.

How do you behave in situations involving conflict?

Often in business you find yourself at odds with others who hold seemingly incompatible views. For a leader to be effective he needs to understand how he handles these conflict situations and be able to modify his behaviour to obtain the best results from others. Based on research by Kenneth Thomas and Ralph Kilmann, the Thomas-Kilman Conflict Modes questionnaire published by Xicom shows how a person's behaviour can be classified under two dimensions:

- Assertiveness – the extent to which individuals attempt to satisfy their own needs.
- Co-operativeness – the extent they attempt to satisfy the needs of others.

These two dimensions lead the authors to identify five behavioural classifications which the questionnaire can identify in individuals:

1. **Competing** is assertive and unco-operative. Individuals are concerned for themselves and pursue their own agenda forcefully, using power, rank or ability to argue in order to win the conflict. This can be seen as bullying with less forceful individuals or, when others use the same mode, it can lead to heated, possibly unresolved, arguments.
2. **Accommodating** is unassertive and co-operative, the opposite of competing. Individuals want to see the concerns of others satisfied. They might do so as an act of 'selfless generosity' or just because they are 'obeying orders', either way they run the risk of not making their own views heard.
3. **Avoiding** is both unassertive and unco-operative. It may involve side-stepping an issue or withdrawing from the conflict altogether. In this mode any conflict may not be even addressed.
4. **Collaborating** is both assertive and co-operative, the opposite of avoiding. Issues get addressed but individuals are willing to work with others to resolve the conflict, perhaps finding alternatives that meet everybody's concerns. This is the most constructive approach to conflict for a group as a whole.
5. **Compromising** is the 'in between' route, the diplomatic, expedient solution to conflict which partially satisfies everyone. It may involve making concessions.

Each style of handling conflict has its advantages and disadvantages and can be effective in certain situations. However, management teams or boards of directors, if they are to get the most from each member over a longer period of time, work best when all members adopt the collaborating or compromising modes. A team made up of just competers would find it difficult to get on and, indeed, to survive. A team made up of just accommodaters would lack assertiveness and drive.

Building the management team

An entrepreneurial firm will only succeed if it has a good management team. However, attracting good staff may be difficult. An entrepreneurial firm faces an uncertain future and because of this there may be a perceived lack of job security and uncertainty about promotion. Cash may not always be readily available to fund higher salaries, hence the need, often, to offer shares in the company.

> 'Know what you are good at and, importantly, know your weaknesses, and get in good people to support you in these areas.'
>
> **Geoff Barrell**
> founder of **BlueArc Ltd**
> *The Times*, 16 March 2002

Selecting a team will depend upon the mix of functional skills and market or industry experience required in the firm, as well as the personal chemistry between its members. For a team to be effective individuals need to have the right mix of a certain set of personal characteristics. Dr Meredith Belbin (1981) identified nine clusters of personal characteristics or attributes which translate into 'team roles', each with positive qualities and allowable weaknesses (overleaf). Individuals are unlikely to have more than two or three of them, yet all nine clusters of characteristics need to be present in a team for it to work effectively. It has been suggested that the 'prototypical entrepreneur' might be a plant (creative, ideas person), shaper (dynamism, full of drive and energy) and a resource investigator (enthusiastically explores opportunities) (Chell, 2001). In this case the first team member should not be strong in any of these categories, but ideally should be an implementer (reliable, efficient and able to turn ideas into practical action). The implementer will want a completer-finisher (conscientious, delivers on time), a team-worker (co-operative and unchallenging) and possibly a specialist (with particular knowledge or skills) working under him or her.

The leader's role is to select the team and then to build cohesion and motivation. In most cases this involves building consensus towards the goals of the firm, balancing multiple viewpoints and demands. However, too great a reliance on achieving consensus can lead to slow decision making, so a balance is needed that will strain the interpersonal skills of the leader. In the best entrepreneurial firms

> 'The ability to find and hire the right people can make or break your business. It is as plain as that. No matter where you are in the life cycle of your business, bringing in great talent should always be a top priority.'
>
> 'The right people in the right jobs are instrumental to a company's success ... If you assume that people can grow at the same rate as your company – and still maintain the sharp focus that is critical to success – you will be sadly disappointed. When a business is growing quickly, many jobs grow laterally in responsibility, becoming too big and complex for even the most ambitious, hard-working person to handle without sacrificing personal career development or becoming burned out.'
>
> **Michael Dell**
> ➡

What sort of team player are you?

Developing a successful team depends not just on the range of professional skills it has, but also on the range of personal characteristics – the chemistry of the team. Based upon research into how teams work, Dr Meredith Belbin identified nine clusters of personal characteristics or attributes which translate into 'team roles'. The roles are:

The Shaper: This is usually the self-elected task leader with lots of nervous energy. Shapers are extrovert, dynamic, outgoing, highly strung, argumentative, pressurisers seeking ways around obstacles. They do have a tendency to bully and are not always liked. However, they generate action and thrive under pressure.

The Plant: This the team's vital spark and chief source of new ideas. Plants are creative, imaginative and often unorthodox. However, they can be distant and uncommunicative and sometimes their ideas can seem a little impractical.

The Co-ordinator: This is the team's natural chairman. Co-ordinators are mature, confident and trusting. They clarify goals and promote decision making. They are calm with strong interpersonal skills. However, they can be perceived as a little manipulative.

The Resource Investigator: This is 'the fixer' – extrovert, amiable, six phones on the go, with a wealth of contacts. Resource investigators pick other people's brains and explore opportunities. However, they can be a bit undisciplined and can lose interest quickly once initial enthusiasm has passed.

The Monitor-Evaluator: This is the team's rock. Monitor-Evaluators are introvert, sober, strategic, discerning. They explore all options and are capable of deep analysis of huge amounts of data. They are rarely wrong. However, they can lack drive and are unlikely to inspire or excite others.

The Team-worker: This is the team's counsellor or conciliator. Team-workers are mild mannered and social, perceptive and aware of problems or undercurrents, accommodating and good listeners. They promote harmony and are particularly valuable at times of crisis. However, they can be indecisive.

The Implementer: This is the team's workhorse. Implementers turn ideas into practical actions and get on with the job logically and loyally. They are disciplined, reliable and conservative. However, they can be inflexible and slow to change.

The Completer-Finisher: This is the team's worry-guts, making sure things get finished. Completer-Finishers are sticklers for detail, deadlines and schedules and have relentless follow-through, picking up any errors or omissions as they go. However, they sometimes just cannot let go and are reluctant to delegate.

The Specialist: This is the team's chief source of technical knowledge or skill. Specialists are single minded, self-starting and dedicated. However, they tend to contribute on a narrow front.

Most individuals are naturally suited to two or three roles. However, to work effectively a team must comprise elements of all nine roles. If a team lacks certain 'team roles' it tends to exhibit weaknesses in these areas.

leadership seems to work almost by infection. The management team seem to be infected by the philosophies and attitudes of the leader and readily buy into the goals set for the firm, something that is helped if they share in its success.

All personal relationships are based upon *trust*. Trust is the cornerstone of a good team and the cornerstone of an effective organizational culture. It is imperative that the management team trust their entrepreneurial leader. For leaders this involves having transparent vision and values, being firm but fair, flexible but consistent. It involves being straightforward – doing what they say and meaning what they say – 'walking the talk'. It involves being open and spontaneous, honest and direct. Whilst always placing the interests of the firm first, it also involves being supportive of individuals and having their interests at heart. Trust also needs to be built up between individual members of the management team. Trust takes time to build and needs to be demonstrated with real outcomes, but can be lost very quickly by careless actions and then takes even longer to rebuild.

> 'I can't remember a single day when I didn't want to go to work. I had such a good team. There was an incredible feeling of trust. None of the boys would let me down.'
>
> **Tom Farmer**
> founder of **Kwik-Fit**
> *Daily Mail*, 11 May 1999

Effective teams, therefore, do not just happen, they have to be developed, and that can take time. Teams go through a development process:

Phase 1   The group tests relationships. Individuals are polite, impersonal, watchful and guarded.

Phase 2   Infighting starts in the group and controlling the conflict is important. However, whilst some individuals might be confrontational others might opt out and avoid the conflict altogether. Neither approach is good. Collaboration is best. This is a dangerous phase from which some groups never emerge.

Phase 3   The group starts to get organized; developing skills, establishing procedures, giving feedback, confronting issues.

Phase 4   The group becomes mature and effective, working flexibly and closely, making the most of resources and being close-knit and supportive.

> 'Even though I'm often asked to define my business philosophy, I generally won't do so because I don't believe it can be taught as a recipe. There aren't ingredients and techniques that will guarantee success. Parameters exist that, if followed, will ensure a business can continue, but you cannot clearly define business or business success and then bottle it as a perfume. It's not that simple: to be successful you have to be out there, you have to hit the ground running, and if you have a good team around you and more than your fair share of luck you might make something happen.'
>
> **Richard Branson**

The whole process of team formation and development has been likened to courtship and marriage, involving decisions based partly on emotion rather than logic. For that reason it is important that the team shares the same values and are committed to the same goals – and that brings us back to issues of leadership. They may disagree on tactics but they all agree on the destination and how they are going to get there. It is also important that team roles are clearly defined, although given the uncertainty involved with rapid growth, it is also important that flexibility is maintained – which brings us back to the way conflict is handled. An effective team will generate team norms of behaviour and that can be a powerful force for conformity and suggests skilful handling.

Entrepreneurial leadership skills

Kirby (2003) likens the entrepreneurial leader to the leader of a jazz band. He decides on the musicians to play in the band and the music to be played but then allows the band to improvise and use their creativity to create the required sounds. In the process they have fun as the leader brings out the best in them. The leader's authority comes from his expertise and values rather than his position. Bandleaders lead by example – playing themselves. They empower their teams and nurture leaders at all levels – encouraging solo performances.

In an entrepreneurial organization the leader must combine many of the traditional skills of management with those of the entrepreneur. They must also reconcile the conflict between the impatience of the entrepreneur with the constraints imposed by an organization in its desire to control events. That is where different structures can be important as well as the role of change agents such as intrapreneurs. The leader's role, however, is more than that of the change agent, championing individual initiatives. Pursuing innovative ideas may be exciting but the leader needs to give the firm a sense of direction and purpose by aligning these developments to the vision and direction of the organization. That means standing back from the developments and providing a measure of impartial and objective evaluation. They must take an overview; reconciling differing perspectives – which may involve conflict resolution, creating a climate of co-operation – which will also involve co-ordination, but also exercising authority when needed to bring forward some initiative whilst pushing back others.

However, on the spectrum of traditional management to entrepreneurship, context is everything. What might be appropriate in one context can be inappropriate in another. And should innovation come from the bottom or be led from the top? Lessem (1987) identified a number of roles or archetypes other than that of 'leader' needed to move innovation along in different business contexts:

Adventurers   These are major risk takers who go in search of opportunity into new and difficult markets. They forge ahead and make things happen, but can rub people up the wrong way and can be difficult to control.

Innovators   These are the first users of new ideas. They link creativity and research with commercial reality, but can be too obsessed with the project they see as their own and may lack objectivity in evaluating its commercial potential.

Animators   These are essentially the 'team workers' needed to get co-operation and good team working.

Change agents   These are the people who are not bound by convention and change the status quo. They launch new products, implement new systems, reorganize working arrangements. To make all this happen they require enormous political skills.

Enablers   These people use their behavioural skills to encourage appropriate behaviour – to challenge convention and, through collaboration with others, to come up with new ideas.

This chapter has highlighted the need for an entrepreneurial leader to have good interpersonal and team-working skills. It has emphasized the need for strong influencing skills alongside good conflict resolution skills. Indeed entrepreneurial leaders need a wide range of interpersonal skills – all focused towards taking the organization with them by consensus and agreement, rather than dictating. These skills are summarized in Table 5.1. Lessem's approach reminds us that the appropriate approach and use of these skills depends on the context. It also emphasizes the need for an effective team comprising individuals who possess the appropriate qualities for the task they face.

Table 5.1   Entrepreneurial leadership skills

• Visionary	• Ability to work in a team
• Ability to communicate	• Ability to form deep relationships
• Ability to influence, informally	• Ability to generate trust
• Ability to motivate	• Ability to delegate
• Ability to think strategically	• Ability to build cohesion and a sense of belonging
• Ability to manage change	• Ability to clarify ambiguity and uncertainty
• Ability to resolve or reconcile conflict	• Ability to be firm but fair
• Ability to build confidence	• Ability to be flexible but consistent

All the skills in Table 5.1 can be developed and improved over time. But this can be a painful way to manage, necessitating considerable dedication and commitment by the leader. However, in the long term the gains from a motivated and dedicated workforce, acting as an effective team, can be considerable.

Summary

Management and leadership are different and distinct terms, although the skills and competencies associated with each are complementary. Management is concerned with handling complexity in organizational processes and the execution of work. It is about detail and logic, efficiency and effectiveness. Fayol defined the five functions of management as planning, organizing, commanding, co-ordinating and controlling.

Leadership on the other hand is concerned with setting direction, communicating and motivating. It is about broad principles and emotion. It is particularly concerned with change. It is seen as an 'event' which can be joined up, one to another, but the leadership style appropriate to one 'event' may be inappropriate for another.

The job of leader has five elements:

1. Having a vision.
2. Effective communication, including listening, seen as particularly important by **David Arculus**.
3. Being able to think strategically.
4. Creating an appropriate organizational culture.
5. Controlling and monitoring performance.

Entrepreneurs are defined by Timmons (1999) as 'patient leaders, capable of instilling tangible visions and managing for the long haul ... a learner and a teacher, a doer and a visionary.' This is strikingly similar to the definition of leader of a learning organization – an organization that 'facilitates the learning of all its members and continuously transforms itself ... adapting, changing, developing and transforming themselves in response to the needs, wishes and aspirations of people, inside and outside'.

The skills needed to lead a learning organization include those of organization designer, steward of its vision – always contrasting this to the reality of its current position – and teacher of how to exploit change – by understanding the root causes of problems and putting in place organizational structures to address the generic problem. These are the skills needed by an entrepreneurial leader such as **Michael Dell**.

Having and communicating a vision is a key skill of both entrepreneurship and leadership. **Derrick Collin**, founder of **Brulines**, agrees that a shared vision is an effective motivational tool. **Michael Dell** emphasizes the importance of good communication. Developing the vision is a continuous process, checking with staff that it resonates with them, modifying it to suit changing circumstances.

A vision is a desired future state. It is best communicated as a 'story' that, in some way, appeals to the emotions of staff and motivates them to achieve. It communicates the values and sense of purpose of the leader. It must be credible – acknowledging the tension created by a realistic appraisal of the current situation. The vision for an organization is formally communicated through the vision or mission statement.

Underpinning vision are the values of the organization – the core beliefs upon which it is founded. Values are enduring and long-term. They influence culture and strategy and bind the organization together. Visions and values are best articulated by leaders as 'stories' that have an emotional resonance. However, the leaders must behave as they talk – walk-the-talk.

As **Richard Branson** emphasizes, there is no single best leadership style. The appropriate style depends upon the leader, the group, the task and the situation or context they are in. **Jonathan Elvidge**, founder of **Gadget Shop**, believes it is important to be yourself. However, in the context of a growing firm that wishes to continue to be entrepreneurial, an autocratic or dictatorial style is unlikely to be appropriate, especially with the management team.

Entrepreneurial leaders must be adept at using informal influence to get their way. Persuasion and motivation are important and as the firm grows organizational culture increasingly becomes the best way of exerting this.

Leadership Style Questionnaire

For each of the following statements, tick the 'Yes' box if you tend to agree or the 'No' box if you disagree. Try to relate the answers to your actual recent behaviour as a manager. There are no right and wrong answers.

	Yes	No
1. I encourage overtime work	☐	☐
2. I allow staff complete freedom in their work	☐	☐
3. I encourage the use of standard procedures	☐	☐
4. I allow staff to use their own judgement in solving problems	☐	☐
5. I stress being better than other firms	☐	☐
6. I urge staff to greater effort	☐	☐
7. I try out my ideas with others in the firm	☐	☐
8. I let my staff work in the way they think best	☐	☐
9. I keep work moving at a rapid pace	☐	☐
10. I turn staff loose on a job and let them get on with it	☐	☐
11. I settle conflicts when they happen	☐	☐
12. I get swamped by detail	☐	☐
13. I always represent the 'firm view' at meetings with outsiders	☐	☐
14. I am reluctant to allow staff freedom of action	☐	☐
15. I decide what should be done and who should do it	☐	☐
16. I push for improved quality	☐	☐
17. I let some staff have authority I could keep	☐	☐
18. Things usually turn out as I predict	☐	☐
19. I allow staff a high degree of initiative	☐	☐
20. I assign staff to particular tasks	☐	☐
21. I am willing to make changes	☐	☐
22. I ask staff to work harder	☐	☐
23. I trust staff to exercise good judgement	☐	☐
24. I schedule the work to be done	☐	☐
25. I refuse to explain my actions	☐	☐
26. I persuade others that my ideas are to their advantage	☐	☐
27. I permit the staff to set their own pace for change	☐	☐
28. I urge staff to beat previous targets	☐	☐
29. I act without consulting staff	☐	☐
30. I ask staff follow standard rules and procedures	☐	☐

Adapted from Pfeiffer, J. and Jones, J. (eds) (1974), *A Handbook of Structured Experiences from Human Relations Training*, vol. 1 (rev.), University Associates, San Diego, California.

Scoring for this test can be found on p. 109.

Entrepreneurs must also be adept at resolving conflict, through a collaborative or compromising approach.

Michael Dell believes a firm is only as good as its people and finding the right people for the right job is essential. As **Geoff Barrell** founder of **BlueArc** agrees, the management team is built around the range of appropriate skills needed to manage a business. However, it is also about assembling a mix of different personalities. Belbin identified nine characteristics that need to be present to form an effective team: shaper, plant, co-ordinator, resource investigator, monitor-evaluator, team-worker, implementer, completer-finisher and specialist.

Teams have strong interpersonal relationships and, as **Tom Farmer**, founder of **Kwik-Fit**, points out, all relationships are based upon trust. Building this up takes time. It involves having transparent vision and values and acting consistently in a firm but fair way in the interests of the organization and staff.

A team takes time to become effective. It is likely to go through a four-stage development process before it reaches this point:

1. Testing.
2. Infighting.
3. Getting organized.
4. Mature effectiveness.

Leaders of entrepreneurial organizations need the range of skills listed in Table 5.1, including the skill of managing and facilitating change, although they do not always control that change. They need to use all the levers available to them to shape the organization. Above all, however, they need good interpersonal skills.

Essays and discussion topics

1. How does the role of leader differ from that of entrepreneur?
2. How does the role of leader differ from that of manager?
3. Leadership is an event. Discuss.
4. Leaders must be charismatic. Discuss.
5. What do you think are the prime tasks of a leader in an entrepreneurial organization? Why?
6. Has Michael Dell made the transition from entrepreneur to leader?
7. What is vision? How can it be developed? How can it be communicated?
8. Why are values important? Are they dangerous?
9. Compare and contrast the different mission statements on pages 91 and 94. Do they fit the format suggested by Wickham? Are they effective?
10. Are the values of Body Shop reflected in their mission statement? What do you think of Body Shop's mission?
11. Give examples of firms with strong values and beliefs and describe how these affect the way the firms operate.
12. Is there such a thing as an effective leadership style for an entrepreneurial business?
13. Why is an ability to handle conflict important in the entrepreneurial firm?
14. How do you build an effective team?
15. What are the phases that the team goes through as it develops?
16. How do you generate trust?
17. Discuss the comments by Jonathan Elvidge, founder of Gadget Shop.
18. In what contexts might each of Lessem's five entrepreneurial archetypes succeed?
19. Which do you think are the five most important leadership skills? Why?
20. Leaders are born not made. Discuss.

Exercises and assignments

1. Obtain the Thomas-Kilman Conflict Mode questionnaire from Xicom and evaluate how you handle conflict.
2. Using the questionnaire in Meredith Belbin's book evaluate your preferred team roles.
3. Using detailed examples, show how the appropriate leadership style might differ for:
   - three different tasks, given the same group and situation;
   - three different groups, undertaking the same task in the same situation;
   - three different situations, where the same group is undertaking the same task.
4. Find a company with strong values and show how these underpin the way it goes about its business.
5. Write a mission statement for an imaginary business.
6. Research and write a profile of a successful entrepreneurial leader, emphasizing his or her leadership style.

References

Adair, J. (1984) *The Skills of Leadership*, London: Gower.

Adizes, I. (1978) 'Organizational Passages: Diagnosing and Treating Life Cycle Problems of Organizations', *Organizational Dynamics,* Summer.

Bartlett, C. A. and Ghoshal, S. (1994) 'Changing the Role of Top Management: beyond Strategy to Purpose', *Harvard Business Review*, November/December.

Belbin, R. M. (1981) *Management Teams – Why They Succeed and Fail*, London: Heinemann Professional Publishing.

Bennis, W. and Nanus, B. (1985) *Leaders: The Strategies for Taking Charge*, New York: Harper & Row,

Blake, R. and Mouton, J. (1978) *The New Managerial Grid*, London: Gulf.

Blank, W. (1995) *The Nine Laws of Leadership*, New York: AMACOM.

Burns, P. and Whitehouse, O. (1996) 'Managers in Europe', *European Venture Capital Journal*, 45, April/May.

Chell, E. (2001) *Entrepreneurship: Globalization, Innovation and Development*, London: Thomson Learning.

Gardner, H. (1995) *Leading Minds: An Anatomy of Leadership*, New York: John Wiley & Sons.

Kirby, D. (2003) *Entrepreneurship*, London: McGraw-Hill.

Lessem, R. (1987) *Intrapreneurship*, Aldershot: Gower.

Nanus, B. (1992) *Visionary Leadership: Creating a Compelling Sense of Direction for your Organization*, San Francisco: Jossey-Bass.

Nonaka, I. (1991) 'The Knowledge-Creating Company', *Harvard Business Review*, November/December.

Ray, G. H. and Hutchinson, P. J. (1983) *The Financing and Financial Control of Small Enterprise Development*, London: Gower.

Senge, P. M. (1992) *The Fifth Discipline*, London: Century Business.

Timmons, J. A. (1999) *New Venture Creation: Entrepreneurship for the 21st Century*, Singapore: Irwin/McGraw-Hill.

Wickham, P. A. (2001) *Strategic Entrepreneurship: A Decision-Making Approach to New Venture Creation and Management*, Harlow: Pearson Education.

Leadership Style Questionnaire: Scoring

To obtain your leadership orientation rating, score 1 point for the appropriate response under each heading, then total your scores. If your response is inappropriate you do not score. As a guide, a score of 5 or less is low and 12 or more is high.

PEOPLE SCORE (maximum score 15)
'Yes' for questions 2, 4, 8, 10, 17, 19, 21, 23, 27.
'No' for questions 6, 13, 14, 25, 29, 30.

TASK SCORE (maximum score 15)
'Yes' for questions 1, 3, 5, 7, 9, 11, 15, 16, 18, 20, 22, 24, 26, 28.
'No' for questions 12.

Next plot your position on the Leadership Grid below.

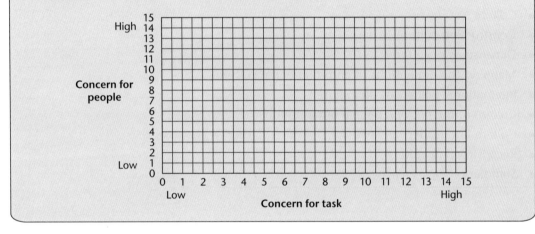

6

Creating the Entrepreneurial Culture

Contents

- Culture
- Constructing culture
- Dimensions of culture
- Mapping the dimensions of entrepreneurial culture
- International influences on culture
- Culture in the entrepreneurial organization
- Culture and leadership style
- Reconstructing culture
- Summary

LEARNING OUTCOMES

By the end of this chapter you should be able to:

- Explain what is meant by culture and give examples of the dimensions along which it can be measured;

- Describe the influences on organizational culture, in particular the importance of national culture;

- Describe the managerial tools available to help construct or reconstruct the culture of an organization;

- Explain what is meant by entrepreneurial culture and how it can be mapped onto the dimensions of culture;

- Recognize an entrepreneurial culture and distinguish which elements are most important;

- Evaluate an organization in terms of these 'high-level' attributes of entrepreneurial culture;

- Explain what is required to develop an entrepreneurial culture in a larger organization and what management style encourages it.

Culture

Cornwall and Perlman (1990) define culture as 'an organization's basic beliefs and assumptions about what the company is about, how its members behave, and how it defines itself in relation to its external environment'. Hofstede (1980) defines it as the 'collective programming of the mind which distinguishes one group of people from another'. It is therefore a pattern of taken-for-granted assumptions and beliefs shared by individuals collectively about how they are. It is the personality of the group. Schein (1990) says that cultures are 'invented, discovered, or developed by a given group ... as it learns to cope with its problems ... that has worked well enough to be considered valid and, therefore ... is to be taught to new members as the ... correct way to perceive, think, and feel in relation to those problems.'

Cultures evolve over time under a multitude of influences. Cultures therefore change over time and can also be shaped and influenced over time. Any one individual may be associated with a number of different groups, each of which might have its own set of characteristics that, together, describe the culture of the group. One group culture might be strong, another weak. A corporate culture is therefore just one of the cultures that any individual may contribute to or be affected by. Even if management do not try to 'impose' a corporate culture, one will emerge. Ignoring culture can therefore be dangerous because the one that might emerge, if the process is not managed, may not help the organization meet its objectives.

Language is an essential element of culture since it transmits the view that the group has of itself and the world, but also because the words themselves help shape people's beliefs. Without the words to describe situations, values or beliefs, they cannot be communicated. In the same way some groups start to carve out their own vocabulary with a view to influencing culture. In some companies employees may be referred to as 'associates'. In John Lewis they are 'partners'. The words are value-laden and convey the organizations' view of their relationships with these people.

At the core of any culture are the values that it holds. Some values are core, some are peripheral. Core values are stabilizing mechanisms that change only slowly over time, whilst peripheral values are less important and can change more quickly. As Guirdham (1999) explains: 'The status of women is a core value in Argentina, Chile, India and Israel, but less so in China, where the Confucian hierarchical concept of relations between individuals is more core ... Similarly, to a third generation

---

Case insight

The **John Lewis Partnership**, the department-store group, is Britain's largest unquoted company. Its founder, **John Spedan Lewis**, had strong moral beliefs. He believed in ensuring the well being of all his employees by giving them a stake in the business. Today they own 100% of it. He opened his first drapers store in Oxford Street, London in 1864 with another pledge that is still kept today; that it is never knowingly undersold.

Today the company has 26 department stores and over 160 Waitrose supermarkets with over 60,000 employees, all partners in the business sharing in its profits. Profits are £174 million on sales exceeding £5 billion. Over £87 million is distributed to the partners. Chairmen of the company still have to swear an oath that they will never investigate demutualizing the business.

American, the value of the democratic right of free speech might be core, but to her Singaporean cousin it might be peripheral, something to be traded off against the value of having a low-crime, drug-free society to live in.'

Cultures might be visible on a fairly superficial level – the costumes or uniforms people wear distinguish them as belonging to a particular group that might be associated with the deeper things – the values and beliefs that the group holds and their view of themselves and the world. However, simply the fact that costumes or uniform are worn does not necessarily guarantee a strong culture. The strength of a culture is rarely visible at the superficial level. Cultures become strong when they are reinforced in a consistent way by the different elements that influence them.

Constructing culture

Edgar Schein (1990) says that the only important thing that leaders do may well be constructing culture. He says that an organization's culture is grounded in the founder's basic beliefs, values and assumptions. So, how do you go about creating culture in an organization? We have identified and explored the crucial role of values – what is worth having or doing – and vision – where we are going and how we will get there – and how it is communicated in creating culture. Having entrepreneurship at the core of these values is fundamental and essential for the success of the entrepreneneurial organization. Values related to entrepreneurship include creativity, achievement, ownership, change and perseverance.

This is the first step, a necessary but not a sufficient condition. It underpins everything else. Beyond this, Bowman and Faulkner (1997) talk about organizational culture being formed or embedded in an organization from three influences; organizational processes, cognitive processes and behaviours. All these influences are represented in Figure 6.1.

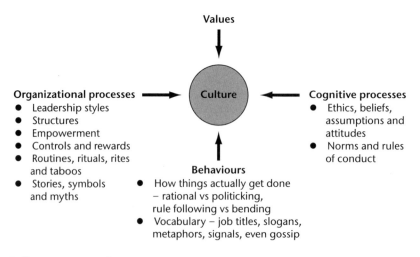

Figure 6.1 Influences on culture

Organizational processes

These can be deliberate or emergent, evolving organically from within the organization and may not be intended. There are many influences on this:

- Management and leadership styles, as we have seen, are an important influence. They send signals about appropriate behaviour. How managers treat people, react to situations, even allocate their time sends powerful signals about priorities that employees react to.
- Organizational structure influences culture. Hierarchical organizations can discourage initiative. Functional specialization can create parochial attitudes and sends signals about which skills might be valued. Flat, organic structures with broader spans of control encourage creativity, innovation and entrepreneurship – a factor to which we shall return in the next chapter.
- The power to make decisions is an important dimension for entrepreneurial organizations. Real empowerment sends the defining signal. Flat, decentralized structures with delegated decision making send signals about encouraging decision making, although sometimes informal power can lie outside formal hierarchies. The reaction to failure is an important message in this.
- Controls and rewards send important signals about what the firm values. People take notice of what behaviour gets rewarded – as well as what gets punished – and behave accordingly. If salaries are based mainly on sales bonuses and there is a monthly league table of the best sales people, what does this tell you about the firm, its values and its goals? Criteria used for recruitment, selection, promotion and retirement are all important. Status, praise and public recognition are powerful motivators.
- Routines, rituals, rites and taboos can have a strong subconscious influence. They form the unquestioned fabric of everyday life, but they say a lot about the organization. 'Guarded' or 'open' management offices, reserved or unreserved parking spaces, dress codes, normal methods of communication all influence the culture of the organization. What impression does a firm with reserved parking spaces and managers in offices 'guarded' by secretaries give you? An entrepreneurial organization needs to send out messages of egalitarianism with open relationships not based on status.

> 'Creating a culture in which every person in your organization, at every level, thinks and acts like an owner means that you need to aim to connect individual performance with your company's most important objectives ... A company composed of individual owners is less focused on hierarchy and who has a nice office, and more intent on achieving their goals.'
>
> **Michael Dell**
> ➜

- Stories and symbols have a part to play in preserving and perpetuating culture. Who are the heroes, villains and mavericks in the firm? What do staff talk about at lunch? Are there symbols of status that are important such as car or office size? How do staff talk about customers? How do staff talk about the entrepreneur and other senior managers?

> **Case insight**
>
> **Wilkin & Sons** is a family-owned business founded in 1885 and best known for its luxury Tiptree jams which sell to over 50 countries. The more esoteric jams such as 'Little Scarlet Strawberry' have attained almost a cult status among jam lovers.
>
> The company is committed to sharing success with its workforce. At the company's 450-hectare estate at Tiptree in Essex, managers and directors test products as well as man the production lines when required. More than 100 of the 180 workforce live in houses owned by the firm. It has operated a non-contributory pension scheme for over a century. The firm has also created a trust which will eventually leave employees with a 51% shareholding in the firm.
>
> There is another ethical dimension to the firm. It has never borrowed and does not want to.

Cognitive processes

These are the beliefs, assumptions and attitudes that staff hold in common and take for granted. They are embedded and emanate from the organization's philosophy, values, morality and creed. They are likely to be strongest in firms that have a long history and where staff join young and stay in the firm for most of their careers. Many successful old family firms such as J. Cadbury & Sons (the chocolate maker) and Wilkin & Sons were built around strong religious ethics whereby the success of the firm was shared with the workforce. Cadbury was founded in 1824 based on Quaker values and ideals. It promoted chocolate drinking as a virtuous alternative to alcohol and, in 1834, started manufacturing drinking chocolate and cocoa, building the legendary Bournville factory and picturesque village for its workers with its red-brick terraces, cottages, schools, duck ponds and wide open park lands. Workers were given a fair day's pay, good working conditions and homes and education for their children.

Norms – rules or authoritative standards – in an organization exist to enforce values and ensure conformity with the culture. An entrepreneurial firm may struggle with norms because one natural norm might well be to always ask the question 'why?', and to question the norms themselves. Because norms are questioned it is all the more important to have some deep values and beliefs underpinning the business. Morris and Kuratko (2002) talk about entrepreneurial organizations having a culture of 'healthy discontent' – one where there is a constant questioning, critiquing and changing of the way things are done. However, they do point out that this requires a balancing act, since too much discontent can easily become negative and destructive and lead to political gamesmanship.

In a new, entrepreneurial firm these beliefs can be moulded and developed by the enthusiasm and personality of the entrepreneur. In larger firms this can be developed through more formal training and communication processes. They are strongly influenced by what the leaders in the organization really pay attention to – not just what they say. But the important point is that they take time to frame. They do not happen overnight.

Behaviour

This is what actually happens in an organization. It decides whether outcomes are rational, transparent or the result of politicking. It influences whether the

---

Five Steps to Destroy a Rich Culture

1. Manage the bottom line (as if you make money by managing money).
2. Make a plan for every action: no spontaneity please, no learning.
3. Move managers around to be certain they never get to know anything but management well (and kick the boss upstairs – better to manage a portfolio than a real business).
4. Always be objective, which means treating people as objects (in particular hire and fire employees the way you buy and sell machines – everything is a 'portfolio').
5. Do everything in five easy steps.

Taken from Mintzberg, H., Ahlstrand, B. and Lampel, J. (1998) *Strategy Safari*, New York: The Free Press.

---

organization does actually follow rules, or is about bending them in the appropriate circumstances. Behaviour is about vocabulary – job titles, slogans, metaphors, signals, even gossip. Language is laden with value judgements that we do not realize most of the time – but they subconsciously influence the culture of the organization. Take an extreme example – a 'private' in the army 'salutes' an 'officer'. What messages do the words and actions convey and what culture do they reinforce? So, what are the behaviours that reinforce the message that this is an entrepreneurial organization?

Behaviour in organizations normally reflects and reinforces culture. However behaviour can also be influenced by a wide variety of external influences, within society as a whole, within a profession or within a sector or industry. Schneider and Barsoux (1997) observe that the culture in Nordic and Anglo-Saxon countries dictates that they frequently adopt 'controlling' strategies – rational-analytic with a desire to control the external environment – whereas the Latin Europeans and Asians tend to adopt 'adapting' strategies – with a belief in a less certain and less controllable environment. Behaviour that becomes routine can be difficult to change. However, attitudes can be influenced over time by getting people to behave in certain ways. Change behaviour first and attitudes will, eventually, follow.

Dimensions of culture

Measuring the dimensions of culture in a scientific way is extremely difficult. The most widely used dimensions are those developed by Hofstede (1981) who undertook an extensive cross-cultural study, using questionnaire data from some 80,000 IBM employees in 66 countries across seven occupations. From his research he established the four dimensions shown in Figure 6.2.

Individualism versus collectivism

This is the degree to which people prefer to act as individuals rather than groups. Individualistic cultures are loosely knit social frameworks in which people primarily operate as individuals or in immediate families or groups. Collectivist cultures are

Figure 6.2 Hofstede's dimensions of culture

composed of tight networks in which people operate as members of 'ingroups' and 'outgroups', expecting to look after, and be looked after by, other members of their 'ingroup'. In the individualist culture the task prevails over personal relationships. The atmosphere is competitive. In collectivism it is co-operative within the 'ingroup', however, it may well be uncharacteristically competitive with 'outgroups'. Whilst the entrepreneur is initially very individualistic, to create the 'team leadership' style required as the organization grows he needs to strike a careful balance between concern for people and concern for task and to become a team player. In that sense an entrepreneurial organization could also be seen as an 'ingroup' working against competitors.

Hofstede found the 'Anglo' countries (USA, Britain, Australia, Canada and New Zealand) are the highest scoring individualist cultures, together with the Netherlands. France and Germany just made it into the upper quartile of individualist cultures. South American countries were the most collectivist cultures, together with Pakistan.

Power distance

This is the degree of inequality among people that the community is willing to accept. Low power-distance cultures endorse egalitarianism, relations are open and informal, information flows are functional and unrestricted and organizations tend to have flat structures. High power-distance cultures endorse hierarchies, relations are more formal, information flows are formalized and restricted and organizations tend to be rigid and hierarchical. Individuals in high power-distance cultures have difficulty working in unsupervised groups whereas those in low power-distance cultures might be thought to exhibit a lack of 'respect' for authority. As we saw in the preceding section, the architecture of an entrepreneurial organization requires low power distance, which is more in line with a consultative or participative leadership style.

Hofstede found low power-distance countries tend to be Austria, Ireland, Israel, New Zealand and the four Scandinavian countries. The USA, Britain and Germany also make it into the lower quartile. High power-distance countries are Malaysia, the Philippines and four South American countries with France also making it into the upper quartile.

Uncertainty avoidance

This is the degree to which people prefer to avoid ambiguity, resolve uncertainty and prefer structured rather than unstructured situations. Low uncertainty avoidance cultures tolerate greater ambiguity, prefer flexibility, stress personal choice and decision making, reward initiative, risk taking and team-play and stress the development of analytical skills. High uncertainty avoidance cultures prefer rules and procedures, stress compliance, punish error and reward compliance, loyalty and attention to detail. Clearly our entrepreneurial culture involves low uncertainty avoidance.

The lowest uncertainty avoidance countries are Hong Kong, Ireland, Jamaica, Singapore and two Scandinavian countries. The USA and Britain are in the lowest quartile group. The highest uncertainty avoidance countries are Greece, Portugal, Guatemala and Uruguay with France also in the highest quartile group. Germany is about halfway.

Masculinity versus femininity

This defines quality of life issues. Hofstede defines masculine virtues as those of achievement, assertiveness, competition and success. Masculine cultures reward financial and material achievement with social prestige and status. Feminine virtues include modesty, compromise and co-operation. Women value relationships. In feminine cultures issues such as quality of life, warmth in personal relationships, service and so on are important. In some societies having a high standard of living is thought to be a matter of birth, luck or destiny, rather than personal achievement. Whilst individual entrepreneurs have a high need for achievement (masculine), we saw that they must temper this as the organization grows with a greater concern for others in the organization and relationships remain important (feminine). This need for achievement must become 'achievement through co-operation and relationships'. This is consistent with Hofstede's first dimension.

Hofstede found the most masculine countries are Japan, Austria, Venezuela, Italy and Switzerland, with the USA, Britain and Germany all falling into the highest quartile. Four North European countries are the highest scoring feminine countries. France is about halfway.

At a later date Hofstede and Bond (1991) added a fifth dimension – short/long-term orientation. A short-term orientation focuses on past and present and therefore values respect for the status quo. For example, they include an unqualified respect for tradition and for social and status obligations. A long-term orientation focuses on the future and therefore the values associated with this are more dynamic. For example, they include the adaptation of traditions to contemporary conditions and only qualified respect for social and status obligations.

HOFSTEDE'S DIMENSIONS

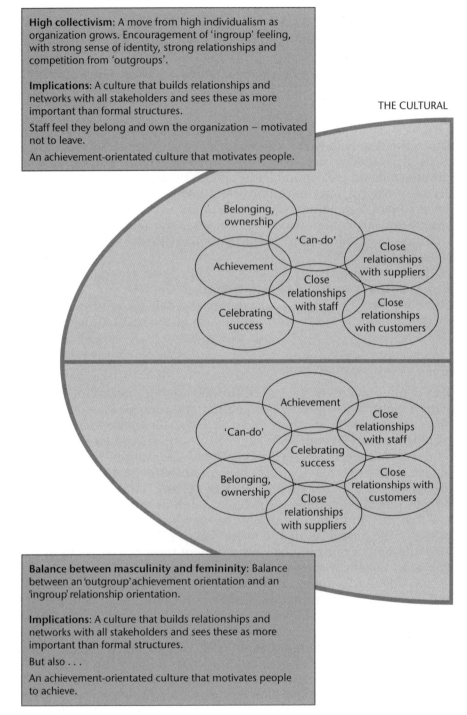

High collectivism: A move from high individualism as organization grows. Encouragement of 'ingroup' feeling, with strong sense of identity, strong relationships and competition from 'outgroups'.

Implications: A culture that builds relationships and networks with all stakeholders and sees these as more important than formal structures.

Staff feel they belong and own the organization – motivated not to leave.

An achievement-orientated culture that motivates people.

THE CULTURAL

Belonging, ownership

'Can-do'

Achievement

Close relationships with suppliers

Close relationships with staff

Celebrating success

Close relationships with customers

Achievement

'Can-do'

Close relationships with staff

Celebrating success

Belonging, ownership

Close relationships with customers

Close relationships with suppliers

Balance between masculinity and femininity: Balance between an 'outgroup' achievement orientation and an 'ingroup' relationship orientation.

Implications: A culture that builds relationships and networks with all stakeholders and sees these as more important than formal structures.

But also . . .

An achievement-orientated culture that motivates people to achieve.

Figure 6.3 The entrepreneurial culture mapped onto Hofstede's four dimensions

HOFSTEDE'S DIMENSIONS

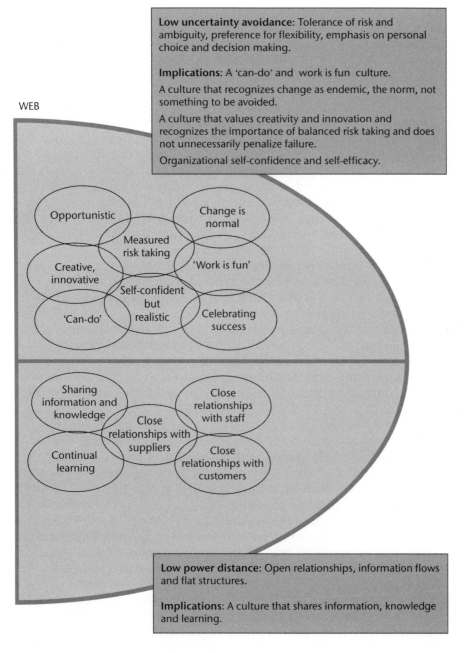

Low uncertainty avoidance: Tolerance of risk and ambiguity, preference for flexibility, emphasis on personal choice and decision making.

Implications: A 'can-do' and work is fun culture.

A culture that recognizes change as endemic, the norm, not something to be avoided.

A culture that values creativity and innovation and recognizes the importance of balanced risk taking and does not unnecessarily penalize failure.

Organizational self-confidence and self-efficacy.

WEB

Opportunistic

Change is normal

Measured risk taking

Creative, innovative

'Work is fun'

Self-confident but realistic

'Can-do'

Celebrating success

Sharing information and knowledge

Close relationships with staff

Close relationships with suppliers

Continual learning

Close relationships with customers

Low power distance: Open relationships, information flows and flat structures.

Implications: A culture that shares information, knowledge and learning.

Mapping the dimensions of entrepreneurial culture

We can describe the elements of an entrepreneurial culture using Hofstede's dimensions. Figure 6.3 takes the cultural web of an entrepreneurial organization, summarized in Figure 3.4, and maps it onto Hofstede's four dimensions. This allows us to describe our entrepreneurial culture in a more structured way. Entrepreneurial culture involves:

- A move from individualism to collectivism as the organization grows and the entrepreneur must depend more upon a team. This implies co-operation and the development of relationships and networks with a strong sense of 'ingroup', with a clear identity and a feeling of competition against 'outgroups'. However, there is a careful balance to be achieved between the need for individual initiative and co-operation and group working. A cross-cultural, empirical investigation (Morris *et al.*, 1994) supports this, observing that entrepreneurship appears to decline the more collectivism is emphasized, but, equally, dysfunctionally high levels of individualism can have the same effect.
- Low power distance. This implies an egalitarian organization with flat structures and open and informal relationships and unrestricted information flows. To reinforce this point Hall (2005) found in his study of organizational culture that innovation cannot occur in a power culture.
- Low uncertainty avoidance. This implies a tolerance of risk and ambiguity, a preference for flexibility and an empowered culture that rewards personal initiative. It implies that failure may occasionally occur.
- A balance between 'masculine' and 'feminine' dimensions to build a culture of achievement against 'outgroups' through co-operation, networks and relationships with the 'ingroup'.

This is summarized in Figure 6.4, where the culture required to encourage entrepreneurship is mapped onto Hofstede's four dimensions. In terms of Hofstede's fifth dimension, an entrepreneurial organization clearly has a long-term orientation as it is egalitarian with open communication and a lack of hierarchy.

Hofstede's dimensions of organizational culture were not designed specifically to measure entrepreneurial culture. Indeed his work was based upon IBM employees and they could hardly be described as the most entrepreneurial in the world at the time the study took place – just as Microsoft was setting up in business. So it is quite probable that there are other dimensions to consider. In that sense it may not completely describe what we want to achieve. What is more it is essentially constructed as a macro-measurement tool that reflects differences in national culture rather than organizational culture. In that sense it may not reflect the differences between an entrepreneurial and an administrative organization with sufficient discrimination. However, it is a widely used framework and appears sufficiently robust to provide a framework for the entrepreneurial characteristics discussed in previous chapters.

Nevertheless, you must remember that large organizations – including IBM – are complex. They contain many different environments, each with competing cultures based on the different tasks, individuals and environment, even time horizons, they face. Often these cultures compete, resulting in different value choices. The role of

Entreprenerial culture summarized by Hofstede's dimensions

management, therefore, is not just about selecting the culture to be emphasized, it is also about resolving these conflicts – emphasizing one or another and striking an appropriate balance between others. This is not an easy task and one that involves judgement rather than any sound scientific basis. Furthermore, the real challenge is to work out how any culture might be created.

One point to note is that one of the characteristics of a low uncertainty avoidance culture is that norms are less rigid and more open to different interpretation. Similarly, more feminine cultures are less rigid in the enforcement of norms. The conclusion is therefore that norms are likely to be less prevalent and less important in shaping culture in an entrepreneurial firm.

International influences on culture

Hofstede's study also reminds us that there are many influences on culture and the many organizations or groups that an individual might belong to, such as race, sect, religion, gender, family and peer group, each with different cultures, also influence the culture within an organization. An entrepreneurial culture does not exist within an organization in isolation. It must somehow reconcile the behavioural norms generated by these other cultures. One of the major influences is the country in which the organization operates. The empirical investigation by Morris *et al.* (*op. cit.*), which covered the USA, South Africa and Portugal, supported this. Powerful national cultures can overpower weaker organizational cultures. For this reason Hofstede argues that is often very difficult for organizational cultures to cross national boundaries. What is more, cultural comparisons and analysis are inextricably bound to a particular time and a particular place. Over time they change.

In this context it is worth remembering that most management theory and research was developed in the West in the second half of the twentieth century and is both culture and gender bound. It was developed for and about men. It reflects the 'scientific method' – independence, lack of emotion, objectivity, rationality, logic. Hofstede (1991) himself states that 'not only organizations are culturally bound; theories about organizations are equally culture bound. The Professors who wrote the theories are children of a culture: they grew up in families, went to schools, worked for employers. Their experiences represent the material on which their thinking and writing have been based. Scholars are as human and culturally biased as other mortals.' There is no guarantee therefore that theories developed around the cultural context of one country at any particular time can be applicable to another country or another time.

So, for example, many of the early motivational theories were developed by American academics (e.g. Herzberg, Maslow, McClelland) and are based around self-interest and the satisfaction of personal needs such as money, status and 'self-actualization'. These theories are based very firmly in the Anglo-Saxon capitalist culture which values individualism and masculinity (using Hofstede's dimensions) with low uncertainty avoidance. Hofstede (1991) suggests that in German and Austrian cultures the motivation to work derives instead from 'the need to relieve tension and stress' in their highly formal societies which are performance-orientated and value masculinity and low power distance with high uncertainty avoidance. Their desire for high uncertainty avoidance leads to high levels of personal stress. By way of contrast, the French, with their 'communitarian' society, deal with this by having high power distance which allows them to have 'father-figure' roles to absorb the stress of uncertainty. Similarly, Morden (1995) observes that, whilst strongly individualistic, the Scandinavian and Dutch interest in the 'quality of work, individual rights, farming co-operatives, etc. stem from a feminine characteristic which stresses interpersonal co-operation and de-emphasises interpersonal competition.' He goes on to make the point that combining this with low power distance means that personalized merit or bonus systems of payment may be inappropriate or counterproductive.

Hofstede (1980) suggests that these characteristics themselves may confer competitive advantage on certain countries. For example highly feminine countries such as The Netherlands or Denmark tend to be successful in consultancy, the service sector, helping relationships, horticulture and agriculture. He also observes that cultures can work in a complementary manner, citing the Anglo-Dutch multinationals Shell and Unilever where the values on power distance, uncertainty avoidance, and individualism are similar but where the people orientation of the Dutch complements the masculine, achievement orientation of the British.

The point here is that, whilst establishing an appropriate corporate culture is vital, there are many influences upon individuals, not least of which is the dominant culture in which the company is based. The dimensions of culture needed in an entrepreneurial organization (Figure 6.4) tend to suggest that it would be difficult to establish in countries with both a high power distance and high uncertainty avoidance. If you look back at Figure 6.2 you will see France falls firmly into both categories. Also these entrepreneurial dimensions (Figure 6.4) require a balance between individualism vs collectivism and between masculinity vs femininity, suggesting that a country with extreme results in either would pose problems for the entrepreneurial firm. Again it is noticeable that France has a high score in individualism. However, it is firmly in the middle ground on masculinity vs femininity. These observations imply that France should not be an easy place to establish an entrepreneurial organization. Interestingly, as we shall see in Chapter 14, another study shows France as having low and worsening levels of creativity, which begs the question whether these two factors could be linked.

No single country has the 'ideal' cultural profile outlined for an entrepreneurial organization although the USA is often put forward as a culture encouraging individual entrepreneurialism. It emerges as a highly individualistic, masculine culture, with low power distance and uncertainty avoidance. It is a culture that tolerates risk and ambiguity, has a preference for flexibility and an empowered culture that rewards personal initiative. It is a highly individualistic and egalitarian culture, one that is fiercely competitive and the home of the 'free-market economy'. Assertiveness and competition are central to the 'American dream'. If there is a key virtue in the USA it is achievement, and achievement receives its monetary reward. It is an informal culture. All men are created equal, however, they also have the freedom to accumulate sufficient wealth to become very unequal. The USA is the original 'frontier culture'. It actually seems to like change and uncertainty and certainly rewards initiative and risk taking. Interestingly again, as we shall see in Chapter 14, another study shows the USA as having the second highest level of national creativity.

Using Hofstede's dimensions this, then, is the anatomy of an enterprise culture: one that encourages enterprise and entrepreneurship, one where the probability of an entrepreneur being made, rather than just born, is highest. Notice that the UK also has this profile. This is the sort of culture that many other countries have been trying to promote and develop because it seems to encourage the characteristics that are needed to develop the largest number of entrepreneurs. However, if those entrepreneurs are to grow their businesses, whilst maintaining the business's entrepreneurial flair, they must move the organizational culture away from the national culture and more towards collectivism and femininity – developing a culture of achievement against 'outgroups' through co-operative team working and network relationships with 'ingroups'. The 3M case in Chapter 4 showed how one US company did this. Companies in different countries will probably need to emphasize different things.

Culture in the entrepreneurial organization

In a later work, Hofstede *et al.* (1990), looked at the different dimensions of organizational culture in an attempt to discriminate between entrepreneurial and administrative organizations. These were not so much dimensions as descriptors of what an entrepreneurial culture might look like compared to an administrative one. These descriptors are shown in Table 6.1.

Morris and Kuratko (*op. cit.*) have a slightly different view of what an entrepreneurial culture might look like within an organization. Based on synthesis of the work of Timmons (*op. cit.*), Peters (1997) and Cornwall and Perlman (*op. cit.*), they say it would have the following elements:

- People and empowerment
- focus;
- Commitment and personal responsibility;

Table 6.1 Entrepreneurial vs administrative cultures

Entrepreneurial	Administrative
● Results	● Process orientation
● Job	● Employee orientation
● Parochial	● Professional interest
● Open	● Closed system
● Loose	● Tight control
● Pragmatic	● Normative orientation

Source: Hofstede *et al.* (1990).

- 'Doing the right thing';
- Value creation through innovation and change;
- Hands-on management;
- Freedom to grow and to fail;
- Attention to basics;
- Emphasis on the future and a sense of urgency.

The authors distinguish between three types of failure: moral failure which occurs when there is a breach of ethics or moral standards; personal failure which relates to inadequate skills, knowledge or understanding; and uncontrollable failure which happens because of events or conditions out of the control of the individual. Whilst moral failure should not be tolerated, personal failure can be addressed through training, development and counselling. Uncontrollable failure is bound to happen in an entrepreneurial organization and valuable learning can take place as a result of it. You might be able to manage the risk, but the danger of failure is always present. Indeed success and failure are constant bedfellows in an entrepreneurial firm where commercial decisions involving risk are constantly being made. Rather than being viewed as the opposite ends of a spectrum, success and failure in the entrepreneurial firm can be viewed as the continuum shown in Figure 6.5. The difference between overall success and failure is for the organization to make certain the volume of successes outweighs the volume of failures. It has been said that the only way to avoid ever making a wrong decision is never to make a decision in the first place – not an option for the entrepreneurial organization.

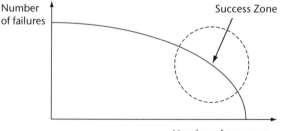

Figure 6.5 Success and failure in the entrepreneurial organization

Table 6.2 Cultures that enhance vs cultures that inhibit learning

A culture that enhances learning	A culture that inhibits learning
• Balances interests of all stakeholders	• Believes tasks are more important than people
• Focuses on people rather than systems	• Focuses on systems rather than people
• Empowers people and makes them believe they can change things	• Allows change only when absolutely necessary
• Makes time for learning	• Is preoccupied with short-term coping and adapting
• Takes a holistic approach to problems	• Compartmentalizes problem solving
• Encourages open communication	• Restricts the flow of information
• Believes in teamwork	• Believes in competition between individuals
• Has approachable leaders	• Has controlling leaders

Source: Derived from Schein (1994).

Entrepreneurial organizations are also learning organizations. Schein (1994) listed some of the features of a learning culture and compared them to a culture that inhibits learning. These are shown in Table 6.2. If you are starting from scratch you might be able to establish these features from the outset but to change an established organizational culture is altogether more difficult. Most established organizations inhibit learning. Schein concluded that to nurture these qualities you need to establish a 'psychologically safe haven' or 'parallel system' within the organization where learning – as we have defined it – can occur. And as we shall see in the next chapter, large organizations have responded to this organizational challenge with some success.

The constant theme coming through both the entrepreneurship literature and the learning organization literature is the need to empower and motivate employees to do 'the right thing' without having to be ordered to do so. This implies more of a consensus form of decision making that can mitigate against speed of action. In some circumstances this might just not be possible if an opportunity is to be seized. This is when the organization moves back from collectivism to individualism as the entrepreneur asserts himself. Often the different scenarios will already have been considered as the organization continuously strategizes and evaluates the options open to it. However, ultimately there may be a problem here that only considerations of size and structure can address. If the decision-making group is too large, the organization may well not be able to react with sufficient speed to changing circumstances.

An entrepreneurial culture needs to motivate people to do the 'right things', in the right way, for the organization as well as for themselves. It needs to help them cope with an uncertain future by giving them a vision and a belief that they can achieve it. Entrepreneurs are naturally good at motivating staff by the example they set – 'walking the talk' – but as the firm grows the leader needs to find different ways of communicating with more people, infecting them with the entrepreneurial virus. The culture of a firm comes from the leader, it reflects her personal values and her vision, but it is made up of a lot of small items of detail. Cultures can come about by chance, but if leaders want to plan for success, they need to plan to achieve the culture they want.

'Empower your staff. "People, people, people" is the mantra. If you do not have the right staff, fire them, quickly. Be nimble and act on your convictions'
Gururaj Deshpande
serial entrepreneur and founder of
Sycamore Networks
The Financial Times, 21 February 2000

Entrepreneurial culture is far harder to describe than it is to recognize – not unexpectedly given the lack of scientific measures available. Many of the detailed elements described aid recognition and are important in contributing to the overall culture. However, many elements are just detail and can get in the way of the big picture. Figure 6.6 attempts to disentangle many of these descriptors and classify them as either higher-level attributes or detail elements of culture. The high-level elements are those that really set the culture of the organization apart as being entrepreneurial. They represent the real DNA of the entrepreneur. All of the detail

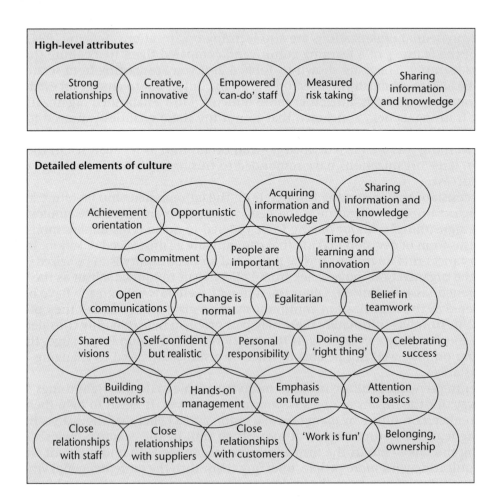

Figure 6.6 The cultural web hierarchy in an entrepreneurial organization

follows logically from these five elements. They are (in no particular order of priority):

- Creativity and innovation;
- Empowerment;
- Strong relationships;
- Continual learning;
- Measured risk taking.

Culture and leadership style

Many studies have shown significant national and gender differences in management style. For example, using Hofstede's dimensions, Torrington (1994) highlighted some of the differences in manager–subordinate relationships in six countries – Britain, USA, France, Germany, Japan and in a number of Arab countries. For example:

- British managers are willing to 'listen' to subordinates (low uncertainty avoidance) and like 'old boy networks' (high masculinity);
- US managers have a 'tough', results-orientated style in dealing with subordinates (high individualism and high masculinity);
- French managers like formality (high power distance) and 'intellectualism' (high individualism);
- German managers like routines and procedures and close control of apprentices (high uncertainty avoidance);
- The Japanese are high on both masculinity and collectivism producing a 'nurturing father' style of management;
- Arab countries value loyalty and the avoidance of interpersonal conflict (high power distance).

The dimensions of an entrepreneurial culture have resonance in motivation theory, in particular in 'Theory Z' (Ouchi, 1981). 'Theory Z' is a development of 'Theory Y', popularized by the American academic David McGregor back in 1960. McGregor contrasted his 'Theory X' – which assumes that employees have an inherent dislike of their work, taking an instrumental view of it, so that managers must exercise strong control over their activities because they cannot be trusted – with 'Theory Y' – which assumes that employees can like their work and can be motivated and then trusted to exercise discretion within a framework of rules. 'Theory Z' develops the participative nature of 'Theory Y' further by assuming that consensus and trust can be established within an organization, particularly through participative, team based, decision-making. These teams are responsible for achieving consensus and making decisions whilst the team's supervisor is still personally held responsible for the decision and its implementation. Relationships within the organization are based on trust and are long-term. Career development depends on total commitment and a willingness to do whatever is needed to further the organization (flexibility). The organization builds upon the experience of individuals, internalizing it and using it in a way that parallels the learning organization.

Management is based upon walk-about – 'walking the talk'. All these characteristics have resonance in the entrepreneurial organization.

The interesting thing about 'Theory Z' is the cultures in which it will or will not flourish. As Morden (*op. cit.*) points out, 'Theory Z' would be difficult to establish 'in cultures characterised by large power distance, strong individualism, aggressive masculinity, strong uncertainty avoidance and a strong attachment to hierarchies'. Such cultures are clearly not entrepreneurial (refer back to Figure 6.4). Morden observes that these cultures include southern Europe and South America. He goes on to make the point that 'Theory Z' contains a tension between group power and individualism (which is exactly the problem facing the growing entrepreneurial organization as it develops from being very dependent on the entrepreneur) and ideally it requires low individualism – or high collectivism – and low power distance. He observes that, whilst there are no such cultures recorded on Hofstede's culture maps, the nearest cultures shown are those of Austria, Israel and Finland.

So what sort of leadership style do you adopt in order to help achieve an entrepreneurial culture? Do you simply adopt a style, such as 'Theory Z', that reflects the values contained in the cultural web, even if the national culture in which the organization is placed finds this alien? Morden (*op. cit.*) supports the view that it is unrealistic to take a 'one style suits all' approach to the principles and practice of management as they are applied from one country to another: 'What works well in one country may be entirely inappropriate in another.' He advocates adapting to suit local circumstances and that means remembering two things:

1. Management is the art of the achievable and it may be impossible to achieve the 'ideal' entrepreneurial culture within some national cultures. That means a suboptimal solution – 'not quite an entrepreneurial culture' – may be appropriate. On the other hand, however, there is no theoretical guarantee that this solution will be effective in delivering entrepreneurial activity.
2. It is one thing knowing where you want to get to but quite another thing getting there. Leadership style can be adapted and changed gradually over time to suit circumstances so that it moves towards a more entrepreneurial style. There is a lot of evidence that it takes quite some time to change inherent cultures, whether we are talking about the impact of national cultures or changing the cultures of existing organizations.

Even in the context of a multinational organization, Morden does not advocate the development of 'geocentricity' – an international culture within the multinational. He sees this as only an option when the multinational has clearly understood values and common technologies; 'the resources to create such a body of international managers, and the desire to maintain a high level of integration and control over diversity through its international management team.'

Reconstructing culture

Constructing culture is like baking a cake. It takes the right ingredients and time for the mixture to bake. However the ingredients are far more volatile and unpredictable than a cake mix, particularly the relationships between individuals. Constructing the appropriate culture in a start-up is difficult enough, but that culture needs to shift and change as the organization grows. Most small firms start life with a 'task culture' – getting the job done. If the entrepreneur finds it difficult to delegate that may turn into a 'power culture' – where people vie to have power and influence over the entrepreneur. As this sort of firm grows, especially if the delegated authority is not genuine, there is a danger of developing a 'role culture' whereby job titles become too important – a culture that is quite different from the entrepreneurial culture outlined in the previous section.

But, whilst constructing and developing culture in a start-up is difficult enough, changing the culture in a large organization from one thing to another is altogether

Case insight

Louis Gerstner is credited with turning around the ailing giant **IBM** in the 1990s. He was brought in when the company was losing $800 million in the first four months of 1993 plus write-offs, eventually totalling $8.1 billion, and was facing planned break-up. Today IBM is the world's number 3 brand measured by equity value. His comments about changing culture are insightful.

'Frankly, if I could have chosen not to tackle the IBM culture head-on, I probably wouldn't have ... Changing the attitudes and culture of hundreds of thousands of people is very, very hard to accomplish. Business Schools don't teach how to do it. You can't lead the revolution from the splendid isolation of corporate headquarters. You can't simply give a couple of speeches or write a credo for the company and declare that the new culture has taken hold. You can't mandate it, engineer it.

What you can do is create conditions. You can provide incentives. You can define the market place realities and goals. But then you have to trust. In fact, in the end, management doesn't change culture. Management invites the workforce itself to change the culture.

In the end, my deepest culture-change was to induce IBMers to believe in themselves again – to believe they had the ability to determine their own fate, and that they already knew what they needed to know ... In other words, at the same time I was working to get employees to listen to me, to understand where we needed to go, to follow me there – I needed to get them to stop being followers. It wasn't a logical, linear challenge. It was counter-intuitive, centred around emotion, rather than reason.

Change is hard work. It calls for commitment from employees way beyond the normal company–employee relationship. It is what I call a high performance culture ... The best leaders create high performance cultures. They set demanding goals, measure results and hold people accountable. They are change agents, constantly driving their institutions to adapt and advance faster than their competitors do.

Personal leadership is about visibility – with members of the institution. Great CEOs roll up their sleeves and tackle problems personally. They don't hide behind staff. They never simply preside over the work of others. They are visible every day with customers, suppliers and business partners. Most of all, personal leadership is about passion. They want to win every day, every hour. They urge their colleagues to win. They loathe losing. It's not a cold intellectual exercise. It's personal.'

Source: Gerstner Jnr, L.V. (2002) *Who Says Elephants Can't Dance?*, New York: HarperCollins.

➡

more difficult. Inability to bring corporate cultures together is, as we shall see in Chapter 12, a major reason why mergers and acquisitions fail – witness what happened when AOL and Time Warner merged. Louis Gerstner is credited with turning around the ailing IBM in the 1990s. He claims management cannot change culture, it merely 'invites the workforce itself to change the culture'.

Reconstructing an existing culture requires great skill in managing change – an important skill in an entrepreneurial organization that is addressed in Chapter 9. Reconstructing culture can be a slow process. It involves many detailed changes that, on their own, might not be considered significant, but, taken together, add up to the definition of 'how it is around here'. Consistent changes reinforce each other. Fundamentally, reconstruction involves a process of redefinition of values and priorities which then have to be effectively communicated. Many people will be unable to 'buy into' the changes in culture and will leave. Organizations with a strong culture tend to attract like-minded staff, as in the case of Body Shop. In this way strong cultures become self-reinforcing. However, strong cultures are also the most difficult to change.

The difficulty in changing culture is one reason why larger organizations create new, smaller organizational units to push through new initiatives, leaving the core business and the prevalent culture unchanged in the larger parent. Size and structure can be important influences on culture as well as a useful tool to facilitate change.

Case with questions

HFL Ltd

HFL Ltd is the UK's pre-eminent drug surveillance and contract research company. It is the only laboratory in the world engaged in both sport drug surveillance and contract research. It currently undertakes funded research for the World Anti-doping Agency and the UK Horserace Betting Levy Board (HBLB). HFL has pioneered sports doping control research and surveillance in the UK, testing athletes and racing animals as part of forensic doping control processes and providing research and bio-analysis testing services to pharmaceutical, food, consumer products and healthcare clients. Based in Newmarket at the heart of the UK's best-known horse racing and breeding areas, it started life in 1963 owned by the HBLB, an inherently conservative quango (a quasi-governmental body), and enjoyed a steady stream of income from the monitoring of racehorses and greyhounds to ensure that their performance was not artificially enhanced by illegal substances. This is, therefore, an unlikely organization to look to as an exercise in change management. But change it did, and by 2007 it had diversified into drug testing on humans and been sold for £20.25 million to Quotient Bio Research Ltd – owned by a consortium of investors, including HFL's Chief Executive David Hall and other senior managers. HFL currently has a turnover of more than £10 million, employs some 130 people and enjoys a far more entrepreneurial culture.

The change catalyst was the appointment of David Hall as Chief Executive in 2001. His brief was to broaden the business base away from racehorses and greyhounds and he effectively 'privatized' the company. David is a scientist – Chartered Engineer with a PhD – but he also has

➡

an MBA, which is the source of his theoretical knowledge of how to change the culture of an organization. The challenge was to put it into practice at HFL. David would say that his passion for creativity and innovation and the pursuit of a perfect culture provided a common thread throughout his career before joining HFL. For example, he set up a technology transfer organization in London – Thames Gateway Technology. The challenge, as David sees it, is to get the very best from your staff and to truly differentiate your company on the basis of its people.

The HFL culture demands involvement, and communication is a vital element in this process. David wants it to run downwards, upwards and sideways through all feasible routes, so there is no excuse for 'not knowing'. David's preferred leadership style is to 'animate and facilitate' rather than 'command and control'. Because of this his preferred communication style involves limiting group size to 20, which he sees as far more conducive to participation. He gives 'state of the union' addresses to these groups every six months. He also instituted informal 'coffee and cakes' sessions on Monday mornings to help communication and get people to mix across boundaries and functions. There are also more formal mechanisms like team briefs and a mythical 'Uncle Bernard' who will answer e-mailed questions from staff. The elected 'Staff Association' also conducts quarterly surveys and plays an important part in promoting and monitoring change, even chasing the introduction of new ideas. HFL also uses cross-functional teams for project work and senior managers often have spells of doing other people's jobs.

HFL's scientific work depends critically on new ideas, which is why David is keen to encourage creativity. To do this he set up a Creativity Club and an Innovation Club. Each provides an environment for the free exchange of ideas, to push boundaries, and to harness the creative energies of staff. Every idea is posted on the company's intranet and staff are invited to comment. The best ideas might be taken forward by project teams. The company also has a book club that encourages the reading of business books, which also can lead to the introduction of new ideas. There is also the Business Intelligence Group, established to trawl the outside world for new ideas and to establish bench marks for its activities. Everyone who sees or hears things outside the company is debriefed and the ideas are passed on or project teams are set up to take the idea further. It was this process that led to the company's move into human drug testing.

David is a great believer in the power of positive thinking – another thing he likes to encourage in staff. He believes it can raise the proportion of time people spend working at maximum output. He arranged in-house training sessions on the topic which resulted in individuals producing 'affirmations' to complete challenging personal tasks. David participated in the training and his 'affirmation' resulted in him cycling coast-to-coast and back to raise money for charity.

HFL uses what it calls a 'strategy map' divided into four interconnecting areas: customer, reputation, people and finance. The aim in the 'customer' area is to become, or remain, 'first choice for analytical chemistry by improving loyalty, building relationships and innovating'. HFL aims to be the best customer choice, but not necessarily the cheapest. To achieve this it has to remain at the leading edge of its science and at the forefront of innovation. But innovation need not always be scientific. So, for example, to help cement customer relationships it set up a Customer Club for clients around the world.

Staff involvement and enthusiasm at HFL is no accident. It is carefully nurtured with formal and informal techniques. There are performance reviews and a bonus scheme. HFL has

→

Case with questions continued

HFL Ltd

'Investors in People' status and in 2005 was voted by its staff into the list of *The Times* '100 Best Companies to Work For'. But David will also admit that there have been casualties along the way, with less willing staff being replaced, particularly at senior management levels. And new managers have had a crucial part to play in changing the culture. David recruited Anne Stringer from a Cambridge wine business, nominally as finance director, but also with responsibility for HR and IT, to head up 'Central Services'.

Up-to-date information on HFL Ltd can be found on their website: www.hfl.co.uk

Case questions
1. Why is effective communication so important in changing culture?
2. What are the techniques HFL uses to promote internal and external communication? How do the 'informal' reinforce the 'formal' techniques?
3. Why is creativity and innovation important at HFL?
4. How is it promoted and what benefits has it brought?
5. Give examples of how HFL has used technology to achieve its aims.
6. How important was David Hall to the process of change experienced at HFL? Give examples.
7. Why is it important to replace senior managers who block change?

Summary

Culture is an organization's basic beliefs and assumptions about what the company is about, how its members behave, and how it defines itself in relation to its external environment. It is the collective programming of the mind, a pattern of taken-for-granted assumptions that influence how people in an organization perceive, think and feel in relation to situations. As in the cases of **John Lewis** and **Wilkin & Sons**, it is grounded in the founder's basic beliefs, values and assumptions. Particularly when based on religious or ethical beliefs, these can produce strong cultures. As **Michael Dell** says, culture can help connect individuals' performances with a company's objectives.

Establishing an appropriate corporate culture is vital if you want to develop an entrepreneurial organization. However, the culture of an organization does not exist in isolation. An individual may participate in many different groups, each with its own dominant culture. Each group influences and is influenced by the other – and cultures can change over time. The dominant culture of the country in which the organization operates will be a major influence on individuals and may be a barrier to establishing an entrepreneurial culture.

Culture within an organization is based on a firm set of enduring values. It can be constructed through organizational and cognitive processes and behaviours. It can be transmitted individually by the entrepreneur or, as in the case of **Body Shop**, through PR activities, induction, training and good communications generally.

Culture can be measured in four dimensions:

- *Individuality vs collectivism.*   An entrepreneurial culture would involve a move from individualism to collectivism as the organization grows. This implies co-operation and the development of relationships and networks with a strong sense of 'ingroup', with a clear identity and a feeling of competition against 'outgroups';
- *Power distance.*   An entrepreneurial culture has low power distance. This implies an egalitarian organization with flat structures and open and informal relationships and open, unrestricted information flows;
- *Uncertainty avoidance.*   An entrepreneurial organization has low uncertainty avoidance. This implies a tolerance of risk and ambiguity, a preference for flexibility and an empowered culture that rewards personal initiative;
- *Masculinity vs femininity.*   An entrepreneurial organization has balance between the masculine and feminine dimensions to build a culture of achievement against 'outgroups' through co-operation, networks and relationships with the 'ingroup'.

Figure 6.3 (pp. 118–19) maps the characteristics of an entrepreneurial culture onto Hofstede's four dimensions.

Figure 6.6 (p. 126) shows the cultural web of entrepreneurship, but it distinguishes between 'high-level' attributes – strong relationships, creativity and innovation, empowerment, measured risk taking and continual learning – and the detailed elements of culture.

The leadership style appropriate to 'Theory Z' reflects many of the dimensions of entrepreneurial culture. However, it is unrealistic to take a 'one style suits all' approach to the principles and practice of management as they are applied from one country to another. The style needs to be adapted to suit local circumstances and national cultures.

Reconstructing the culture of an organization is very difficult, as **Louis Gerstner** of **IBM** discovered. It requires good change management skills. However, as we saw in the case of **HFL Ltd**, with a good change agent at the top it can be done. The difficulty is one reason why larger organizations often attempt to separate or spin out new initiatives so that they can create their own culture, leaving that of the core business unchanged. Size and structure matter.

Whether you try to manage it or not, every organization will evolve a culture, be it strong or weak. Strong cultures attract like-minded people. They self-reinforce. However they can be very difficult to reconstruct.

Essays and discussion topics

1. How do you describe culture? Can it be measured?
2. How does language affect culture? How does culture affect language?
3. Is strong culture good or bad? Give examples.
4. What are your core values?
5. What are the core values of your national culture?
6. What are the core values of entrepreneurship?
7. How do cognitive processes influence the culture of an organization? Give examples.
8. What organizational processes would reinforce the message that an organization is entrepreneurial?

9. What cognitive processes would reinforce the message that an organization is entrepreneurial?
10. What managerial behaviours would reinforce the message that an organization is entrepreneurial?
11. Do you notice any patterns in the national results of Hofstede's research?
12. The USA is normally seen as an entrepreneurial national culture. If this is the case, how would you describe an entrepreneurial culture? What about the UK?
13. What methodological problems might emerge when using a study that sets out to discriminate national cultures as a basis for discriminating organizational cultures?
14. Why is the balance between individualism and collectivism so important? Why might it vary?
15. How would you describe an entrepreneurial organizational culture?
16. In what circumstances might an organization wish to see no mistakes or failures?
17. What methodological problems might emerge when organizing a study which tries to discriminate entrepreneurial from other organizations?
18. What particular problems face your country in developing an entrepreneurial organizational culture?
19. Why might it be better to separate or spin out new initiatives so that they can create their own culture, leaving that of the core business unchanged?
20. What additional elements of the cultural web of entrepreneurship do the works of Hofstede *et al.* (1990), Morris and Kuratko (2002) and Schein (1994) bring to the elements highlighted in Figure 6.3? Do you think they are important?
21. Do you agree that the most important elements of an entrepreneurial culture are creativity and innovation, empowerment, strong relationships, continual learning and measured risk taking?
22. Could you recognize an entrepreneurial organization? How?

Exercises and assignments

1. Select two organizations, one that you would describe as entrepreneurial, the other that you would describe as administrative or bureaucratic. Describe their cultures in a brief report and evaluate on the five dimensions of creativity and innovation, empowerment, strong relationships, continual learning and measured risk taking.

References

Bowman, C. and Faulkner, D. O. (1997) *Competitive and Corporate Strategy*, London: Irwin.
Cornwall, J. and Perlman, B. (1990) *Organizational Entrepreneurship*, Homewood, Ill.: Irwin.
Guirdham, M. (1999) *Communicating across Cultures*, Basingstoke: Macmillan – now Palgrave Macmillan.
Hall, D. (2005) 'Insight from Facilitating Entrepreneurial Business Development within Established Organisations', presented at *Institute for Small Business and Entrepreneurship conference*, Blackpool, UK.
Hofstede, G. (1980) *Culture's Consequences: International Differences in Work-related Values*, Beverly Hills: Sage.
Hofstede, G. (1981) *Cultures and Organizations: Software of the Mind*, London: HarperCollins.
Hofstede, G. (1991) *Cultures and Organizations*, London: McGraw-Hill.
Hofstede, G. and Bond, M. H. (1991) 'The Confucian Connection: From Cultural Roots to Economic Performance', *Organizational Dynamics*, Spring.
Hofstede, G., Neuijen B., Ohayv, D. D. and Sanders, G. (1990) 'Measuring Organizational Cultures: A Qualitative and Quantitative Study across Twenty Cases', *Administrative Sciences Quarterly*, 35.

McGregor, D. (1960) *The Human Side of Enterprise*, London: McGraw-Hill.

Morden, T. (1995) 'International Culture and Management', *Management Decision*, 33(2).

Morris, M. H., Davies, D. L. and Allen, J. W. (1994) 'Fostering Corporate Entrepreneurship: Cross Cultural Comparisons of the Importance of Individualism versus Collectivism', *Journal of International Business Studies*, 25(1).

Morris, M. H. and Kuratko, D. F. (2002) *Corporate Entrepreneurship*, Orlando: Harcourt College Publishers.

Ouchi, W. (1981) *Theory Z*, Reading, Mass: Addison-Wesley.

Peters, T. (1997) *The Circle of Innovation*, New York: Alfred A. Knopf.

Schein, E. H. (1990) 'Organizational Culture', *American Psychologist*, February.

Schein, E. H. (1994) 'Organizational and Managerial Culture as a Facilitator or Inhibitor of Organizational Learning', *MIT Organizational Learning Network Working Paper 10.004*, May.

Schneider, S. C. and Barsoux, J.-L. (1997) *Managing across Cultures*, London: Prentice Hall.

Timmons, J. A. (1999) *New Venture Creation: Entrepreneurship for the 21st Century*, Singapore: Irwin/McGraw Hill.

Torrington, D. (1994) *International Human Resource Management,* Hemel Hempstead: Prentice Hall.

7

Building an Entrepreneurial Structure

Contents

- Size
- Traditional large firm structures
- Environmental change and task complexity
- Organic structures
- Networks and other new forms of organizing
- Strategic alliances
- Summary

By the end of this chapter you should be able to:

- Explain and give examples of how size, structure and different organizational forms can encourage and contribute to the development of corporate entrepreneurship;

- Explain how this is related to the tasks being undertaken and the environment in which the organization finds itself;

- Explain why firms are increasingly exploring new forms of organizing;

- Describe different forms of networking and explain how and why they are built up.

Size

Structures create order in an organization. Although there is no one 'best' structure, different types of structure are good for particular types of task. The most appropriate structure depends on a number of factors: the nature of the organization, the strategies it is employing, the tasks to be undertaken, the environmental conditions under which the firm operates and the size of the firm.

Size does seem to matter. Large organizations are more complex than small and complexity impedes information flows, lengthens decision making and can kill initiative. To be entrepreneurial, a large organization needs to find ways of breaking itself down into a number of sub-organizations with varying degrees of autonomy. The span of control for management does seem to matter – 'walking the talk', a management approach advocated earlier, only seems possible up to a certain size. But large organizations can structure themselves so that they comprise smaller 'units'. Again there are no prescriptive 'correct' approaches. However, for some time large companies have been seeking to replicate the flexibility of the small firm and encourage entrepreneurial management by 'deconstructing' themselves – that is, breaking themselves down into smaller units. Peter Chemin, CEO of the Fox TV empire, believes that 'in the management of creativity, size is your enemy' (*Economist*, 4 December 1999). He has tried to break down the studio into small units, even at the risk of incurring higher costs.

Many companies believe that the initial stages of innovation – a particular form of task – require such a different culture that completely separate premises from the corporate offices need to be found. This leads them to set up separate 'research' establishments. But research is not the same as development and even then the innovation has to be exploited commercially. Having separate locations for many of these activities allows firms to maintain different cultures as well as different structures, staffing and remuneration.

Taking this idea further, big companies often 'spin off' new ventures, creating completely new, small companies that are lean and flexible and focused on getting their product to market. However, often the big company has to put in place mechanisms to make this happen, mini-organizations within the big company with the task of spotting innovative opportunities and facilitating their development. This can be the corporate venture capital firm – an autonomous company that underwrites and assists new product/service developments that meet formal venture capital criteria.

Amar Bhidé (2000) believes that, rather than trying to re-invent themselves, large firms should concentrate on projects with high costs and low uncertainty, leaving those with low costs and high uncertainty to small entrepreneurial firms – with entrepreneurial management. As ideas mature and risks and rewards become more quantifiable, large firms can adopt them. Even in capital-intensive businesses such as pharmaceuticals, entrepreneurs or smaller entrepreneurial organizations can conduct early-stage research, selling out to large firms when they reach the expensive, clinical trial stage. About a third of drug firms' revenue now comes from licensed-in technology. Many large companies, like General Electric and Cisco, have adopted the policy of buying up small firms who have developed new technology.

John Naisbitt (1994) also feels the future lies very much with small independent firms, whether owner-managed or 'deconstructed' from large firms. His book is based upon the apparent paradox that 'the bigger the world economy, the more powerful its smallest players'. He sees much of the growing importance of smaller firms, and with them entrepreneurs, coming from larger firms which will have to restyle themselves into 'networks of entrepreneurs' if they are to survive. In his view 'downsizing, re-engineering, the creative networking organization, or the latest virtual corporation, whatever it is called, it comes down to the same thing. Corporations have to dismantle bureaucracies to survive. Economies of scale are giving way to economies of scope, finding the right size for synergy, market flexibility, and above all, speed.' He observes that 'to survive, big companies today – ABB, AT&T, GE, Grand Metropolitan, Coca-Cola, Benetton, Johnson & Johnson, British Petroleum, Honda, Alcoa, Xerox – are all deconstructing themselves and creating new structures, many as networks of autonomous units. Deconstruction is now a fashion, because it is the best way to search for survival.'

The other side to this trend towards downsizing and deconstructing large firms is that the large firm will increasingly concentrate on its core activities, where they have competitive advantage, and sub-contracting of non-core activities will increase. This enables the large firm to reduce its fixed cost base and thus the risk it faces and flatten its organization structure thereby ensuring a quicker response time to changes in the market place. As with Dell, 'partnership sourcing' is likely to increase, whereby a close relationship is built between the bigger company and the smaller subcontractor, with one helping the other to grow. Entrepreneurial firms can take the lead in this. The development of e-commerce for supply chain management will just accelerate this trend.

The trend towards flattening organizational structures started in the USA in the 1980s and then came to Europe. In the UK, 1994 saw BT cut 5000 middle and senior managers in one year reducing its layers of management from twelve to six. WH Smith cut 600 store managers in the same year reducing its layers of management from four to two. In the following year Shell got rid of 1200 managers from its head office. In the late 1980s and early 1990s the entire UK banking industry saw over one-third of its managers leave the industry. This is not just about deconstructing, it is about changing the attitudes of the remaining managers about the security of their jobs as well as putting many middle-aged managers in the position of having few alternatives other than self-employment. No wonder self-employment blossomed over the same period. Charles Handy (1994) predicted that many larger firms will become 'shamrock organizations' – the three leaves being core staff, temporary staff to ease them over peaks and troughs in work and small organizations supplying specialist services, deeply embedded in, and dependent upon, the larger firm. Many of us will mix five kinds of work: wage work, fee work, home work, gift work and study work. This takes us back to entrepreneurial management and the architecture on which it is based.

Large firms are increasingly experimenting with different structures, organizational forms and processes. Pettigrew and Fenton (2000) noted the following trends:

- Decentralizing
- Delayering
- Outsourcing
- Downscoping
- Using project forms of organizing

- Developing strategic alliances
- Communicating horizontally as well as vertically
- Investing in information technology
- Practising new HRM techniques

One implication from all this experimentation is clear – size matters and small is, indeed, beautiful. The reason for this is to do with the need in entrepreneurial organizations for flatter structures which result in better communication, greater delegation of authority and faster decision making. The larger the unit of organization the more people and the broader the span of control, or number of people reporting to a given manager – which make it difficult to handle. Put another way, size, or the larger the number of people in the unit of organization, requires structures that involve hierarchies and these tend to rely on power to make decisions, and the exercise of power tends to be slow and inflexible.

The question is how to achieve the best of both worlds – the benefits in terms of resources of large scale and the benefits in terms of entrepreneurship of small scale. The answer is not straightforward, and, as already said, needs to be adapted to particular circumstances. However, part of the answer is in smaller sub-structures, which form part of a larger whole. These, as we shall see, can take many different forms. Each sub-structure may have its own sub-culture and, what is more important, smaller units can be more entrepreneurial. Within any structure there needs to be a hierarchy of some sort that gives managers confidence that they have the authority to manage. Generally, to encourage entrepreneurship levels or layers of management need to be kept to a minimum to ensure flexibility and responsiveness. To start with, it is worthwhile reflecting on how and why structures typically evolve as the organizations age and grow in size.

Traditional large firm structures

Chapter 3 looked at the classic work of Larry Greiner (1972) on organizational life cycles. For Greiner organizational structures evolve as the organization grows through a process of continuous change and development. He typified this as comprising a number of identifiable stages. First there is the 'spider's web' that is so typical of a newly formed entrepreneurial organization. Early on this can be a real advantage to the organization but, as the number of people reporting either formally or informally directly to the entrepreneur increases, it can become dysfunctional. As the organization grows more structure is put in place, often with a functional hierarchy and centralized control. Departmentalization – forming people into functional groups such as marketing, production and accounting – will occur. Figure 7.1A shows a classic hierarchical structure. Each level might represent a

'It doesn't make sense to stay true to a structure that makes it more difficult for your people to succeed. Your organizational structure must be flexible enough to evolve along with your people, rather than work against them. This is one of the biggest and most challenging cultural issues we face as a fast growing company.'

Michael Dell
➡

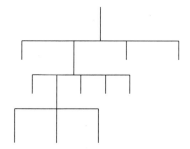

Figure 7.1A The hierarchical structure

particular grouping or sub-grouping within the organization. A similar diagram could be drawn representing individuals within the organization.

Next comes greater decentralization either based on geographic or product groupings, built around profit centres. Again, each division or profit centre would be represented at a certain level in Figure 7.1A and would itself have a hierarchical structure. This is followed by a move towards merging product groups into strategic business units together with the development of a head office with centralized administrative and staff functions. Finally, to aid integrative working, matrix structures and other cross-functional structures are adopted with head office staff reassigned to consultative teams. This form of organization is shown in Figure 7.1B.

The bureaucratic form of hierarchical structure (Figure 7.1A), with its universal organization structure, marks the earliest influential theory of organizational design. Based on the work of Weber (1947), it stresses rationality and functional efficiency. The literature was broadened by Chandler (1962), as technical and organizational complexity increased, by the inclusion divisions – a development that was seen as a rational solution to increasing scale and complexity. However, much of the later literature focuses on the dysfunctional consequences of this structure where people got in the way of rational efficiency (Pugh and Hickson, 1976).

It was the contingency theorists of the late 1950s and 1960s that concluded there was no single best way of organizing a business. That depends on the extent to which the structure furthers the objectives of the firm, but in particular it depends on:

- The environment it faces (Stinchcombe, 1959; Burns and Stalker, 1961; Emery and Trist, 1965; Haige and Aiken, 1967; Lawrence and Lorsch, 1967);
- The technology it uses (Woodward, 1965; Perrow, 1967);
- Its scale of operation (Pugh *et al.*, 1969; Blau, 1970);

In all cases, variations in structure can be rationalized in terms of task predictability and diversity. However, these approaches tend not to explain the underlying processes – how things happen.

The matrix structure (Figure 7.1B) came out of the contingency school. First posited by Galbraith (1973), it is based on the work of Lawrence and Lorsch (*op. cit.*) and is essentially an overlay on what is still a bureaucratic structure with hierarchical distributed power and decision making. It spawned the development of teams and task forces. Galbraith also observed how task complexity increased with task uncertainty and the amount of information that needs to be processed by the decision maker.

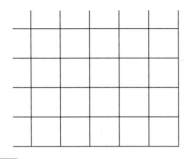

Figure 7.1B The matrix structure

Environmental change and task complexity

A traditional hierarchical structure of the kind shown in Figure 7.1A is most suited to organizations that require security and stability. The matrix or task structure shown in Figure 7.1B is often seen in organizations undertaking project work, for example consultancies. But it can also be combined very effectively with the hierarchical structure so that individuals in different branches of the hierarchical structure come together as a team to undertake projects or tasks within the matrix structure. So, for example, the hierarchical structure might reflect functional areas such as design, production, marketing, sales and finance. Individuals from these areas, at appropriate levels in the hierarchy, might come together to form a matrix team to tackle a project such as new product development.

On its own, the traditional hierarchical structure shown in Figure 7.1A is mechanistic, bureaucratic and rigid. It has been called a 'machine bureaucracy' because it is most appropriate where the organization (or sub-organization) is tackling simple tasks with extensive standardization, in stable environments, and/or where security is important and where plans and programmes need to be followed carefully. Well developed information systems reporting on production/processing activity need to exist for it to be effective. Power is concentrated in the top executives. It is more concerned with production than marketing and is good at producing high volumes and achieving efficiency in production and distribution. As such, it is particularly appropriate when a product is at the mature phase of its life cycle and is being 'milked' as a 'cash cow' (see Chapter 12). It is the antithesis of an entrepreneurial structure and is designed to stifle individual initiative.

As the environment becomes more liable to change, standardization becomes less viable and responsibility for coping with unexpected changes needs to be pushed down the hierarchy. Complex tasks in stable environments mean that it becomes worthwhile developing standard skills to tackle the complexities. In both these cases the matrix organization can be an effective sub-structure within a more hierarchical organization. In a stable environment the matrix team can work on their complex tasks within set protocols – as they do, for example, in a surgical operation. In a changing environment the matrix team must have a high degree of discretion because established protocols may be inappropriate to the changing circumstances, even for the simple tasks they face. The implications of task complexity and environmental stability on organization structure are shown in Figure 7.2.

Source: Adapted from Burns, P. (2001) *Entrepreneurship and Small Business*, Basingstoke: Palgrave.

Figure 7.2   Organization structure based upon task complexity and environment

The main characteristic of the entrepreneurial environment is that it is one of change. In a changing environment where there is high task complexity an innovative, flexible, decentralized structure is needed, often involving structures within structures. Authority for decision making needs to be delegated and team working is likely to be the norm with matrix-type structures somehow built into the organization. Clear job definitions should never lead to a narrowing of responsibilities so that people ignore the new tasks that emerge. In many ways, far more important than the formal organization structure for a firm of this sort is the culture that tells people what needs to be done and motivates them to do it. This is often called an 'organic structure'.

Where there is low task complexity in a changing environment there is scope for greater centralization but the structure still needs to be responsive to change, probably through a degree of central direction and supervision. The structure, although hierarchical, should be relatively flat with few middle-management positions. However, culture is still important because the workforce still need to be motivated to make these frequent changes to their work practices. A business is a little like a house. If the organization structure is the plan and people are the bricks then culture is the cement that holds the whole thing together. Ignore any one element at your peril. Intrapreneurs and venture teams are examples of how hierarchical organizations can establish matrix teams to pursue entreprenurial opportunities. We shall look at these in the next chapter.

Organic structures

Some authors (e.g. Morris and Kuratko, 2002) implicitly assume that all entrepreneurial organizations face complex tasks, based on the observation that the innovative process is complex. As they say, 'major innovations are most likely under

'Hyper-growth companies are quintessentially learn-by-doing organizations. Their survival depends on swift adaptation. Because resources and people are stretched, they most likely don't have excessive formal or overly structured systems in place. The key is to have enough structure in place that growth is not out of control – but not so much that the structure impedes your ability to adapt quickly ... Balancing the need for supporting infrastructure without building infrastructure too far ahead of growth is one of the more difficult and on going challenges any hyper-growth company will face.'

Michael Dell
➡

structures that most closely mimic the organic structure.' But the complexity of innovation varies with the very nature of innovation and not all parts of the organization will be involved in 'cutting-edge' innovation. However, where this is the case, we are starting to define the nature of an effective entrepreneurial structure. Morris and Kuratko use Miller's (1986) definition of an organic structure saying it has 'limited hierarchy and highly flexible structure. Groups of trained specialists from different work areas collaborate to design and produce complex and rapidly changing products. Emphasis on extensive personal interaction and face-to-face communication, frequent meetings, use of committees and other liaison devices to ensure collaboration.

Power is decentralized and authority is linked to expertise. Few bureaucratic rules or standard procedures exist. Sensitive information-gathering systems are in place for anticipating and monitoring the external environment.'

So what will an organic structure look like? Unfortunately that is difficult to answer because, by its very definition, it is constantly forming and reforming to meet the changes it faces as it undertakes those complex tasks. Figure 7.3 is an example of one highly organic structure which comprises a series of spider's-web organizations within one large spider's web. There is no hierarchy. The organization is flat. In this organization the reporting lines between the smaller spider's webs are informal. Each operates almost autonomously and, in that sense, this may be seen more as a loose coalition of entrepreneurial teams, perhaps forming and reforming as opportunities

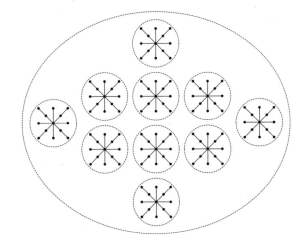

Figure 7.3   An organic structure

appear. The danger is that each might operate with too much autonomy and too little direction, resulting in anarchy. In many organizations, particularly larger ones, more structure and hierarchy may therefore be needed.

Remember that it is unlikely that one organizational structure – even an organic one – will suit all situations. Greiner (*op. cit.*) emphasized how organizations naturally change and adapt and Galbraith (1995) underlines the importance of change and variety rather than rigidity and conformity: 'Organizational designs that facilitate variety, change, and speed are sources of competitive advantage. These designs are difficult to execute and copy because they are intricate blends of many different policies.' So flexibility and ability to change quickly are the key. Like the chameleon, the entrepreneurial organizational structure will adapt to best suit the environment it finds itself in.

The common themes are that the organic structure will be flexible, decentralized with a minimum of levels within the structures. It will be more horizontal than vertical. Authority will be based on expertise not on role and authority for decision making will be delegated and individuals empowered to make decisions. It will be informal rather than formal, with loose control but an emphasis on getting things done. Spans of control are likely to be broader. Team working is likely to be the norm. There will be structures within structures that encourage smaller units to develop, each with considerable autonomy, but there will be structures in place that encourage rapid, open, effective communication between and across these units and through any hierarchy. The success of these units will depend on the degree of fit with the mainstream organization requiring a high degree of awareness, commitment and connection between the two (Thornhill and Amit, 2001). What is more, with such a loose structure, strong entrepreneurial leadership and culture will be needed to keep the organization together and moving in the right direction.

Case with questions

Virgin

Virgin is one of the best known brands in Britain today, with 96% recognition, and it is well known world wide. It is strongly associated with its founder – 95% can name him. In 2004 Interbrand ranked it eighth in the global rankings for Brand of the Year. Research shows it is associated with value for money, quality, good service, innovation, fun and a sense of competitive advantage. But despite its high profile, Virgin is actually made up of lots of small companies – 20 umbrella companies with some 270 separate, semi-independent businesses, most set up in partnership with other companies. This mirrors a Japanese management structure called 'keiretsu', where different businesses act as a family under one brand, each empowered to run its own affairs independently, but offering help and support when needed. Richard Branson explains:

'Despite employing over 20,000 people, Virgin is not a big company – it's a big brand made up of lots of small companies. Our priorities are the opposite of our large competitors . . . For us our employees matter most. It just seems common sense that if you have a happy, well motivated workforce, you're much more likely to have happy customers. And in due course the resulting profits will make your shareholders happy. Convention dictates that big is

→

beautiful, but every time one of our ventures gets too big we divide it up into smaller units. . . Each time we do this, the people involved haven't had much more work to do, but necessarily they have a greater incentive to perform and a greater zest for their work.'

Virgin uses its brand as a capital asset in joint ventures. It is continually searching out opportunities where it can offer something 'better, fresher and more valuable'. Virgin contributes the brand and Richard Branson's PR profile, whilst the partner provides the operating capability and often the capital input – in some ways like a franchise operation. New firms are set up and sold off to finance Virgin's global expansion. In the three years to 2002 Virgin raised an estimated £1.3 billion in this way. Among these the biggest was the sale of 49% of Virgin Atlantic to Singapore Airlines for an estimated £600 million, followed in 2001 by a £75 million mortgage secured on his remaining stake. Virgin sold 50% of Virgin Blue, the Australian low-fare carrier to Patrick Corp. for £96 million. It also sold Virgin One to Royal Bank of Scotland for £45 million, the Virgin Active health clubs for £75 million and the French Megastore business to Lagardère for £92 million. Virgin has also raised smaller amounts by selling stakes in Raymond Blanc's restaurants.

The brand has been largely built through the personal PR efforts of its founder. According to Richard Branson:

'Brands must be built around reputation, quality and price . . . People should not be asking "is this one product too far?" but rather, "what are the qualities of my company's name? How can I develop them?" '

According to Will Whitehorn, director of corporate affairs at Virgin Management:

'At Virgin, we know what the brand name means, and when we put our brand name on something, we're making a promise. It's a promise we've always kept and always will. It's harder work keeping promises than making them, but there is no secret formula. Virgin sticks to its principles and keeps its promises.'

Virgin defines its consumers as 'the public at large – anyone who will buy from us.' It defines its customers as 'people who are using Virgin products or services' and would like to extend its relationship with them, for example through Virgin Mobile. It believes its products and services are about making life easier – 'developing better value for money, a better service, challenging the status quo, and injecting an element of fun into what have traditionally been dreary marketplaces.' For example, in the airline industry it aims to offer excellent customer service and has consistently innovated in many ways like offering on-board messaging. In 2004 Virgin Atlantic was voted best long haul business airline by Business Travel and best transatlantic airline by Travel Weekly. Virgin Mobile offers one simple tariff with no extra charges rather than the complicated contracts offered by other mobile phone companies. In 2003 Mobile Choice Consumer placed it first for the best pre-pay package and best for customer service.

Service quality is at the core of many of the businesses and this is delivered by staff having the culture of 'going the extra mile'. Staff are seen as the company's most valuable asset. They give the company its personality, shape its culture and innovate. Staff training encourages empowerment and challenging of existing rules and reinforces the brand culture. There are numerous activities designed to promote team spirit and reinforce brand values, including Richard Branson's summer party for staff. All staff have annual appraisals and a continuous service policy allows them to move freely around the Virgin Group of companies. They enjoy a

➡

Case with questions continued

Virgin

group-wide discount scheme. The Group conducts regular employee satisfaction surveys and focus groups. It has staff committees and makes use of ideas/suggestions boxes. The company encourages employees to 'go that extra mile' by schemes that reward this, such as Virgin Atlantic and Virgin Holidays' Heroes, Virgin Mobile Shout Scheme, Virgin Money's Academy Awards and the group-wide Star of the Year prize dinner. In 2003 Virgin was voted, by Business Superbrands, the brand that most values its employees.

Richard Branson now runs the Virgin empire from a large house in London's Holland Park. Although there does not appear to be a traditional head office structure, Virgin employs a large number of professional managers. It has a devolved structure and an informal culture. Employees are encouraged to come up with new ideas and development capital is available. Once a new venture reaches a certain size it is launched as an independent company within the Virgin Group and the intrapreneur takes an equity stake. Will Whitehorn, Branson's right hand man for the last 16 years, says of Richard: 'He doesn't believe that huge companies are the right way to go. He thinks small is beautiful... He's a one-person venture capital company, raising money from selling businesses and investing in new ones, and that's the way it will be in the future' (*The Guardian*, 30 April 2002). In 2007 Richard Branson announced that he would be taking a less active role in the day-to-day management of his companies.

Up-to-date information on Virgin and Richard Branson can be found on the company website: www.virgin.com

Questions
1. How would you describe the structure of the Virgin Group?
2. Do you agree that Virgin is now just a 'branded venture capital company'? Explain what this means.
3. What does the Virgin brand bring to a product or service? How far can the brand be stretched?
4. How dependent is the Virgin brand on its founder, Richard Branson?

Networks and other new forms of organizing

Over the last fifty years, firms have continued to organize based upon the enduring principles of Weber and Chandler. Whittington *et al.* (1999) noted that out of the top 500 companies in the three leading European economies the overwhelming majority used a multidivisional form of structure – 89% in the UK, 79% in Germany and 70% in France. However, Whittington *et al.* concede that their structural categories refer mainly to formal organizational characteristics and say little about the processes that go on under the surface – how managers actually behave. They also observe that the character of the divisional organization of the 1960s was not the same as in the 1990s. New technologies have emerged and continue to be a strong driver of organizational change, particularly in multinational companies. Management styles have altered and internal processes are different.

So what is going on under the surface? Over the last twenty years, there has been a proliferation of writing on new organization forms that broaden our concepts of organizational structures. In part this reflects the increasing complexity of organizations as they struggle and experiment with different organizational forms to maintain an effective global presence in a global economy where the pace of change is accelerating. In part it reflects the changing nature of society in terms of social norms and how computers and the internet make communication easier and quicker. In part it reflects the shift towards a knowledge economy with competitive advantage based upon the organization's ability to exploit knowledge quickly. Although this burgeoning literature seems to have no overarching perspective or theory it is fundamentally concerned with both structure and particularly process, but it has broadened to recognize the importance of relationships – which is at the core of entrepreneurial architecture. As Fenton and Pettigrew (2000) observe:

'It would seem that large organizations at the end of the twentieth century have the same structural characteristics as they did 50 years ago The evidence appears to be that formal hierarchical organization is still present as an institutional backdrop but not so crucial in determining organizational activities or capabilities. Instead "new" subtle coordination mechanisms stress the informal and social processes of the organization. There is also a move away from defining organizations purely in distributional terms toward more relational notions As firms add value via relationships and require ever greater internal and external interdependence to create, share and transfer knowledge, so the basis for organizational activity and configuration is centred on relationships and the wider social context within which firms are embedded.'

So the traditional hierarchical reporting structures mask important informal lateral relationships that add value to the firm through knowledge transfer. In looking at these new forms of organization Fenton and Pettigrew (*op. cit.*) identify three themes in the literature:

1. Networks and the socially embedded firm.
2. The knowledge firm in the knowledge economy.
3. The globalizing firm and its changing boundaries.

Networks and the socially embedded firm

One of the characteristics of entrepreneurs is their ability to command resources that they do not own and there are a number of organizational structures which can facilitate this characteristic. The network structure comprises either an internal or external network of independent members (individuals or organizations), unified by a common purpose and sharing in the benefits that stem from collaboration. An example of an internal network would be a large company organized around strategic business units (SBUs). An external network could take the form of a strategic alliances or joint ventures.

Networks are based on personal relationships and reciprocity, and all relationships are based on trust, self-interest and reputation (Dubini and Aldrich, 1991; Larson,

1992). Organizational networks develop based upon multiple networks of individuals. Each member of the network may have a different organization structure so relationships may be multi-level rather than flat, formed by clusters of coalitions at different hierarchical levels. The many links in these networks are strengthened by increased interaction and can be further strengthened by an entrepreneurial leader pulling the network together and giving it stability. These complex networks can facilitate many forms of organizational relationships. A network structure can be complex and difficult to chart – it could look very similar to Figure 7.3 – and it faces the same challenge of co-ordination as its size and complexity increases.

These networks create distinctive capabilities. In the case of strategic partnerships the relationships are usually designed to create value through synergy as partners achieve mutual gains that neither could gain individually (Teece, 1992). For example, since assets are owned by the constituent individuals or organizations, the financial resources needed and the risk associated with any joint venture are spread and flexibility increased. It has been shown that international networks are an important stimulant for international start-ups (McDougall *et al.*, 1994; Oviatt and McDougall, 1995; Johnson, 2004). Similarly alliances can create economic advantage by leveraging market presence (Ohmae, 1989; Lewis, 1990; Lorange and Roos, 1992). They can provide vertical integration and scale economies at a greatly reduced cost (Anderson and Weitz, 1992). As we explain further in Chapter 13, there is growing evidence of the benefits of networking as a way of stimulating innovation and knowledge transfer. At a macro economic level strategic alliances and supplier networks are said to be crucial for the future success of US manufacturing (Goldhar and Lei, 1991).

A virtual structure is one that uses information technology – computers and the internet – to link many individuals or independent organizations, based in many different locations. It is frequently used to build supplier networks, as in the case of Dell. Virtual structures come together to exploit specific opportunities, forming and reforming in different groupings to exploit different opportunities. It is a structure that is best used to undertake specific tasks that do not need contact or the building of relationships. Because relationships are not built up it is likely to have a shorter life than a network structure. With this exception, it shares many of the advantages of the network structure. Handy (1996) described it as a 'box of contracts' and because of its lack of tangibility it has profound consequences for how we think of organizational forms.

Networks blur the boundaries of the firm extending them to a community of interest, rather than restricting them to a legal or economic unit. They mean that resources and risks can be shared across economic units so that networks of small firms can compete more effectively against large firms. They mean that organization relationships are not necessarily dictated by hierarchies and power structures, rather by trust, respect and mutual self-interest. And ultimately it is quite conceivable that these networks are more important than formal organizational structures.

The knowledge firm in the knowledge economy

We observed in Chapter 4 that truly entrepreneurial organizations are learning organizations – organizations that add value in highly competitive, often technology-based, industries by sharing knowledge and learning throughout their structure.

Indeed 'sharing information and knowledge' is one of the high-level attributes in the cultural web of an entrepreneurial organization (Figure 6.6) whereby it becomes both a vehicle for knowledge access and knowledge creation. The importance of this in the context of stimulating innovation is explored further in Chapter 13. And it is the ability to innovate, again and again, that creates sustainable competitive advantage.

The literature on knowledge management sees organizations as complex, without clear structure but with a high degree of integration brought about partly by a strong culture. It explores how to achieve co-ordination and integration of individuals' knowledge within an organization as greater complexity and hence knowledge specialization occurs. The literature stresses the importance of tacit knowledge (embedded in minds and activities), which is difficult to share, rather than explicit knowledge (stated in verbal communications or documents), which can be easily copied. For example, Grant (1996) assumes that knowledge creation is primarily an individual activity and the primary role of the organization is harnessing it for the production of goods or services. It is therefore logical that the primary focus of the organization is to stimulate individual creativity and learning and translate that into products and services that the market values. We shall return to the issue of how individual creativity might be stimulated in Chapter 14. In this context Grant proposes that: 'Once firms are viewed as institutions for integrating knowledge, a major part of which is tacit and can be exercised only by those who possess it, then hierarchical coordination fails.' Structures need to be flat and non-hierarchical where knowledge must be shared but the boundaries of the organization can extend beyond formal lines where knowledge sharing takes place. For knowledge firms new forms of organizing revolve around social and relational dimensions (Nahapiet and Ghoshal, 1998). Networks can play an important role.

The globalizing firm and its changing boundaries

This theme stresses the need to focus an organization on its core competencies to add value in an increasingly global market place, whilst outsourcing other activities. It focuses on technology, in particular IT as a way of integrating the firm by making knowledge transparent and developing global IT networks (Konstadt, 1990). There is also a focus on managing business processes rather than departments which has emphasized horizontal structures and fed into the literature on teams and team working (Stewart, 1992). However, as we have seen, when vertical structures are de-emphasized it inevitably emphasizes co-operation and relationship building as a basis for co-ordination, an approach supported by empirical work on the relationships between headquarters and their subsidiaries conducted by Roth and Nigh (1992). This emphasis on informal relationships presents us with some familiar themes. The global firm literature challenges the efficacy of the divisional structure with its emphasis on the integration of sub-units and the sharing of their resources (Ghoshal and Bartlett, 1995).

What so much of this literature reveals is that the traditional organization chart is a poor representation of how many organizations really function. Informal structures are important, based on strong relationships – the word that appears again and again. Networks are important – in one context and then in another – flexing and changing over time. As soon as we identify one structure (and name it), another appears, perhaps reflecting the rapidly changing environment in which organizations today operate. And processes are just as important as structure, processes that are 'continually shaped and reshaped by the actions of actors who are in turn constrained by the structural positions they find themselves' (Nohria, 1992). What this literature does not give us is any clear agreement on how to think about these new structures. As with many things in management, firms are continually experimenting, both intentionally and unintentionally, both formally and informally, trying to face up to the organizational challenges they face. And organization innovation often involves moving between extremes, yet maintaining business continuity as firms battle with the contradictions between hierarchies and networks, vertical and horizontal integration and sharing knowledge across units that both compete and collaborate and the dilemmas then posed in making decisions (Pettigrew, 1999).

Case with questions

Dell

Dell assembles computers. Originally assembled in the USA, they are now assembled also in Ireland, Malaysia, China and Brazil. However, from the start Michael Dell knew what the critical success factor for his business was. He used an expert to build prototype computers whilst he concentrated on finding cheap components. And the company still sources its components from around the world. Dell grew at an incredible pace, notching up sales of £3.7 million in the first nine months. The company pioneered direct marketing in the industry whereby systems are built to the customer's specifications after an order is placed, and then shipped directly to the customer. More lately, it has pioneered the development of integrated supply chain management, linking customers orders directly to its supply chain. At all times it has focused clearly on a low-cost/low-price marketing strategy.

'We built the company around a systematic process: give customers the high-quality computers they want at a competitive price as quickly as possible, backed by great service.'

Every division in Dell is tasked to continuously improve efficiency and reduce costs, and workers undertake extensive training through its team-based Business Process Improvement programme. This is aimed at reinforcing the importance of cost reduction, but also putting in place processes and procedures that allow efficiency savings to be made, giving the team control over implementing new ideas. As Dell says, 'Empower workers with the tools to make a difference and the innovation will follow.' Productivity at Dell, measured by the number of computers built per employee, has increased 240% in the last five years.

Dell was a pioneer of e-business. What makes Dell special today is its 'fully integrated value chain' – B2B2C. Suppliers, including many small firms, have real-time access to information about customer orders and deliveries via the company's extranet. They organize supplies of hard drives, motherboards, modems etc. on a 'just-in-time' basis so as to keep the production line moving smoothly. From the parts being delivered to the orders being shipped out takes just a few hours. Inventories are minimized and, what is more important, the cash is received from the customer before Dell pays its suppliers. These systems and processes are part of Dell's competitive advantage. They help keep Dell's costs low and allow it to build to order. In the 1990s, in order to protect this, the company started applying for patents, not for its products, but for different parts of its ordering, building and testing processes. It now holds over 80 such patents.

➡

Dell has created a three-way 'information partnership' between itself and its customers and suppliers by treating them as collaborators who together find ways of improving efficiency:

'The best way I know to establish and maintain a healthy, competitive culture is to partner with your people – through shared objectives and common strategies . . . Dell is very much a relationship orientated company . . . how we communicate and partner with our employees and customers. But our commitment doesn't stop there. Our willingness and ability to partner to achieve our common goals is perhaps seen in its purest form in how we forge strong alliances with our suppliers . . . Early in Dell's history we had more than 140 different suppliers providing us with component parts . . . Today our rule is to keep it simple and have as few partners as possible. Fewer than 40 suppliers provide us with about 90 percent of our material needs. Closer partnerships with fewer suppliers is a great way to cut cost and further speed products to market.'

Dell's market place is highly competitive. Dell prides itself on good marketing of quality products but, most importantly, speedy delivery of customized products – factors it believes are reflected in the Dell brand.

'The idea of building a business solely on cost or price was not a sustainable advantage. There would always be someone with something that was lower in price or cheaper to produce. What was really important was sustaining loyalty among customers and employees, and that could be derived from having the highest level of service and very high performing products.'

Nevertheless, whilst Dell might not sell the cheapest computers in the market place, the price it asks must always be competitive and that means costs must still be kept as low as possible.

Up-to-date information on Dell can be found on their website: www.dell.com.

Questions
1. How much of a generic product is a Dell computer?
2. What do you think of Dell's marketing strategy?
3. From what you know about the company, is Dell's competitive advantage based solely on its external architecture? What else might contribute to this?

Strategic alliances

Strategic alliances have featured quite prominently in the literature on corporate entrepreneurship. They can take a number of different forms. A strategic alliance can be internal – between departments or other structures of the same organization – or external – between different organizations. It can encompass all of the functional areas of an organization or just a single function, such as R&D. It can straddle markets and hierarchies, providing a structure for co-operation. Parkhe (1993) defines strategic alliances as 'relatively enduring interfirm cooperative arrangements, involving flows and linkages that use resources and/or governance structures from autonomous organizations, for the joint accomplishment of individual goals linked to the corporate mission of each sponsoring firm.'

Strategic alliances can be an effective way of sustaining competitive advantage. They can be particularly important in relation to innovation and in that context we will return to them in Chapter 13. Aside from the explicit strategic and operational motives such as gaining access to new markets, acquiring new technologies, enhancing new product development capabilities or leveraging on economies of scale or scope (see the BBC/IBM, Sun Microsystems/Intel and KongZhong/DangDang/SouFun case insights), mutual learning is an important element in many alliances. Alliances facilitate organizational learning (Parkhe, *op. cit.*). Karthik (2002) states that 'alliances are pooling mechanisms comingling diverse unique skills and capabilities, and thus are able to create potentially powerful learning opportunities for firms. In fact, learning opportunities create "learning organizations" that are able to increase their absorptive capacities and to assimilate new ideas easily to remain competitive.' So, strategic alliances increase the learning community and the potential knowledge base of the organization. The risks involved in this are minimal but there are costs in finding a partner and maintaining the relationship.

Alliances evolve and change in nature over time. Firms involved in an alliance often have a mix of emotions, involving competition and collaboration in varying proportions, as the partnership evolves over time. Over time the partners build trust and mutual respect – essential in any relationship. Karthik (*op. cit.*) posited four distinct phases in the evolution of the relationship based on the work of Dwyer *et al.* (1987) and Wilson (1995):

1. *Awareness and partner selection*: In this phase the need for an alliance is recognized and the search for a suitable partner begins. Learning starts but it is largely unilateral as each organization finds out about the other and decide whether they can work with the other and also seeks to better understand the external market environment in which the alliance will work.
2. *Exploration*: In this phase partners begin interacting and set the ground rules for future interaction. Partners start to build trust and establish a common culture in order to build the social bonding process. Learning is still largely unilateral but there are elements of experimentation and mutual learning as a way of bridging the compatibility gap between partners.
3. *Expansion*: As trust builds, greater interaction takes place and partners grow closer. They stop probing each other and start working as a partnership. Learning is partly mutual as partners share common perceptions and goals and bridge expectation gaps with a view to sustaining the relationship. Unilateral learning also takes place as partners attempt to internalize the other's embedded knowledge and skills.
4. *Commitment to the relationship*: This is the stage where 'significant economic, communication, and/or emotional resources may be exchanged' (Dwyer *et al.*, *op. cit.*) and boundaries between the partners have little significance. There is commonality of purpose, multiple levels of relationships and mutual learning processes. Learning at this stage is one of mutual capacity-building (Hamel, 1991) and both parties seek to maintain the relationship, building psychological contracts instead of legal ones.

Case insight

In 2007 the **BBC** and **IBM** forged a strategic alliance following an agreement for a framework outlining several joint projects. One of the first was applying IBM image/video search technology to CBeebies and CBBC programmes. The IBM research system, called 'Marvel', has the ability to visually analyze images so as to categorize content based upon appearance. This allows images/videos to be more easily searched online for specific content. The project is the first of a number that will allow the BBC to unlock the commercial value of its massive TV and radio archive.

In 2007 **Sun Microsystems** and **Intel** announced a broad strategic alliance that centred on Intel's endorsement of Sun's Solaris operating system and Sun's commitment to deliver a comprehensive family of enterprise servers and workstations based on Intel's Xeon processors. The alliance also included joint engineering, design and marketing efforts as well as other Intel and Sun enterprise-class technologies. The alliance is expected to help with the widespread adoption of Sun's Solaris system but, perhaps more importantly, it is expected to move Intel's Xeon-based systems up the server value chain to datacentres and other high performance facilities. These environments are currently dominated by IBM and HP with a range of servers powered by an Itanium chip, which itself was co-developed with Intel.

In 2007 **KongZhong Corporation** announced a strategic partnership with **DangDang** and **SouFun**. KongZhong is China's leading provider of wireless value-added services and the operator of one of China's main wireless internet portals whilst DangDang is a leading e-commerce website specializing in books and consumer electronics and SouFun is one of the largest online real estate information providers. DangDang and SouFun will establish exclusive co-branded channels on KongZhong's wireless internet portal to provide wireless users with content and services.

Summary

Structures create order in an organization but there is no single 'best' solution. The most appropriate structure depends on the nature of the organization, the strategies it employs, the tasks it undertakes, the environment it operates in and its size.

Small organizational units are more responsive to the environment and large firms have responded to the entrepreneurial challenge by experimenting with different organizational forms. There is an accelerating trend to downsize and deconstruct large firms – breaking them down to smaller components so that even the core is better able to act entrepreneurially. More firms are outsourcing non-core activities, downscoping and using project forms of organization. They are developing strategic alliances with smaller firms and using them to 'outsource innovation'. They are flattening organizational structures, investing in information technology and new HRM techniques to make this happen.

Structures evolve as organizations grow and, as **Michael Dell** says, survival depends on swift adaptation. For larger firms, both hierarchical and matrix structures, or a combination, can be appropriate in different circumstances. However the traditional hierarchical structure is mechanistic, bureaucratic and rigid. It is most appropriate for simple tasks in stable environments. Entrepreneurial organizations typically face a high degree of environmental turbulence. If the tasks they need to undertake are complex, they are best served by an organic organization structure.

An organic structure has limited hierarchy and is highly flexible, decentralized with a minimum of levels within the structures. It is more horizontal than vertical. Authority is based on expertise not on role, and authority for decision making is delegated so that individuals are empowered to make decisions. It is informal rather than formal, with loose control but an emphasis on getting things done. Spans of control are likely to be broader. Team working is likely to be the norm. There are structures within structures that encourage smaller units to develop, each with considerable autonomy, but there are also structures in place that encourage rapid, open, effective communication between and across these units and through any hierarchy.

Richard Branson understands this, and his **Virgin** empire comprises some 270 separate, semi-independent companies, often set up in partnership with other individuals and organizations.

What so much of this literature on new forms of organizing reveals is that the traditional organization chart is a poor representation of how many organizations really function. Because of the increasing pace of change and increasing complexity in a global environment where knowledge is possibly the most important resource, formal structures struggle to cope. Informal structures are becoming increasingly important, based on strong relationships. Strong network connections are becoming vital – in one context and then in another – flexing and changing over time. Networks, virtual or real, encourage resource sharing and therefore can mitigate risk. **Dell** uses this as part of its B2B2C fully integrated supply chain that generates an information partnership between Dell, the customer and suppliers.

Strategic partnerships – like those between **BBC/IBM**, **Sun Microsystems/Intel** and **KongZhong/DangDang/SouFun** – are also important, particularly in the context of innovation, for both strategic and operational reasons but also as essential ways of transferring knowledge and increasing the size of the learning community.

Essays and discussion topics

1. Why does size matter for an organization?
2. Should large firms concentrate on projects with high cost and low uncertainty and leave those with low cost and high uncertainty to small firms? Will this happen?
3. Will small firms become more important in the twenty-first century?
4. Why do large firms deconstruct and downsize?
5. Consider Handy's 'shamrock organization'. What is in it for the company? What is in it for staff? What is in it for subcontractors?
6. Are 'shamrock organizations' becoming reality?
7. What are the implications for an appropriate organizational structure of a turbulent environment?
8. What is an organic structure? Can it be defined?

9. Do you agree that Virgin is just a 'branded venture capital company'? Why?
10. What are the advantages and disadvantages of the network structure – both real and virtual?
11. Why has globalization encouraged the growth of networks?
12. Why has IT encouraged the growth of networks?
13. Why has the increasing importance of knowledge encouraged the growth of networks?
14. How can networking encourage innovation?
15. Why are relationships important in networks?
16. What is meant by process being just as important as structure?
17. What are the prerequisites for an effective strategic partnership?
18. Is an organic structure just another way of describing a large network of small operating units such as strategic business units?
19. Is there such a thing as an ideal organization structure for an entrepreneurial firm? If so, outline what its elements should be.
20. Why should the entrepreneurial firm find developing the 'new forms of organizing' easy?

Exercises and assignments

1. Give some specific examples of an industry where a hierarchical, bureaucratic structure should be the best way to organize. Select three companies in this industry and investigate their organizational structure. Explain why their structure conforms or does not conform to your expectations, taking into account the success of the business in that industry.
2. List the type of organizations and market sectors or environments that face high degrees of turbulence. Select a particularly turbulent sector and research how the organizations within it are organized and the success, or otherwise, they have in dealing with it.
3. List and describe the different ways by which large organizations break themselves down into smaller sub-organizations. Under what circumstances are each of these approaches appropriate?
4. Select a large company that has deconstructed itself (e.g. Asea Brown Boveri, ABB). Research and write up its history and describe its success or failure. What lessons are to be learnt from this?
5. Provide three examples of strategic alliances and indicate why they are important.
6. Provide three examples of business networks and explain what use they serve.

References

Anderson, E. and Weitz, B. (1992) 'The Use of Pledges to Build and Sustain Commitment in Distribution Channels', *Journal of Marketing Research*, 29 (February).

Bhidé, A. (2000) *The Origin and Evolution of New Businesses*, Oxford: Oxford University Press.

Blau, P. M. (1970) 'A Formal Theory of Differentiation in Organizations', *American Sociological Review*, 35(2).

Burns, T. and Stalker, G. M. (1961) *The Management of Innovation*, London: Tavistock.

Chandler, A. D. (1962) *Strategy and Structure: Chapters in the History of the American Industrial Enterprise*, Cambridge, Mass: MIT Press.

Dubini, P. and Aldrich, H. (1991) 'Personal and Extended Networks are Central to the Entrepreneurial Process,' *Journal of Business Venturing*, 6.

Dwyer, R. F., Schurr, P. H. and Oh, S. (1987) 'Developing Buyer–Seller Relationships', *Journal of Marketing*, 51 (2).

Emery, F. E. and Trist, E. L. (1965) 'The Causal Texture of Organisational Environments', *Human Relations*, 18.

Fenton, E. and Pettigrew, A. (2000) 'Theoretical Perspectives', in A. Pettigrew and E. Fenton (eds), *The Innovating Organisation*, London: Sage.

Galbraith, J. R. (1973) *Designing Complex Organisations*, Reading, Mass: Addison-Wesley.

Galbraith J. R. (1995) *Designing Organizations: An Executive Briefing on Strategy Structure and Process*, San Francisco: Jossey-Bass.

Ghoshal, S. and Bartlett, C. A. (1995) 'Building the Entrepreneurial Corporation: New Organisation Processes, New Managerial Tasks', *European Management Journal*, 13(2), June.

Goldhar, J. D. and Lei, D. (1991) 'The Shape of Twenty-first Century Global Manufacturing', *Journal of Business Strategy*, 12(2).

Grant, R. M. (1996) 'Towards a Knowledge-based Theory of the Firm', *Strategic Management Journal*, 17 (Winter Special Issue).

Greiner, L. (1972) 'Revolution and Evolution as Organizations Grow', *Harvard Business Review*, 50 (July/August).

Haige, J. and Aiken, M. (1967) 'Relationship of Centralisation to other Structural Properties', *Administrative Science Quarterly*, 12.

Hamel, G. (1991) 'Competition for Competence and Inter-Partner Learning within International Strategic Alliances', *Strategic Management Journal*, 12 (Summer).

Handy, C. (1994), *The Empty Raincoat*, London: Hutchinson.

Handy, C. (1996) 'Rethinking Organisations' in T. Clark (ed.), *Advancement in Organisation Behaviour: Essays in Honour of Derek, S. Pugh*, Aldershot: Ashgate.

Johnson, J. E. (2004) 'Factors Influencing the Early Internationalisation of High Technology Start-ups: US and UK Evidence,' *Journal of International Entrepreneurship*, 2.

Karthik, N. S. (2002) 'Learning in Strategic alliances: An Evolutionary Perspective', *Academy of Marketing Science Review*, 10.

Konstadt, P. (1990) 'Into the Breach', *CIU*, 11 August.

Larson, A. (1992) 'Network Dyads in Entrepreneurial Settings: A Study of the Governance of Exchange Relationships,' *Administrative Science Quarterly*, 37.

Lawrence, P. R. and Lorsch, J. W. (1967) *Organisation and Environment: Managing Differentiation and Integration*, Boston, Mass: Division of Research, Graduate School of Business, Harvard University.

Lewis, J. D. (1990) *Partnerships for Profit: Structuring and Managing Strategic Alliances*, New York: Free Press.

Lorange, P. and Roos, J. (1992) *Strategic Alliances: Formation, Implementation and Evolution*, Oxford; Blackhills.

McDougall, P. P., Shane, S. and Oviatt, B. M. (1994) 'Explaining the Formation of International New Ventures: The Limits of Theories from International Business Research', *Journal of Business Venturing*, 9.

Miller, D. (1986) 'Configurations of Strategy and Structure: Towards a Synthesis', *Strategic Management Journal*, 7.

Morris, H. M. and Kuratko, D. F. (2002) *Corporate Entrepreneurship*, Fort Worth: Harcourt College Publishers.

Naisbitt, J. (1994) *Global Paradox*, London: Books Club Association.

Nahapiet, J. and Ghoshal, S. (1998) 'Social Capital, Intellectual Capital and the Creation of Value in Firms', *Academy of Management Best Paper Proceedings*.

Nohria, N. (1992) 'Introduction: Is a Networking Perspective a Useful Way of Studying Organizations?' in N. Nohria and R. G. Eccles (eds), *Networks and Organizations: Structure, Form and Action*, Boston, Mass: Harvard Business School Press.

Ohmae, K. (1989) 'The Global Logic of Strategic Alliances', *Harvard Business Review*, March/April.

Oviatt, B. M. and McDougall, P. P. (1995) 'Global Start-ups: Entrepreneurs on a Worldwide Stage', *Academy of Management Executive*, 9(2).

Parkhe, A. (1993) 'Strategic Alliance Structuring: A Game Theoretic and Transaction Cost Examination of Interfirm Cooperation', *Academy of Management Journal*, 36 (August).

Perrow, C. (1967) 'A Framework for the Comparative Analysis of Organizations', *American Sociological Review*, 32.

Pettigrew, A. M. (1999) 'Organising to Improve Company Performance', *Hot Topics, Warwick Business School*, 1(5).

Pettigrew, A. and Fenton, E. (2000) *The Innovating Organization*, London: Sage.

Pugh, D. S. and Hickson, D. J. (1976) *Organisational Structure in its Context: The Aston Programme 1*, Farnborough: Saxon House.

Pugh, D. S., Hickson, D. J. and Hinings, C. R. (1969) 'The Context of Organisation Structures', *Administrative Science Quarterly*, 13.

Roth, K. and Nigh, D. (1992) 'The Effectiveness of HQ–Subsidiary Relationships: The Role of Coordination, Control and Conflict', *Journal of Business Research*, 25.

Stewart, T. A. (1992) 'The Search for the Organisation of Tomorrow', *Fortune*, 125(10), 18 May.

Stinchcombe, A. L. (1959) 'Social Structure and Organization', in J. G. March (ed.), *Handbook of Organizations*, Chicago: Rand McNally.

Teece, D. J. (1992) 'Competition, Cooperation and Innovation: Organisational Arrangements for Regimes of Rapid Technological Progress', *Journal of Economic Behaviour and Organisation*, 18.

Thornhill, S. and Amit, R. (2001), 'A Dynamic Perspective of Internal Fit in Corporate Venturing', *Journal of Business Venturing*, 16(1).

Weber, M. (1947) *The Theory of Social and Economic Organisation*, Glencoe, Ill.: The Free Press.

Whittington, R., Mayer, M. and Curto, F. (1999) 'Chandlerism in post-war Europe: Strategic and Structural change in France, Germany and the United Kingdom, 1950–1993', *Industrial and Corporate Change*, 8(3).

Wilson, D. T. (1995) 'An Integrated Model of Buyer-Seller Relationships', *Journal of the Academy of Marketing Science*, 23(4).

Woodward, J. (1965) *Industrial Organisation: Behaviour and Control*, Oxford: Oxford University Press.

8

Intrapreneurship and Corporate Venturing

Contents

- Intrapreneurship
- Encouraging intrapreneurship
- Venture teams and new venture divisions
- Organizing new venture developments
- Corporate venturing
- Summary

By the end of this chapter you should be able to:

- Describe the role of the intrapreneur in larger entrepreneurial firms;

- Explain how organizations might encourage and facilitate the work of the intrapreneur;

- Describe the role of venture teams and new venture divisions in promoting innovation;

- Describe the options for dealing with new venture developments and explain which are best in different circumstances;

- Explain why large organizations undertake corporate venturing and what is needed to make such a strategy successful.

Intrapreneurship

The term intrapreneur is now generally used to describe the individual charged with pushing through innovations within a larger organization, in an entrepreneurial fashion. They are entrepreneurs in larger organizations. Rarely the inventor of the product, they work with teams to cut through the bureaucracy of the organization to develop it for the market place as quickly as possible. They share many of the characteristics of the entrepreneur, and may ultimately become the Managing Director of a company set up by its larger parent to exploit the idea. However, essentially, like Art Frye with his Post-it Notes at 3M (see case with questions in Chapter 4), the intrapreneur works within the larger organization and will have come from within it. They are therefore likely to be hybrids, having to work hard to create entrepreneurial structures and cultures around them, but always having to communicate with the more bureaucratic organization that employs them. They must be skilled at innovation but also at putting a team together and handling the political constraints of a large organization.

Ross and Unwalla (1986) say the best intrapreneurs are result-orientated, ambitious, rational, competitive and questioning. They dislike bureaucracy and are challenged by innovation but have an understanding of their organization and a belief in their colleagues. They are adept at politics and good at resolving conflict – and need to be because they will face a lot of it as they smooth the connections with 'conventional' management. Kanter (2004) found that intrapreneurs were comfortable with change, had clarity of direction, thoroughness, a participative management style and an understanding that they needed to work with others to achieve their goals.

Pinchot (1985) also characterizes them as goal-orientated and self-motivated but, unlike entrepreneurs, he says they are also motivated by corporate reward and recognition. They are able to delegate but not afraid to roll their sleeves up and do what needs to be done themselves. Like entrepreneurs, they need to be self-confident and optimistic, but may well be cynical about the bureaucratic systems within which they operate, although they do believe they can circumvent or manipulate them. In that sense they are good at working out problems within the 'system' – or even bypassing the system – rather than leaving the organization. They are often good at sales and marketing and can bring those skills to bear both internally and externally. Like entrepreneurs they are strongly intuitive, but unlike entrepreneurs their corporate background means they are willing to undertake market research. They are risk takers and believe that, if they lose their jobs, they will quickly find new ones. However, they are sensitive to the need to disguise risks within the organization so as to minimize the political cost of failure. They are adept communicators with strong interpersonal skills that make them good at persuading others to do what they want. In this respect they are somewhat more patient than entrepreneurs. This process of influencing without authority, based upon reciprocity, is at the heart of the skill of intrapreneurs (Cohen and Bradford, 1991). They need to identify potential allies, diagnose their world – its language and what they value (and which things of value the intrapreneur controls) – and then establish a working relationship in which exchanges of value might take place.

Often intrapreneurs need to build a team around them. To do this they need to be able to identify key players that complement their own competencies (Stopford and Baden-Fuller, 1994). Often the intrapreneurial team works outside traditional lines of authority – in the USA it is called 'skunk working'. This eliminates bureaucracy, permits rapid progress and promotes a strong sense of team identity and cohesion – Hofstede's 'ingroup'. They subvert the prevailing corporate culture in an attempt to counter the stagnation or inertia often encountered as organizations get larger or older. Often they will 'bootleg' resources – time, materials and so on – because none are formally made available to them.

Intrapreneurship is an important strategic tool of entrepreneurial management. It may be an isolated activity, designed to see a new project into the market place, either as part of the existing organization or as a spin-off from it. On the other hand it may be part of a broader strategy to reposition or re-invigorate the whole organization or even re-invent an entire industry. It can be undertaken at the corporate, divisional, functional or project level. It may be happening at a number of different levels, based on different individuals, at the same time. It is an attempt to compartmentalize the change agent(s) and reduce risk, whilst still pursuing fleeting opportunities.

The level of intrapreneurship varies and can be adapted to suit different organizations but, whilst not dependent upon the size of the organization (Antoncic and Hisrich, 2003), the practice of intrapreneurship does become more difficult as the firm grows (Ross, 1987). Some intrapreneurs just emerge in organizations. Others will have to be identified. Pinchot (*op. cit.*) observes that if there are too few intrapreneurs within an organization there are two solutions: attracting successful intrapreneurs from other companies or recruiting managers with an intrapreneurial character and growing them. Galloway (2006) stresses the importance of transferring and disseminating intrapreneurial knowledge through appropriate structures and cultures, observing that it is not enough to simply recruit intrapreneurs from outside. Without the appropriate structure and culture they will not flourish.

Case insight

Boeing, in the USA, has what it calls its Phantom Works project whose stated mission is: 'To be the catalyst of innovation for the Boeing Enterprise'. Within this there are various programmes designed to encourage intrapreneurship.

The Chairman's Innovation Initiative (CII) was launched in 2000 to encourage employees to develop new business ideas from company-developed technologies and processes. Since then hundreds of new ideas for businesses have been submitted, with some notable successes. The Autonomous Underwater Vehicle (AUV) is now a joint venture involving two other companies that undertake undersea surveying for the gas, oil and telecom industries, IntelliBus Network Systems has developed technology for automotive application and AVChem is a chemical management service provider to the aerospace industry.

Another, larger, programme is called CREATE. This focuses on commercializing military applications, perhaps trying to transform existing technologies that have had disappointing results into money spinners. It brings together intrapreneurial teams made up from both Boeing staff and outside staff – for example from suppliers or universities – to work on each project. These teams come together from far flung locations to 'brainstorm in meetings punctuated by organic meals and hourly exercise like power walking, yoga and racquetball.' Sometimes projects emerge from the CII programme to be worked on further within the CREATE framework.

Encouraging intrapeneurship

To work effectively, intrapreneurs need a certain amount of 'space', since they will end up 'breaking the rules', but equally they need to be kept under control. A balance is required. They also need a high-level sponsor to protect them when times are difficult or vested interests are upset and to help them unblock the blockages to change as they occur. The sponsor will help secure resources, provide advice and contacts. He or she will need to nurture and encourage the intrapreneur, particularly early on in the life of the project or when things go wrong, and will need to endorse and create visibility for the project at the appropriate time. Underpinning this must be a good relationship between the sponsor and the intrapreneur, based on mutual trust and respect.

Pinchot (*op. cit.*) laid down 'Ten Commandments' for how intrapreneurs should approach their task. They should:

1. Come to work each day willing to be fired.
2. Get round any orders aimed at stopping their dream.
3. Be prepared to do anything needed to make their project work, regardless of their personal job description.
4. Build up a network of good people who are willing to help.
5. Build a highly motivated but flexible team. Choose the best.
6. Work 'underground' for as long as possible. Once they 'go public' barriers will emerge to restrain them.
7. Be loyal and truthful to their corporate sponsor. In this way they build a solid relationship.
8. Remember it is better to ask for forgiveness than permission.
9. Be true to their goals, but realistic in how they can be achieved.
10. Be thoroughly engaged and take ownership of the project – and always persevere, no matter what.

To this list Morris and Kuratko (2002) have added that intrapreneurs should manage expectations and never over-promise. It is better to promise less and deliver more. They also suggest that showing a few early wins with tangible deliverables is good because it creates confidence. What is more, small wins can evolve into significant accomplishments and develop a momentum for the project that becomes difficult to stop. Finally they advise intrapreneurs to try to set the parameters of what they do and how they do it – in other words change the rules of the game – so that they start to control as much of the project and how it is evaluated as they can.

However, at the end of the day, intrapreneurs still work within the confines of a large organization and they therefore need to be nurtured and encouraged by supportive entrepreneurial management. Drucker (1985) maintains that entrepreneurial management does not happen by chance in big companies. Just as the intrapreneur needs a high-level sponsor, entrepreneurial management has to have the backing of those at the top of the organization. Firstly, it requires a culture that is receptive to innovation and willing to see change as an opportunity rather than a threat. The company must do the hard work for the intrapreneur and remove, or have mechanisms for removing, as many barriers as possible. Secondly, systematic measurement of intrapreneurial and innovatory performance is necessary. The company must also build in learning from its successes and failures so as to improve its performance. Thirdly, intrapreneurship needs to be structured, supported and remunerated appropriately. This can be in money through bonuses, profit-sharing, share ownership or intracapital (the freedom to use corporate resources to fund additional product development). It can also take non-money form by way of recognition or promotion, which will normally also mean an increase in salary.

Based on empirical analysis, Kuratko *et al.* (1990) found that the four most significant enablers of intrapreneurship were: (top) management support; organizational structure; resources (including time); and reward. To these a subsequent study added tolerance of risk-taking (Hornsby *et al.*, 2002). Without these, intrapreneurship would not flourish. Christensen (2005) expanded on what these meant. This is shown in Table 8.1.

Within this framework there also needs to be a clear vision and plan for a longer time horizon that is effectively communicated to employees and highlights the importance of intrapreneurship (Sathe, 2003). And all these factors should be nested in a supportive culture. Hisrich (1990) defines an intrapreneurial culture as one that develops visions, goals, and action plans; takes action and rewards action; encourages suggesting, trying and experimenting; encourages creating and developing regardless of the area; and one that encourages the taking of responsibility and ownership. Hornsby *et al.* (1993) also noted the importance of personal characteristics like risk-taking propensity, desire for autonomy, need for achievement, goal orientation, and internal locus of control – all the things you would expect to see in an entrepreneur – also having a significant influence on corporate entrepreneurship. Other researchers have noted the importance of external factors such as dynamism, technological opportunities, industry growth and demand for new products (Antoncic and Hisrich, 2004).

Table 8.1 Factors encouraging intrapreneurship

Factor	Basic factors	Intrapreneurial factors
Reward	Regular pay, job security	Promotion, expanded job responsibility, autonomy, recognition, free time to work on pet projects, bonuses
(Top) management support	Sponsors	Commitment
Resources	Finance and materials	Knowledge resources
Organizational structure	Hierarchy	Corporate venturing, cross functional teams, internationalization, external networks
Risk	Tolerance of lower risks	No penalization

Could you be an intrapreneur?

Gifford Pinchot proposed the short eleven question test below to see whether you might have what it takes to be an intrapreneur.

1. Does striving to make things work better occupy as much of your time as working on existing systems and duties?
2. Do you get excited about work?
3. Do you think about new business ideas in your spare time?
4. Can you see what needs to be done to actually make new ideas happen?
5. Do you get into trouble sometimes for doing things that exceed your authority?
6. Can you keep your ideas secret until they are tested and more developed?
7. Have you overcome the despondency you feel when a project you are working on looks as if it might fail and pushed on to complete it?
8. Do you have a network of work colleagues you can count on for support?
9. Do you get annoyed and frustrated when others cannot successfully execute your ideas?
10. Can you overcome the desire to do all the work on a project yourself and share responsibility with others?
11. Would you be willing to give up some salary to try out a business idea, provided the final rewards were adequate?

He says that if you answer 'yes' to six or more questions it is likely that you are already behaving like an intrapreneur.

Adapted from Pinchot (*op. cit.*)

Venture teams and new venture divisions

The importance of team work was emphasized in Chapter 5. Its importance is just as great in pushing through innovative opportunities, although you might expect there to be an intrapreneur or champion at the helm. Morris and Kuratko (*op. cit.*) believe venture teams are a vitally important element in any entrepreneurial organization: 'No matter what particular structures emerge, an important building block for structure should be the concept of the venture team ... Venture teams represent a means for achieving a major break-through in terms of innovation productivity in the firm.'

Venture teams can take many forms. They could be led by an intrapreneur. However, they could become a group of intrapreneurs working together. Reich (1987) uses the term 'collective entrepreneurship' where individual skills are integrated into a group and the team's capacity to innovate then becomes greater than the sum of individuals. Whatever the form, the 'rules' under which a venture team would operate are the same as for the intrapreneur.

The venture team is just one step removed from the *new venture division*. This is a permanent division set up for the purpose of innovation. New venture divisions may operate at corporate or other operating levels within the organization. By separating out the process of innovation the organization hopes that the division will be able to establish its own leadership, management, structures and culture that encourage and facilitate innovation as a continuous process. Mainstream activities can continue as 'business-as-usual' in the rest of the organization. Each and any innovation coming out of the division may take the organization in a new strategic direction and therefore how the innovation is integrated into the organization – or indeed sold off or separated out – depends entirely on the nature of the innovation. Thus, the new venture division may be expected to produce a stream of innovations that include a greater number of bolder breakthroughs than the ad hoc venture team. The scale of each innovation is likely to be greater. Maletz and Nohria (2001) found that placing innovative projects in the organizational 'whitespace' – outside the formal organization with its usual rules and procedures – accelerated natural experimentation. By not imposing the traditional processes of planning, organizing and controlling, projects were nurtured until they were ready for moving over to the regular organization. Managers need to set the boundaries of this whitespace broadly. They need to provide organizational, moral and adequate (but not sufficient) financial support, build enthusiasm among those outside the project and then monitor the project's progress to decide upon the next steps.

This approach is based on the idea of product life cycles (see Chapter 11) and the need for different approaches at different stages in the life cycle. New product/market offerings may need entrepreneurial approaches to management, but those at the mature stage require the secure guiding hand of a strong Financial Director. The approach recognizes the strength of the *portfolio* of different product/market offerings, each with its different cash-flow profile, but equally the challenge of the very different management approaches. The new venture division is an attempt to institutionalize the continuous flow of innovations within a large and complex organization that has a diverse portfolio to manage. However, having an intrapreneur involved in developing a new venture, rather than a new venture division seems more likely to lead to commercial success (David, 1994). David speculates that this is because the intrapreneur is self-motivated, whereas a new venture manager has his or her role assigned.

These approaches are one step beyond the traditional R&D department – staffed by technical staff and dedicated to taking existing products further in their technical sophistication. In the R&D department the focus is entirely on technological advancement. The work is research-based and technology-driven. Many R&D departments are better at inventing than innovating – an important distinction explored in Chapter 13. In a new venture team or division the activity is market-focused and market-driven – where are the opportunities and how can we capitalize on them? Part of the work may be technology based but the emphasis is on how this will be delivered to a market and how it will best meet a real market need. Whereas R&D departments will undertake most of the technological development work themselves, new venture teams or divisions may outsource, sub-contracting work or even buying in patents and so on where an opportunity related to other organizational core competencies is spotted. Speed of innovation may therefore be increased.

> **Case insight**
>
> **Xerox** may have problems with its core copier business but it has managed to push through many innovations. Many were pioneered by its Palo Alto Research Centre (PARC). But initially few were taken up by Xerox, who left them to be exploited, often very successfully, by others. The one (major) exception was, of course, the laser printer. It was only when it set up a separate company, **Xerox Technology Ventures**, located almost as far away in the USA as you can get from both Xerox head office and PARC that things began to change. This company was to exploit technologies that did not 'fit' into Xerox's product portfolio.
>
> If a product was turned down by head office it could be offered to the new venture group. Once a working model was perfected, the founders, who would be rewarded with a 20% stake in the new business, were moved out of the plush PARC laboratories and into low-cost commercial premises and professional management put in to bring the product to market.
>
> The company now has more than a dozen young firms established.

Organizing new venture developments

Once the flow of new venture ideas has started from intrapreneurs the question will arise as to what to do with them? Bergelman (1984a, 1984b) uses the typology shown in Figure 8.1 which suggests that the answer depends on how strategically important the development is for the business and how operationally related it is. Generally, the more important the development and the more operationally related it is, the more it is likely to be kept 'in-house'. If there is little or no operational relatedness and the

		Very important	Uncertain	Not important
Operational relatedness	Unrelated	Special business unit	Independent business unit	Complete spin-off
	Partly related	New product business department	New venture division	Contracting
	Strongly related	Direct integration	Micro new business department	Nurturing and contracting

Strategic importance

Source: Adapted from Bergelman, 1984 and 1984b.

Figure 8.1 Dealing with new venture developments

development has little or no strategic importance to the existing business then it should be completely spun-off, with no ownership retained – often called a sell-off. The most important condition for a spin-off, according to Garvin (1983), is that the core competencies are embodied in skilled labour rather than physical assets because the individuals transfer the knowledge to new firms. He argues that when new market segments develop opportunities for industries in the mature stage of their life cycle these industries are most likely to generate spin-offs because of the information advantage of insiders:

> 'An industry whose technology is embodied in skilled human capital is a prime candidate for spin-offs, for techniques, designs, and ideas are readily appropriable by individuals and transferable to new firms ... Spin-offs in particular are encouraged by the existence of multiple market segments, information and start-up advantage accruing to members of established firms, readily transferable technologies, and environments in which skilled human capital is the critical factor of production.'

Looking at Bergelman's other typologies:

- *Direct integration* – this is recommended where the development is both strategically important and operationally related, for example, when a new product development is integrated into a product range.
- *New product business departments* – these remain in-house because of their importance but for some operational reason a new department needs to be established to get the product to market. This might be the case with product extension.
- *Special business unit* – where operational relatedness is minimal, new staff with different skills may have to be recruited and the unit given greater independence and operational freedom, whilst still retaining ownership.
- *Micro new business departments* – where the strategic importance is uncertain the situation needs to be clarified before a final decision is made. This option keeps the development 'in-house' within a department because of the strong operational relatedness, pending that final decision.
- *New venture division* – such a division should be used to deal with developments that require further investment before their final fate is decided. They could ultimately be spun out or integrated into the mainstream, depending on the final assessment.
- *Independent business units* – these have greater independence than other formats. Often they are joint ventures with other strategic partners and may ultimately be spun off completely.
- *Nurturing and contracting* – these are appropriate where the core competencies are embodied in some physical assets or processes that are owned by the company but they are of little strategic importance. These can then be offered for use by other firms on a contracting basis.

There is some ambiguity in the literature about spin-offs with not all writers assuming that no ownership is retained (e.g. Ito, 1995). However, unless the spin-off is a sell-off or the result of a management buy-out or buy-in, it is likely that the management will come under some degree of control by the corporate parent. And, as you would expect, the degree of control they exercise is likely to affect the entrepreneurial behaviour of the spin-off. Too much formal control will diminish innovative behaviour and stifle creativity (MacMillan *et al.*, 1986). However, most parents might like to at least influence and provide direction to that innovation – and herein lies the balancing act that is part of managing the entrepreneurial organization, a topic to which we shall return in the next chapter.

Corporate venturing

Larger companies may also invest in smaller businesses – called *corporate venturing*. This may involve a real partnership or a complete take-over of the smaller business (see Chapter 12). The reasons for corporate venturing rarely involve short-term financial gain but more normally relate to issues of innovation and strategic foresight. Small firms are often good at innovation and larger firms therefore have to buy them out to capitalize on their 'first mover advantage' in a critical area of new technology development. This happens far more in the USA than in the UK with firms like General Electric, Monsanto, Xerox, Apple, IBM, Kyocera, Intel, Dupont, Johnson and Johnson, Dell and Cisco particularly active.

> **Case insight**
>
> When **Bayer** came up with an innovative new technology capable of providing high quality, short-run colour printing quickly and at low cost, the company was not planning to expand into that area. However, it realised that there was a gap in the market between office printers or photocopiers and conventional printing.
>
> It therefore spun off a new company, **Xeikon**, which it set up in Belgium in 1988, providing it with full support including seed capital, advice and facilities. By 1998 the company had a turnover of over £45 million and employed 160 people.

The key to success here is 'strategic fit' – finding corporate venturing opportunities where there is a strong relationship with the core competencies of the venturing company or acquiring skills, technologies or customers and market segments that complement the strategic direction of the venturing company. Ideally there should be strong synergy between the venture company and its smaller 'partner' (see Chapter 12). For the smaller company there can be advantages in gaining resources – money and advice – or access to markets, that it might not otherwise have.

The advantages of corporate venturing to the large firm are:

- It facilitates innovation and knowledge to be imported from external sources;
- External sources of finance may be more easy to access;
- It facilitates the creation of semi-autonomous operating units with their own cultures, incentives and business models;
- It is often highly motivating to the staff involved.

The disadvantages are that:

- It requires investment, normally in the form of equity, which can be risky;
- It requires the investing company to invest in mechanisms that set up venture management and networks that search out, evaluate and generate deal flows;
- The investing company will not be in complete control of the innovation.

For corporate venturing to work a number of things need to be in place. Firstly, as with most initiatives, it needs the commitment of senior management. Secondly, it needs to be consistent with corporate strategy, in such a way that an investment 'roadmap' can be produced, listing the areas to be investigated and invested in, the rationale for this and the mechanisms for searching out investments. However, the search mechanism needs to be sufficiently flexible to react to unexpected opportunities. It is important that the strategy is integrated into the overall corporate strategy for growth and innovation. A company can only beat venture capitalists at their own game if it adds value to the process in some way and the venture portfolio is aligned to its overall corporate strategy. It is this ability to share and leverage industry knowledge between portfolio companies and the business units of the investing company that creates added value. Thirdly, there need to be effective HR policies in place to encourage the retention of talented staff and encourage continuity. There is not much point in acquiring a company only to find that key staff leave shortly after acquisition. Finally, the investing firm needs to have access to sufficient capital to use corporate venturing in this strategic way.

Corporate venturing is also used to spin out non-core, but still very profitable, opportunities coming from in-house research, whilst maintaining an equity stake in the new technologies. Monsanto, Apple, 3M and Xerox have used independent venture capital conduits for this purpose. Finally, large companies also sometimes run funds with other investment criteria, such as creating jobs in areas where the company has made redundancies. Many of these funds have 'non-profit' objectives and are part of a larger social or environmental agenda for the company.

Effective knowledge transfer is at the heart of successful corporate venturing for commercial purposes and many mechanisms can be used to facilitate this. For example, within the Intel Corporation, Intel Capital investment professionals work alongside Intel business units to identify venture investments. Similarly within Motorola, Motorola Ventures has a knowledge transfer team that is tasked with developing relationships between each start-up or investment company and the parent. In this way engineers can monitor whether the technology acquired meets expectations and identify opportunities between it and existing business units.

A related activity, falling short of investment or acquisition is the growing number of larger firms that are buying in some form of intellectual capital – in effect 'outsourcing innovation'. This also can take many forms, for example the purchase of patents, copyright and so on or simply acquiring distribution rights. It all depends on what stage the innovative development has reached and how the larger company can best add value. It happens because, as we have already noted, many small firms are often better than larger firms at innovation – they can often do it more cheaply and quickly (see Chapter 13). The larger firm may be better at the development process or be better able to bring the product to the market quickly because of its extensive distribution network.

Case with questions

Pret A Manger

Julian Metcalfe and **Sinclair Beecham** opened their first **Pret A Manger** sandwich bar in Victoria Street, central London, in 1986. They made sandwiches in the basement from fresh ingredients bought every morning at Covent Garden market and cooked by themselves. They built Pret on the simple concept of providing gourmet, fresh and organic fast-food in modern, clean surroundings from outlets in high-traffic areas. The 'healthy-food' formula proved successful. By 2001 Pret had grown to 103 stores in the UK and one in New York, producing profits of £3.6 million on turnover of £100 million.

The pair had ambitious plans to expand Pret overseas, particularly in Asia, but their first experiences taught them how difficult, time-consuming and expensive this could be. Outlets in Japan had to be closed after the franchisee expanded too rapidly and the business in New York had to be pared back after opening 16 shops in one year. They also wanted to launch 'Family Pret', a similar concept but with larger, less urban shops especially for children. The problem was that they needed both cash and world-wide contacts and expertise.

Nevertheless it came as a surprise to analysts when a 33% stake in Pret was sold to McDonald's in 2001 for £50 million. The motives were, however, simple enough. McDonald's could provide not only cash but also support for Pret's global expansion plans and they were happy not to change the Pret formula in any way – a promise they have kept. McDonald's, who also owned the Aroma coffee bar chain, saw this as a strategic purchase that would advance their long-term strategy of gaining a greater share of the diverse informal eating-out market.

In the UK Pret is made up of small groups of ten shops run by team leaders, with trainers within their core staff. Training (which is mainly to do with sandwich making) is taken very seriously. The company has an in-house 'ideas department' that vets ideas from staff for which prizes are offered every month. Twice a year Pret throws a massive party for staff. The company also helps dozens of charities by offering them the unsold sandwiches at the end of the day, and they also donate cash. Pret is a partner of Forum For The Future, a leading sustainability development charity, that is working with them to help embed sustainability principles into everything they do – packaging, recycling, food waste, energy use and food sourcing.

By 2006 Pret had some 180 stores mainly in the UK but also in New York, Hong Kong and Singapore, producing profits of £8 million on turnover of £190 million. It was estimated to have captured 1.3% of the lucrative £2.9 billion British sandwich market.

Up-to-date information on Pret A Manger can be found on their website: www.pret.com

Questions
1. Why has Pret been so successful?
2. Has it continued to be successful since the investment by McDonald's? If so, why?
3. Why is Pret an important investment for McDonald's?
4. Where is the 'strategic fit' with McDonald's and what are the synergies?

Case with questions

Nokia

Nokia has a number of integrated mechanisms and organizations for encouraging and searching for innovation: Nokia Ventures Organization; Nokia Research Centre; Nokia Venture Partners; Nokia Innovent; and Nokia Growth Partners.

Nokia Ventures Organization has as its mission 'the renewal of Nokia'. Nokia's venturing activities have created independent businesses, contributed to the growth and profitability of core business, provided financial returns in their own right and provided intangible assets and insights. It approaches its mission from two directions. Firstly it tries to identify broad opportunities based upon industry analysis and developing new ventures from Nokia employees' ideas as well as those from external sources. Nokia has an annual Venture Challenge ideas campaign for employees. But it also collects ideas from a broad network that extends beyond Nokia and includes external research centres, academics, business partners and entrepreneurs. In collaboration with other Nokia units it systematically scans emerging trends and disruptions from the perspectives of technology, business and users to spot opportunities.

The *Nokia Research Centre* explores new concepts, applications and technologies. On the one hand the Centre develops disruptive technologies that go beyond the current state-of-the-art and on the other hand it supports the locally based product development units with technological expertise. The business units fund the majority of the research undertaken by the Centre. In both cases the Centre helps develop new business/venture ideas.

Ideas are collected and evaluated by New Business development teams across Nokia. New business cases are developed for the most promising ideas and, where appropriate, these are developed further in incubation units of the business unit where the objectives and competencies best match the scope of the idea and the resources needed to develop it. Projects where the business case is not yet clear or where there are many opportunities to be explored continue to be incubated in the Research Centre's incubator unit. Later, when the business case is clear, they are transferred to the *Ventures Organization*. If the technology to support the business idea has not yet been developed, Nokia Ventures Organization will commission technology research and development from the Research Centre or outside partners. Nokia uses the same venturing process throughout the organization. The process ensures essential services and tools are available, facilitating the whole venturing process. Support includes personal guidance, dedicated resources, business planning and technology validation. A series of milestone reviews ensure projects move along.

Nokia has three corporate venturing arms. *Nokia Venture Partners* offers seed finance for early-stage business ideas to both internal and external ventures. It also offers support on legal, communications and human resources issues. Technology experts from the Research Centre also support Venture Partners in evaluating technologies that may be invested in. *Nokia Innovent* is its early-stage focused development team and *Nokia Growth Partners* invests in mid- to late-stage mobile technology companies. Both provide external funding only and focus on Nokia's broad vision of 'Life Goes Mobile'.

Examples of Nokia's innovations coming through this integrated network include:

- *Nokia One Mobile Connectivity Service* – This offers corporate employees easy and secure access to mobile email, calendar, directory, contacts and mission critical corporate applications from a mobile phone.

→

Case with questions continued

Nokia

- *Nokia Mobile RFID Kit* – This Radio Frequency Identification (RFID) Kit integrates reader technology with the phone and allows mobile phones to be used to access data and initiate familiar mobile phone functions simply by touching a smart object with the phone. It is designed for use by security and maintenance service personnel.
- *Nokia Lifeblog* – This is a PC and mobile phone software combination that allows you to keep a real-time multimedia diary – text, photos, videos, text messages – with clear chronology.

Up-to-date information on Nokia can be found on their website: www.nokia.com

Questions
1. Compare and contrast the processes of Nokia designed to encourage innovation with those of 3M (Chapter 4).
2. Do you consider them more focused? If so, on what and is this a good thing?

Summary

An intrapreneur pushes through innovations within a larger organization, in an entrepreneurial fashion. Intrapreneurship can be an isolated activity, designed to see a new project into the market place, either as part of the existing organization or as a spin-off from it, or it can be part of a broader strategy to reposition or re-invigorate the whole organization – or even re-invent an industry.

Intrapreneurs are results-orientated, ambitious, rational, competitive and questioning and must be adept at handling conflict and the politics of the larger organization in which they operate. Facilitating the work of intrapreneurs is another organizational tool available to the entrepreneurial organization. It needs a high-level sponsor in senior management and an organizational structure that encourages him or her. **Boeing**, with its Phantom Works project, seeks to encourage intrapreneurship.

The five most significant enablers of intrapreneurship are: (top) management support; organizational structure; resources (including time); reward; and tolerance of risk-taking. Without these, intrapreneurship would not flourish.

One of the structures that can help are venture teams. However, if venturing is to be more than an ad hoc activity, the organization may form its own venture division, like **Xerox Technology Ventures**, tasked with the job of bringing on stream a continuous flow of innovations. What to do with a new development depends on how strategically important it is to the business and how operationally related it is. Generally, the more important the development and the more operationally related it is, the more likely it is to be kept in-house. If there is little or no operational relatedness and the development has little or no strategic importance to the existing business then it should be completely spun-off, with no ownership retained – often called a sell-off.

Some firms prefer corporate venturing – investing in smaller businesses in order to capitalize on their innovations. This is the reason McDonald's bought **Pret A Manger**. Corporate venturing can also be used to spin out non-core activities, just as **Bayer** spun off **Xeikon**. For corporate venturing to work it needs the commitment of senior management; consistency and integration with corporate strategy; to add value through effective knowledge transfer, leveraging knowledge from itself and the firm it acquires (as in the case of **Pret A Manger**); effective HR policies to encourage the retention of talented staff and encourage continuity; and finally to have access to sufficient capital. This is what **Nokia** seeks to do through its various initiatives.

Essays and discussion topics

1. Is an intrapreneur the same as an entrepreneur? If not, how are they different?
2. Is it easier to be an intrapreneur or an entrepreneur?
3. Under what conditions might intrapreneurship thrive?
4. How important is the intrapreneur as a tool of entrepreneurial management?
5. How much 'space' does an intrapreneur need?
6. What does an organization need to do to encourage intrapreneurship?
7. Do intrapreneurs really exist? Discuss.
8. Real entrepreneurs leave an organization to set up their own new venture rather than run one belonging to a big company. Discuss.
9. The number of people leaving to set up their own business is a sign of an entrepreneurial organization. Discuss.
10. Does there always have to be at least one intrapreneur in a venture team?
11. What are the advantages of having a new venture division? What are the risks?
12. How does a new venture division differ from a R&D department?
13. Why are operational relatedness and strategic importance important determinants of what to do with new ventures?
14. Why should new product/service ideas not simply be integrated into an existing business?
15. Is there any relationship between Bergelman's typology (Figure 8.1) and the Ansoff matrix (Figure 12.1).
16. Is corporate venturing any more than an excuse for buying up successful small firms?
17. What needs to be in place for corporate venturing to work?
18. Explain the importance of effective knowledge transfer for corporate venturing to work best.
19. What is the difference between corporate venturing and venture capital?
20. Why should a large company want to spin out a new venture with good opportunities?

Exercises and assignments

1. Select a large company spin-out. Research and write up its history and describe its success or failure. What lessons are to be learnt from this?
2. Find an example of corporate venturing that has proved unsuccessful and analyze why. What lessons can be learned from this?

References

Antoncic, B. and Hisrich, R. D. (2003), 'Clarifying the Intrapreneurship Concept', *Journal of Small Business and Enterprise Development*, 10(1).

Antoncic, B. and Hisrich, R. D. (2004) 'Corporate Entrepreneurship Contingencies and Organizational Wealth Creation', *Journal of Management Development*, 23(6).

Bergelman, R. A. (1984a) 'Designs for Corporate Entrepreneurship in Established Firms', *California Management Review*, 16(3).

Bergelman, R. A. (1984b) 'Managing the Internal Corporate Venturing Process', *Sloan Management Review*, Winter.

Christensen, K. S. (1985) 'Enabling Intrapreneurship: The Case of a Knowledge-Intensive Industrial Company', *European Journal of Innovation Management*, 8(3).

Cohen, A. R. and Bradford, D. (1991) *Influence without Authority*, New York: Wiley.

David, B. L. (1994) 'How Internal Venture Groups Innovate', *Research Technology Management*, March–April.

Drucker, P. (1985) *Innovation and Entrepreneurship*, London: Heinemann.

Galloway, L. (2006) 'Identifying Intrapreneurship in Organizations: A Human Resources Study', presented at Institute for Small Business and Entrepreneurship conference, Cardiff.

Garvin, D. A. (1983) 'Spin-offs and New Firm Formation Process', *California Management Review*, 25(2).

Hisrich, R. D. (1990) 'Entrepreneurship/Intrapreneurship', *American Psychologist*, 45(2).

Hornsby, J. S., Kuratko, D. F. and Zahra, S. A. (2002) 'Middle Managers Perception of the Internal Environment for Corporate Entrepreneurship: Assessing a Measurement Scale', *Journal of Business Venturing*, 17(2).

Hornsby, J.S., Naffziger, D.W., Kuratko, D.F. and Montagno, R.V. (1993) 'An Interactive Model of the Corporate Entrepreneurship Process', *Entrepreneurship, Theory and Practice*, 17(2).

Ito, K. (1995) 'Japanese Spin-offs and New Firm Formation Process', *California Management Review*, 25(2).

Kanter, R. M. (2004) 'The Middle Manager as Innovator', *Harvard Business Review*, 82(7/8).

Kuratko, D. F., Montagno, R. V. and Hornsby, J. S. (1990) 'Developing an Intrapreneurial Assessment Instrument for an Effective Corporate Entrepreneurial Environment', *Strategic Management Journal*, 11(1).

MacMillan, I. C., Block, Z. and Narashima, P. N. S. (1986) 'Corporate Venturing: Alternatives, Obstacles Encountered, and Experience Effects', *Journal of Business Venturing*, 1(2).

Maletz, M.C. and Nohria, N. (2002) 'Managing in the Whitespace', *Harvard Business Review*, 2/01.

Morris, H. M. and Kuratko, D. F. (2002) *Corporate Entrepreneurship*, Fort Worth: Harcourt College Publishers.

Pinchot, G. H. (1985) *Intrapreneurship*, New York: Harper & Row.

Reich, R. (1987) 'Entrepreneurship Reconsidered: The Team As Hero', *Harvard Business Review*, 65(3), May/June.

Ross J. (1987) 'Intrapreneurship and Corporate Culture', *Industrial Management*, 29(1).

Ross, J. E. and Unwalla, D. (1986) 'Who is an Intrapreneur?', *Personnel*, 63(12).

Sathe, V. (2003) *Corporate Entrepreneurship: Top Managers and New Business Creation*, Cambridge: Cambridge University Press.

Stopford, J. M. and Baden-Fuller, C. W. F. (1994) 'Creating Corporate Entrepreneurship', *Strategic Management Journal*, 15(7).

9

Managing the Entrepreneurial Organization

Contents

- Barriers to corporate entrepreneurship
- Change
- Managing change
- Freedom and control
- Balance
- Management and structure
- Managing risk
- Summary

By the end of this chapter you should be able to:

- Describe the barriers to corporate entrepreneurship and explain how they can be overcome;

- Explain how change can be facilitated, resistance reduced and blocks removed;

- Describe the balance between freedom and control needed in an entrepreneurial organization and explain the dimensions on which this can be measured;

- Justify why entrepreneurial firms need loose control but tight accountability, with early warning signs that indicate when risks might materialize;

- Describe how management style and structure must be congruent and explain the dimensions on which this can be measured;

- Use basic risk management techniques such as risk classification and the development of key risk indicators.

Barriers to corporate entrepreneurship

Many traditional management techniques unintentionally discourage corporate entrepreneurship. They dissuade individuals within the organization from behaving entrepreneurially. Examples of this include the way in which some organizations:

- *Focus on efficiency or return on investment*: An entrepreneurial organization is one that is going places, fast. It is probably first into a new market and needs to grow quickly, in order to penetrate the market, persuading customers to buy the product or service before competitors have time to react. It needs to focus on the critical issues that it faces to achieve this, rather than being managed like a mature company – a 'cash cow' – with the simple objective of generating maximum short-term profit through greater efficiency.
- *Plan for the long term and then control against plan*: In a turbulent, changing environment the future is not certain. The entrepreneurial organization needs to have goals and a vision but it also needs to learn from the changing reality as it moves towards its goals, changing the plans as appropriate. Interim milestones need to be set, but progress needs to be re-assessed after each one is reached and benchmarked against reality.
- *Enforce standard procedures, rules and regulations*: This tends to block innovation and lead to missed opportunities. The entrepreneurial organization needs to be flexible, creating rules for specific situations but then being prepared to ditch them when circumstances change. That means having a culture where rules are challenged and only accepted when proved to be for the good of the organization.
- *Avoid risk*: Avoiding risk means missing opportunities. By way of contrast, an entrepreneurial organization will be willing to take measured risks. However, rather than launching headlong into the unknown, it progresses toward its goal in small, spider-like steps, building an understanding of the risks it faces as it progresses. Risks need to be identified, even if they cannot be avoided. Once identified, early warning mechanisms can be put in place so that appropriate action can be taken in good time.

> 'To encourage people to innovate more, you have to make it safe for them to fail.'
> **Michael Dell**
> ➡

- *Make decisions based on past experience*: In a changing environment the past is not always a good predictor of the future. The entrepreneurial organization takes small steps, testing its assumptions as it goes, learning from the changing reality.
- *Manage functionally*: Functional management disciplines and rigid job descriptions can be a barrier to creativity, which often relies on a holistic approach to problem solving. Entrepreneurial organizations often create multidisciplinary teams to investigate and develop entrepreneurial opportunities.
- *Promote individuals who conform*: This is a certain way to lose innovators. An entrepreneurial organization must be able to accommodate, indeed encourage, those who do not conform. Ideas people and 'doers' need to be encouraged and rewarded.

There is nothing wrong with these management techniques, in the right environmental context. However they will not encourage the development of an entrepreneurial organization. Approaching the issue in a more systematic way, Morris (1998) believes that barriers to corporate entrepreneurship can be classified into six groups. These are based upon an extensive review of the literature on corporate innovation and entrepreneurship, surveys of medium-sized and large companies and in-depth assessments of three Fortune 500 companies:

1. *Systems*: Inappropriate evaluation and reward systems, excessive and rigid control systems, inflexible budgeting systems, overly rigid and formal planning systems and arbitrary cost allocation systems. Formal systems evolve over a period of time and in most organizations are in place to generate order and conformity in a large complex organization. By way of contrast small, entrepreneurial companies rarely have strong systems. Their strategies evolve and planning becomes contingent, based upon different scenarios. The lesson is clear, if systems are too strong they can act as a disincentive for entrepreneurship.
2. *Structures*: Too many hierarchical levels, top-down management, overly narrow span of control, responsibility without authority, restricted communications and lack of accountability. Hierarchy is anathema to an entrepreneurial organization, instead authority and responsibility are pushed down to the point where they are most effective.
3. *Strategic direction*: No formal strategy for entrepreneurship, no vision from the top, no entrepreneurial role models at the top, no innovation goals, lack of senior management commitment. Visionary leaders with a commitment to make the entire organization entrepreneurial are essential. Equally tangible but achievable goals for product, process and marketing innovation are vital.
3. *Policies and procedures*: Long, complex approval procedures, excessive documentation requirements, unrealistic performance criteria and over-reliance on established rules of thumb. As with systems, small, entrepreneurial firms rarely have sophisticated policies and procedures – and this gives them greater flexibility – but they are needed as the firm grows. The problem is that, as policies and procedures grow in complexity, the lead time to make things happen increases and the temptation 'not to bother' grows. The entrepreneurial organization needs to build some slack and leeway into its procedures so that innovation is encouraged.
5. *People*: Fear of failure, resistance to change, parochial bias, complacency, protection of own sphere of activity, short-term orientation, inappropriate skills and talents. People can be the greatest barrier of all. Changing people – their attitudes and the way they do things – is the biggest challenge facing management. It is never easy. There is a natural tendency to resist change and preserve the status quo, and nobody said generating an entrepreneurial culture was easy.
6. *Culture*: Ill-defined values, lack of consensus over priorities, lack of congruence, values that conflict with those of an entrepreneurial culture. Culture is the cement that binds the entrepreneurial organization together. The stronger it is, the stronger the entrepreneurial architecture. Culture comes from the top but it rests on a set of commonly held values and beliefs. If they are not commonly held, or not seen to be held by top management, there is little chance of success.

You can do three things with these barriers:

- Ignore them – but this only works with the less important barriers;
- Work around them – intrapreneurs are particularly good at this;
- Remove them. An entrepreneurial organization is one that embraces change. Often change is resisted by individuals within it. Unblocking barriers to change can be particularly difficult when it comes down to dealing with individuals – and that comes down to the interpersonal skills of its leader.

Case insight

The English pub may be a uniquely friendly place, home for a diverse range of customers but the UK licensed trade is also known for high staff turnover and the problems of keeping a motivated and loyal workforce. **JD Wetherspoon** is a national chain of some 650 pubs that expanded rapidly since it was founded in the late 1980s by **Tim Martin** – still Chairman of what is now a publicly quoted company. It provides good-quality food and drink at reasonable prices in a modern environment free of music. It also specializes in 'real ales' – cask conditioned beers from England's regional brewers. It is famous for its 'Sorry Ronny' meal deals – a beer and a burger at prices cheaper than McDonald's.

The company has grown largely organically and has only made one acquisition, the Lloyds No 1 chain, purchased from Wolverhampton & Dudley Breweries in 2001. Lloyds No 1 offers a similar formula, but with music and entertainment. Under its new owners sales more than doubled in the space of five years. One of the reasons for this organic growth is Wetherspoon's preference for selecting and fitting out its own sites rather than converting other people's ideas into the Wetherspoon format. Pubs typically have an above-average floor space and are in high customer-density areas, like high streets.

Wetherspoon has won many awards recognizing the excellence of its staff and management. Most JD Wetherspoon staff are hourly paid – called 'associates'. It recognizes that many will not stay for all their working lives but it wants to encourage motivation and loyalty. To do this it uses a range of approaches to create a positive culture including pay and benefits, training and development and involvement in deciding on new ways of doing things.

- *Pay and benefits*: Staff are generally paid more than competitors. Staff receive a bonus, based on the pub's performance. There are incentive schemes, including a monthly competition for customer care. There is a share option scheme for employees.
- *Training and development*: The company is known for the excellence of its training, which is closely linked to the qualifications offered by the British Institute of Innkeeping. Staff are encouraged to identify their development needs and the obtaining of National Vocational Qualifications is actively encouraged. Training leads to promotion. 54% of pub managers started out as associates, 40% of area managers were once pub managers.
- *New ideas*: Staff are encouraged to come up with new ideas as to how products or service might be improved and good practice is disseminated throughout the organization. Kitchen staff might come up with menu, food preparation and serving suggestions. They might suggest which meals should be promoted. Many small but frequent changes are made in this way. Every fortnight the company holds a 'big meeting' which includes the chairman, directors, pub managers and some associates. This considers performance and future initiatives.

Change

The skill of managing change is crucial. Any entrepreneurial organization will face change aplenty, often seeming like a succession of crises. As the organization passes through each change, individuals can encounter a roller coaster of human emotion as they find themselves facing a different role with new demands. The classic change/ denial curve used by Kakabadse (1983) is shown in Figure 9.1. This illustrates these changes very well and can offer insights into the attitude of staff at each stage.

- *Phase 1:* The unfamiliarity of individuals with their new roles makes them feel anxious about their contribution and so their effectiveness drops slightly. They need to get used to the new circumstances. Within a short time, having become used to the role using previously successful skills, and finding support to help them, their effectiveness improves and they start to believe that they do not have to change. This is the denial phase.
- *Phase 2:* Hard demands are now being made and individuals experience real stress as they realize that they do have to develop new skills to keep up with the job. They need to relearn their role. Although they may eventually learn how to do their new job, a period of anxiety makes them less effective because they can no longer rely on their old skills and they may believe that they can no longer cope. In fact this 'low' indicates that the person is realizing that they have to change and then, at some point, they abandon the past and accept the future. However, this is the most dangerous point in the change cycle as they feel really stressed and may be tempted to give up.
- *Phase 3:* This testing period can be as frustrating as it can be rewarding. Mistakes can recreate the 'low', but, as the newly learnt skills are brought into play effectively, entrepreneurs' performances improve and they achieve a higher level of effectiveness than at the beginning of the stage. They now have a set of new skills alongside their old ones. However, this transition is not inevitable and some

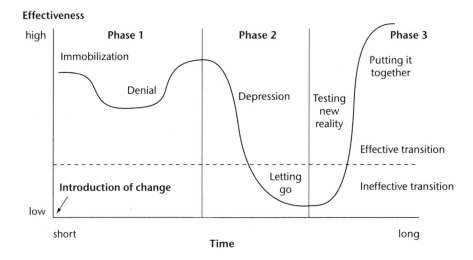

Figure 9.1 Work effectiveness through change

people fail to acquire new skills or cannot pull themselves out of the 'low'. The risk is that they may give up. The challenge for the entrepreneurial leader is to lead staff successfully through the three phases again and again and again.

Managing change

As we have seen, the key to a culture of continuous improvement and change is the acquisition of new knowledge – the development of what is called a learning organization. Learning organizations 'combine an ability to manage knowledge with an ability to change continuously so as to prove their effectiveness' (Jackson and Schuler, 2001). As Hamel (2000) observed 'organizational learning and knowledge management are first cousins to continuous improvement'. Corporate entrepreneurship embraces change, encouraging it to the point where it is seen to be the norm and individuals continuously question the status quo.

But as Machiavelli said: 'There is nothing more difficult to handle, more doubtful of success and more dangerous to carry through than initiating change'. Some individuals inevitably resist change – even if it is ultimately in their own interest. They will even resist it to the point of trying to sabotage it. This could be because:

- They think it will have a negative impact on them;
- It affects their social relationships within the organization;
- It means long-standing habits have to be changed;
- The needs for and benefits of change have not been properly communicated;
- Structures, systems, rewards are not aligned with the changes and inhibit them;
- They feel coerced, not in control.

If any, or all, of these reasons for resisting change can be removed the likelihood of resistance will reduce. Change needs to have the full and unequivocal commitment of those at the top of the organization. At the same time change is more likely to be pushed through if any, or all, of these things occur:

- A compelling reason for change can be communicated effectively – staff buy into a shared vision of the future;
- The change aims to achieve clear, tangible results quickly – and achievement can be readily demonstrated;
- Information about the changes and the change effort are generally and freely available;
- Management are all equally committed to the changes – their need and what they are intended to achieve;
- Change is not piecemeal – do as much as possible, as quickly as possible and make a clean break with the past;
- Address the cultural components of change that could endanger the chances of success;
- Staff are consulted on the need for and the process of change.

Change is never easy to manage. Indeed Jim Clemmer (1995) believes that whilst change can be created, it cannot be managed. 'Change can be ignored, resisted, responded to, capitalized upon, *and created*. But it cannot be managed and made to march to some orderly step-by-step process . . . Whether we become change victims or victors depends on our readiness for change'. Which means that to some extent you must realize you cannot always predict its course but rather need to 'go with the flow'.

Staff need to 'buy into' the change and be clear about what they have to do to achieve it. They need to be encouraged and rewarded if they act appropriately and reprimanded and penalized if they do not. It is easier to change behaviour than beliefs. Any potential barriers to the changes need to be tackled in advance. Managing change in a successful, growing organization is easier than in one that is contracting because change brings tangible results that reward everyone. And an entrepreneurial organization will be looking to grow. If it does not succeed at first it will readjust and try again. But an entrepreneurial organization can only experience downsizing for just so long. Its architecture is not appropriate to an organization in the decline phase of its life cycle.

Yukl (2002) argues that successfully implementing change involves engaging in two overlapping sets of actions – 'political and organizational' and 'people orientated'. The political and organizational actions involve eight steps:

1. Deciding who might oppose change and doing something about them. You can try to convince sceptics or you can isolate or remove them.
2. Putting change agents into key positions in the organization. Often new people need to be brought into an existing organization if you are going to bring about major change, particularly when it involves shifts in culture. These sorts of changes need to start near the top and with the full approval of the Board of Directors, otherwise they are likely to be frustrated by the prevailing inertia. The big advantage of 'parachuting in' change agents like these at a senior level is that they are likely to get results – one way or another – quickly. And time is important in business. Either they will displace the status quo or they will leave. This sounds rather like using force instead of persuasion and that threat can be important – 'change behaviour or leave' is the ultimate threat to those blocking change. But actually the change agents can employ any or all of the persuasive, political skills at their disposal. It just means you have more people doing it and that means you are more likely to see results more quickly. You only have to look to see how often a new Managing Director replaces the top management team to realize that this has almost become a standard procedure when major change is to be pushed through in a limited time span.
3. Building political support for the changes with stakeholders such as shareholders, employees, suppliers, and so on, whether inside or outside the organization, so as to ensure that there is a coalition of support for the changes.
4. Using task forces to push through implementation. The composition of the team depends on the nature of the task it faces and the resulting skills required. It should also reflect the composition required for effective team working (see Belbin in Chapter 5). Using multidisciplinary staff from different departments or units ensures a holistic approach to problems and helps subsequently to embed the changes within the organization.
5. Making dramatic, symbolic changes early on – such as changing key personnel. This helps emphasize the importance placed on implementing the changes – and what might happen to blockers.

6. If possible, beginning on a small scale and demonstrating success quickly. This helps convince doubters. It also allows you to learn from mistakes, if you make them, without necessarily jeopardizing the project.
7. Remembering to change relevant parts of the organizational structure as you go along. This is covered in greater detail later in this chapter.
8. Monitoring the process of change so as to learn from it and ensure that the changes are successfully embedded. Resistant people can reverse change all too easily if left to their own devices. On the other hand some of the changes may actually prove to be inappropriate – so always learn from mistakes.

People-orientated actions focus on getting staff motivated to undertake the changes. This involves seven steps:

1. Creating a sense of urgency about the need for change. You find that organizations often embark on change as a result of a crisis (see Marks & Spencer case with questions). They often need that to jolt them out of their lethargy.
2. Preparing people for the effects of change by proper briefings. People want to know how big changes will affect them personally – only this makes it real for them.
3. Helping people deal with change through proper training, counselling and so on. If you are asking people to undertake new or different jobs they will need to be trained. Putting this in place in advance gives them assurance that they will be able to cope.
4. Keeping people informed about the changes being made as they progress and the successes being achieved. Celebrate success so as to build confidence and help convince the sceptics.
5. Breaking up the change process into small parts or stages. These provide opportunities to celebrate success as well as evaluate effectiveness.
6. Empowering staff to make the necessary changes themselves. Task forces should have the necessary authority to undertake the tasks asked of them. There is nothing worse than being held accountable for something over which you have no authority.
7. Demonstrating continued commitment to the changes from the highest levels in the organization right until the project is complete. 'Walking the talk' is important, unblocking where necessary – all demonstrate that pushing through the changes is high on the agenda of senior management. Often a project is unsuccessful because management is diverted from it when the changes are only three-quarters complete and there is no final follow-through.

A final perspective on the scale of the task involved in managing change is given to us by Henry Mintzberg (1998). He developed the concept of a 'change cube', shown in Figure 9.2. The cube is three dimensional: strategy/organization, concrete/conceptual and formal/informal. The face of the cube shows strategy/organization. As we have explained, both have to be addressed in making change happen. However strategy can be highly conceptual (abstract) or concrete (tangible). The most conceptual element of strategy is vision, followed by strategic positioning (repositioning, reconfiguring) then programmes (reprogramming, re-engineering), whilst the most concrete are products (redesigned, replaced). Similarly for the organization, culture is the most conceptual, followed by structures (re-organization), then systems

Adapted from Mintzberg (*op. cit.*)

Figure 9.2 The change cube

(reworking, re-engineering), whilst the most concrete are people (retrained, replaced). Vision and culture are highly abstract. Products and people are highly concrete and can be changed or replaced relatively easily – without affecting any element above them. However if you change vision or culture you will end up having to change everything below. In fact, wherever you intervene in this cube you have to change everything below it. For example, if you change structures, you must change systems and people.

The final dimension is formal/informal. For example, strategic positioning can be a formal process (deliberate) or an informal process (emergent). Similarly, people can change formally (training) or informally (coaching, mentoring). Mintzberg's point is that, to be effective, change in an organization must include the entire cube: strategy and organization, from the most conceptual to the most concrete, informally as well as formally.

Toolkit for Managing Change

Exercises to help initiate and manage change can be downloaded free from the US web site *www.esdtoolkit.org*. Written by Rosalyn McKeown with Charles Hopkins, Regina Rizzi and Marrianne Chrystalbridge, they comprise seven exercises with related worksheets:

1. Examining assumptions.
2. Steering around barriers.
3. Inventory of support and resistance.
4. Commitment charting.
5. Creating an action plan.
6. Identifying communication strategies.
7. Recognizing values in action

Freedom and control

Most organizational control systems are aimed at eliminating risk and uncertainty – something the entrepreneurial firm must tolerate – and promoting efficiency and effectiveness – which can be at the expense of innovation. Innovation requires organizational 'slack' or 'space' – a looseness in resource availability which allows employees to 'borrow' expertise, research, materials, equipment and other resources as they develop new concepts. 3M have slack built into their organization by allowing researchers to spend 15% of their time on their own projects. Garud and Van de Ven (1992) confirm that entrepreneurial activity in a large organization is more likely to continue, despite negative outcomes, when there is slack in resource availability and a high degree of ambiguity about the outcomes. A highly efficient organization has no slack. Everything is tightly controlled, every penny accounted for, all jobs are defined and individuals made to conform. This environment might lead to high degrees of efficiency but it does not encourage entrepreneurship and innovation.

Foster and Kaplan (2001) echo this concern. They advocate a minimalist approach to control: 'Control what you must, not what you can: control when you must, not when you can. If a control procedure is not essential, eliminate it.' They promote the need for 'divergent thinking' to encourage creativity which they say 'requires control through selection and motivation of employees rather than through control of people's actions; ample resources, including time, to achieve results; knowing what to measure and when to measure it; and genuine respect for others' capabilities and potential.'

Morris and Kuratko (2002) say that the core principle in developing entrepreneurial control requires that managers need to 'give up control to gain control'. Rather than tight budgetary controls, they advocate a 'no-surprises' approach – one that 'generates adequate information on a timely basis for all who need to know'. The authors believe that 'open book' management, where there is transparency of information, is important. Control mechanisms should produce indicators or early warning signals of problems before they occur. A by-product of such a system is that it also conveys a sense of trust. Employees are trusted to get on with the job but the outcomes, rather than the processes, are monitored. They envisage the control system becoming 'a vehicle for managing uncertainty, promoting risk tolerance, encouraging focused experimentation, and empowering employees'.

For them giving up control is also about greater accountability and a greater sense of responsibility:

> 'Where there is an elaborate system of control measures, the employee can be secure in the knowledge that, if the control system has been complied with, then his or her accountability is absolved, that his or her responsibility has been fulfilled. He or she need not take any further responsibility for outcomes or the implications of personal behaviour for company performance. However, by giving up control to the employee, there is a much deeper sense of responsibility not only for accomplishing a task or behaving in a certain manner but also for the quality of task performance and the impact it has on the organization ... to give up control is to empower.'

'Open book' management focuses on the outcomes – the bottom line – rather than the processes. It is built around free flows of information and seeks to motivate employees to improve the performance of the organization by thinking outside their narrow job definition and focusing on the consequences of their action. It encourages them to take ownership of and responsibility for their actions. In many ways it is the logical extension of the principles of the learning organization to financial information. But equally it encourages employees to think the way owner-managers would think about their own business. Case (1997) says it is built around six principles:

1. Free access to all financial information that is critical to tracking the firm's performance.
2. A continuous and overt attempt to present this information to employees.
3. Training processes that encourage understanding of this information.
4. Employees learn that part of their job is to improve the financial result in whatever way they can.
5. People are empowered to make decisions in their jobs based on what they know.
6. Employees have a stake in the organization's success or failure.

The leader in an entrepreneurial firm, therefore, faces a crucial dilemma – the amount of freedom given to the management team. Too much, and anarchy or worse might result. Too little, and creativity, initiative and entrepreneurship will be stifled. It is all well and good talking about empowerment, but at what stage does it become licence?

Balance

The answer is a question of 'balance'. Birkinshaw (2003) explains the model used by BP to help guide and control entrepreneurial action. BP's philosophy is that 'successful business performance comes from a dispersed and high level of ownership of, and a commitment to, an agreed-upon objective'. Within BP there are a number of business units. Heads of units have a 'contract' agreed between them and the top executives in the organization. Once agreed they have 'free rein to deliver on their contract in whatever way they see fit, within a set of identified constraints'. BP's model uses four components to help guide and control entrepreneurial action: direction, space or slack, boundaries and support. All four need to be in balance. If they are too tight they constrain the business unit, but if too slack they might result in chaos. This is shown in Figure 9.3.

Direction

This is the company's broad strategy and goals. Heads of units should have considerable scope to develop the strategy for their own unit, in line with BP's general direction, developing new products and markets within these constraints. However, without an overarching sense of values, mission and direction, entrepreneurship becomes a 'random set of initiatives. Although each initiative has its own rationale, when you put them together, the result is a mélange that stakeholders are likely to denounce as incoherent, vague, or chaotic.'

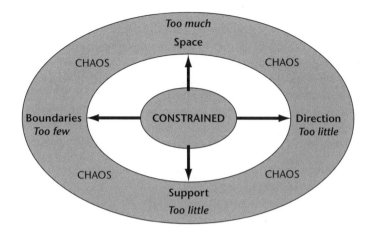

Adapted from Birkinshaw (*op. cit.*).

 Figure 9.3   Freedom vs control

Birkinshaw gives two pieces of advice on getting this balance right:

● Set broad direction and re-evaluate periodically as markets and the environment change.
● Let the company's strategy inform that of the unit and the unit's inform that of the company. A central role for senior executives is to magnify and reinforce those initiatives that most clearly fit the company's goals.

Space or slack

As already explained, space or slack is to do with the degree of looseness in resource availability – monetary budgets, physical space and supervision of time. Companies have a responsibility to their shareholders to see that resources are put to their best use and are being used efficiently. However, in a tightly run, highly efficient organization there is no time or other resources to think, experiment and innovate. People do not have the time to work outside their job descriptions. As we shall see in Chapter 13, all creative organizations require a degree of space or slack to allow experimentation. New ideas almost always require initial work to refine and adapt them.

To circumvent this problem employees' roles need to be defined by outcome rather than behaviour. As in the case of 3M, slack is built into the system, so that employees can do things that are not formally part of their job. However, if employees are given too much space they run the risk of losing focus on the day-to-day detail of the job and it can be wasteful.

Birkinshaw also gives two pieces of advice on getting this balance right:

● Goal setting should be carefully managed and clear and specific, but individuals should be given freedom in how the goals are to be achieved.
● Individuals should be allowed to learn from their own mistakes.

Boundaries

These are the legal, regulatory and moral limits within which the company operates. They should be tightly defined but adherence should come from the creation of a set of shared values rather than through conforming to a set of rigid rules. Rigid rules without a shared agreement to adhere to them begs for the rules to be circumvented. Not having boundaries courts extreme danger, particularly if breaking them might lead to the failure of the organization.

Birkinshaw again gives two pieces of advice on getting this balance right:

- Identify critical boundaries that, if crossed, threaten the survival of the organization and control them rigorously.
- Manage other boundaries in a non-invasive way through training, induction, codes of conduct and so on.

Support

This refers to the information and knowledge transfer systems and training and development programmes provided by the company to help business unit managers do their job. Systems should encourage knowledge sharing and collaboration. Training and career planning should be top-down. Both should, however, be discretionary. The danger here is that knowledge will not be shared and there will be little collaboration, encouraging the business unit to go its own way and raising the danger of duplication of effort. On the other hand if there is too much support the unit will always be oppressive or 'spoon-fed' and initiative will be stifled.

Birkinshaw gives this final two pieces of advice on getting this balance right:

- Put in place enough support systems to help individuals and ensure they know where to go for help.
- Systems should encourage collaboration.

These elements need to be considered in the whole rather than individually. And balance is the key. Birkinshaw observes that most companies operate in the 'constrained' area in Figure 9.3 – direction defined too tightly, too little space, too tight boundaries and overly complex support structures – rather than the 'chaos' area, so most central management probably needs to 'let go' a little. The point is that management is an art, not a science, and it involves some fine judgements about the individuals you work with – their strengths and weaknesses – as well as their personal characteristics. This brings us back to the idea that *entrepreneurial firms need loose control but tight accountability, with early warning signs should the risks they face materialize.*

One final ingredient is needed to encourage entrepreneurship in this sort of organization – financial and resource support to get the ideas off the ground. The financial support might take the form of internal seed or venture capital that is separate from normal budgets. Different funds might be set up for different purposes, reflecting the stage of development of the idea. They might be administered by a committee or board with well-laid-down procedures for applying for resources – for example the presentation of a brief business plan. 3M support their '15% policy' with funding for equipment and extra help. To get an idea accepted in 3M the researcher must get the personal backing of a member of the main board. At that point an interdisciplinary team is set up to take the idea further.

Case insight

In his article Julian Birkinshaw (*op. cit.*) raises the interesting question about whether the failure of **Enron** might signal a rethink about the value of corporate entrepreneurship. After all, the company was held up as a model of entrepreneurship, attracting aggressive and creative managers and encouraging internal entrepreneurship to achieve its growth. Whilst hindsight is a wonderful thing that gives everybody 20:20 vision, he concludes that Enron does not merit such a rethink because the company was at the outer boundaries of all four dimensions of BP's model.

Too little direction: In the 1990s the company moved out of the natural gas sector into electricity trading, online trading, weather derivatives and broadband networks. It started out with the goal of being the 'best gas distribution company', this became 'the world's best energy company' and finally 'the world's best company'. Enron's lack of direction became a strength as managers were encouraged to pursue any opportunity that might help in its headlong rush for growth.

Too much space: Enron gave managers enormous freedom to pursue these opportunities. Top management practised a philosophy of 'laissez-faire'. For example one gas trader started an online trading business (EnronOnline) while still working at her original job. It had some 250 people working for it before the President of Enron became aware of its existence.

Too few boundaries: Enron had explicit rules about capital allocation and risk and had a Risk Assessment Control Unit. However, Enron managers regularly broke the rules, for example by setting up new subsidiary companies and financing activities off the balance sheet. Instead of being dismissed for these things, managers were often rewarded. The culture within the organization was one of rule breaking and there was no moral or ethical underpinning.

Too little support: Management at Enron were recruited from top US business schools. After a six-month induction working with different business units, they were largely left to their own devices. The reward system encouraged 'pushy', aggressive people and development start-ups or high growth opportunities. Support was not a function that was rewarded and 'steady performers' did not stay long in the company.

●

Management and structure

Management is an art not least because the structures of the organization affect how you undertake it – and vice versa. As an entrepreneurial firm moves away from centralized, formal hierarchies to flatter structures with more horizontal communication the need for managers and tight management control lessens. If you are looking for 'dazzling breakthroughs' then autonomy and flexibility are crucial. But if the degree and frequency of entrepreneurship is less, the need for controls will increase. Again, it is all a question of balance.

In this context, Covin and Slevin (1990) argue that entrepreneurial behaviour within an organization is positively correlated with performance when structures are more organic, as shown in Figure 9.4. In reality the dimension of structure from organic to mechanistic is a continuum and ought to correspond to the managerial dimension from entrepreneurial to administrative. A mechanistic structure is appropriate for a bureaucratic or administrative style of management because it will result in an efficient albeit bureaucratic organization. However, it will stifle, if not kill,

STRUCTURE

	Organic structure	Mechanistic structure
Channels of communication	Open, free-flow throughout the organization	Highly structured and restricted
Operating styles	Allowed to vary freely	Uniform and restricted
Authority for decisions	Based upon expertise of individual	Based on formal line-management position
Ability to adapt	Free to adapt to changing circumstances	Reluctant to change from tried and tested principles
Emphasis	On getting things done, unconstrained by procedures	Reliant on procedures and tried and tested principles
Control	Loose and informal with emphasis on co-operation	Tight control through sophisticated systems
On-the-job behaviour	Shaped by the situation and the personality of the individual	Constrained to conform to job descriptions
Decision making	Participation and consensus frequently used	Superiors make decisions with minimum consultation
	Entrepreneurial	Bureaucratic

MANAGEMENT STYLE

Adapted from Covin and Slevin (*op. cit.*).

Figure 9.4 Organizational structure and management style

an entrepreneurial style. On the other hand an organic structure facilitates an effective entrepreneurial management style. Organizations are much more problematic when there is an incongruity between structure and style, as shown in Figure 9.5.

Figure 9.5 also demonstrates what the authors call 'cycling', where a successful firm can cycle between quadrants 1 and 3 as it moves from periods of opportunity, innovation and change to periods of consolidation and stability when greater bureaucratic control is needed. This mirrors quite closely the strategy formulation cycle described in Figure 3.1 and may give one reason why the transition from growth to consolidation is so often interspersed with a crisis – management style and organizational structures are not synchronized and the firm gets stuck in quadrants 2 and 4. Change, if it is to be successful, must be along both dimensions simultaneously.

As we have already observed, however, it is quite possible to have different units, departments or divisions within an umbrella organization that have the two different, but in their own way, appropriate organizational structures and management styles – particularly as a product or service moves through its life cycle. The only issue is that the interface between them needs to be managed carefully.

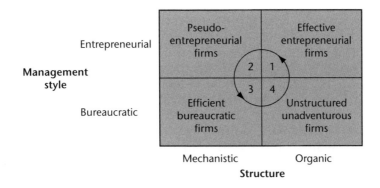

Figure 9.5 Organizational structure, management style and the concept of cycling

Managing risk

Risk is inherent in business and it is at its highest in an entrepreneurial business. Whilst it cannot be avoided, it can be managed – or, more accurately, identified and even quantified so that it can be managed down to acceptable levels. This might improve decision making not least because it encourages discussion about a factor that is inherent in the entrepreneurial organization. It might also help avoid the risks materializing or by putting in place appropriate controls at least provide an early warning of potential problems materializing. If risks can be avoided then less time is spent 'fire-fighting' when they materialize.

The first step is to identify the risks associated with following – or indeed not following – the course of action or strategy being considered. Some risks may be more likely than others whilst some may have a more serious impact on the organization than others. Figure 9.6 shows a useful way of classifying risks along these dimensions. Any risks that have a major impact on the organization are undesirable, but those which are very likely to happen pose the greatest danger (quadrant A). By way of contrast risks with a low impact and a low likelihood of occurrence (quadrant D) pose

  Risk classification

the least risk. Another dimension to this is controllability. Some risks may be under your control or influence, others might be completely out of your control. Generally, the less you control or influence the risk, the greater the danger it poses. In this way the risk matrix becomes a Rubic cube, with the greatest danger being in the cube with the highest impact, highest likelihood and least controllability.

There are four reactions to risk. You might:

1. *Attempt to eliminate the risk.* You might withdraw completely from the area of activity that generates the risk – an unlikely course of action initially for an entrepreneurial business, although if the risks continue to be monitored, at some point in the future they may become unacceptable and this may be the best course of action. Generally these will be the risks that pose the greatest danger to the organization – high impact, high probability and least controllable.
2. *Attempt to reduce the risk.* You might increase internal controls, training or supervision depending on the nature of the risk. Alternatively you might select strategic alternatives that are less risky. Many of these strategies might involve transferring or sharing the risk with others.
3. *Transfer the risk.* There are many useful techniques that can be used to transfer both internal and external risks; for example insurance, outsourcing, sub-contracting and foreign exchange or interest rate hedging. So, companies constantly 'insure' against currency fluctuations – a risk they neither control nor influence – by buying forward in the currency market. If entering a new market or developing a new product you might find ways of spreading the risk by finding collaborative partners. This might also diminish the resources needed to exploit the opportunity but it will almost certainly also reduce the return that you achieve.
4. *Accept the risk.* You might simply accept all the risks in quadrant D. If you accept the risk completely, all you can attempt to do is plan to manage the risk and put in place early-warning indicators of it materializing, but even this might be uneconomic if the impact on the organization is small.

The riskiest situation in the risk cube is where you have a high likelihood of occurrence, with a high impact in a situation where you have little control. In this situation you might consider any of options 1 to 3, but even if you end up accepting the risk it is vital that you monitor the risk and then take corrective action if it materializes.

Early-warning mechanisms are indicators that alert you before a risk materializes so that you can take remedial action. For major risks it is important to identify parameters or events that indicate an increased propensity for the risk to materialize and to ensure that they are being monitored on a regular basis. A simple example would be bad debts which, in a low-margin business, can have an enormous impact on profitability. If that business is teetering on the edge of bankruptcy it is vital to monitor a *key risk indicator* for this on a regular and frequent basis. Key risk indicators for this might be the ratio of days sales in debtors and the aged listing of debts. To be effective key risk indicators must be easy to monitor as part of the regular activity of the organization, highlight when corrective action is needed and provide guidance on what action is needed. Entrepreneurial firms need to highlight the highest risks they face and monitor the associated key risk indicators for the strategy they are

> 'Communicating is one of the most important tools in recovering from mistakes. When you tell someone, be it a designer, a customer, or the CEO of the company, "Look, we've got a problem. Here's how we're going to fix it," you diffuse the fear of the unknown and focus on the solution.'
>
> **Michael Dell**
> ➔

following. Only by doing this can they mitigate against the high risks inherent in what they do.

As we have already noted, corporate entrepreneurship involves a number of other factors that mitigate risk. The fact that decision making is passed down and staff feel empowered should mean that problems can be dealt with quickly by the person or people nearest to them. This improves speed of response but also minimizes information loss. Even if information needs to be passed on within the organization, knowledge transfer should be a strength. Its external orientation, particularly towards the market, should make it sensitive to changes in the environment that might trigger danger. The way the organization approaches strategy and decision making should mean that it is able to change its plans quickly and effortlessly. In other words the architecture of the organization is sensitive to changes that signal danger and can respond quickly once the risk is identified.

Case with questions

M&S

Marks & Spencer (known as M&S) is a famous British retail chain selling clothes, food, household goods and furniture. It has over 450 shops in the UK and some 200 managed under franchise in 30 territories mostly in Europe, the Middle East, Asia and the Far East as well as wholly-owned stores in the Republic of Ireland and Hong Kong. In 2007 it had a turnover of over £7 billion and employed over 70,000 people. M&S's origin was as a chain of 'penny bazaars' (market stalls selling everything for one penny) set up in the late 1800s by a Russian-born Polish-Jewish immigrant, Michael Marks, in Leeds with a £5 loan from Isaac Dewhirst, a wholesaler. Interestingly Dewhirst went into manufacturing and remains the biggest supplier of M&S to this day. Marks opened his first store below his home in Manchester in 1893. He went into partnership with Thomas Spencer (then a Dewhirst cashier) and the first Marks & Spencer store was opened in the prestigious Cross Arcade in Leeds in 1904. After the death of the founders, Simon Marks (son of Michael) took over as Chairman and started to work with his friend Israel Sieff. Together they turned M&S into the iconic British retailer it is today.

The original success was based upon a number of ideas that meant M&S, although never cheapest in the market place, offered high quality but most important of all very good value for money. They did this by adopting the then revolutionary idea of buying directly from manufacturers and placing their own label on goods – originally the St Michael brand (registered in 1928). By the 1950s all goods were sold under this label. By then it was known for selling only British-made goods, entering into long-term partnerships with British manufacturers which required them to commit solely to manufacturing M&S products. It was also known for its policy of accepting the return of unwanted goods, giving a full cash refund if the receipt was shown. Its first overseas store was opened in 1975 and it resisted the lure of television advertising until the mid-1990s.

➔

Case with questions continued

M&S

But it was in the 1990s that M&S started to lose direction and, as can be seen from the financial highlights below, both turnover and profitability started to fall. With the benefit of hindsight, Sir Richard Greenbury's tenure as Chairman (1991–99) saw profit margins pushed to untenable levels, and the loyalty of customers was seriously eroded. A number of things happened. The costs of using British suppliers increased so M&S reduced quality. Meanwhile competitors were sourcing overseas and beating M&S on value for money. M&S's reaction was to switch to overseas suppliers but this undermined a core part of the company's philosophy and appeal. At the same time the company was losing touch with potential younger customers who increasingly saw M&S designs as frumpy and old-fashioned. Alongside this the company steadfastly refused to accept credit cards except for their own store card. In the financial press M&S came to be seen as an aging and famously lethargic and bureaucratic company. They simply failed to see that the high street had changed and competitors were now offering better products at lower prices in more attractive surroundings. The slump took the company by surprise and its share price fell by over two-thirds. The late 1990s saw serious boardroom instability. But how do you encourage a firm with over 100 years of history to re-invent itself and become, again, entrepreneurial? How do you drive through the necessary changes? Answer – you bring in new people... and you start at the top.

Year ending March/April	Turnover (£bn)	Profit before tax (£m)	Basic earnings per share (p)
2007	8.6	965	40.4
2006	7.8	746	31.4
2005	7.5	505	29.1
2004	8.3	782	24.1
2003	8.0	678	20.7
2002	8.1	336	5.4
2001	8.1	146	0
2000	8.2	418	9.0
1999	8.2	546	13.0
1998	8.2	1,155	28.6
1997	7.8	1,102	26.7
1996	7.2	966	23.3

Sir Richard Greenbury retired in 1999 and Luc Vandevelde, a Belgian, took over as both Chairman and Chief Executive. He had previously been Chairman and Chief Executive of Promodès, the French hypermarket chain, where he oversaw a merger with Carrefour, its rival. Roger Holmes was brought in at about the same time and he became Chief Executive later in the year. Drastic action was needed simply to survive. Stores were closed on the Continent and in the USA, and jobs were cut as the company also closed down its Direct catalogue so as to enable it to focus on its core UK retail business. Sourcing was moved overseas, cutting back on UK suppliers, in order to increase margins and make prices more competitive. At the same time the supply chain was modernized, allowing clothes to be brought to market more quickly, bureaucracy was reduced and new talent brought in to drive innovation. Shops opened on Sundays and accepted credit cards.

Clothing fashions were improved by bringing in new people. George Davies, founder of Next, was brought in to produce a young, fashionable collection called Per Una. In the same year Yasmin Yusuf, the brains behind the Warehouse clothing chain, was appointed as creative director. The fashion strategy became one of targeted sub-brands, such as the Limited Collection label, Blue Harbour men's casual wear, the Perfect range of classic pieces and the more expensive Autograph label which has designers such as Betty Jackson, Sonja Nuttall and Anthony Symonds. Fashion sales started to increase. By 2002 the company was gaining market share in areas like lingerie and men's casual wear. New ways of presenting clothes meant the average spend increased as shoppers were encouraged to buy entire outfits rather than just single products. M&S started innovating again with products ranging from seam-free underwear to 'steam cuisine' microwave meals. It opened new convenience food outlets called Simply Food, targeting new markets. Some, within railway stations and motorway service areas, are run by Compass Group, the specialist catering company, under franchise. Vittorio Radice, the brains behind the regeneration of the department store Selfridges was brought in to experiment with stand-alone homeware stores, the first of which was opened in Gateshead in 2004 with the name Lifestore. But not all the initiatives worked and many of the underlying management problems remained.

In 2004, amid rumours of a possible take-over bid, M&S announced that Chairman Luc Vandevelde would be leaving with immediate effect and that the Chief Executive, Roger Holmes would be replaced by Stuart Rose. At the same time Paul Myers, chairman of Guardian Media Group, took over as Chairman. Timing is crucial in business because shortly after this Philip Green, boss of the fashion retailers Arcadia Group, which includes Bhs stores, announced a take-over bid for M&S. Stuart Rose came to M&S with a track record of turning around struggling retailers. Indeed he is credited with turning around Arcadia Group, which is quite a coincidence. He was also a friend of Philip Green. Stuart quickly put together a recovery plan which included selling off the financial services business to HSBC Bank, buying control of the Per Una range, closing the Gateshead Lifestore (Vittorio Radice along with many senior managers subsequently left M&S) and stopping the expansion of the Simply Food outlets (there were about 20 at the time). Philip Green later withdrew his bid after failing to get sufficient backing from shareholders.

Son of a civil servant, Stuart Rose was educated at a Quaker boarding school and started his career in retailing in 1972 after joining M&S as a management trainee. He remained with the company for 17 years, holding a variety of jobs in the textiles and food divisions before being appointed commercial director for M&S's European operation in Paris. In 1989 he joined Burton Group, which included Debenhams, Top Shop and Dorothy Perkins stores. The group later demerged into Arcadia and Debenhams. In 1998 he was appointed chief executive of the Argos catalogue/shop chain. Later as boss of Booker, the cash-and-carry business, he arranged a merger with the frozen food retailer Iceland and became the new group's chief executive. He joined Arcadia in 2000, a company with £250 million of debt, which he turned around and then sold two years later to Philip Green for £855 million – making £25 million for himself. He took over as Chief Executive of M&S in 2004 at the age of 55.

Although always smartly dressed, Stuart Rose is known for his informal management style that circumvents formal structures. If he wants to know something he is quite likely to go directly to the person who should have the answer rather than ask for a management report. He

→

Case with questions continued

M&S

is seen as 'very good at motivating people and giving them clear instructions. He brings the best out in people ... a dedicated networker, always lunching with someone from the City or the media ... He maintains a helicopter position ... [but nevertheless] ... sits in on merchandising reviews, knows how many of which style is sold where, and can reel off financial data about each of his many retail chains at will' (Times Online, 25 January 2007). He is also known for bringing in his own trusted managers to focus on the minutiae – which is precisely what he did, reshuffling and firing many of M&S's top managers. For example, Steve Sharp was brought in as new Marketing Director. He met Stuart Rose at Debenhams where he was Marketing Director. At M&S he introduced the new Your M&S brand, together with the new clothing advertising campaign featuring the celebrated model Twiggy and younger models associated with the Bohemian styles of 2005–6. He was also responsible for the TV advertising campaign for their food range featuring Dervla Kirwan with the tag line 'This is not just food, this is M&S food'. Managerial and directorial changes followed, including the appointment in 2007 of Martha Lane Fox, co-founder of Lastminute.com, as non-executive director to advise on the company's Direct business.

Stuart Rose focused on three things: product, environment and service. Getting the product right was also top of the agenda. Many slow-moving, expensive suppliers were replaced by quick-turnaround specialists, often overseas. Prices were frequently cut whilst quality was maintained. Improving value, style and the amount of new product was important. In clothing the company initially focused on the classic designs it had historically always excelled at – the Classic Collection – but other lines have been expanded, particularly the Per Una range. It rationalized its menswear. For both menswear and womenswear it introduced innovative products such as machine washable suits and seam-free underwear. In food M&S focused on offering high quality, innovative products such as the additive free 'Marks and Spencer Cook!' range. After a pause the Simply Food stores started to expand once more so that by 2007 there were about 200. Getting the environment right meant stores were completely redesigned with white tiles (black in Foods) replacing carpets and laminate flooring, brighter lighting, new product stands, display styles, mannequins, till points and staff uniforms. By 2007 some 35% of stores had been completely refurbished in this way and many others temporarily updated as part of a massive investment programme costing over £520 million. M&S also moved to improve its service levels by investing in its biggest ever customer service training programme based around the Mary Gober Method – called 'Your M&S – Our Service Style'. Our Service Style is defined as 'We are friendly, helpful, courteous people, who are knowledgeable and enthusiastic about taking care of our customers'. The company also overhauled its pay rates and improved career planning for its 'customer assistants', reducing the number of grades to just four with clear progression. As well as attractive salaries staff are paid a performance bonus, which in 2006 totalled £70 million or an average of £500 per employee. The company also has a saving scheme that allows staff to buy M&S shares at a 20% discount. As the turnaround gathered pace in January 2007 sizable bonuses were triggered – a total of £56 million or an average of £4700 per member – based upon a share price that had tripled in less than three years.

What Stuart Rose did in focusing on product, environment and service was to return to the core M&S value(s) propositions:

- M&S's vision is 'to be the standard against which all others are measured'.
- M&S's mission is 'to make aspirational quality accessible to all'.
- M&S's values are 'quality, value, service, innovation and trust'.

'Our plan remains the same – to drive further growth from our core business through the delivery of better products, service and environment. We are also starting to broaden the business, by stretching the brand into new product areas, expanding space, driving our Direct business and growing our brand internationally.'

Up-to-date information on M&S can be found on their website: www.marksandspencer.com.

Questions
1. What are the lessons you learn from M&S about how to turn around an ailing, bureaucratic firm?
2. What lessons do you learn from Stuart Rose about the role of leader in this situation?
3. How important was it to change senior management at M&S?

This case is continued in Chapter 12.

➜

Summary

Many traditional management techniques discourage corporate entrepreneurship. These need to be avoided in an entrepreneurial organization. The barriers can be classified into six groups:

1. Systems
2. Structures
3. Strategic direction
4. Policies and procedures
5. People
6. Culture

J D Wetherspoon encourages entrepreneurship through pay and benefits, training and development and by pushing decision making down and encouraging new ideas.

The key to a culture of continuous improvement and change is the acquisition of new knowledge. Nevertheless people resist change even if it is for their own good. To make change happen two overlapping sets of actions must be engaged – 'political and organizational' and 'people-orientated'. The change cube demonstrates the complexity of what is required with all aspects of strategy and organization potentially having to change in the concrete and conceptual dimensions and the formal and informal dimensions.

Marks & Spencer faced a severe crisis before radical changes in top management were made which resulted in a complete reappraisal of their strategies. New strategies, policies and procedures were brought in but, in particular, new people were brought in to effect the change quickly, underlining its importance.

In working through change, organizations experience three phases:

1. Immobilization and denial.
2. Depression and letting go.
3. Testing the new reality and putting it together.

Managers must give up control to gain control. Entrepreneurial firms need loose control but tight accountability. Too much control stifles creativity, innovation and entrepreneurship. However, too little control can lead to chaos. Most firms place too many constraints and controls on managers. Some, like **Enron**, do not have enough. What is needed is 'balance', as in **BP**'s model which involves:

- Space or slack – a looseness in resource availability;
- Direction – the broad strategy and goals;
- Support – knowledge transfer and training systems;
- Boundaries – not just rules but underlying morals and ethics.

The concept of space or slack – a looseness in resource availability – is important for entrepreneurship. Some slack is necessary for experimentation and innovation. Internal seed or venture funding is also needed to take ideas further.

Open book management encourages employees to focus on the bottom line and the effects their actions have on the financial performance of the organization.

For change to work the structure of the organization and the style of management must be synchronized. As an entrepreneurial firm moves away from centralized, formal hierarchies to flatter structures with more horizontal communication the need for managers and tight management control lessens. If you are looking for 'dazzling breakthroughs' then autonomy and flexibility are crucial. But if the degree and frequency of entrepreneurship is less, the need for controls will increase. Again, it is all a question of balance.

Many successful firms cycle between organic/entrepreneurial and mechanistic/bureaucratic structure and styles as they grow – mirroring the growth → crisis → consolidation process noted in strategy development.

Risk is an ever-present danger in an entrepreneurial firm. It can be classified in terms of likelihood, impact and controllability. The riskiest situation is where you have a high likelihood of occurrence with a high impact in a situation where you have little control. Once risks are identified it is important to monitor key risk indicators that give early warning signs of the risks materializing. Entrepreneurial firms need to locate the highest risks in the strategies they are following and then monitor the associated key risk indicators.

Essays and discussion topics

1. Discuss why the seven conventional management techniques listed might discourage corporate entrepreneurship. Can you think of other examples that fit with the classifications proposed by Michael Morris?

2. Does your national culture accept failure? Does it encourage success? What are the implications of your views for corporate entrepreneurship?
3. You can never change people. Discuss.
4. Change can be created, but never managed. Discuss.
5. The inter-relationships in Mintzberg's change cube are so complicated that no major change is ever likely to be 100% successful. Discuss.
6. Why has Wetherspoons been so successful?
7. Why does tight control stifle creativity, innovation and entrepreneurship?
8. Why is slack or space so important for creativity, innovation and entrepreneurship?
9. How do you achieve 'balance' between freedom and control? Who makes the judgement?
10. How can you have loose control but tight accountability? Give examples.
11. With freedom comes accountability. Discuss.
12. Freedom without accountability leads to anarchy. Discuss.
13. Is 'open book' management practical?
14. Why do so many managers resist 'open book' management?
15. Why are boundaries important?
16. What moral and ethical boundaries would you place on business?
17. Why are management style and organizational structure interlinked?
18. What is meant by 'cycling'? Why should this also be linked to strategy formulation?
19. If you cannot manage risk, you might as well ignore it. Discuss.
20. Risk is the biggest issue facing corporate entrepreneurship. Discuss.

Exercises and assignments

1. Using an example of a major change of which you have experience, chart how the changes were made, the problems encountered and the solutions put in place. Were the changes successful? Explain.
2. Describe the risks facing an organization of which you have experience (it might be your university). Classify them using the risk cube in Figure 9.6 and indicate what would be the key risk indicators that need monitoring.
3. Research the reasons for Enron's failure and critically evaluate Birkinshaw's contention that it was at the extremes of boundaries of BP's model for entrepreneurial development.
4. Arthur Andersen was once considered to be the most entrepreneurial of accounting firms. Research the reasons for its failure and apply Birkinshaw's model.
5. Download the Toolkit for Managing Change from www.esdtoolkit.org and use the Worksheets to plan around a change situation.

References

Birkinshaw, J. (2003) 'The Paradox of Corporate Entrepreneurship', *Strategy and Business*, 30.
Case, J. (1997) 'Opening the Books', *Harvard Business Review*, 75, March/April.
Clemmer, J. (1995) *Pathways to Performance: A Guide to Transforming Yourself, Your Team and Your Organization*, Toronto: Macmillan Canada.
Covin, D. and Slevin, J. (1990) 'Judging Entrepreneurial Style and Organizational Structure: How to Get Your Act Together', *Sloan Management Review*, 31 (Winter).
Foster, R. and Kaplan, S. (2001) *Creative Destruction: Why Companies that are Built to Last Underperform the Stock Market*, New York: Doubleday/Currency.
Garud, R. and Van de Ven, A. (1992) 'An Empirical Evaluation of the Internal Corporate Venturing Process', *Strategic Management Journal*, 13 (special issue).
Hamel, G. (2000) 'Reinvent your Company', *Fortune*, 12, June.

Jackson, S. and Schuler, R. (2001) 'Turning Knowledge into Business Advantage', in J. Pickford (ed.), *Mastering Management 2.0*, London: Prentice Hall.

Kakabadse, A. (1983) *The Politics of Management*, London: Gower.

Mintzberg, H. (1998) in H. Mintzberg, B. Ahlstrand and J. Lempel, *Strategy Safari*, New York: The Free Press.

Morris, M. H. (1998) *Entrepreneurial Intensity*, Westport: Quorum Books.

Morris, M. H. and Kuratko, D. F. (2002) *Corporate Entrepreneurship*, Fort Worth: Harcourt College Publishers.

Yukl, G. (2002) *Leadership in Organizations*, Upper Saddle River, NJ: Prentice Hall Inc.

Part 3

Strategies for the Entrepreneurial Organization

10 Entrepreneurial Strategies

11 Life Cycle and Portfolio Strategies

12 Developing Strategies for Growth

10

Entrepreneurial Strategies

Contents

- The strategic process
- Strategic planning
- Strategic analysis
- Strategy misfit
- Strategic vision
- Generic marketing strategies
- Value drivers
- Successful entrepreneurial strategies
- Differentiation
- Summary
- Financial analysis checklist

By the end of this chapter you should be able to:

- Explain the nature of strategy and describe the strategic process in an entrepreneurial organization;

- Use the basic tools of strategic analysis involved in a SWOT analysis;

- Develop strategic vision and strategic options using the tools of a SLEPT analysis, 'scenario planning' and 'futures thinking';

- Identify core competencies in an organization and use the framework of 'generic marketing strategies' to develop strategies that give the best chance of generating the highest profits;

- Pick out the strategies that are most likely to lead to successful growth in an entrepreneurial organization;

- Differentiate a firm and its products or services by understanding its value drivers and sustain this through effective branding.

The strategic process

The strategic process is more of a distinguishing feature of an entrepreneurial organization than the actual strategy it adopts. Mintzberg *et al.* (1998) characterize what they call the 'entrepreneurial school' of strategy as focused 'exclusively on the single leader' – the entrepreneur. 'Under entrepreneurship, key decisions concerning strategy and operations are centralized in the office of the chief executive. Such centralization can ensure that strategic response reflects full knowledge of the operations. It also encourages flexibility and adaptability: only one person need take the initiative.' For them, the entrepreneurial school 'stresses the most innate of mental states and process – intuition, judgement, wisdom, experience, insight. This promotes a view of strategy as *perspective*, associated with image and sense of direction, namely *vision*'.

Many academics in what is called the 'Process School' (such as Mintzberg) would argue that the strategic process is so inextricably interlinked that what you need to do to understand strategy is look at how it is *actually* developed rather than how it *ought* to be developed. For them, the process is all because, in Mintzberg *et al.*'s (*op. cit.*) opinion 'no one has ever developed a strategy through analytical technique. Fed useful information into the strategy-making process: yes. Extrapolated current strategies or copied those of a competitor: yes. But developed a strategy: never.' They pour cold water on both the reality and the effectiveness of schools, such as the 'Positioning School', that see strategy as a rational, deductive, more deliberate process that can be depicted as a logical sequence of operations. The main flag bearer for this school is probably Michael Porter, to whom we shall return later.

This book shares Mintzberg *et al.*'s view of the importance of the central character – the entrepreneur – but has sought ways of replicating the character of the individual within the organization in a systematic manner – learning from the process of strategy development entrepreneurs use. Chapter 3 highlighted how the development of strategy can be *both* deliberate and emergent, but must always be underpinned by a strong vision. The chapter went on to highlight the need for continuous *strategizing at all levels within an entrepreneurial organization* – the process is vital, more important than the actual strategy at any point of time. This process must be underpinned by good information flows which should lead to the development of strategic options that can be evaluated. Preceding chapters have highlighted the importance of developing a 'learning organization' culture so that this can become embedded within the organization alongside the information flows. They also emphasized that decision making should be incremental and adaptive to maintain maximum flexibility. In that sense entrepreneurial strategy can indeed be both deliberate in overall vision and emergent in how the details of the vision unfold. This is the typical strategic process in an entrepreneurial organization.

However, my experience leads me to agree with John Kay (1998) that strategic techniques can help roll out the process systematically. What is more, if you are trying to replicate strategizing across an organization, a set of commonly known and understood techniques and processes can help – not least because they generate a common language and mechanism for communication. And once you accept these frameworks as an aid to thinking, then inevitably you will ask whether there is any empirical evidence about which strategies are most successful – and there is. But that is not to diminish the importance of Mintzberg *et al.*'s (*op. cit.*) focus on the strategic processes: 'A successful strategy is one that committed people infuse with energy: they make it good by making it real – and perhaps making it themselves.' Nor is it to deny that many formalized strategic planning processes have not served companies well because they fail to do this. As Foster and Kaplan (2001) say: 'The conventional strategic planning process has failed most corporations ... New ways of conducting a dialogue and conversation among the leaders of the corporation and their inheritors are needed'.

Strategic planning

Figure 10.1 sets out a process for how strategy might be developed in a systematic way in an entrepreneurial organization. Strategy should be more than a wish list driven by a leader's vision. We have already made the point that a vision must be realistic and credible and the leader's job involves developing 'creative tension' by contrasting the vision to the reality of the current situation. So too with strategy. Effective strategy must be rooted in the distinctive capabilities of the individual organization. It starts with a thorough understanding of its strengths and weaknesses. It then goes on to contrast this with the opportunities and threats it faces in the environment. This is the classic SWOT (strengths, weaknesses, opportunities and threats) analysis so beloved by most Business Schools. What is more, other tools have been developed to help implement this analysis in a systematic and rational way.

Figure 10.1 The strategic planning process

The second element in the strategic process is strategy formulation. A strategy is just a linked pattern of actions. First you identify the strategic options, evaluating each one in terms of fit with the strengths and weaknesses of the organization and finally selecting the most appropriate option. There are some common or *generic* strategies, particularly in relation to marketing, that an organization might consider, and we shall return to these later. In an entrepreneurial organization strategy formulation should be a continuous process undertaken at many different levels with varying degrees of formality. The 'right' strategy will emerge as part of consultative process but it will never be sufficiently rigid to inhibit the pursuit of opportunity.

The final element is strategy implementation. This involves leading and managing the process, developing the organizational structure and culture to sustain it and planning and allocating resources to make it happen. In fact strategy formulation and implementation are inextricably linked in the hands of a skilled strategist, because the likelihood of the strategy being successfully implemented, given the organizational capabilities, is part of the formulation process. What is more, the process of implementation will feed back on both the analysis and formulation stages, particularly in an entrepreneurial organization. The success or otherwise of implementation will even affect the vision. The whole process is, therefore, an inextricably interlinked and never ending process – which is where we came into this argument.

Quinn *et al.* (1988) summed up the dilemma between the 'Positioning' and the 'Process' Schools rather well: 'One cannot decide reliably what should be done in a system as complicated as a contemporary organization without a genuine understanding of how the organization really works. In engineering, no student ever questions having to learn physics; in medicine, having to learn anatomy. Imagine an engineering student's hand shooting up in a physics class. "Listen, prof. It's fine to tell us how the atom does work. But what we want to know is how the atom *should* work"'. Which did come first, the chicken or the egg?

Strategic analysis

So, no matter how strategy might actually be developed, strategic frameworks are useful. They help people strategize, giving them a framework and a language to approach the task. They might also be used more formally at certain times and less formally at others. They should help us identify strategic options. In the entrepreneurial firm they should help give direction but should never get in the way of seizing opportunities that present themselves – just so long as they help us towards our ultimate goal. And for the entrepreneurial organization strategy making is dominated by the active search for new opportunities.

The basic tool of strategic analysis is the SWOT analysis. This seeks to identify an overlap between the business environment and the firm's resources. In other words, a match between the firm's strategic or core competencies and capabilities and a market opportunity. This match, as such, may not create *sustainable* competitive advantage – it may be copiable or may change over time. Entrepreneurial architecture is likely to form the core of *sustainable* competitive advantage because it is not easy to copy – not least because it increases complexity by encouraging the process to go on at many levels within the firm. However, other competencies will exist for individual firms, each contributing to their sustainable competitive advantage. Kay (*op. cit.*) identified three further capabilities that may form the basis for sustainable competitive advantage, but all three may be viewed as just part of entrepreneurial architecture, as we have defined it:

- *Reputation.* This is often encapsulated in brand identity but equally can be communicated through the relationships embedded in the architecture.
- *The way the organization innovates.* This is one of the defining characteristics of the organization's entrepreneurial architecture enabling innovation to take place again and again and again.
- *The organization's strategic assets.* These are the ones that competitors do not have access to. However, the most valuable is likely to be its entrepreneurial architecture.

The secret to success, therefore, starts with identifying this unique set of competencies and capabilities. This portfolio of resources can be combined in various ways to meet opportunities or threats. They could, for example, allow a firm to diversify into new markets by re-applying and reconfiguring what it does best.

The chief proponents of this approach are Prahalad and Hamel (1990). They see core competency as the 'collective learning of the organization, especially how to coordinate diverse production skills and integrate multiple streams of technology ... [through] ... communication, involvement, and a deep commitment to work across organizational boundaries ... Competencies are the glue that binds existing businesses. They are also the engine for new business development.' They suggest that there are three tests which can be applied to identify core competencies:

1. They provide potential access to a wide variety of markets rather than generating competitive advantage only in one.
2. They make 'a significant contribution to the perceived customer benefits of the end-product' – they add value.
3. They are difficult for competitors to copy. Products are easier to copy than processes.

The SWOT analysis is also the basis for undertaking customer analysis and deciding on market segmentation. It informs marketing strategy but equally must be interpreted in the context of a particular market, taking into account both customers and competitors. Strengths can be transformed into weaknesses in a different market and vice versa. The market context is crucial. Thus a SWOT analysis on the fast-food chain McDonald's in the context of the US market would yield completely different results from one undertaken in the context of the Russian market. In the USA it is a mature product, facing declining sales amidst severe competition. In Russia it is still a novel product in high demand.

The whole process is an art rather than a science. There is no prescriptive approach. Successfully pursuing opportunities is about identifying attractive business opportunities which, given the firm's capabilities, have a high probability of success. This probability is influenced by the firm's strengths, in particular how its distinctive competencies match the key success requirements to operate in the market, given the existing competition. Most opportunities also carry associated threats. Threats may be classified according to their seriousness and probability of occurrence. A view of the overall attractiveness of a market is based upon the opportunities it offers balanced by the threats that it poses. In making this judgement it is often useful to list the factors – whether you control them or not – that are critical to the success of the venture.

To undertake a SWOT analysis you have to be brutally honest about yourself and your business. That means not pretending that something is a core competency when really it is not. As Gary Hamel urges, it means listening to people with different opinions and judging what is the prevailing wisdom in the company. Treacy and Wiersema (1995) pose five questions about the status quo that need to be answered honestly:

- What are the dimensions of value that customers care about? They claim there are only three value disciplines:

  - *Operational excellence*: a good product/market offering (e.g. McDonald's or Dell)
  - *Product leadership*: the best quality, most innovative product (e.g. Dyson or Rolls Royce)
  - *Customer intimacy*: understanding and developing relationships with customers (e.g. Body Shop)

- For each dimension, what proportion of customers focus on it as their primary or dominant decision criterion?
- Which competitors provide the best value in each of these value dimensions?
- How does the firm compare to the competition on each dimension?
- Why does the firm fall short of the value leaders in each dimension of value?

From the answers to these questions realistic options can be listed and choices made. But, once again, honesty is essential because this means being realistic about the options even if some of them are not very pleasant.

There are a number of techniques that can help in a SWOT analysis. These are summarized in Table 10.1. Most are explained in other parts of this book. Central to a SWOT analysis are the concepts of benchmarking and market research. Benchmarking performance has been around in one form or another since the 1960s. It usually involves developing performance ratios. These can be compared over time,

Table 10.1 Tools of the SWOT analysis

Internal appraisal (strengths, weaknesses)	External appraisal (opportunities, threats)
• Benchmarking	• Market research
• Life cycle analysis (see Chapter 11)	• Economies of scale (covered later in this chapter)
• Portfolio analysis (see Chapter 11)	• SLEPT analysis (covered later in this chapter)
• Value chains (see Chapter 12)	• Porter's Five Forces Industry Analysis (covered later in this chapter)

measuring improvement or deterioration, or compared to other companies in the same industry or used as absolute measures of performance. Financial ratios are important (a list of typical performance ratios is given at the end of this chapter and an exposition of how to use them can be found in Burns (2007)). These can be judged against budgets, trends over time or against industry norms, based on published financial data, produced by organizations like The Centre for Interfirm Comparison or ICC Business Ratios.

However, performance ratios need not always be financial. In 1996 the Government launched the UK Benchmarking Index aimed at SMEs. The index gathers data on a wide range of performance indicators including customer satisfaction rates, profitability, earnings per worker, productivity and stock turnover. (In the UK it can be accessed via local Business Links and Training and Enterprise Councils and costs from about £400.) It has now gathered data on over 2500 companies. *Closing the Gap*, a recent report based on this data shows that companies in the top quartile achieve profit margins five times higher than those in the bottom quartile. They achieve 98% supplier accuracy and delivery reliability against 60% accuracy and 85% reliability for companies in the bottom quartile. Also in these companies spending on training is ten times higher and staff absenteeism 75% lower. The initiative is now being extended to the continent and the EC is funding its use in some 1500 middle-sized firms across nine European countries. It is also now being used in the USA, Singapore, South Africa and Australia.

The President of Harvard Business School once said that if you thought knowledge was expensive, you should try ignorance. Market research is about getting information about customers and competitors. Whole books are written on this topic and it is beyond the scope of this one to go into any detail about how to go about it. Desk research can provide information quickly and cheaply. Information on markets, sectors and industries is published in newspapers, trade magazines, industry surveys and reports, trade journals or directories, many of which will be available at the local business library. There may be websites that provide information. Desk research can provide information on product developments, customer needs or characteristics, competitors and market trends. If more extensive research is required, then field research might be used. This can involve conducting face-to-face individual or group interviews, telephone surveys or administering postal questionnaires.

Market research is particularly important for niche businesses, which specialize in a thorough understanding of the needs of a small market segment of customers. An entrepreneurial firm should also be a knowledge-based firm and staff should not only have a lot of information on customers and competitors, they should also be willing to share it. Systems, therefore, need to be in place to ensure market information is shared. There are numerous excellent texts on this subject in its own right (for example: Bagozzi (1994), Birn (1999), Chisnall (1997), McQuarrie (1996) and Tull and Hawkins (1990)).

This list of tools is not exhaustive. It is imperative that the appraisal is grounded firmly in reality. Delusional entrepreneur beware! This traditional 'tool-box' approach is very general. It is probably weakest when it comes to identifying specific threats (which can often materialize without any prior warning – witness the effect of September 11, 2001 on the airline industry) and opportunities, which will be addressed separately in a later chapter.

Table 10.2 The influence of life cycle on organizational culture

Life cycle stage	Key cultural features	Implications for strategic choice
Introduction	• Cohesive culture • Founders dominant • Outside help not valued	• Try to repeat success • Related developments favoured
Growth	• Less cultural cohesion • Mismatches and tensions arise	• Diversification often possible • Vulnerability to take-over • Structural change needed for new developments • New developments need protection
Maturity	• Culture institutionalized • Culture breeds inertia • Strategic logic may be rejected	• Related development favoured • Incrementalism favoured
Decline	• Culture becomes a defence	• Re-adjustment necessary but difficult • Divestment may prove necessary

Source: Johnson, G. and Scholes, K. (1993) *Exploring Corporate Strategy*, Hemel Hempstead: Prentice Hall International.

One final point to consider in any SWOT is, of course, the culture in the organization and the quality of the leadership and management. The life cycle of the firm can have an influence on this. Johnson and Scholes (1993) summarize the key cultural features at different stages and the implications for strategic choice. This is summarized in Table 10.2. In many ways this mirrors Greiner's Growth Model discussed in Chapter 3 and highlights how situational factors influence many aspects of management. They point out that it is the growth phase that involves the greatest variety of cultural change and, by implication, is therefore the most difficult to manage.

Strategy misfit

The SWOT analysis may lead the firm to conclude that its strengths and resources do not match its high aspirations. This is strategy misfit. Hamel and Prahalad (1994) studied firms that had successfully challenged established big companies in a range of industries. They say that to reconcile this lack of fit between aspirations and resources the successful firms used *'strategic intent'*. This necessitates developing a common vision about the future, aligning staff behaviour with a common purpose and delegating and decentralizing decision making – all consistent with what we have called the entrepreneurial architecture.

Hamel and Prahalad (*op. cit.*) argued that 'the challengers had succeeded in creating entirely new forms of competitive advantage and dramatically rewriting the rules of engagement.' They were daring to be different. Managers in these firms imagined new products, services and even entire industries that did not exist and then went on to create them. They were not just benchmarking and analysing competition, they were creating new market places that they could dominate because it was a market place of

> **Case insight**
>
> **Swatch** created a whole new market for cheap watches by daring to be different. In the 1980s cheaper watches like Citizen and Seiko competed by using quartz technology to improve accuracy and digital displays to make reading the time easier. The industry competed primarily on price and functional performance. People usually owned just one watch.
>
> Swatch set out to make fashion accessories that were also accurate time pieces. SMH, the Swiss parent, set up a design studio in Italy whose mission was to combine powerful technology with artwork, brilliant colours and flamboyant designs. Swatch changed the reason for buying a watch from the need to tell time to the desire to be fashionable. They differentiated themselves not on the function of the time piece but on its design and also its emotional appeal – what it said to others about the wearer. In doing this they encouraged repeat purchases because each watch was a different fashion accessory making a different statement.

their own making. Hamel and Prahalad claim that the trick is to answer three key questions:

1. What new types of customer benefits should we seek to provide in five, ten, or fifteen years?
2. What new competencies will we need to build or acquire in order to offer these benefits?
3. How will we need to reconfigure our customer interface over the next few years?

Whilst these managers may be revolutionaries they still have their feet firmly on the ground because they understand very clearly the firm's core competencies – that is the skills and technologies that enable the company to provide benefits to customers. This brings us back to understanding our existing marketing strategies and reworking our SWOT analysis.

Strategic vision

So if strategic intent or vision is so important, how might it be developed? A lot of this is down to creative flair and inspiration. However, the strategy toolbox does contain a couple of techniques that can help firms develop their vision of the future.

SLEPT analysis can be a useful aid in thinking about future developments in the environment and how they might affect the business, but not necessarily the firm's position in that environment. The analysis looks at the changes that are likely to occur in the areas spelt out by the acronym SLEPT:

Social	Social changes such as an ageing population, increasing work participation often from home, 24-hour shopping, increasing crime, increasing participation in higher education, changing employment patterns, increasing number of one-parent families etc.
Legal	Legal changes such as Health and Safety, changes in employment laws, food hygiene regulations, patent laws etc.
Economic	Economic changes such as entry into the Euro currency area, changes in interest rates, growth, inflation, employment etc.

| Political | Political changes like local or central government elections, political initiatives for example on competitiveness in car prices or at supermarkets, new or changed taxes, merger and take-over policy etc. |
| **Technological** | Technological developments such as the internet, increasing use of computers and chip technology, increasing use of mobile phones, increasing use of surveillance cameras etc. |

The trick is to brainstorm and think outside the square about how these developments might affect the business. For example, the development of the internet and broadband networks might be thought to dramatically bring into question the future viability of shops selling CDs or videos. The development of teleconferencing might be seen as a threat to those firms providing business travel over long distances, such as airlines. The development of internet shopping might cause developers to rethink the purpose and structure of our town centres as well as individual shops to re-engineer the way they meet customer needs. The future may be uncertain, but it cannot be ignored.

'Scenario planning' can be a valuable tool for assessing a firm's environment in conditions of high uncertainty over a longer term, say five years or more (McNulty, 1977; Wack, 1985; Zentner, 1982). With this technique views of possible future situations that might impact on the firm are constructed. Often major trends in the environment are identified from the SLEPT analysis and built into scenarios. These situations must be logically consistent possible futures, usually an optimistic, a pessimistic and a 'most likely' future, based around key factors influencing the firm. This technique can also be used to create the strategic options, recommended by Sir George Mathewson. In this case Hamel and Prahalad's three key questions form the agenda.

Optional courses of action or strategies can then be matched to these scenarios. In effect, the scenarios are being used to test the sensitivity of possible strategies. They also allow assumptions about the status quo of the environment in which a firm operates to be challenged. So, for example, a company planning overseas expansion may be uncertain about factors like exchange rate fluctuations or tariff barriers and might construct possible futures that help it decide whether to manufacture in the UK and export or to set up a manufacturing base in the country.

Scenario planning takes the firm away from the short-term, day-to-day imperatives and helps it think about long-term trends and changes in its environment. The technique has been used particularly effectively by Shell as a tool for assessing the effect on it of economic changes that are out of its control (de Geus, 1988). In a risky environment or one where high capital costs are involved scenario planning has a lot to recommend it – and it is a lot cheaper than making mistakes.

'Futures thinking' is a technique that follows on easily from a SLEPT analysis and the development of likely scenarios. With it a vision about a desired future state is developed and planning then takes place, backwards from that state to where the firm is at the moment. Futures thinking tries to take a holistic perspective, avoiding a rigid approach to strategic planning. Current constraints to action are ignored and in this way the barriers to change are identified. Some barriers may be permanent, but some might not be. This is the closest a technique gets to generating creative flair and inspiration. Objections are outlawed and disbelief suspended at the initial ideas stage. Only later on might options get discarded.

One variant to this is to look at a highly undesirable future state and demonstrate how the organization might drift into it unless it takes some radical action. This is a very useful technique for unblocking change in an unresponsive organization. Although its people might not want to change, the state envisaged might be so undesirable and all too easy to drift into, that they are motivated to take the corrective action out of fear.

Schwartz (2003) lists some of the less surprising future shocks like the lengthening of the human life span; the changing patterns of migration; the emergence of the military and economic dominance of the USA; the emergence of unstable nations able to unleash disease, and terror and other forms of disruption. His recipe for companies seeking to cope with this is building better intelligence and information management systems; avoiding denial; and cultivating a sense of timing. He asks the question: 'What processes, practices, and organizations have you actually dismantled in the last year or two? If the answer is none, then perhaps it's time to get some practice in before urgency strikes.'

The key to thinking about the future is not to assume it will necessarily be like the past. Change is now endemic. As Foster and Kaplan (*op. cit.*) point out, you cannot even assume that the company will continue to exist, certainly in its present form, let alone customers, competitors and the environment generally. They argue that too many Managing Directors assume the future will be much like the past and what worked before will work again. They cite numerous examples of how this is simply untrue and how failure to recognize this has led to corporate failure. The moral is clear: assume nothing, question everything and think the unthinkable.

Generic marketing strategies

There are some generic strategies that are routine patterns based on experience. On the one hand they act as useful checklists of what is expected if these strategies are followed. On the other hand they can act as benchmarks against which to test how different you dare to be. However, many of the strategies have been researched and some have far better chances of success than others.

If we start with marketing basics, there have really only ever been three ways of selling products or services. You see two of them being used every day in any street market. At one end of the market there is a street trader offering the cheapest goods in the market – fruit, vegetables or whatever. At the other end there is another offering something different – freshest or organically grown fruit, vegetables or whatever. The more different you are, the higher the price you can charge. But there is also a third way to charge a higher price – not to go to the market, but rather to take the product to the customer. This is focusing on customers and their needs.

In recent times, Michael Porter (1985) gave this piece of common sense the catchy title of '*generic marketing strategies*' and argued that there are only three fundamental ways of achieving sustainable competitive advantage:

- Low price;
- High differentiation;
- Customer focus.

Figure 10.2 Generic marketing strategies

These are quite consistent with Treacy and Wiersema's (*op. cit.*) three value disciplines but lead to the four market positions, or 'generic marketing strategies' that are shown in Figure 10.2.

Commodity supplier

This is where the firm sets out to be the lowest-priced producer in the industry appealing to a very broad market with a relatively undifferentiated product. To have the lowest price means you must have the lowest costs. This assumes that costs can be reduced, for example through economies of scale, and that this is important to the customer. If a firm sets up in a market where economies of scale are achievable and are important to customers it must grow quickly, just to survive. A firm can find itself in this situation when the market or product may be new and economies of scale have yet to be developed. Firms may not yet have grown to their optimal size to achieve these economies and the battle is on to see who can get there first. This is shown in Figure 10.3. Technological change can cause a step change downward in this curve. Minimum cost is at output A with average cost per unit A1.

Similar to economies of scale are experience curve economies. These are the consequence of the business learning how to generate its outputs more efficiently and effectively. Like economies of scale, experience curve economies are related to output. However, whereas economies of scale depend on output in a particular period, experience curve economies are the result of cumulative output. Another source of low cost might be lower input costs than competitors for things like materials, energy or labour. These might be sustained through special contract arrangements or geographic proximity.

If a firm is a commodity supplier, price is important to its customers and it therefore needs to understand how costs can be minimized. Dominance of the market will depend very largely on being the lowest cost producer in the sector. It is likely that sustainable cost leadership can only be achieved by means of 'substantial relative market share advantage' because this provides the firm with the cost advantages of economies of scale, market power and experience curve effects. Following this

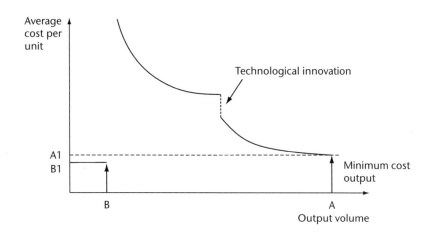

Figure 10.3 Economies of scale and economies of small scale

strategy means having a focus on new technology, as this is often the best way to reduce costs. It also means fighting competitors hard to sustain any cost advantage through market dominance. Achieving dominance in this sort of market place is risky and the road to high growth will have many casualties along the way. The risks this strategy faces are that cost leadership cannot be sustained: competitors might imitate, technology might change, indeed any basis for that all-important cost leadership might be eroded.

Case with questions

Stelios Haji-Ioannou and easyJet

One firm that has successfully followed the low-price strategy is easyJet. The company was founded by Stelios Haji-Ioannou, a graduate of London Business School, in 1995 with £5 million borrowed from his father, a Greek shipping tycoon. Copying similar operations in the USA and Ryanair flying out of Ireland, easyJet was one of the first 'low-cost' airlines in the UK, flying from Luton to Scotland. Stelios then launched similar low-cost, no-frills services to continental Europe. The company has transformed the European air travel market and has spawned many rival imitators. easyJet was floated on the Stock Market in 2000 at 310p a share, making Stelios £280 million in profit.

> 'You start the business as a dream, you make it your passion for a while and then you get experienced managers to run it because it's not as much fun as starting. I think there's a lot to be said about starting a business and a lot to be said about running a business when it's mature.' (*Sunday Times*, 29 October 2000)

A central strategy of being low price is being low cost and that has a number of implications for how easyJet and its rivals are run. Low cost comes from two driving principles – 'sweating' the assets and high operating efficiency. easyJet flies its Boeing 737s for 11 hours a day, 4 hours longer than BA. Their pilots fly 900 hours a year, 50% more than BA pilots.

→

Case with questions continued

Stelios Haji-Ioannou and easyJet

In terms of operating efficiency, it means:

● Aircraft fly out of low-cost airports. These are normally not the major airport serving any destination and can be some distance from it.
● Aircraft are tightly scheduled. They are allowed only 25 minutes to off-load one set of passengers and load another, less than half the time of their scheduled full-fare rivals.
● Aircraft must leave and arrive on time (they will not wait for passengers), and if there are delays they can have horrendous knock-on consequences for the timetable. Nevertheless punctuality is varied, with the low-cost carriers just as good as full-fare airlines on some routes.
● There is no 'slack' in the system. easyJet admits to having 'one and a half planes' worth' of spare capacity compared with the dozen planes BA has on stand-by at Gatwick and Heathrow. If something goes wrong with a plane it can lead to cancellations and long delays.
● There are fewer cabin crew than full-fare rivals and staff rostering is a major logistical problem.

In terms of customer service, it means:

● No 'frills' such as free drinks, meals or assigned seats.
● There is no compensation for delays or lost baggage.
● The low-cost airlines do not guarantee transfers as the planes could be late.
● The low-cost airlines concentrate on point-to-point flights, whereas the full-fare airlines tend to concentrate on hub-and-spoke traffic.

easyJet is aggressive in promoting its brand and running advertising promotions to get more 'bums on seats'. It realizes that its planes must have a high seat occupancy to be economic. To this end it is particularly inventive with pricing, encouraging real bargain hunters onto the less popular flights during the day and promoting early bookings with cheaper fares.

easyJet has been at the forefront of the use of the internet for virtual ticketing, to the point where it now sells most of its tickets over the web. This means it does not have to pay commission to travel agents and check-in can be quicker and more efficient. Its website has been held up as a model for the industry and many have copied it.

However, easyJet does have competition and some airlines are cheaper. Whilst easyJet claims an average price of £45 per 600 kilometres, Ryanair claims £34. This compares to British Airways' price of £110. Interestingly Ryanair has so little faith in its timetable that it advises passengers not to book connecting flights. In 2002 easyJet bought one of its major rivals, Go, with whom it had been in fierce price competition on certain routes, to the point where tickets were being given away with only airport tax to pay. One of the first things easyJet did was to close the Go flights on these routes and restore prices. As well as eliminating competition, the purchase of Go had other strategic reasoning behind it. easyJet was purchasing market share in a fast growing market (in 2002 it grew by 60%) where there are economies of scale. They were also buying new routes and landing rights, which can be difficult to secure.

One of the fears about low-cost airlines is that they will be tempted to compromise on safety for the sake of cutting costs. The British Airline Pilots Association has claimed that pilots of low-cost airlines can be tempted to cut corners to achieve flight timetables. Stelios himself has fuelled the safety debate by expressing doubts about Ryanair's use of 20-year-old planes on some of its routes, pointing out that though they might improve profits in the short term, they put the future of the whole airline at risk in the event of an accident. Ryanair is phasing these planes out and does have an unblemished safety record. But the industry is all too aware that the low-cost US airline, Valuejet, went bankrupt after one of its planes crashed in 1996, killing all 110 people on board. As the *Economist* says (17 August 2002): 'the low cost airline business is not for the faint-hearted'.

In 2002, only seven years after starting the company and still owning 29 per cent of easyJet, Stelios realised that he was better suited to being a serial entrepreneur than managing an established public company, so he resigned as Chairman, aged only 35. He was to be replaced by Sir Colin Chandler, aged 62, part of London's financial establishment as chairman of Vickers Defence Systems, deputy chairman of Smiths Group and director of Thales. Shortly after easyJet took over Go, the low cost airline set up by British Airways and sold off to its management. Newspaper comment at the time suggested that Stelios had been blocking such a deal and this might have been one reason for his departure.

'Running a company that is listed on the Stock Exchange is different from building up and running a private company. The history of the City is littered with entrepreneurs who hold onto their creations for too long, failing to recognise the changing needs of the company. I am a serial entrepreneur...It is all part of growing up. I've built something and now it is time to move on.' (*The Times*, 19 April 2002)

Stelios still had many other 'easy' ventures to grow. These include easyRental – a car rental business, easyEverything – a chain of internet cafes and cinemas and easyValue – which provides impartial comparisons for online shopping. He still has everything to play for doing something he enjoys more and possibly does better.

Up-to-date information on easyJet can be found on their website: www.easyjet.co.uk

Questions
1. Based upon this information, undertake a SWOT analysis on easyJet.
2. Compared to Ryanair and British Airways, where would you place easyJet in terms of Porter's generic marketing strategies? Is this sustainable?
3. What is the underlying strategy behind all of Stelios' 'easy' ventures? Can this strategy be replicated in any market? What is required for it to work?

Market trader

And yet, we do see very small businesses surviving in highly price-competitive markets where economies of scale exist. Just visit your local Saturday market to see some examples. How do they do it? Burns (2007) explains that this can happen in some markets because of economies of small-scale, where overheads can be minimal at very low levels of output (see Figure 10.3, where economies of small scale occur at output B and unit cost B1). The problem is that this will only hold true of production levels up to a certain low level and to grow the business beyond this size means that the firm must increase its overheads disproportionately, and then start to move down the cost curve. The firm will need high investment and it will need to grow quickly. The chances of making this dash successfully are therefore relatively low.

216 O Strategies for the Entrepreneurial Organization

Niche player

Differentiation means setting out to be unique in the industry along some dimensions that are widely valued by customers. This is called developing a unique selling proposition (USP). The firm sets out to establish itself as unique and different from its competitors in some ways. It can then charge a premium price.

> 'Find out what you want to do and look at the competition and decide on how you can improve on the competition. What is your USP? What is it about your business that makes you different from anyone else. And once you have found those little uniquenesses state them time and time again because those little uniquenesses are the thing the competition will find it difficult to duplicate.'
>
> **Anita Roddick**
> founder of **Body Shop**
> personal interview
> ➡

Entrepreneurial firms should be good at this because of their ability to innovate. Where the firm combines this with a focus on a narrow target market segment it is said to be following a strategy of 'focused differentiation' better known as a niche strategy. Economists call this occupying the 'interstices' of the economy. Clear differentiation often goes with well-aimed segmentation as it is easier to differentiate yourself in a small, clearly identified market. The key to segmentation is the ability to identify the unique benefits that a product or service offers to potential customers. Thus, for example, there may be two electrical engineers producing similar products but, whereas one is a jobbing engineer producing a range of products for many customers with no particular competitive advantage, the other might differentiate itself on the basis of its market – that it sells to a few large companies with whom it has long-term relationships, being integrated into their supply chains.

Establishing a market niche is most effective when aimed at a narrowly defined market segment. One problem of a niche market is its very narrowness. However the environment can change; markets grow or shrink; technology changes and customers move around. As the picture changes, so do opportunities, and what might offer a good niche in one decade may turn into a free-for-all in another. Having said that, an entrepreneurial firm may successfully develop a portfolio of products or services, each in its own distinct market niche.

Outstanding success

Sometimes firms that differentiate themselves effectively turn out to have a very broad market appeal and what may have started as a niche business turns out to be an outstanding success that experiences rapid and considerable growth. It is unlikely that many businesses will start life here, except perhaps in areas of real innovation. Differentiation can, however, prove costly if the basis that is chosen subsequently proves inappropriate. So, for example, Sony devised the Betamax format for its video recorders but ultimately had to adopt JVC's VHS system. Companies try to protect the basis for differentiation in any way possible. It might be that a product can be patented, the design registered or, for written material, copyrighted. Commodity suppliers try desperately to differentiate themselves, with varying degrees of success.

Case insight

Born in Shanghai and living much of his early life in Hong Kong, **Barry Lam** is founder, chairman and chief executive of **Quanta Computer Inc.**, the world's largest maker of laptop computers, with factories in both Taiwan and China. And yet few will recogniZe his name or that of his company because he keeps a low profile. That is because Quanta is a contract manufacturer – a company that designs and manufactures electronic equipment, but leaves the branding and marketing to others. Most of Dell's laptops are made by Quanta at its factory near Taipei airport in Taiwan. It also manufactures laptops for IBM, Apple and Compaq. Indeed Taiwanese companies now manufacture over half of the world's laptop computers with Quanta being the largest with over 15% of the market.

Barry specializes in contract manufacturing. It is what he knows and what he does best. His entrepreneurial career started in the 1970s when he started **Kimpo**, a company that went on to become the largest contract manufacturer of calculators. Quanta was set up in 1988 and by 2000 had overtaken Toshiba as the world largest manufacturer of laptops.

Contract manufacturers tend to be either providers of electronic manufacturing services (EMS) or original design manufacturers (ODMs). EMSs build machines that others design. They look to achieve greater economies of scale with lower risk by amalgamating orders from several companies. However, they sell to fewer and fewer global brand names and have little bargaining power because they do not control design or marketing. Consequently margins are becoming increasingly squeezed. Quanta, however, is an ODM and because it designs laptops, it is able to charge a premium price, which reflects itself in the high profitability of the firm. Quanta is not just a 'me-too' manufacturer, it invests in research and product innovation, which are vital elements in the firm's success.

Quanta is now the world's largest manufacturer of data-storage servers. However, this market place is different again, with the end user likely to be a big company that places far more emphasis on reliability and quality than on price. And that begs the question of the place of the contract manufacturer.

It has been suggested by Porter (*op. cit.*) that firms cannot change their generic strategy successfully. That is generally now not held to be correct. For example, when Direct Line launched itself in the UK, selling on price, it did so for a relatively narrow range of very popular cars. It rapidly widened this as the concept proved successful. However, as competitors emerged it rapidly started differentiating itself on the quality of service in the event of an accident. Porter also said that a firm had to obviously follow one of the four strategies otherwise it would have no clear direction. Given that there are many firms offering similar products on the price/differentiation spectrum to a range of sizes of different markets, this is also difficult to prove, although there are examples of the lack of success of such policies.

Value drivers

Real advantages in cost or differentiation need to be found in the chain of activities that a firm performs to deliver value to its customers. Michael Porter (*op. cit.*) says that

PRIMARY ACTIVITIES

SUPPORT ACTIVITIES

Figure 10.4 The value chain

the value chain, shown in Figure 10.4, should be the start of any strategic analysis. He identified five primary activities:

1. Inbound logistics (receiving storing and disseminating inputs)
2. Operations (transforming inputs into a final product)
3. Outbound logistics (collecting, storing and distributing products to customers)
4. Marketing and sales
5. After-sales service

and four secondary or supporting activities:

1. Procurement (purchasing consumable and capital items)
2. Human resource management
3. Technology development (R&D etc.)
4. Firm infrastructure (general management, accounting etc.).

Porter argues that each generic category can be broken down into discrete activities unique to a particular firm. The firm can then look at the costs associated with each activity and try to compare it to the value obtained by customers from the particular activity. By identifying the cost or value drivers – the factors that determine cost or value for each activity – and the linkages which reduce cost or add value or discourage imitation the firm can develop the strategies that lead to competitive advantage.

This is a way of focusing on the drivers of value in a business that ought to influence the strategy of the firm. For example, the low-cost supply situation may be linked to its proximity to a key supplier and could therefore disappear if the firm decides, as part of its expansion plans, to move to another location. The value chain is

> 'We put a great deal of emphasis on understanding what drove customer satisfaction, whether it was response times on the telephone, quality of products, valuable features, or ease of experience in using the product. Engaging the entire company – from manufacturing to engineering to sales to support staff – in the process of understanding customer requirements became a constant focus of management energy, training, and employee education.'
>
> **Michael Dell**
> ➜

also a useful way of thinking about how differentiation might be achieved. For example, a high-quality product might be let down by low-quality after-sales service – the value to the customer not being matched by the investment. In other words differentiation is likely to be achieved by multiple linkages in the value chain as exemplified by a consistent marketing mix. If multiple compatible linkages can be established they are more difficult to imitate than single linkages. Similarly, building switch costs into the value chain can also enhance competitive position. However, the advent of e-commerce has generally made it easier to disaggregate the value chain, establishing markets at different points along it, allowing firms to radically rethink or 're-engineer' the way their product/market offering is put together.

Entrepreneurial firms can add value to the customer in a number of ways, not least by developing the close relationships they offer to both customers and suppliers. A particularly effective entrepreneurial strategy is to identify a sector in which the relationships are weak and to create value by tightening them up.

Case insight

In the ubiquitous mobile phone market you might think it hard to differentiate yourself. When **Charles Dunstone** set up **Carphone Warehouse** in 1989 with his savings of £6000 he was only 24 years old. He started selling mobile phones from a two-room office in Harley Street, relying on newspaper advertisements, but his original vision was to sell them from shops so that people could browse before they bought. Nobody else was selling mobile phones in this way at the time.

Whilst making the most of a high growth market, the real opportunity to differentiate the firm came when Vodafone and Cellnet started offering packages with different combinations of rental and call charges. Customers had to decide which tariff was best for them and many were confused about the packages on offer. Carphone Warehouse set itself up to offer independent, reliable advice, something few other retailers offered. In a highly competitive market place the firm was able to claim some element of differentiation, a claim that it used extensively in its advertising.

Part of the success of the company comes from the emotional and personal involvement of Charles Dunstone – he still cannot let go. He has been described as a 'monofocused, workaholic ... a retail-detail obsessive with a calm exterior ... in love with the great Carphone Warehouse: its shops, its products, its people, its advertising and, above all, its customers and its sales' (*Sunday Times*, 28 July 2002). Although he enjoys sailing – he owns two big boats – he is quite likely to spend a weekend as a duty manager in one of the shops and will serve at counters if he finds customers waiting during one of his frequent store visits. Not unexpectedly he was still

➜

Case insight continued

unmarried in 2006 at the age of 42. The *Sunday Times* described him as 'driven by anxiety and a tough competitive streak. That way he remains always alert to rivals and constantly worried about strategy' (16 April 2006). Pierre Danon, former Chief Executive of BT Retail and now advisor at JP Morgan says: 'Charles is clever, he is customer focused, he has very good strategy allied with a down-to-earth management style' (*Sunday Times*, 16 April 2006).

By 2006 Carphone had some 1771 stores across Europe (669 in Britain) and is considered one of the country's great retail successes. Charles Dunstone is now a millionaire, estimated to be worth over £300 million. He sold £56 million worth of shares when Carphone floated in July 2000 but still holds 34% of the equity. However, like most telecom shares, the share price has dropped since its float price of 200p and with mobile phone ownership across Europe now averaging 70%–75% it looks unlikely to ever return to these levels. However, the arrival of 3G networks, which allow music and pictures to be downloaded and sent to other phones, has rejuvenated this market to some extent. Dunstone's response has been to reposition the company to be less dependent on new phone sales. Over 45% of revenues now come from 'recurring revenues', generated from managing customers for the networks. Consistent with this strategy, in 2006 he launched his latest venture – 'free' broadband connections in Britain. Actually it was only 'free' if purchased as part of his fixed-line service, called Talk Talk, which also offered unlimited landline calls all for a fixed line rental. Dunstone's rationale for 'selling cheap' comes from his belief that phones, television and internet are all converging, so what is important is to build market share as quickly as possible, since economies of scale will become increasingly important.

●

Successful entrepreneurial strategies

So, Porter wants you to select cost leadership, differentiation or focus. Hamel and Prahalad want you to focus on core competencies. On the other hand, Treacy and Wiersema want you to select operational excellence, product leadership or customer intimacy. Which theory do you choose? *The key theme is that strategy should emphasize something that makes the firm as unique as possible and delivers as much value to the customer as possible today, and more importantly, tomorrow.* And we might add that, whatever you do, you must do it quickly so as to seize the market opportunity and that means, inevitably that your strategy cannot be spelt out in detail. You need a firm idea of your general direction – your vision – and the rest of the firm will have to deal with the detail on a day-to-day basis.

And what does research tell us are the specific strategies that are most likely to ensure growth? In their survey

'We learned to identify our core strengths . . . The idea of building a business solely on cost or price was not a sustainable advantage. There would always be someone with something that was lower in price or cheaper to produce. What was really important was sustaining loyalty among customers and employees, and that could only be derived from having the highest level of service and very high performing products.'

Michael Dell
➡

of 179 supergrowth companies, Harrison and Taylor's (1996) entrepreneurs identified five 'winning performance factors', most of which can be supported by other research:

1. *Compete on quality rather than price.*   Competing on the quality of a product or service rather than price is an important element of success for entrepreneurial firms across Europe (Burns, 1994; Ray and Hutchinson, 1983; Storey *et al.*, 1989). By way of contrast, slow growing firms tend to emphasize price (Burns, *op. cit.*).
2. *Dominate a market niche.*   Many surveys support this conclusion about niche marketing (3i, 1993; Birley and Westhead, 1990; Macrae, 1991; Siegel *et al.*, 1993; Solem and Steiner, 1989; Storey *et al.*, 1989). There is also a strong relationship between market share and financial return (Boston Consulting Group, 1968, 1972; Buzzell *et al.*, 1974; Buzzell and Gale, 1987; Yelle, 1979).
3. *Compete in areas of strength.*   This relates particularly to the previous point since the ability to differentiate effectively is a considerable strength.
4. *Have tight financial and operating controls.*   Researchers often link strong financial control with planning (3i, 1991).
5. *Frequent product or service innovation (particularly important in manufacturing).* Innovation and new product introduction is also seen as important by many researchers (Dunkelberg *et al.*, 1987; Solem and Steiner, 1989; Storey *et al.*, 1989; Woo *et al.*, 1989; Wynarczyk *et al.*, 1993).

The conclusion is obvious. If you want to play the odds, *the strategy with the best chance of generating the highest profits is to differentiate with the aim of dominating that market and do it effectively and quickly, and continue to innovate based on your differential advantage.* And one important element of differentiation in our entrepreneurial firm is the entrepreneurial architecture that will allow it to pursue this strategy successfully and, more importantly, sustain it.

However, one final word of caution, but also reinforcement. Nohria and Joyce (2003) report the results of a ten-year study of 160 companies and their use of some 200 different management techniques. They conclude what we all know: that it does not really matter so much which technique you apply but it matters very much that you execute it flawlessly. They claim flawless execution is something too many management theorists have forgotten. Attention to detail is important. They also highlight three other things that distinguish successful companies over time:

1. A company culture that aims high.
2. A structure that is flexible and responsive.
3. A strategy that is clear and focused.

Differentiation

Whilst the entrepreneurial architecture allows you to pursue this strategy there will probably be some other, more tangible, elements of differentiation evident in the product or service offering. Differentiation is about being different and distinctive. It can come from being innovative in some way – we shall return to this important area in a later chapter. However, many firms might not be described as innovative but are still clearly differentiated from the competition. Product or service differentiation can

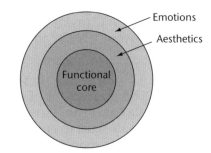

Figure 10.5 Dimensions of differentiation

come about through any number of factors such as function, quality, performance, technology or other tangible characteristics. So, for example, Mercedes Benz cars and Dom Perignon champagne aim to differentiate themselves through quality in their respective sectors. McDonald's does it, in part, through quality of service (speed, cleanliness and so on). Differentiation might come from the other elements of the marketing mix, for example, the channels of distribution. When Direct Line started selling motor insurance over the telephone in the UK it was so radically different that it was seen as an innovation in financial service delivery that had applications in other sectors. And yet the innovation was simply the use of another, much cheaper, channel of distribution. In the event this innovation did not provide sustainable competitive advantage because it was so easy to copy. However, it did give Direct Line first-mover advantage and a lead on the market.

> 'When you've got single-digit market share – and you're competing with the big boys – you either differentiate or die.'
> **Michael Dell**
> ➡

Often differentiation is more sustainable when based on less tangible factors. Aesthetics of design are one area which are difficult to replicate that the hi-fi manufacturers Bang & Olufsen use to differentiate themselves. Emotional benefits can be a further element of differentiation that are even more difficult to copy. So, for example, Body Shop differentiates itself primarily on its ethical values. Customers relate to products or services along all of these dimensions, as shown in Figure 10.5. If a product can score in all three dimensions, as Mercedes Benz would claim, the product or service is bound to be a winner.

Differentiation is helped by clear branding. A brand should be the embodiment of the product or service offering to customers. So, for example, the Mercedes Benz, Jaguar and BMW brands all convey quality. Virgin is the embodiment of Richard Branson; brash, entrepreneurial, different, anti-establishment. Body Shop is environmentally friendly. In the UK the Co-op bank is about ethical investment, whereas Coutts Bank is about service and

> 'Basically any brand is an assurance to customers. It is an assurance of quality, an assurance of consistency. There is an immediate recognition, when you see the Cadbury signature on the front of the chocolate bar or box of Milk Tray, all those things are guaranteed.'
> **Sir Adrian Cadbury**
> *The Times*, 8 July 2000
> ●

Figure 10.6 The customer loyalty ladder

status for the wealthy. Many so-called brands, however, fall far short of this instant recognition of values and virtues, being little more than expensive logos. What do the Barclays, Shell or the BT brands convey, other than a knowledge of what the firm sells?

In a world where products and services are often all too homogeneous, a good brand is a powerful marketing tool that must be the cornerstone of any strategy of differentiation. Not only can it help turn prospects into customers, if everything else is right it can turn them into regular customers. What is more, it can help turn them into supporters – regular customers who think positively about the brand – or even advocates – who are willing to recommend the product and bring in new customers. In other words it helps move them up the customer loyalty ladder (Figure 10.6). And here again the entrepreneurial architecture, with its emphasis on long-term relationships, can help. If the architecture is in place it is not just the entrepreneurial leader who will 'walk the talk', but every member of staff. Each of them will be the embodiment of the product or service offering and, because of their sincere belief in it, they will be its best advocates.

Companies try to protect the basis for differentiation in any way possible by creating barriers to entry in the market for as long as possible. It might be that a product can be patented, the design registered or, for written material, copyrighted. Branding also creates barriers to entry. However, the bigger the market, the more difficult and expensive this is to achieve. That is why differentiation is most successful when combined with a strategy of focus. It is vital that any firm understands the basis of its competitive advantage. For a firm pursuing a differentiation strategy this means understanding the basis for its differential advantage. This can be based in law (a licence, copyright, patent and so on), upon elements of the product (quality, design and so on), the service offered or intangible things like image. For a shop it may be based on location (the only shop in the area). The more elements that the firm can claim to set it apart from the competition the better. However, these elements must be a real benefit and add value to the customer. If the firm has elements of differentiation then it should aggressively promote them, usually through a strong brand identity.

Case insight

Specialist cereals producer **Jordans** is a family company tracing its origins back to 1855 with milling and the supply of animal feed. In the 1960s the company switched from producing white to wholemeal flour in the face of fierce price competition from big conglomerates. It also started producing small quantities of oat-based cereals, which it sold to health food stores.

By the 1970s health foods had really caught on and Jordans were selling to the supermarkets. Two keys to their growth since then have been product quality and innovation. Quality, backed with a respected brand identity, have allowed them not to be drawn too far into the vicious food-price wars. Innovation has kept them one step ahead of the big-company competition. They were among the first to introduce 'food on the run' cereal bars. They were also amongst the first to introduce freeze-dried fruits to their breakfast cereals, even innovating in the packaging by introducing cellophane bags. They pioneered the introduction of 'conservation grade' ingredients which are cheaper than organically grown but contain few pesticides.

However, Jordans has also entered the own-brand market and 20% of its £50 million turnover comes from this source. Even here it trades on its 'brand integrity' – its ability to produce tasty and nutritious cereals in an environmentally-friendly way. But it has had to control costs. It is also entering the adult savoury market with its low-fat cereal-based oven-crisped chips. It now plans a major expansion into Europe. Bill Jordan explains the key to his strategy:

'The company needs to differentiate its products rather than slog it out on price. We need to sustain advertising support to develop customer demand, which is the key to getting our goods placed on the supermarket shelf'.

Sunday Times, 12 March 2000

Case with questions

Anita and Gordon Roddick and Body Shop

In 2006 Anita and Gordon Roddick sold the international retail chain Body Shop, that they had founded back in 1976, for £652 million. They had come a long way in thirty years and the achievements were not just due to luck:

'I know everyone wants to think that it is like an act of God – that you sit down and have a brilliant idea. Well, when you start your own business it does not work like that. I remember walking through Littlehampton with the kids, one in a pushchair and one walking beside me. We went into the sweet shop, then into the greengrocer and then to Boots. In both the sweet shop and the greengrocers I had choice. I could buy as much, or as little, as I wanted. I could buy half a pound of gob-stoppers or a kilo of apples, the quantities were up to me. In Boots I suddenly thought 'What a shame that I can't buy as little as I like here too. Why am I stuck with only big sizes to choose from? If I'm trying something out and don't like it, I am too intimidated to return it, so I'm stuck with it.' That one thought, that single reaction, was me voicing a need, a disappointment with things as they were. But if that's a need I have, lots of other women must have the same need, I thought. Why can't we buy smaller sizes – like in the greengrocers?'

Anita's basic idea was a huge success. However, whilst the idea was novel at the time it was also easily copiable. The firm's initial roll-out owes much to the clear focus of Anita and Gordon Roddick on where their competitive advantage lay. They realized that the idea they had could be easily copied and success would only come from developing the brand and a rapid expansion. Unfortunately they had little cash to do either. It was Gordon who had the idea of a franchise, which meant that franchisees paid to become part of Body Shop and managed the shop themselves.

Franchisees pay an initial fee plus an annual operating charge for a fixed-term, renewable franchise. They buy a 'turn-key' system with a tightly controlled retail format providing shop fitting and layout, staff training, financial and stock control systems and even help with site identification. Body Shop can also help arrange finance to purchase the franchise. Body Shop also, of course, makes a margin on the products it sells to the franchisees.

Franchisees receive regular visits from company representatives who provide assistance with display, sales promotion and training. Information packs, newsletters, videos and free promotional material are made available and franchisees have to return a monthly report on their sales. This enables the company to monitor both trading results and the local sales performance of individual products. The company closely monitors the use of the Body Shop trade mark in all franchisees' literature, advertising and other uses.

Franchisees are selected partly upon their 'fit' with Body Shop ideals. Employees receive regular newsletters and videos concentrating on Body Shop campaigns and achievements. In 1995 the firm introduced in-store satellite transmitted radio. Body Shop takes every opportunity to put forward its values and beliefs which it believes sets it out as distinctive and different from its high street competitors. It also believes that the company brings together like-minded people and motivates staff in a sector with an otherwise high staff turnover. The franchisees generated sufficient cash to finance early expansion of Body Shop until 1984 when the company went to the Stock Market, although it still maintained the franchise model.

Overseas expansion followed the same model as in the UK. In most countries a head franchisee was granted exclusive rights as user of the trade mark, distributor and, after an initial trial of running a few shops themselves, the right to sub-franchise. In this way the firm built upon local market knowledge and minimized its risks. This model was not always followed because of the quality of the head franchisee. For example, the firm might take back control of the franchise. Body Shop remains an international franchise chain of shops with Body Shop International Ltd as the franchisor.

The Roddicks initially decided not to manufacture their products or even invest in a distribution system, but rather to concentrate on getting the franchise formula right, developing the brand and protecting it from imitators. In the 1980s Body Shop reversed its decision and started its own warehousing and distribution network, based upon a sophisticated stock-control system, and built up a substantial fleet of lorries. Products could typically be delivered within 24 hours. It also started manufacturing many of its cosmetics, mainly in the UK, although many of the ingredients came from overseas under its 'trade-not-aid' policy. These two elements of strategy initially worked well and generated substantial sales and profit growth, but the manufacturing policy was reviewed in the late 1990s.

In the early years Body Shop could not afford to advertise. Developing the brand was heavily reliant upon the personality of Anita and her ability to get free PR for the environmental causes associated with the firm. Indeed, advertising would have been very much against the firm's image. In those early days her outspoken, controversial views (concerning just about anything)

➡

Case with questions continued

Anita and Gordon Roddick and Body Shop

guaranteed her media coverage and helped her win the Businesswoman of the Year award just before the Stock Market launch. Even today the Body Shop brand is inexorably linked with its culture, which in turn is based firmly in its ethical and environmental beliefs and values. Based very much around the charismatic Anita Roddick's views that business can be a vehicle for social and environmental change, the firm has championed numerous causes. These not only show themselves in window displays and PR activities, they also underscore everything the company does. Employees are given time off to work on local social projects. Body Shop takes every opportunity to put forward the values and beliefs which set it out as distinctive and different.

Body Shop is now a global brand, but what does it stand for and what are customers buying? Even Anita Roddick admitted they were not just buying cosmetics – 'oil and water will not make their hearts sing'. The marketing mix comprises cosmetics made from high quality, natural ingredients which do not involve cruelty to animals. They can be bought in a range of refillable containers, including trial sizes, that are plain and simple with clear factual statements about their ingredients. Tester bottles are freely available in shops and staff are trained not to sell products 'hard' and to respond to questions honestly, if necessary going to the Product Information Manual. The company does not advertise, relying instead on PR and their prime-site shop windows that often promote environmental issues rather than products. The green shop decor with its ambience of a sweet shop reinforces the environmental, no-frills image. Staff receive regular training, not only on business but also on environmental issues. Unlike other cosmetics companies, Body Shop is selling a feel-good factor of a different sort, with a strong ethical dimension. It campaigns on behalf of many environmental issues such as the destruction of the Brazilian rain forests, 'trade, not aid', recycling and, famously, animal testing of cosmetics. The Body Shop brand is deeply emotional, based upon a marketing mix that reinforces the 'save the planet' image and really does 'make the heart sing'. The company's values and mission reflect this (see page 94).

In 1996 an attempted re-privatization was abandoned because of the gearing implications. After that the Roddicks increasingly took a back seat. In 1998 a new Chief Executive was recruited, with the Roddicks becoming co-chairmen. Over the last decade Body Shop has been attracting more competition from both newcomers and established retailers who are introducing 'natural' products. Because of the emergence of an aggressive US competitor called Bath and Body Works, Body Shop was forced into even more rapid expansion with a unfortunate effect on costs and profitability. However, profits and share price subsequently recovered. It also faced criticism about the reality behind its ethical stance. In 1999 the company withdrew from manufacturing.

In 2000 the Roddicks resigned from Body Shop, multimillionaires, but retained a majority shareholding. In March 2006 it was announced that Body Shop was to be sold to L'Oreal for £652 million. With the Roddick's stake in the company estimated at 18%, they were expected to make £130 million – and they moved into the top 100 richest people in the UK. This was the final exit. L'Oreal assures the public it will take a 'hands-off' approach to managing the business, but, with its very different image to Body Shop, many analysts wonder whether the Body Shop values and ethos will really survive – indeed whether the brand can survive, not only without the Roddicks, but now as part of a larger multinational company – the very thing it hated so much.

Up-to-date information on Body Shop can be found on their website: www.bodyshop.com

Questions
1. Why has Body Shop been so successful?
2. Which strategic decisions contributed most to the successful initial roll-out of Body Shop? Why were they correct?
3. Why did the company make the decision to stop distribution and manufacturing?
4. What are the dangers of having the brand so closely linked to the entrepreneur?
5. Can a company like Body Shop, linked so closely to the values and vision of its founders, survive after their exit? Is this a wise purchase for L'Oreal?

Summary

The strategic process is more of a distinguishing feature of an entrepreneurial organization rather than the strategy it adopts.

A strong vision is essential. Strategy development is both emergent and deliberate but continuous strategizing at all levels is vital so as to develop strategic options. Good information flow is important. But decision making tends to be incremental and adaptive so as to maintain maximum flexibility.

A strategic framework is useful but a good framework is minimalist. Effective strategy must be rooted in the distinctive capabilities of the firm. The strategic process involves four stages:

1. Developing vision.
2. Strategic analysis, which involves undertaking a SWOT analysis and highlighting the core competencies of the organization.
3. Strategy formulation, which involves identifying, evaluating and selecting strategic options.
4. Strategy implementation, which involves leading and managing a change process, putting in place the appropriate organization structure and culture and planning and allocating resources.

The basic tool of strategic analysis is the SWOT analysis. However, there are a number of other strategic tools that can also help in completing the SWOT analysis. The main ones are summarized in Table 10.1. They seek to highlight the core competencies of the organization and match them to the opportunities in the market place to create sustainable competitive advantage. Core competencies can be used in a variety of markets, add value and are difficult to copy. Entrepreneurial architecture is likely to be a key sustainable competitive advantage.

When there is a misfit between aspirations and resources, strategic intent is the one binding force that allows managers to change the face of the markets they enter. SLEPT analysis, scenario planning and futures thinking are techniques that can help develop that vision.

Porter's generic strategies highlight three fundamental ways of gaining competitive advantage. **easyJet** follows a strategy of low cost, **Body Shop** and **Quanta Computers** a strategy of differentiation. As we shall see in the next chapter, other strategic imperatives emerge from the analysis of life cycles and product portfolios. However, as **Michael Dell** underlines, these strategies must essentially add value for the customer in a way that competitors find difficult to replicate. **Carphone Warehouse** added value by offering independent personal advice on the purchase of mobile phones. But can this be copied?

The key theme that comes out from theorists and empirical research in strategy formulation is that strategy should emphasize something that makes the firm as *unique* as possible and delivers as much *value* to the customer as possible today and, more importantly, tomorrow. As **Michael Dell** emphasizes, it is important to differentiate your product/market offering. He believes building a business *solely* on cost or price will not lead to sustainable advantage.

Research tells us that the strategy with the best chance of generating the highest profits is to differentiate with the aim of dominating that market and do this effectively and quickly, and continue to innovate based on your differential advantage.

Whilst the entrepreneurial architecture itself is a key differentiating factor that gives competitive advantage, other more tangible aspects include a focus on quality, innovation, use of different channels of distribution and so on. However, unless patented or copyrighted, these can often be copied. Aesthetics and emotions generated by the product or service are more difficult to copy.

As **Adrian Cadbury** emphasizes, branding helps differentiation and promotes customer loyalty. In a highly competitive market, the specialist cereals producer, **Jordans**, is trying to do just this.

Essays and discussion topics

1. Which comes first, strategy or action?
2. What are the differences between the 'Positional' and 'Process' Schools of strategy?
3. What is the 'Entrepreneurial School' of strategy?
4. 'Entrepreneurs are incapable of developing strategy.' Discuss.
5. What exactly is strategizing?
6. How would you go about undertaking a SWOT analysis on an established small firm?
7. How useful is a strategic tool-kit?
8. What is a core competency? How can it be identified?
9. 'If you thought knowledge was expensive you should try ignorance.' Discuss.
10. You cannot determine profit in a small firm because there are too many ways for the entrepreneur to manipulate it. Any form of financial analysis will therefore not work. Discuss.
11. How might you go about determining the profitability of a small firm so that financial analysis can be undertaken?
12. 'Entrepreneurial strategy is simple. Find out what others are doing and do the opposite.' Discuss.
13. Was Swatch really innovative?
14. Can you really develop strategic vision?
15. We can only guess what the future might hold, so there is no point in trying to predict it. Discuss.
16. How do you think music will be sold in the future? How can firms make a profit?
17. What did Porter actually say about generic marketing strategies? Is it really 'a glimpse of the blindingly obvious'?

18. Porter wants you to select cost leadership, differentiation or focus, Hamel and Prahalad want you to focus on core competencies and Treacy and Wiersema want you to select operational excellence, product leadership or customer intimacy. All these strategies are just fad and fancy. Nobody really knows how to generate competitive advantage. Discuss.
19. Value chains are an elegant concept but cannot be operationalized. Discuss.
20. How can you differentiate a product or service and ensure that competitors do not copy it?
21. How important is the brand? Can it be valued?
22. What constitutes the 'ideal' brand?
23. How can you safeguard your competitive advantage?
24. Is there really such a thing as strategy or is it something that academics dreamed up?

Exercises and assignments

1. Select a successful entrepreneur, like Michael Dell or Richard Branson, and research his or her background. Show how the business developed and analyze why has he or she been so successful.
2. Select a well-known product that is now in the mature phase of its life cycle and chart how the marketing strategy has changed over that life cycle.
3. For your University, College or Department:

   – Undertake a SLEPT analysis. Based upon this, try scenario planning on one major trend that you identify.
   – Undertake a SWOT analysis.
   – Undertake a comprehensive SWOT analysis on your course.

   Draw up a list of Action Points that follow from your analysis.
4. For a selected company, undertake a SLEPT analysis. Based upon this, try scenario planning on one major trend that you identify.
5. Consider the case of Jordans, undertaking more research as necessary. Where does its competitive advantage lie and how can it secure it?
6. Consider the case of Dell Computers, undertaking more research as necessary. Where does its competitive advantage lie and how can it secure it?

References

3i European Enterprise Centre (1991) *High Performance SMEs: A Two Country Study*, Report 1, September.

3i European Enterprise Centre (1993) *Britain's Superleague Companies*, Report 9, August.

Bagozzi, R. P. (ed.) (1994) *Principles of Market Research*, Oxford: Blackwell.

Birley, S. and Westhead, P. (1990) 'Growth and Performance Contrasts between Types of Small Firms', *Strategic Management Journal*, vol. II.

Birn, R. (1999) *The Effective Use of Market Research*, London: Kogan Page.

Boston Consulting Group (1968) *Perspectives on Experience*, Boston, Mass: Boston Consulting Group.

Boston Consulting Group (1972) *Perspectives on Experience*, Boston, Mass: Boston Consulting Group.

Burns, P. (1994) *Winners and Losers in the 1990s*, 3i European Enterprise Centre, Report 12, April.

Burns, P. (2007) *Entrepreneurship and Small Business*, 2nd edn, Basingstoke: Palgrave Macmillan.

Buzzell, R. D. and Gale, B. T. (1987) *The PIMS Principles – Linking Strategy to Performance*, New York: Free Press.

Buzzell, R. D. Heany, D. F. and Schoeffer, S. (1974) 'Impact of Strategic Planning on Profit Performance', *Harvard Business Review*, 52/2.

230 O Strategies for the Entrepreneurial Organization

Chisnall P. M. (1997) *Marketing Research*, Maidenhead: McGraw-Hill.

de Geus, A. (1988) 'Planning as Learning', *Harvard Business Review*, 70/4.

Dunkelberg, W. G., Cooper, A. C., Woo, C. and Dennis, W. J. (1987) 'New Firm Growth and Performance', in N. C. Churchill, J. A. Hornday, B. A. Kirchhoff, C. J. Krasner and K. H. Vesper (eds), *Frontiers of Entrepreneurship Research,* Babson College, Boston, Mass.

Foster, R. and Kaplan, S. (2001) *Creative Destruction: Why Companies that are Built to Last Underperform the Stock Market*, New York: Doubleday/Currency.

Hamel, G. and Prahalad, C. K. (1994) *Competing For the Future: Breakthrough Strategies for Seizing Control of your Industry and Creating the Markets of Tomorrow*, Boston, Mass: Harvard Business School Press.

Harrison, J. and Taylor, B. (1996) *Supergrowth Companies: Entrepreneurs in Action*, Oxford: Butterworth-Heinemann.

Johnson, G. and Scholes, K. (1993) *Exploring Corporate Strategy*, Hemel Hempstead: Prentice Hall International.

Kay, J. (1998) *Foundations of Corporate Success*, Oxford: Oxford University Press.

Macrae, D. J. R. (1991) 'Characteristics of High and Low Growth Small and Medium Sized Businesses', paper presented at 21st European Small Business Seminar, Barcelona, Spain.

McNulty, C. A. R. (1977) 'Scenario Development for Corporate Planning', *Futures*, 9, April.

McQuarrie, E. F. (1996) *The Market Research Toolbox: A Concise Guide for Beginners*, London: Sage.

Mintzberg, H., Ahlstrand, B. and Lampel, J. (1998) *Strategy Safari*, New York: The Free Press.

Nohria, N. and Joyce, W. (2003) 'What Really Works', *Harvard Business Review*, July/August.

Porter, M. (1985) *Competitive Advantage: Creating and Sustaining Superior Performance*. New York: The Free Press.

Prahalad, C. K. and Hamel, G. (1990) 'The Core Competence of the Corporation', *Harvard Business Review*, 68/3, May/June.

Quinn, J. B. Mintzberg, H. and James, R. M. (1988) *The Strategy Process*, Hemel Hempstead: Prentice Hall International.

Ray, G. H. and Hutchinson, P. J. (1983) *The Financing and Financial Control of Small Enterprise Development*, London: Gower.

Schwartz, P. (2003) *Inevitable Surprises: Thinking Ahead in a Time of Turbulence*, Gotham Books.

Siegel, R., Siegel, E. and MacMillan, I. C. (1993) 'Characteristics Distinguishing High Growth Ventures, *Journal of Business Venturing*, 8.

Solem, O. and Steiner, M. P. (1989) 'Factors for Success in Small Manufacturing Firms – and with special emphasis on growing firms', paper presented at Conference on SMEs and the Challenges of 1992, Mikkeli, Finland.

Storey, D. J., Watson, R. and Wynarczyk, P. (1989) *Fast Growth Small Business: Case Studies of 40 Small Firms in Northern Ireland*, Department of Employment, Research Paper No 67.

Treacy, M. and Wiersema, F. (1995) *The Discipline of Market Leaders*, Reading, Mass: Addison-Wesley.

Tull, D. S. and Hawkins, D. I. (1990) *Marketing Research*, New York: Macmillan.

Wack, P. (1985) 'Scenarios, Shooting the Rapids', *Harvard Business Review*, November/December.

Woo, C. Y., Cooper, A. C., Dunkelberg, W. C., Daellenbach, U. and Dennis, W. J. (1989) 'Determinants of Growth for Small and Large Entrepreneurial Start-Ups', paper presented to Babson Entrepreneurship Conference.

Wynarczyk, P., Watson, R., Storey, D. J., Short, H. and Keasey, K. (1993) *The Managerial Labour Market in Small and Medium-Sized Enterprises*, London: Routledge.

Yelle, L. E. (1979) 'The Learning Curve: Historical Review and Comprehensive Survey', *Decision Sciences*, 10.

Zentner, R. D. (1982) 'Scenarios, Past, Present and Future', *Long Range Planning*, 15/3.

Financial analysis checklist

Performance

Return on shareholders funds (%) $\dfrac{\text{Net profit (after interest)}}{\text{Shareholders funds}}$

Return on total assets (%) $\dfrac{\text{Operating profit (before interest)}}{\text{Total assets}}$

Profitability

Net margin (%) $\dfrac{\text{Net profit}}{\text{Sales}}$

Gross margin (%) $\dfrac{\text{Gross profit}}{\text{Sales}}$

Cost of materials (%) $\dfrac{\text{Cost of materials}}{\text{Sales}}$

Cost of labour (%) $\dfrac{\text{Cost of labour}}{\text{Sales}}$

Overhead cost (%) $\dfrac{\text{Overhead costs}}{\text{Sales}}$

Asset efficiency

Capital/Net asset turnover $\dfrac{\text{Sales}}{\text{Net assets}}$

Debtor turnover $\dfrac{\text{Sales}}{\text{Debtors}}$

Stock turnover $\dfrac{\text{Sales}}{\text{Stock}}$

Fixed asset turnover $\dfrac{\text{Sales}}{\text{Fixed assets}}$

Liquidity

Current ratio $\dfrac{\text{Current assets}}{\text{Current liabilities}}$

Quick ratio $\dfrac{\text{Current assets excluding stock}}{\text{Current liabilities}}$

Gearing

Gearing ratio (%) $\dfrac{\text{All loans + overdrafts}}{\text{Shareholders funds}}$

Short-term debt ratio (%) $\dfrac{\text{Short-term loans + overdrafts}}{\text{All loans + overdraft}}$

Interest cover $\dfrac{\text{Trading profit}}{\text{Interest}}$

Risk

Margin of safety $\dfrac{\text{Sales} - \text{Break-even sales}}{\text{Sales}}$

11

Life Cycle and Portfolio Strategies

Contents

- Life cycles
- Product portfolios
- Portfolio strategies
- Managing the product life cycle
- Financial implications of the product portfolio
- Implications for management
- Corporate and industry life cycles
- Summary

LEARNING OUTCOMES

By the end of this chapter you should be able to:

- Explain the effect of product life cycles on marketing strategy;

- Explain how the life cycle can be lengthened through product expansion and extension;

- Use the Boston matrix to present marketing strategies for a portfolio of products;

- Describe the effects of the product portfolio on cash flow and profitability;

- Describe the implications of the product portfolio on management styles and the problems this creates for corporate entrepreneurship across a large, complex organization;

- Explain how the concept of life cycle can be extended to companies and industries, and describe the implications of this for management.

Life cycles

Most companies are complex organizations selling a range of different products or services into a range of different markets, each with a different strategy. These are called different 'product/market offerings'. The same product can even be sold to different market segments with a slightly different strategy. Slightly different products might also be developed to better meet the needs of different market segments. The permutations are endless.

One important influence on strategy is the point the product or service is at in its life cycle. This can be used to identify the different market segments attracted to the product and the degree and nature of competition it faces. From this comes another set of 'routine patterns, based on experience', which can be used either as a strategy checklist or as a benchmark against how different you dare to be – but remember the odds! This concept can, in turn, be used to better understand the complexity of the portfolio of different product/market offerings and how that portfolio can be managed. It also raises issues about how corporate entrepreneurship can be managed across a large, complex organization.

The concept of the product life cycle is based on the idea that all products or services have a finite life cycle and that, to some extent, the appropriate marketing strategy, is dictated by the stage it is at in this life cycle. Life cycles can vary in length from short for fashion products such as clothing and other consumables to long for durable products like cars. Often the life cycle can be extended by a variety of marketing initiatives. Figure 11.1 shows a four-stage product life cycle with the implications for marketing strategy at the different stages. The simplicity of the model has much to recommend it. However, these broad generalizations must be treated with caution as all products are different, as are different market segments and the customers that comprise them.

At the introductory phase the objective should be to make potential customers aware of the product and to get them to try it. The benefits need to be explained and the relevance to customer needs to be underlined. Early customers are likely to be 'innovators', that is people who think for themselves and try things. Rogers (1962) estimated that they make up some 2.5% of the population. Entrepreneurial firms launching innovative new products are particularly interested in this phase.

At the growth phase the objective should be to grab market share as quickly as possible because competitors will be entering the market. This means that prices will have to be competitive, depending on the uniqueness of the product and how well it can be differentiated. The promotion emphasis should shift to one of promoting the brand and why it is better than that of competitors. 'Early adopters' will now be buying the product. These tend to be people with status in their market segment and opinion leaders. They adopt successful products, making them acceptable and respectable. These are estimated to represent some 13.5% of the population. The product range should start to be developed at this stage so as to give customers more choice and gain advantage over competitors.

The 'middle and late majority' now start buying the product and take it into the mature phase of its life cycle. The middle majority (comprising some 34%) are more conservative, with slightly higher status and are more deliberate. They only adopt the product after it has become acceptable. The late majority (also comprising some 34%) are typically below average status, are sceptical and adopt the product much later. In

Sales

Introduction	Growth	Maturity	Decline
Low sales	High, rapidly increasing sales	Static but high sales	Declining sales
Low growth		Static but high profits	Declining profits or losses
Low profits or losses as costs are high	Higher profits as costs come down	Focus on cost reduction	
		Fight for market share	Competitors exit
Few competitors	Competitors emerging and competition intensifying	Established competitors	

Time

Innovators   *Early adopters*   *Middle and late majority*   *Laggards*

Elements of marketing strategy			
Basic product	Develop product extensions and service levels	Wide range in place but expansion slows down or eventually ceases	Range narrows
Price low for repeat purchase products where trial is important	Price competitively to combat competition and penetrate market	Modify and differentiate	Weak products are dropped
		Develop next generation	Price high if reducing number of competitors means demand still high
Price high where novelty or uniqueness is valued, particularly if purchases are infrequent		Price defensively – meeting or beating competitors – to ensure maximum return	
	Promote actively and aggressively	Emphasize brand	
		Differentiate	Price low to dispose of stocks at end of life, in line with declining demand
	Build brand		
Promote actively and aggressively	Intensive push on distribution	Selective, based around special offers or promotions	
Explain product benefits	Limited trade discounts	Intensive push on distribution	Minimum required to maintain loyalty
Build awareness, encourage early adoption		Trade discounts offered	
			Emphasis on low price
Selective distribution			Distribute selectively
			Phase out weak outlets

Figure 11.1   The product/service life cycle

this phase competitors are becoming established as some fall by the wayside. In order to maintain market share, pricing tends to be defensive at, or around, the level of competitors. There should be an emphasis on cost reduction so that profits are as high as possible. The accountant's influence should be evident at this stage in the life cycle. It is at this point that products tend to get revamped – by changing designs, colours, packaging etc. – in order to extend their life cycle. Toward the end of this period, price reductions may be hidden by offering extra elements to the product for the same price. Cars, for example, often get this treatment with limited edition models offering many extras for the same price.

'Laggards' (comprising some 16%) tend to view life through the rear view mirror and will continue buying products because of habit. The interesting thing about the decline phase of the life cycle is that there may still be the opportunity to charge high prices and make good profits, at least in the short term, because competitors may be exiting the market quicker than demand is tailing off. Exactly when to exit is therefore a matter of careful judgement.

The problem with this concept is one of trying to establish where a product might actually be. Firms plotting their own product sales are not recording the product's life but their ability to manage it. Bad management can lead to an early downturn in sales which is not necessarily the mature phase of the life cycle, and vice versa. What is more, products can be in the mature phase of their life cycle in one market but at the introductory phase in another. You only have to see the queues and check the prices for McDonald's hamburgers in Russia to realize that the product has a long way to go in that market. Entrepreneurial management is most effective in the early phases of the life cycle.

Not only can the length of the life cycle vary from country to country and product to product, but also the length of each phase can vary. The take-off phase comes when slow initial sales accelerate towards a mass market. This introductory phase averages six years after launch in both the USA and Europe. White goods – refrigerators, washing machines, freezers etc. – have generally taken longer. Brown goods – TVs, CD players, VCRs etc. – have generally taken less time. But the average 'time to take-off' also varies from country to country. Tellis *et al.* (2003) studied 137 new product launches across 10 consumer durable categories in 16 European

Table 11.1 New products: average time to take-off in Europe

Upper quartile: 8 to 10 years	Greece
	Britain
	France
Upper-middle quartile: 6 to 8 years	France
	Spain
	Italy
	Germany
Average: 6 years	
Lower-middle quartile: 4 to 6 years	Finland
	Sweden
Lower quartile: up to 4 years	Norway
	Denmark

countries and found that, despite the Common Market, there were considerable differences, summarized in Table 11.1.

Scandinavian countries tended to have the shortest 'time to take-off' – for example 3.3 years in Denmark. This was well ahead of the largest EU economies of France, Germany, Italy, Spain and the UK. The average time in Scandinavian countries was 4 years compared to 7.4 years in Mediterranean countries. They concluded that cultural factors partly explain the differences. In particular, the probability of take-off increases in countries that are placed high in an index of achievement and industriousness and low in uncertainty avoidance. Economic factors were found not to be strong or robust explanatory variables. They also found that the probability of a new product's take-off in one country increased with prior take-offs in other countries. The authors therefore recommend that managers adopt a 'waterfall' strategy for product introduction in Europe, putting them first into the countries that are likely to have the shortest 'time to take-off'.

Product portfolios

As already mentioned, if a company has more than one product or service, then it might be following different strategies for each of the different product/market offerings it has and one important reason for this is that each of these offerings might be at a different stage of its life cycle in the particular market. So, for example, McDonald's may have a different marketing mix for its products in Russia, where it is at the introductory phase of its life cycle, compared to the USA, where it is a mature product – although the length of the life cycle in Russia is likely to be a lot shorter than in the USA.

This added complexity of having a portfolio of product/market offerings can be handled using a technique adapted from the 'Boston matrix', which derives its name from the Boston Consulting Group that developed it. The original matrix was adapted by McKinsey so as to have more realistic multi-dimensional axes. Figure 11.2 shows the adapted matrix. Market attractiveness – the growth and profit potential that relate to the market – is measured on the vertical axis. The strength of product or service offering in the market – sales, relative market share and so on – is measured on the horizontal axis. When a product or service offering is first developed it will be launched into an attractive market (otherwise why do it?), but the firm is unlikely to have a great deal of strength. This is called a Problem Child and is equivalent to the introduction phase of the life cycle. Sometimes the market proves to be unattractive – then the life cycle is very short. This is called a Dog. More often, if the market is attractive, sales will grow and the product or service offering will become more established and will strengthen in the market. This is called a Star. Eventually, however, the market will mature and the product or service will become a Cash Cow. These are market leaders with a lot of stability but little additional growth because they are at the end of their life cycles.

There are many problems with the framework at an operational level, centring around measurement of the elements on the two axes; for example, defining the market a firm is in so that you can measure market share or market growth. You can use just one factor on each axis or, indeed, a number of them weighted appropriately using some sort of simple scale. Nevertheless the problem of measurement remains.

High
STAR PROBLEM CHILD

Market attractiveness
Measures:
- Size
- Growth
- Profitability
- Level of price
- Degree of competition
- Customer loyalty
- Reliability

INTRODUCTION

GROWTH

FAILURE

MATURITY DECLINE

Low
CASH COW DOG

High Low

Market strength
Measures:
- Market share
- Reputation and image
- Base of loyal customers
- Technical expertise
- Production or delivery expertise

Figure 11.2 The Boston matrix

Case with question

Heineken

Heineken is Europe's largest brewer and is second only to the US brewer Anheuser-Busch world-wide. The brand is recognized around the world. However, its dominant market position, particularly in Europe where 40% of the world's beers are consumed, is maintained by actually having a portfolio of brands that allow it to adjust its marketing mix to suit the tastes and needs of local markets. It also allows the company to create the necessary distribution network and achieve high levels of economies of scale in production. Heineken typically has three core brands in each European country:

- A local brand aimed at the largest market segment, offered at a competitive price. In France it has '33', in Spain it has Aguila Pilsner and in Italy it has Dreher.
- A brand aimed at the upper end of the market such as Amstel or the locally produced Aguila Master in Spain.
- The premium Heineken brand itself where every effort is made to maintain quality and brand integrity. In the UK the product itself has been developed (called product expansion) into Heineken Export Strength, a stronger version more like the usual Heineken found throughout the rest of Europe.

Up-to-date information on Heineken can be found on their website: www.heineken.com

Question
Why does Heineken opt for a mix of internationally known brands alongside local beers?

The Boston matrix is therefore probably best used as a loose conceptual framework that helps clarify complexity. Treated with caution, as we shall see, it can be extremely valuable. In a complex world, anything that simplifies complexity and therefore helps our understanding must be of value.

Portfolio strategies

Among other things, the Boston matrix allows us to make some broad generalizations about marketing strategy for product/service offerings in the different quadrants. These are shown in Figure 11.3. If you can place the product/market offering within its life cycle on the matrix, these would be the elements of marketing strategy you would, a priori, expect to see. But remember that whilst this framework reflects product life cycles, it does not reflect Porter's generic marketing strategies, which need to be superimposed on them. However, as a product nears the end of its life cycle, and becomes a cash cow, it is more likely to be on its way to becoming a commodity and therefore having to sell on price.

	High	STAR	PROBLEM CHILD
		Objective Invest for growth ● Penetrate market ● Expand geographically ● Sell and promote aggressively ● Differentiate ● Promote brand, if possible ● Accept moderate short-term profits ● Extend product range	**Objective** Develop opportunities ● Be critical of prospects ● Invest selectively in products or services ● Specialize in strengths ● Shore up weaknesses
Market attractiveness		**Objective** Maintain market position and manage for earnings ● Maintain market position with successful products or services ● Prune less successful ones in range ● Differentiate ● Promote brand, if possible ● Stabilize prices, unless temporary aggressive pricing is required in the face of competition	**Objective** Either kill off or maintain and monitor carefully ● Minimize expenditure ● Improve productivity ● Maximize cash flow ● Live with declining sales until the best time to kill off product
	Low	CASH COW	DOG

High   **Market strength**   Low

Figure 11.3 The Boston matrix – strategy implications

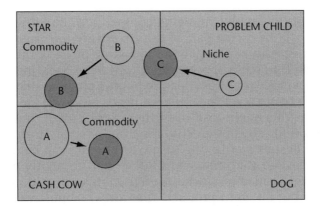

Figure 11.4 Boston matrix for a hypothetical company

The Boston matrix also allows us to present complex information more understandably, particularly when linked to forecasting future market positions and strategies involved in getting there. For example, Figure 11.4 represents a hypothetical three product portfolio for a company. The size of each circle is proportionate to the turnover each achieves. The lighter circles represent the present product positions, the darker circles represent the positions projected in five years time. The portfolio looks balanced and the diagram can be used to explain the strategies that are in place to move the products to where they are planned to be. Again, one essential added complexity is the generic marketing strategies. If products A and B are commodities, selling mainly on price, with low margin under intense pressure, it has implications not only for strategy but also for the cash flow available to invest in product C, particularly if this is a niche market product needing heavy investment.

Managing the product life cycle

Product innovation is not just about entirely new product/market offerings. Every product has a life cycle and that cycle can be managed in such a way as to expand and extend it and grow the market. Early adopters are the customers characterized as buying products in the growth phase of the life cycle. This is the point when the company can start *expanding* the product offering and start meeting the needs of selected market segments in order to counter the threat of competition moving in. Expanding the offering means developing product variations. So, for example, a car manufacturer might start offering sports or estate variants or a soft drink manufacturer might start to offer new flavours for a successful brand. The original product might also be modified in terms of quality, function or style so as to address any weaknesses or omissions in it. In many cases service levels will be improved.

At the same time the company might want to try to find new distribution channels so that more customers gain exposure to the product. Sometimes they move from a selective distribution network to a more intensive network. Associated with this is a more aggressive promotion and pricing strategy that encourages further market penetration ahead of the rapidly emerging competition. Building the brand is important and this will be a vital part of the advertising message.

Further growth may even be possible in the mature phase of the life cycle. In many cases a mature market presents opportunities to start segmenting the market and tailoring the product range that was expanded in the previous phase through product *modification*, so as to better meet the different needs of the different market segments that purchase them. This might lead to further expansion of the range and further product modification in terms of quality, function or style. In this way, using the terminology of the Boston matrix, the cash cow product can be 're-invented' to become a series of smaller star products, all of which are highly profitable.

Another technique is called product *extension*. In this way a successful brand can be extended to similar but different products that might be purchased by the same customers. In this way a number of chocolate bar manufacturers, such as Mars, successfully extended their brand into ice cream. The key to success here is having a strong brand, one that actually means something to customers, and with values that can be extended onto the other products. Thus Timberland, a company well known for producing durable outdoor footwear, extended its product range to include durable outdoor clothing. Many so-called new products are in fact line extensions. This strategy is generally a less expensive and lower-risk alternative for firms seeking to increase sales. The cash cow product can therefore also be 're-invented' to become a series of smaller problem children. However, these will face all the challenges of a problem child and may face stiff competition from existing companies in the market. Risk is, however, mitigated compared to a completely new product launch because of customer loyalty to the brand.

Product modification, extension and expansion opportunities can be represented in the Boston matrix. Again this is a useful visual aid to understanding strategy options. An example of this is shown in Figure 11.5.

 Figure 11.5 Product life cycle management

Case with questions

Barbie® and Mattel Corporation

'I'm a blonde bimbo girl, in a fantasy world . . . Life in plastic. It's fantastic.' (*Aqua*)

Barbie was born in 1959 but she has never aged because she is a doll. To date over 1 billion Barbies have been sold by the US company that own her – **Mattel Corporation**. Ruth Handler, who founded the company along with her husband, Elliot, modelled the doll on an 11½ inch plastic German toy called Lilli sold to adult men. She named the adapted doll after her daughter, Barbara. It is estimated that the average girl aged between 3 and 11 in the USA owns 10 Barbies, in Britain or Italy she owns 7 and in France or Germany she owns 5. With annual sales of over $1.6 billion, it is little wonder that the Barbie brand is valued at some $2 billion – making it the most valuable toy brand in the world. But how has this plastic doll endured for so long in an industry notorious for its susceptibility to fickleness and fashion? Surely it must have come to the end of its life cycle? The answer lies in innovative marketing and product extension.

When originally introduced into the market Barbie was competing with dolls that were based on babies and designed to be cradled and cared for. By way of contrast, Barbie, with her adult looks, exaggerated female figure normally with blonde hair and pouting lips, was seen as adult and independent – a child of 'liberated' times, one that could become anything or anyone the child wanted. But Mattel describe Barbie as a 'lifestyle, not just a toy . . . a fashion statement, a way of life'. Barbie was not only innovative, it was intended to be more than just a doll.

Every year Mattel devises some 150 different Barbie dolls and 120 new outfits. She has always been trendy and continues to re-invent herself. She was a 'mod' in the 1960s and a hippie in the 1970s. Her hair style has changed from ponytail, bubble-cut, page boy, swirl to side-part flip. She has had various roles in life – from holidaying in Malibu, to being an astronaut, soldier, air force pilot, surgeon, vet, doctor, dentist, engineer, fire-fighter, diplomat, fashion model, Olympic athlete, skier, scuba diver, ball player, TV news reporter, aerobics instructor, rock star, rap musician to presidential candidate. Each role has numerous accessories to go with it – from cars to horse and carriage, from jewellery box to lunch box – and including a partner called Ken. Dressing and undressing, grooming and making-up is what Barbie is made for. You can even buy a 'Make-me-pretty talking styling head' play set. And Mattel has worked hard to generate brand extension – more add-ons to the basic Barbie doll. The 2002/03 Rapunzel Barbie came with a handsome prince not to mention a computer-animated video and 14 product tie-ins. By 2006 the company had produced the sixth Barbie movie, *The 12 Dancing Princesses*, each accompanied by special dolls. By wearing a motion-sensor bracelet and shoe clip, the latest *Let's Dance Barbie!* allows the doll to follow a child's dance steps. A previous video based on Barbie in the Nutcracker grossed $150 million in sales, including associated products. In addition, Mattel license production of hundreds of different Barbie products: including make-up, pyjamas, bed clothes, furniture and wallpapers.

Mattel also continue to segment the market – trying to find new markets to sell the doll and its accessories to. The product extensions attempt this. But selling beyond the basic market, for example to older girls, is problematic. The main problem is that 'age compression' – girls getting older sooner – means that it is increasingly hard to hang on to the basic market, let alone trying to extend it. One recent variation called *My Scene* attempts to sell three Barbie

➡

Case with questions continued

Barbie® and Mattel Corporation

variants, with an older, more 'hip' look, together with perfume, cosmetics and music to this older group. This doll has a movable face feature that allows girls to create expressions on the doll's face like frowns, pouts, smirks and smiles.

Over the years Barbie has become a cult. There are Barbie conventions, fan clubs, magazines, websites and exhibitions. She is seen by many as the ideal vision of an American woman. In 1976 the USA included Barbie in the bicentennial time capsule. There are sociology courses in the USA based upon her, speculating on this image and what it implies. Mattel has cultivated these images. It has also worked hard at defending Barbie's image (or reputation). In 1997 the company prosecuted (unsuccessfully) the pop group Aqua who produced the satirical song 'Barbie Girl', some of whose lyrics are reproduced at the head of this case. Nevertheless, Barbie seems now to have become something of a gay icon. Whether gay or not, collectors have been known to pay up to $10,000 for a vintage model. The question is whether, in a changing world, young girls will continue to want the Barbie fantasy world.

The problem remains that Barbie is getting old and must be nearing the end of her product life cycle. Sales peaked at $1.8 million in 1997. Since then they have fallen continuously every year. World-wide sales remained 'flat' in 2006, and this included a 1% benefit from changes in currency exchange rates. So the question is how long can innovations sustain Barbie? And how much longer can life stay fantastic?

Up-to-date information on the Mattel Corporation can be found on their website: www.mattel.com

Questions
1. Why has Barbie been so successful?
2. Barbie is hardly a high-tech product, but has Mattel been innovative in how it has developed the product and extended its life cycle?
3. What are the lessons for product innovation?

Financial implications of the product portfolio

The concept of product portfolios and the need to manage each product/market offering differently has a number of implications for corporate entrepreneurship. The first relates to the cash flow likely to be generated by product/market offerings in each of the different quadrants of the Boston matrix (Guiltinan and Paul, 1982). This is shown in Figure 11.6.

The problem child consumes cash for development and promotional costs at a rate of knots, without generating much cash by way of revenues. The star might start to generate revenues but will still be facing high costs, particularly in marketing to establish its market position against new entry competitors. It is therefore likely to be cash neutral. Only as a cash cow are revenues likely to outstrip costs and cash flow likely to be positive. There are two kinds of dogs. One is a cash dog that covers its costs and might be worth keeping, for example if it brings in customers for other

STAR		PROBLEM CHILD	
Revenue	+ + +	Revenue	+
Expenditure	– – –	Expenditure	– – –
Cash flow	neutral	Cash flow	negative
Revenue	+ + +	Revenue	+
Expenditure	–	Expenditure	–
Cash flow	positive	Cash flow	neutral
CASH COW			DOG

Figure 11.6   Cash flow implications of the Boston matrix

products or services or it shares overheads. The other is the genuine dog which is losing money – both in cash flow and profit terms – and should be scrapped. It is from this model that phrases like 'shoot the dog', 'invest in stars' and 'milk the cow' came.

Ideally entrepreneurial companies need a balanced portfolio of product/service offerings so that the surplus cash from cash cows can be used to invest in the problem children. These funds can be used almost as venture capital to invest, selectively, in new products and services. This ideal firm is self-financing. The problem arises with an unbalanced portfolio. If the entrepreneurial firm has too many problem children and stars in its portfolio (too many good, new ideas) then it will require cash flow injections which will only be forthcoming if it can either borrow the capital – and that largely depends on the strength of the balance sheet – or raise more equity finance. The challenge is to develop and then effectively manage a balanced portfolio using the different structures available.

It must be remembered that cash flow and profit are quite different concepts that should never be confused. Profit is a measure of the increase in all assets including, but not exclusively, cash. It measures increases in long-term value using what accountants call the 'accrual concept' to match costs with revenues. Cash flow, however, is an immediate, short-term concept. It relates to the cash in your pocket – your ability to pay a bill now, from the cash you have available. You can have a profitable product or even company that has negative cash flow. For example, you might have to make high levels of capital investments before you can produce, let alone sell, a product. Similarly customers might be slow to pay for the highly profitable products they buy. Profit is a longer-term measure of successful asset accumulation. Cash flow is a short-term measure that reflects the firm's ability to survive.

The ABC Sales/Contribution analysis measures success in terms of the profitability of a product in relationship to its sales within the overall product portfolio. High sales and high contribution are the ideal combination. ABC analysis helps identify those products that are of longer-term value to the company – really successful products. An example is shown in Figure 11.7. Sales are measured on the vertical axis and contribution on the horizontal axis. (Contribution is the difference between sales price and variable cost. Total contribution is the difference between total sales or

Figure 11.7 ABC analysis contribution chart

turnover and total variable cost. Contribution margin expresses both of these in percentage terms to the base of sales price or total sales.) The 45° diagonal line from bottom left to top right is the optimum, but of course most products will fall on either side. Class 'A' products are the ideal. They have high sales and make a large contribution to the firm. Class 'B' are less attractive and class 'C' least attractive.

This analysis highlights attractive products – where contribution and sales are high – but it can also be used to identify attractive customers or markets. If sales are low but contribution is high, it shows where a sales push, even if margins are eroded, would yield the greatest reward. Similarly it identifies products, customers or markets where sales are high but contribution is low. Cash flow may be good, but contribution and hence profitability are not helped. Cash flow and profitability measure different things – like a rev. meter and speedometer on a car. Ideally, but rarely, they go hand in hand. When they are out of phase the management of the portfolio is a question of judgement. You need profit for long-term return and growth, but you need sufficient cash flow for survival. If cash flow is insufficient you need to be able to borrow to tide you over the short-term problem.

Implications for management

The product life cycle has some important implications for management. Entrepreneurial skills are most valued in the problem child phase. Once the product is in its mature phase it needs to be managed as a cash cow – milked for all the cash flow it can generate. That means high levels of efficiency are needed, probably achieved through a high degree of control and direction. Whilst the problem child is best managed by an entrepreneur, the cash cow is best managed by an accountant. And, if we are to characterize the management discipline needed to manage the star, it would probably be marketing. In other words, as the product works its way through its life cycle the approach to management needs to change. In a one-product company this presents a challenging but manageable problem. In a multi-product firm the problem is more complex. Do you segregate problem children into different, separate organizations? Do you set them up as individual organizations? Perhaps you should group them together to make the most of entrepreneurial expertise? And what happens as they progress through their life cycle? Do you transfer them to different organizations, delineated not by their product specification but by the stage they are at in their life cycle and the managerial style therefore required? And at what point do you make the transfer?

Earlier chapters have discussed the problem of 'balance' in many of the dimensions of management. That balance has been characterized as needing the shift between the administrative and the entrepreneurial firm. The reality is that an administrative firm is better suited to managing mature products at the end of their life cycle – cash cows – and an entrepreneurial firm is better suited to managing new products at the beginning of their life cycle – problem children. But the problem is that most firms have a balanced portfolio of different products or services. The challenge, therefore, is to combine both styles within an organization that can still be described as entrepreneurial. And there is no prescriptive answer to how this is done – particularly as to how the balance is shifted as the product matures or how a portfolio of different products can best be combined. The umbrella organization needs to remain entrepreneurial, but it needs to use all the levers of management – leadership, structure, culture and strategy – to ensure that it does so.

Management is an art not a science, so there are no prescriptive solutions to these problems. But there are some clues. As we have seen, size matters and new initiatives or ventures are better off – for all sorts of reasons – started small. Whichever mechanism we select from Chapter 8, the initiative is better managed as a separate organization (or organization within an organization) and kept lean, fit and entrepreneurial in every sense. And this generalization ignores the tremendous challenge of generating ideas for new initiatives that are not stifled before birth.

Whether they combine at some later stage depends on the synergy that might be obtained from combining them. 3M have different divisions into which new ventures are expected to be merged. Divisions might comprise different operating units or companies, each with product/market profiles that are different in significant ways but can be combined in some overriding way. New products might spawn new companies or be swallowed up into existing operating units or companies. Xerox has so many completely different new ventures that it is far more relaxed about spinning out completely different companies. The point is that there is unlikely to be any synergy offered through combining them. Indeed, in these circumstances completely spinning off, and even selling off, subsidiaries that are not core to the business may be an appropriate option. There is no prescriptive blueprint. What is more, *when* these changes take place is an even more complex judgement that depends on individuals as well as products, markets and competitors combined with an unimaginable array of external factors, many of which will be outside the control of the company.

The real problem, however, is with the umbrella organization – head office, parent company, whatever it is called. Unless it is essentially entrepreneurial this diversity will just not happen. But this means that its approach to management of the different parts of the organization must be very different. It must be able to handle this heterogeneous approach to management, the very different styles of leadership that are necessary, deal with the apparent inconsistencies and handle confused shareholders that themselves need to be 'managed'. Essentially, however, it must be willing to delegate effective management within defined parameters. And again there are different approaches to this, each of which produce 'dominant cultures'. The BP example in Chapter 9 showed one approach – that of trying to maintain balance within each operating unit belonging to one organization. By way of contrast, the Virgin empire thrives on entirely separate organizations sharing the same culture and brand, but little else. There are infinitely many approaches to solving the challenge of corporate entrepreneurship, which is why it is so difficult to analyze how to meet it.

Corporate and industry life cycles

The stage a product is at in its life cycle therefore influences the marketing strategy for the product. We have already observed that the stage the company is at in its life also influences strategy. And companies also have life cycles that come to an end. They cannot count on longevity or continuity. Research conducted by McKinsey on more than 1000 companies in 15 industries is cited by Foster and Kaplan (2001) to prove this. They compared the original 1917 Forbes magazine list of the top 100 US companies (by size of assets) to a comparable list of companies published in 1987. They found that 61 of the top 100 had ceased to exist and, of the remainder, only 18 remained in the top 100. These included Kodak, DuPont, General Electric, General Motors and Procter & Gamble. However, of these 18, only two – Kodak and General Electric – had outperformed the stock market. The group as a whole made results that were 20% below the market's compound annual growth rate of 7.5% over those 70 years. They also looked at Standard & Poor's 500 list in 1957 and compared it to the 1997 list. Only 74 (37%) survived the 40 years and only 12 (6%) outperformed the index over the period. Endurance or longevity, as such, bears no relationship to performance. The authors conclude: 'Managing for survival, even among the best and most revered corporations, does not guarantee strong, long-term performance. In fact quite the opposite is true ... Unless companies open up their decision-making processes, relax conventional notions of control, and change at the pace and scale of the market, their performances will be drawn into an entropic slide to mediocrity.'

The authors' solution to this problem is 'creative destruction' – strategies of discontinuity and transformation. They, like us, argue that control processes themselves can deaden the company to the vital and constant need for change. They want to abandon outdated, ingrown structures and rules and adopt new decision-making processes, control systems and mental models. However, they argue against incremental change in favour of 'transformational strategies' of continually creating new businesses and selling off or closing down divisions where growth is slowing.

It has also been argued (Deans et al., 2003) that the stage an industry is at in its life cycle should also be a determinant of strategy. They claim that an industry has four distinct phases. In the first there is little or no market concentration as start-ups, spin-offs, firms in deregulated industries and smaller companies typically compete in this phase. Concentration, measured by the combined market share of the three biggest companies, is low – less than 20%. This phase typically lasts at least five years. The second phase is the 'scale phase' where size begins to matter. Leading companies start to merge and concentration increases to 30–45%. In the third phase the authors claim that companies extend their core business, eliminating secondary operations or exchanging them with other firms for assets closer to their core business.

Phase 1	Phase 2	Phase 3	Phase 4
Low concentration	30–45% concentration	70% concentration	90% concentration
Examples: railways, telecoms, utilities, insurance	Examples: chemicals, drugs, pulp and paper, fast foods, hotels, breweries	Examples: steel, toys, tyres	Examples: tobacco, automobiles

 Figure 11.8 Industry life cycles and acquisitions and mergers

Concentration in this phase is almost 70%. The final phase sees concentration reaching 90% and sees the large companies forming alliances in order to boost growth. This is shown in Figure 11.8. The authors claim that the main factor determining corporate survival and success is the speed with which the company actively moves towards the final phase – 'the endgame curve' – through a series of mergers and acquisitions. We shall deal with each of these strategies in the next chapter. It is by no means clear that they are always successful.

Case with questions

Cadbury

In 2007 Cadbury Schweppes announced its intention to either sell off or demerge its Americas Beverages operation because it thought that shareholder value would be enhanced if it operated as focused and independent businesses.

Cadbury had merged with Schweppes in 1969 to form the international confectioner and fizzy drinks giant **Cadbury Schweppes**. Both companies have a long history. Cadbury has come a long way from its days as a chocolate manufacturing family firm with Quaker values and ideals. The original shop was opened in 1824 selling chocolate as a virtuous alternative to alcohol but the company went on to become a large-scale manufacturer of chocolate based at the now legendary Bournville factory, built in 1879, and its picturesque village with its red-brick terraces, cottages, duck ponds and wide open parks. Over the next 100 years it developed the products that have become so familiar: *Dairy Milk* in 1905, *Milk Tray* in 1915, *Flake* in 1920, *Creme Egg* in 1923 and *Roses* in 1938. Jean Jacob Schweppe, a German, invented a system for making carbonated water in 1783 and opened a factory in London in 1790. Ownership changed in 1834 and the company started making flavoured soda drinks like lemonade. It produced Ginger Ale and the famous Tonic Water in 1870, popular in India because the quinine helped prevent malaria.

➡

Case with questions continued

Cadbury

Cadbury Schweppes' growth exceeds market trends – first half results for 2007 showed revenue growth at +6%. This continuing growth came from three sources: organic growth, mainly through finding new channels of distribution; acquisition of new brands; efficiency saving (profit only) as ageing products are produced at a lower cost. By 2007 most of Cadbury Schweppes' core products were at the mature stage of their life cycle and sales were therefore stagnant, so it had to search for ever more inventive ways of achieving the ambitious growth targets it set itself. However, these core areas were also hugely cash generative, giving the company between £300 and £400 million a year. So how did it use this cash surplus to generate continuing growth?

To start with, the company was constantly looking for new markets for its products, but since most of these products already sell around the world, it has now developed a two-pronged growth strategy, both reliant upon the company's strong cash flow. Because about 70% of its products are bought on impulse, it is looking for new channels of distribution so as to encourage sales, or 'indulgence opportunities' as they are called. Chocolate bars and drinks are now sold anywhere from petrol stations to off-licences. Vending machines selling them can be found anywhere from factory floors to tube stations. The company wants more products to be sold in restaurants and pubs.

The second strand to the company's strategy was buying into other related high growth segments, where the company can capitalize on its existing distribution chains or use new distribution chains to sell more of its existing products. The company has followed an acquisitions strategy for many years. In 1986 it bought *Typhoo Tea*, *Kenco Coffee* and *Canada Dry* and *Sunkist* soft drinks. In 1989 it bought *Crush* soft drink and *Bassett* and *Trebor* in the UK. The best selling US brands, *Dr Pepper* and *7UP*, were purchased in 1995. The company has also diversified out of fizzy drinks, which in 1998 accounted for 85% of the important US market, with the acquisition of brands like *Snapple*, *Hawaiian Punch* and *Nantucket Juices*. By 2002 fizzy drinks accounted for only 50% of drink sales. The latest target for acquisitions is the fast growing chewing gum market. In 2000 it bought *Hollywood*, the French gum maker, and *Dandy*, the Danish gum maker. In 2002 Cadbury purchased the US company Adams from Pfizer. Adams' brands include *Halls*, *Trident*, *Dentyne*, *Bubbas*, *Clorets*, *Chiclets* and *Certs*. It also purchased *Intergum* in Turkey and *Kandia-Excelent* in Romania. By 2007 gum and other 'better for you' products accounted for some 30% of confectionery sales. But there have been other confectionery acquisitions such as Green & Black's in 2005. These acquisitions make Cadbury the market leader in non-chocolate confectionery, including gum and 'functional' products such as sore-throat remedies, and will give it a foothold in markets such as Japan and Latin America.

However the beverages market has proved tough despite the fact that Cadbury Schweppes' portfolio of beverage products are sold around the world and many are international brands, such as *Dr Pepper* and *7UP*. In the late 1990s the company decided to focus on strong regional beverages – in particular in the Americas and Australia. In 1999 it sold off its beverage businesses in about 160 countries and in 2006 it concluded the sale of its European beverages business in order to focus on the Americas. North America is the largest market for its drinks. But distribution here is complex and problematic. Coca-Cola (40% of market), Pepsi (30%) and Cadbury Schweppes (20%) all use franchises to manufacture, bottle and distribute their products within geographic areas. However, Cadbury Schweppes originally had no dedicated distribution system of its own and channelled 20% of its product through those of Coca-Cola, 30% through those of Pepsi and 50% through independent bottlers. Relationships eventually broke down to such an extent that Cadbury Schweppes sued Pepsi, alleging that the company tried to block the distribution of its products to a large US restaurant chain. As a result Cadbury Schweppes decided to distribute all of its products through the independent bottlers, but at the same time took shareholdings in five of them and merged them to form the Dr Pepper/Seven UP Bottling Group, in which it now has a 40% stake. In this way it took more control over its distribution in the USA, presenting more consumers with 'indulgence opportunities'. In Australia the company bought the Pepsi Lion Nation joint venture to secure its distribution channels.

In 2007 Cadbury Schweppes decided to focus on its strength. It was claiming to be 'the leading global confectionery company with unrivalled product and geographic reach'. Cadbury is in fact the world's largest confectionery business with a 10% share of the global market and has number one or two positions in nearly half the top 50 confectionery markets, with strong brands and positions in the markets of chocolate, gum and candy. It also generates 30% of its sales from new 'emerging' markets. Confectionery revenues grew by over 5%, on average, between 2004 and 2007 and beverages had become the 'poor sister' in the relationship. This section of the business has a separate management structure but delivers growth below the targets for the company.

So what will the future hold for the new Cadbury plc? As we have seen, it will start life as a huge business – with sales of nearly £5 billion. The company's goal is to maintain its market leadership position, and to leverage its scale and advantaged positions to maximize growth and returns. The stated 'new priorities' are:

- To drive growth through concentration on 'fewer, faster, bigger, better' participation and innovation, supported by its global category structure;
- To drive cost and efficiency gains to achieve margin goals;
- To continue to invest in capabilities to support its growth and efficiency agendas.

The question, of course, is what this means in terms of strategies. The company still has what we might see as a mature product portfolio, albeit, in a global leadership position and in emerging markets where confectionery is not a 'mature product'.

Up-to-date information on Cadbury Schweppes can be found on their website: www.cadburyschweppes.com

Questions
1. Why do you think it was decided to split the company in 2007, after almost 40 years? Is there any evidence that this decision was a good one?
2. Are all of Cadbury's products at the mature stage in their life cycle in each of their markets? Give examples.
3. What do Cadbury's new goals and priorities mean? What do you think of them?
4. What strategies do you think will support these goals and priorities?
5. Do you think these strategies will translate into sales growth? Will they translate into profit growth?

Summary

Products and services face a predictable life cycle that has implications for marketing strategy at different phases. Most firms, like **Heineken** and **Cadbury Schweppes**, have a range of products and services at different stages of their life cycle. These can be represented in a Boston matrix – a loose conceptual framework that helps clarify the complexity of the portfolio. The two axes of the matrix represent market attractiveness and market strength. Products at different points in the matrix have different strategic imperatives and different marketing strategies.

You can manage the product life cycle through product modification, expansion and extension. By using these strategies, the **Barbie** doll has been around for over 40 years.

The Boston matrix has cash-flow implications; problem children use cash, stars are cash-neutral, generating but also using large amounts, and cash cows generate cash. Only when the portfolio is balanced will cash flow be stable. However, cash flow is not the same as profitability. The ABC analysis allows you to analyze product in terms of sales and contribution – those with high levels of both are very attractive (class A products). But equally it can be used to adjust other elements of the marketing mix, such as price, so as to maximize sales.

Problem children are best managed by entrepreneurs – or entrepreneurial firms – cash cows by accountants – or administrative firms. Where a business has a balanced portfolio of product, the challenge is to find a form of organization that allows both to flourish. There are many different approaches to this.

Companies and industries also have life cycles. Companies do not last forever and they must plan for their own replacement. Similarly industries grow, mature and decline, and by the maturity phase a company should have become a dominant player in the market – perhaps through mergers, acquisitions and alliances – so that it can maximize its returns.

Cadbury Schweppes have been past masters of this strategy which, together with expansion into emergent markets where their mature products were new, has yielded them good financial results. However, by 2007 realizing that they were failing to dominate the drinks market, they have decided to focus on confectionery.

Essays and discussion topics

1. Some products – basic necessities such as food and water – do not have a life cycle. Discuss.
2. How useful are the labels of 'innovators', 'early adopters', late adopters' and 'laggards' to customers at different stages of the life cycle?
3. In practical terms it is impossible to find out where a product is at in its life cycle. Discuss.
4. What is the relationship between marketing mix and the product life cycle?
5. How useful is the Boston matrix?
6. How would you go about creating a scale for each axis of the Boston matrix that reflects a range of factors? Give a practical example.
7. In what circumstances might you not want to 'shoot a dog'?
8. Give some examples of product expansions and extensions.
9. Cash flow is not the same as profit. Discuss.
10. Contribution is not the same as profit. Discuss.
11. Can a problem child be profitable? Why?
12. Is a star always likely to be a 'class A' product? Explain.

13. In what circumstances might you have a cash cow that is unprofitable? What would you do with it?
14. If management is an art, there is no point in studying it. Discuss.
15. Does there always have to be one dominant culture within an organization?
16. What is the relationship between life cycles and leadership style?
17. What is the relationship between life cycles and culture?
18. What is the relationship between life cycles and organizational structures?
19. How can a company become a dominant market force by the mature stage of its product life cycle, other than through mergers and acquisitions?
20. Do you see any potential dangers in following an aggressive strategy of merger and acquisition?
21. What is 'creative destruction'? Is it the same as the term 'deconstruction', used in Chapter 7?
22. If most firms are destined to fail, we cannot have learned anything about the management of business. Discuss.

Exercises and assignments

1. Select a well-known product that is now in the mature phase of its life cycle and chart how the marketing strategy has changed over that life cycle.
2. For your University, College or Department, analyze the course portfolio using the Boston matrix. What are your conclusions?
3. For a selected company, analyze the product portfolio using the Boston matrix. What are your conclusions?
4. Select a mature industry. Research the major three companies in this industry and find out how they gained their market dominance.

References

Deans, G., Zeisel, S. and Kroeger, F. (2003) *Winning the Merger End Game*, New York: McGraw-Hill.

Foster, R. and Kaplan, S. (2001) *Creative Destruction: Why Companies that are Built to Last Underperform the Stock Market*, New York: Doubleday/Currency.

Guiltinan, J. P. and Paul, G. W. (1982) *Marketing Management: Strategies and Programs*, New York: McGraw-Hill.

Rogers, E. M. (1962) *Diffusion of Innovation*, New York: Free Press.

Tellis, G. J., Stremersch, S. and Yin, E. (2003) 'The International Takeoff of New Products: The Role of Economics, Culture, and Country Innovativeness', *Marketing Science*, 22(2).

12

Developing Strategies for Growth

Contents

- Opportunities for growth
- Market penetration
- Market development
- Product/service development
- Diversification
- Mergers and acquisitions
- Sustainability and corporate social responsibility
- Sustaining growth
- Summary

Opportunities for growth

The dominant goal of the entrepreneurial firm is likely to be growth. As we have seen, understanding what has made the business successful in the past – in particular what makes it unique and what adds value for the customer – is a prerequisite for moving forward. In general terms, to achieve growth a company should:

- build on its strengths and core competencies;
- shore up its weaknesses;
- develop a marketing strategy for each product/market offering and the opportunity it presents that reflects the appropriate generic marketing strategy and the stage a product/market offering is at in its life cycle;

all placed in the context of its portfolio of product/market offerings.

As we saw in Chapter 10, research tells us that the strategy with the best chance of generating the highest profits is to differentiate with the aim of dominating that market niche – and to do this effectively and quickly – and to continue to innovate based on that differential advantage. Although firms following other strategies do, of course, succeed, the importance of this research cannot be overemphasized. Business, like life, is about playing the odds. You ignore them at your peril.

The unique elements of the differentiation strategy are likely to be based on distinctive capabilities – like the entrepreneurial architecture – that, applied to a relevant market, becomes a competitive advantage. This will become the firm's core market, the one in which it has a distinct advantage by adding the greatest value for its customers. A focus on core business was emphasized in the 1980s (Abell, 1980) and popularized by Peters and Waterman (1982) as 'sticking to the knitting'. However, core competencies may be relevant to other markets and, even if they are not directly relevant, can often be leveraged by entering other markets in which, although the firm may not have the same distinctive competitive advantage, it can use economies of scale or its channels of distribution to gain market share.

Whilst the objective of entrepreneurial strategy is growth, its essence is that it is opportunity driven. Stevenson and Gumpert (1985) describe the entrepreneur as 'constantly attuned to the environmental changes that may suggest a favourable chance.' However, in order to start understanding the opportunities for growth, there is one further tool that helps analyze in a systematic fashion how growth can be achieved. It is called the Product/Market matrix, was originally devised by Igor Ansoff (1968) and shown in Figure 12.1. This simple conceptual framework uses existing/new products on one axis and existing/new markets on the other. It then goes on to explore the options within the four quadrants of the matrix and how the options might be achieved.

Like all useful business frameworks it is attractively simple and intuitively logical. To achieve growth a company has four options:

1. Market penetration
2. Product development
3. Market development
4 Diversification.

Figure 12.1 The product/market matrix

Market penetration (quadrant 1)

Market penetration involves selling more of the same product/service to the same market – just selling more to existing customers. If the firm has strong relationships with its existing customers this may be possible. It can also involve finding new customers from the same market segment. Cadbury Schweppes achieve this by constantly improving their channels of distribution and giving customers more 'indulgence opportunities' for their impulse-buy products. Using the Boston matrix, this is how you move from 'problem child' to 'star'. The best way of finding new customers is to understand existing customers – assuming that they are happy with the product/service offering – and try to find more of the same. This involves understanding why they buy and being able to describe the customers' common characteristics – effectively describing the market segment(s) buying the product or service. In a growth market there may be ample opportunity to achieve further growth in this way. Figures 11.1 and 11.3 detailed some ways this can be achieved. The chapter underlined the importance of gaining market dominance as quickly as possible in these circumstances. However, the ease with which a business can pursue this policy will depend on the nature of the market and the position of competitors. In a static or declining market it is much more difficult to pursue this option, unless competitors are complacent or are leaving the market. To attract customers from an established competitor, they must be convinced that the alternative product or service offers greater value, and that might involve price reductions – not always an attractive strategy.

Market penetration is an essential part of gaining market dominance. However, once the market is mature there is unlikely to be significant sales growth. Consolidation should generate profit growth, but this strategy inherently starts to go against the entrepreneurial grain and is not one that an entrepreneurial firm is designed or inclined to follow. Inevitably the entrepreneurial firm will start to look at the other quadrants of the matrix to achieve its aims.

For the sake of completeness it is worth considering two other strategies associated with this quadrant:

1. *Consolidation* This involves keeping the products/services and markets the same, but changing the way the firm operates so as to generate more profit. For example, niche markets are, by definition, limited in size and further expansion may threaten the niche. However, consolidation is often not a sensible option in a growing market as it leaves competitors free to take market share, which might then affect the firm's competitive cost base. In a mature market it is common for companies to place increasing emphasis on product quality, greater marketing activity such as further segmentation or reducing their cost base so as to create barriers to entry for new competitors. In a declining market, consolidation may involve cost reduction, volume reduction and ultimately selling off all or part of the business. An entrepreneurial firm is unlikely to favour a strategy of consolidation, except insofar as it forms part of a portfolio of strategies for different product/market opportunities.

2. *Withdrawal* An entrepreneurial firm might decide to withdraw from an area of activity if there are no further growth prospects, perhaps selling all or part of the business to capitalize on the growth so far. Richard Branson did this in 1982 when he sold his original business, Virgin Records, to concentrate on the airline business. It might also be just the right time to get a very good deal, for example because of consolidation in the industry. Withdrawal might be triggered, very simply, by the product or service offered by the firm coming to the end of its life cycle. In a declining market, when the firm has low market share and there is little chance of improvement, then a timely withdrawal may minimize future losses. Alternatively entry into the market might have been a mistake in the first place (using the Boston matrix terminology from the last chapter, the 'problem child' could not be turned into a 'star'), and the firm could not gain market share sufficiently quickly, so withdrawal is now the least worst option.

Case insight

Standard Chartered operates in over 50 countries and has 29,000 employees. It was formed in 1969 from the merger of two banks. The Chartered Bank, was founded by a Scot, James Wilson, in 1853 to finance trade across the British Empire. The Standard Bank was also founded by a Scot, John Paterson, in Port Elizabeth, South Africa in 1863. But in November 2001 the Chief Executive, Rana Talwar, was ousted from office after a dispute with the Chairman based upon his failing strategy for expansion. This involved an aggressive acquisition strategy that required the bank to raise increasing amounts of money from investors to buy up banks that were still reeling from the effects of the Asian currency crisis and it was not yielding any profit growth. Indeed its share price was so low that there were rumours of take-over.

The new Chief Executive, **Mervyn Davies**, reversed this strategy, pulling out of planned acquisitions and paying back money to shareholders. He returned to the basics of good strategy for an established business. The new strategy is one of internal growth – expanding by offering consumer services in countries where people are getting richer such as India and China. At the same time he acknowledged that customers are very price-sensitive and he therefore streamlined the back-office operations and shifted them to Channai in India and Kuala Lumpur ➡

Case insight

in Malaysia so as to minimize costs. In fact this has been so successful that these operations have become models for other banks thinking of transferring back-office operations offshore. The third leg of the strategy was to cut bad debts, although this was helped by the creation of credit-rating agencies in its major market of Hong Kong in the wake of a ballooning number of personal bankruptcies. Hong Kong remains the bank's biggest market, generating a third of its revenues. Other key areas include Singapore, Malaysia and Africa.

By 2003 Standard Chartered was generally thought to have turned the corner after a two-year period of extremely rapid change. It is listed on the Hong Kong stock exchange and in London, where it is in the top 25 firms measured by capitalization.

Market development (quadrant 2)

It is one thing to find new customers in a market that you are familiar with, but it is quite another to enter new markets, even when they are selling your existing products or services. Nevertheless, if a firm wants to grow it will have to seek out new markets at some stage. These might be new market segments or new geographical areas. In seeking new overseas markets the lowest-risk option is to seek out segments – or customers – that are similar to the ones the firm already sells to. Product *expansion* is essentially a strategy to seek out new markets for similar products, although it can also be a defensive strategy to counter competition.

One reason for finding new markets is to achieve economies of scale of production – particularly important if the product is perceived as a commodity and cost leadership is dependent upon achieving those economies. Another reason might also be that a company's key competency lies with the product, for example with capital goods like cars, and therefore the continued exploitation of the product by market development is the preferred route for expansion. Most capital goods companies follow this strategy – opening up new overseas markets as existing markets become saturated – because of the high cost of developing new products. By way of contrast, many service businesses such as accounting, insurance, advertising and banking have been pulled into overseas markets because their clients operate there. Finally, another reason to find new markets for a product or service might be simply that it is nearing the end of its life cycle in the existing market. This was the case with McDonald's and its entry into the East European markets.

Of vital importance in considering whether to enter a new market is its structure – the customers, suppliers, competitors – and the potential substitutes and barriers to entry. These determine the degree of competition and therefore the profitability likely to be achieved. Michael Porter (1985) developed a useful structural analysis of industries which he claims goes some way towards explaining the profitability of firms within it. He claims that five forces determine competitiveness in any industry. These are shown in Figure 12.2.

1. *The power of buyers.* This is determined by the relative size of buyers and their concentration. It is also influenced by the volumes they purchase, the information they have about competitors or substitutes, switch costs and their ability to

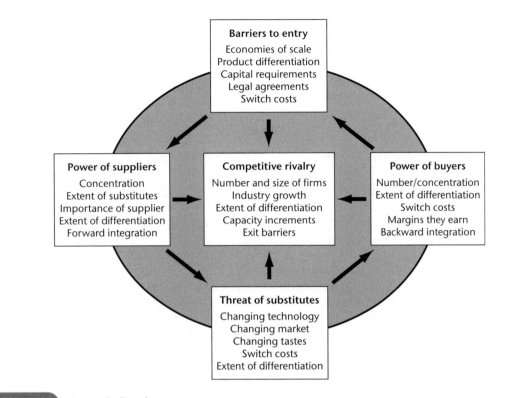

Figure 12.2 Porter's five forces

backward integrate. Switch costs are the costs of switching to another product. The extent to which the product they are buying is differentiated in some way also affects relative buying power. The greater the power of the buyers, the weaker the bargaining position of the firm selling to them. So, for example, if buyers are large firms, in concentrated industries, buying large volumes with good price information about a relatively undifferentiated product with low switch costs they will be in a strong position to keep prices low.

2. *The power of suppliers.* This is also determined by the relative size of firms and the other factors mentioned above. So, for example, if suppliers are large firms in concentrated industries, with well-differentiated products that are relatively important to the small firms buying them, then those small firms are in a weak position to keep prices, and therefore their costs, low.

3. *The threat of new entrants.* Barriers to entry keep out new entrants to an industry. These can arise because of legal protection (patents and so on), economies of scale, proprietary product differences, brand identity, access to distribution, government policy, switch costs, capital costs and so forth. For example, a firm whose product is protected by patent or copyright may feel that it is relatively safe from competition. The greater the possible threat of new entry to a market, the lower the bargaining power and control over price of the firm within it.

4. *The threat of substitutes.* This revolves around their relative price performance, switch costs and the propensity of the customer to switch, for example because of changes in tastes or fashion. The greater the threat of substitutes, the less the

ability of the firm to charge a high price. So, for example, a small firm selling a poorly-differentiated product in a price-sensitive, fashion market should find it difficult to charge a high price.

5. *Competitive rivalry in the industry.* The competitive rivalry of an industry will depend on the number and size of firms within it and their concentration, its newness and growth and therefore its attractiveness in terms of profit and value added together with intermittent overcapacity. Crucially important is the extent of product differentiation, brand identity and switch costs. The greater the competitive rivalry, the less the ability of the firm to charge a high price.

Porter claims that these five forces determine the strength of competition in the market – and therefore firm profitability. They are a function of industry structure – the underlying economic and technical characteristics of the industry. They can change over time but the analysis does emphasize the need to select industries carefully in the first place. The forces also provide a framework for predicting, a priori, the success or otherwise of the firm. For example, a small firm competing with many other small firms to sell a relatively undifferentiated product to a few large customers in an industry with few barriers to entry is unlikely to do well without some radical shifts in its marketing strategies.

Two further factors warrant consideration in deciding whether to enter a new market – entry and exit barriers. These are represented in the matrix in Figure 12.3. All things being equal, the most attractive market in terms of profitability is likely to be one with high entry barriers and low exit barriers – few firms can enter but poor performers can easily exit. With high entry barriers but high exit barriers, poor performers are forced to stay on, making the returns more risky as they fight for market share. Unfortunately, a firm seeking to enter these markets has to overcome the high entry barriers, whatever they be. For example, this could involve overcoming legal barriers or high investment costs. If entry barriers are low returns are likely to be low, but stable if exit barriers are low and unstable if exit barriers are high, and poor performers are forced to stay on if the market worsens.

Exporting is a form of market development. For many firms the easiest way to export is to find a distributor in the selected country who understands the local distribution channels and variations in customer needs. The distributor might

Source: Wilson, R. M. S. and Gilligan, C. (1997) *Strategic Marketing Management: Planning, Implementation and Control*, Oxford: Butterworth-Heinemann.

Figure 12.3   Entry and exit barriers, profitability and risk influence changes in the product or other elements of the marketing mix to suit local needs. The company might be expected to finance advertising and promotion itself and with no certainty of a profitable return. Finding a distributor can be difficult enough but if, for whatever reason, the distributor does not push the firm's products then there is little the firm can do other than change distributors, unless they are willing to take on the job of marketing in the country themselves – and that can be both expensive and risky. Cadbury Schweppes' problems with Pepsi stem from the compromises it made to distribute its drinks economically when it entered the US market. This situation was less than ideal, but it was a low-cost way of gaining entry to the market.

Another approach to penetrating an overseas market, particularly for a service, is to appoint a franchisee. Franchisees apply a fairly standard franchise format to the particular market in which they operate. Their market knowledge and dedication is vital if the market is to be effectively penetrated. If the franchise roll-out is successful they share in the success. To be effective, the firm and their franchisee or distributor must have a symbiotic relationship, one based upon mutual trust and with effective incentives to ensure success. Body Shop's rapid growth owes much to its successful global roll-out using a franchise format. In most countries a head franchisee was granted exclusive rights as user of the trade mark, distributor and, after an initial trial of running a few shops itself, the right to sub-franchise. In this way the firm built upon local market knowledge and minimized its risks. This model was not always followed because of the quality of the head franchisee. For example, the firm took back control of the franchise in France because the head franchisee was not delivering the volume of sales expected.

Case with questions

Royal Bank of Scotland

'Royal Bank of Scotland *are one of the top three banks in Europe. They are just very good at running businesses, with a high degree of entrepreneurial flair.'*
Anik Sen of Goldman Sachs (*The Times*, 21 July 2003)

Royal Bank of Scotland (RBS) is one of the oldest banks in the UK. It was founded in 1727 in Edinburgh, by Royal Charter, as the Royal Bank and opened its first branch in Glasgow in 1783. It developed a network of branches across Scotland in the nineteenth century but it was not until 1874 that it opened its first branch office in London. From the 1920s it grew by acquisition, swallowing Drummonds, William Deacon's Bank, Glyn, Mills and Co., and Child & Co., then merging with Edinburgh based National Commercial Bank of Scotland, which itself comprised the National Bank of Scotland and Commercial Bank of Scotland. At this stage it dominated 40% of Scotland's banking business.

In 1985 RBS merged with Williams & Glyn's to give it a presence in England and ownership of the banker to the Queen, Coutts. This was the first glimpse of the bank's entrepreneurial flair. It also set up Direct Line (the direct car insurance company) which went on quickly to become one of the dominant forces in direct insurance. Realizing it was very dependent on the UK market, RBS acquired Citizens Financial Group of Rhode Island, a small savings bank in the USA.

→

Case with questions continued

Royal Bank of Scotland

It also started to refocus on its core business of retail banking and started on a round of cost cutting. It realized that retail banking was becoming a commodity and, to compete on price, it had to achieve economies of scale that were just not available to it on a conventional banking model. Its answer in 1997 was to set up the UK's first online banking service. Not content with this it realized that other organizations were probably better at marketing banking services than the banks themselves and joined forces with a number of well-known brands such as Tesco, the supermarket, and Virgin One to offer online banking. RBS did the 'back-office' operations, all the time driving down costs because of economies of scale. However, it also chose not to enter the high street price war being waged by its bigger rivals. In 2000 RBS bought its far bigger rival, NatWest (which included Ulster Bank), in what was the biggest take-over in British banking history. Whereas RBS had just 650 branches, NatWest had 1650 and Ulster Bank a further 228 branches. As a result RBS underwent a large round of redundancies to further cut back its cost base – a realization of what the core strategy was for this part of the business.

Since 2000 the bank has been continuing its policy of organic growth and opportunistic but tactical acquisitions. It has grown the wholesale side of its banking operations – corporate lending, derivatives, foreign exchange and leasing. It is now the biggest banker in the UK in small business and corporate banking. Its US bank, Citizens, has also acquired the Mellon Bank's regional retail franchise, Medford Bancorp and Commonwealth Bancorp, increasing its geographical coverage in New England and making it the twentieth largest US bank measured by deposits. It has also purchased Santander Direkt, a Frankfurt-based credit card company in what is thought to be its first steps into mainland Europe. More recently RBS purchased Churchill Insurance, a direct competitor to Direct Line, and now intends to merge it with Direct Line. It is also thought to be interested in taking over former building societies so as to give it more exposure to mortgage (house lending) business as well as a savings bank.

Today RBS is an international bank making profits of £5.1 billion in the first half of 2007 (up 11% on the same period in 2006). In 2002 RBS made pre-tax profits of £4.7 billion – five years earlier they had been just £1 billion. Its entrepreneurial executive Chairman is **Sir George Mathewson**. He joined the bank after being head of the Scottish Development Agency and has been accused of running the bank like a venture capital company. His Chief Executive, Fred Goodwin, is one of the youngest among the FTSE 100 and also came from outside the company.

Questions
1. What are the main elements of the Royal Bank of Scotland's strategy?
2. Why has it used acquisition so much?
3. Explain each acquisition and the reasons behind it.
4. Why is scale of operation so important to it? Has this driven some elements of strategy?
5. Compare and contrast the strategies of Royal Bank of Scotland with those of Standard and Chartered (page 256). Are there any market-based explanations for the different approaches?
6. In 2003 Standard Chartered became the only UK-listed bank to be part of the consortium that aims to help Iraq to rebuild. Why might the bank have entered this risky market?

Product/service development (quadrant 3)

Product/service innovation is one of the key characteristics of entrepreneurial companies and one that is explored in greater detail in subsequent chapters. Ansoff's framework gets us to focus on the effect of product/service development in different markets, dealing first with the firm's existing market.

Product/service development can take a number of forms. Completely new products may be introduced into the portfolio because market opportunities are spotted. They might be completely new, innovative products to either replace or sell alongside the existing product range. Product replacement will be necessary when the product is nearing the end of its life cycle. Replacement may also be necessary if other firms produce a 'better' product and the firm is forced to react. Copied or 'me-too' products might be introduced where another firm has successfully pioneered the product in the market. At the other extreme small and evolutionary changes to existing products might be introduced. This may be necessary as competitors improve their products or when a product is nearing the end of its life cycle – a process called product *extension.*

Firms with a robust entrepreneurial architecture will be well placed to follow a strategy of innovation – rather than incremental change. The ability to innovate speedily is built into the architecture, as is a close relationship with customers – a customer focus. If there is a relationship of trust, customers are more likely to try the new product, provided of course they perceive a need for it and that means the company must also be good at communicating with customers in whatever way is most appropriate. In developing new products the customer-focused firm will have an advantage because, if it understands how its customers' needs are changing, it ought to be able to develop new products that meet them. The key to this strategy, therefore, is building good customer relationships, often associated with effective branding, and the ability to innovate quickly.

One advantage of this approach is that it is often far more cost effective to increase the volume of business with existing customers than it is to go out looking for new ones. What is more, good relationships often result in customers bringing in new customers through word of mouth or referral. However, developing new products, even for existing customers can be expensive and risky. Development must be grounded firmly in the needs of the existing market. And even then, if done too rapidly, it can mean resources are spread too thinly across an unbalanced portfolio.

Virgin is a good example of a brand that has been applied to a wide range of diverse products, mainly successfully, linking customers and their lifestyle aspirations. Virgin, however, rarely undertake 'production', relying instead on partners with developed expertise. On the other hand Mercedes Benz is a brand that has a strong association with quality and the company has capitalized on this by producing an ever-wider range of vehicles, always being able to charge a premium price for its product. This has allowed it to move into new and different segments of the vehicle market.

Diversification (quadrant 4)

Diversification involves selling new products into new markets. The rationale for this is normally one of 'balancing' the risk in a firm's business portfolio by going into new products and new markets and, ultimately, developing a business conglomerate. However, since this strategy involves unfamiliar products and unfamiliar markets it is normally seen as a high-risk strategy, with too many unknowns in the equation. Reflecting this, most conglomerates seem to be unattractive to stock markets, commanding a discount on their constituent parts.

Of course, market development and product development might go hand-in-hand, since the move into a new market segment may involve the development of variants to the existing product offering by altering the marketing mix or even changes to the product range. Product *extension* and *expansion* may similarly be viewed as incremental diversification, in that they involve elements of both new product development and seeking new market segments. However, the risk is mitigated because of the incremental movement in one or other element and it can be further mitigated if these developments are associated with a strong brand with values that are attractive to customers.

Risk is therefore dependent upon the extent of the diversification. The literature distinguishes between related and unrelated diversification and entrepreneurial firms face a distinct opportunity in the former.

Related diversification happens when development is beyond the present product and market, but within the confines of the 'industry' or 'sector' in which the firm operates. There are three variants:

- *Backward vertical integration* where the firm becomes its own supplier of some basic raw materials or services or provides transport or financing. When Anita Roddick first set up Body Shop it was purely as a retail business. In the 1980s it started its own warehousing and distribution network, based upon a sophisticated stock-control system, and built up a substantial fleet of lorries. Products could typically be delivered within 24 hours. It also started manufacturing its cosmetics mainly in the UK, although many of the ingredients came from overseas under its 'trade-not-aid' policy. These two elements of strategy initially worked well for it and generated substantial sales and profit growth but the manufacturing policy was reviewed in the late 1990s and Body Shop started to move away from manufacturing and concentrate on its core retailing activity.
- *Forward vertical integration*, where the firm becomes its own distributor or retailer or perhaps services its own products in some way. In this way Timberland, famous for its sturdy, waterproof boots, opened a number of prominently-sited retail outlets selling its boots and other Timberland-branded outdoor clothes and products.
- *Horizontal integration*, where there is development into activities which are either directly complementary or competitive with the firm's current activities; for example, where a video rental shop starts to rent out video games. In this way Ford now earns more from financial services related to car purchase than from the manufacture of the vehicles themselves.

In an entrepreneurial firm the portfolio of core competencies can be combined in various ways to meet opportunities. So it can re-apply and reconfigure what it does best in a way best suited to meet the opportunities in new markets. In this way the entrepreneurial firm can have an advantage over others in applying this strategy. So, for example, Mercedes Benz uses new products to move incrementally into new markets and market segments, leveraging on its reputation for quality, for example with its small 100 Series. All of this has been within the industry it knows best. The primary competency lies in product development – it builds good quality cars which appeal in terms of aesthetics and emotions but are leveraged by an excellent brand. In this way it has a competitive advantage over other new entrants to the market, although not necessarily existing ones.

By way of contrast, unrelated diversification is a high-risk strategy for any firm. It happens where the firm develops beyond its present 'industry' or 'sector' into products/services and markets that, on the face of it, bear little relationship to the one it is in. The risks are high because the firm understands neither the product/service nor the market.

'Synergy' is often used as a justification for both related and unrelated diversification, particularly when it involves acquisition or merger. Synergy is concerned with assessing how much extra benefit can be obtained from providing linkages between activities or processes which have been previously unconnected, or where the connection has been of a different type, so that the combined effect is greater than the sum of the parts. It is often described as 'one plus one equals three'. Synergy in related diversification is mainly based upon core product or market characteristics or competencies – for example, Mercedes Benz leveraging on its reputation for quality of vehicles. The claimed synergy in unrelated diversification is normally based on financing – the positive cash flows in one business being used for the funding requirements of another. Another often-claimed synergy is based on the managerial skills of the head office.

Research indicates that most successful entrepreneurial firms follow a strategy of incremental, mainly internal, growth (Burns, 1994). They move carefully into new markets with existing products or sell new products to existing customers. Whilst Johnson and Scholes (2001) claim that attempts to demonstrate the effects of diversification on performance are inconclusive, they also admit that successful diversification is difficult to achieve in practice. However, many researchers have found that more focused firms perform better than diversified ones (Wernerfelt and Montgomery, 1986). This is reflected in their share price. What is more, it has been demonstrated that smaller firms that diversify by building on their core business – related diversification – do better than those that diversify in an unrelated way (Ansoff, *op. cit.*). This was established for a broader range of firms in the 1970s (Rumelt, 1974) and used as part of Porter's (1987) argument for firms that build on their core business doing better than those who diversify in an unrelated way.

The conclusion must be that diversification generally, but unrelated diversification in particular, is risky and therefore requires careful justification – although the pay-off can be large. Nevertheless one of the companies that has adopted a strategy of diversification most successfully is Lonrho, and its strategy has been one of unrelated diversification. Its interests range from hotels in Mexico to freight forwarders in Canada, from motor distribution in Africa to oil and gas production in the USA.

Case insight

Crucial to success for dot.com firms is the 'business model' – how income will be generated. Arguably the most successful model is that of the online auctioneer **eBay**. eBay has 69 million registered users worldwide and hosts over 12 million items on its website. It is now the largest site for used car sales in the USA. Someone buys a computer game every 8 seconds. In 2002 it had sales of $1.2 billion. By 2005 sales were over $4 billion and it had over 5000 employees.

eBay's success comes from being nothing more than an intermediary – software running on a web server. Its customers, both buyers and sellers, do all the work. Sellers pay to set up their own auction, buyers use eBay's software to place their bids, shipping and payment are arranged between the seller and buyer and eBay takes 7–18% of the selling price as commission for letting them use its software. eBay is simply the trading platform. It holds no stocks and its involvement in the trade in minimal. After each transaction the buyer and seller rate the other. Next to each user's identification is a figure in brackets recording the number of positive comments – thus encouraging honesty and trust. It is a truly virtual business which also sells advertising space.

eBay developed a 'virtuous circle' in which more buyers attracted more sellers, who attracted yet more buyers and sellers – called 'network effects'. At the core of eBay's business is software rather than people. The company has bought software companies to gain exclusive use of their technologies and make the auction process more efficient. It therefore faces enormous economies of scale in attracting as many auction transactions as possible and, with that in mind, has moved into new areas such as used cars and even plans to host storefronts for small merchants. It has also started to sell private-label versions of its service to companies, for a fee.

In 2002 eBay purchased **PayPal**, the dominant provider of internet payments in the USA with over 12 million customers of whom 3.2 million are fee-paying business customers. The two companies are complementary but depend on each other. Indeed, auctions account for 61% of PayPal's business. PayPal allows customers to register details of their credit card or bank account with it so that when they buy something on the internet they just enter an e-mail account and an amount. Like eBay, it is fully automated, relying on software rather than people. Like eBay, Paypal also relies on the same 'network effects'. It initially paid users $10 to sign up their friends to enable it to reach its critical mass, but now the firm is signing up 28,000 new users a day without this incentive. The commercial synergy between eBay and PayPal is clear. Not only are the business models similar, but also the customers buying or selling on eBay can secure their payments by using PayPal. And now it is made more easily available to them more are using the service.

Mergers and acquisitions

Bowman and Faulkner (1997) add an extra dimension to the Ansoff matrix by considering core competency and method of implementation. They point out that any move into new markets or new products/services becomes riskier, the further the firm strays from its core competency. This is tantamount to a start-up. They also point out that the implementation becomes riskier as the firm moves from internal development through alliances into acquisition. The highest-risk strategy of all would therefore be to develop new competencies and their application into a new market with a new product/service, through an implementation policy involving acquisition. This brings us to the issue of mergers and acquisitions.

Mergers and acquisitions are frequently used by entrepreneurs as a tool for achieving rapid growth and also as a short cut to diversification. The compelling reason for this tactic is the speed with which it allows the entrepreneur to enter a new product/market area. Another reason might be that the firm lacks a resource, such as R&D or a customer base, to develop a strategy unaided. Often, particularly when a market is static, it is seen as the easiest way to enter a new market, for example overseas. Sometimes the reason for buying out a competitor is to buy their order book, perhaps related to shutting down their capacity, cutting costs and gaining economies of scale. Sometimes, as with Cadbury Schweppes and its purchase of Dr Pepper and 7UP, you are both buying a respected brand and a foothold in an overseas market and its channels of distribution to help market your existing products.

However, this tactic can be time-consuming, expensive and risky. By distracting management it can also damage short-term business performance. In fact there is no evidence that commercial acquisitions or take-overs – particularly in unrelated areas (other than in a distress sale) – add value to the firm. Many studies show that mergers and acquisitions suffer a higher failure rate than marriages and business history is littered with stories of failed mergers of titanic proportions such as AT&T's purchase of NCR in 1991, the second largest acquisition in the history of the computer industry. This failed largely because of the clash of cultures in the two companies. NCR was conservative, tightly controlled from the top whilst AT&T was 'politically correct', informal and decentralized. Within four years most of NCR's senior managers had left and the new company had become loss-making. In 1997 NCR was made independent again, having lost some 50% of its value.

The great conglomerate-merger wave of the 1960s did not generally lead to improvements in performance for those firms involved and was reversed by the large-scale selling of unrelated businesses in the 1980s. Porter (*op. cit.*), in his study of 33 major corporations between 1950 and 1986, concludes that more often acquisitions were subsequently sold off rather than retained, and the net result was dissipation of shareholder value. And yet companies of all sizes persist in following this strategy.

All too often acquisitions have too much corporate ego tied up in the deal and that can lead to a loss of business logic. It is important that there is a clear logic to any acquisition, related to the product/market strategy. For example:

- As a defensive acquisition to maintain market position, perhaps to gain economies of scale, or as a result of aggressive competitive reaction from rivals.
- As part of a strategy to develop new products related to the core products/markets of the firm when it does not have the capability to do so itself, for example because of R&D or technology.
- As part of a strategy to develop new markets, for example overseas.
- As part of a strategy of diversification designed to spread product/market risk, although this must be seen as the highest of high-risk growth strategies.

If a firm decides to undertake this high-risk strategy it first needs to decide on the industry into which it is to diversify. Related diversification will normally be into the same industry. If it is unrelated diversification then the industry should be one where

Case insight

The **Reliance Group** is now the biggest business group in India with sales of over $12 billion and profits of over $950 million. It is a family-run conglomerate and was started by **Dhirubhai Ambani**, the son of a poor Gujarati school teacher who began work at a Shell petrol station in Aden. To make extra money he traded commodities and, at one time, even melted down Yemeni rial coins so as to sell the silver for more than the currency's face value. He returned to India and started a yarn trading company in 1959 which, by the end of the 1990s, had become an integrated textiles, petrochemicals and oil conglomerate that then diversified into telecommunications, power, biotechnology and even financial services. Initially the business grew primarily through exploiting contacts with Indian politicians and bureaucrats but, in the wake of the changes caused by economic liberalization in the early 1990s, it started to do things differently – it built production sites that were competitive in global markets. Dhirubhai also popularized share ownership in India – which is where financial services comes in – and the two holding companies now have over 3.5 million shareholders.

Dhirubhai died in 2002 and the business is now run by his two sons Mukesh and Anil. Both have MBAs from the USA and have been involved with the business for some 20 years, managing the company increasingly since their father had his first stroke in 1986 and having a strong role in forging it into the world-class company that it is today.

the acquiring company has the key competencies required for success in the sector and, where there is a deficiency, they should be addressed by being present in the target company. The attractiveness of the industry will depend to some extent on the strategic direction of the company, informed by an analysis of the industry (perhaps using Porter's Five Forces and a SLEPT analysis). The acquisitions that are most likely to succeed are those for which an attractive market presents itself to a company with a good 'mesh' between the acquiring company's core competencies and the sector's required key competencies.

Of course, some acquisitions are simply opportunistic. For example, when a rival firm or a firm in a related area, goes into receivership the temptation to buy it out cheaply and quickly from the receiver might be irresistible and might also make sound commercial sense. Most acquisitions take three to nine months to complete but a sale from a receiver can be completed in as little as three weeks.

The major reason why mergers and acquisitions fail is because of failure of implementation. Claimed synergies may not be achieved, perhaps rationalization is insufficiently ruthless, possibly because clear management lines and responsibilities are not laid down. One of the major reasons for failure boils down to a clash of organizational cultures that does not get resolved. This can arise because of many factors, but it results in the merged organizations being unable to work together effectively. That was the major reason for the seemingly logical, but ultimately disastrous, take-over of NCR by AT&T in 1991, which nearly brought down both companies. For whatever reason, one common outcome of mergers or acquisitions is that many managers in the acquired company will leave within a short space of time. They may, of course, be 'pushed' rather than leave of their own volition, but nevertheless this means that the time scale for proactive management of change can be very short. Management of a merger or acquisition is therefore difficult.

Case with questions

Ineos Group

The Ineos Group was founded in 1998 when Jim Ratcliffe led a £91 million management buyout of Inspec's chemicals division. Jim is a qualified accountant who had previously worked for the US private equity house Advent. By 2007 Ineos had grown to become the world's third largest petrochemical company. Jim's strategy to achieve this was simple. He went out to buy undervalued subsidiaries from global oil and chemical giants, financed almost entirely by debt – high yield bonds and bank debt. The company has bought businesses from ICI, Dow Chemicals, Degussa, BASF, Cybec, BP and Norsk Hydro. It was Ineos' purchase of BP's petrochemical arm Innovene for £5.1 billion in 2006 that catapulted the company into the world rankings of the petrochemical industry. The deal quadrupled the company's turnover and signalled a move away from specialist compounds to the simpler chemicals from which they are made. Following a £1.6 billion bond issue in 2006 to refinance the purchase of Innovene, Ineos continued its acquisition strategy with the £76 million purchase of BP's German ethylene oxide business followed by the £460 million purchase of Norsk Hydro's polymers business in 2007.

Ineos sees itself as a leading global manufacturer of petrochemicals, speciality chemicals and oil products. It comprises 18 businesses with 68 manufacturing sites in 17 countries. It believes its strengths lie in its:

● High quality, low cost production facilities
● Well located, well invested, large plants that allow it to benefit from economies of scale
● Experienced management
● Leading market positions that allow it to be the supplier of choice for many large customers
● Operating diversity in products, customers, geographic regions, applications and end-user markets.

By 2007 the company had a turnover of some £18 billion and had some 15,000 employees. It was ranked the largest private company by the *Sunday Times* – with a turnover three times that of its nearest rival, the John Lewis Partnership. The company currently plans to build a £60 million biodiesel plant at the former BP site at Grangemouth and another at Antwerp as well as a £125 million phenol acetone plant in China. Jim Ratcliffe himself is a fairly low-profile entrepreneur, but he still owns about two-thirds of the business, giving him a paper fortune of some £3.3 billion and placing him in the top ten wealthiest people in Britain in 2007, according to the *Sunday Times* Rich List.

Up-to-date information on Ineos Group can be found on their website: www.ineos.com

Questions
1. What risks does Ineos face and how might they be reduced?
2. How secure is the personal fortune of Jim Ratcliffe and what steps might he take to secure it further?

Sustainability and corporate social responsibility

It is now widely accepted that many business practices have negative social and environmental side effects. Growing pressures are leading firms to give careful consideration to sustainable development and how it might contribute to the sustainability of competitive advantage and growth of the organization. These pressures come from:

- *Environmentalists* – who see companies rapidly using up the valuable but limited resources of the planet and at the same time contributing to global warming, which may ultimately cause the destruction of the planet. Green issues and the corporate 'carbon footprint' are rapidly becoming the most important issues facing business today.
- *Social reformers* – who see companies behaving in ways that they object to, for example by 'exploiting' cheap labour in developing countries, or providing poor working conditions. Trade unions and consumer groups have both focused on social issues in the past, often with the result that legislation limiting the activity of companies has been enacted (for example the minimum wage in Europe).
- *Social activists* – who see companies as having a broader social role in the community beyond the boundaries of the working environment. Corporate citizenship programmes, for example in which employees undertake charitable work in the community, have become a trendy outlet for many companies, whilst others like Body Shop and Timberland have practised this for years.
- *Ethical activists* – who see companies (such as Enron) behaving in unacceptable ethical ways usually by trying to mislead stakeholders. There is, of course, an overlap here with the agendas of the other groups. Nevertheless, business ethics has risen up the agendas of society as a whole and shareholders in particular, and companies are responding.

Often these issues are bundled together under the broad umbrella of corporate social responsibility (CSR). More and more companies are engaging seriously in CSR, and over 500 in the UK issue annual CSR reports on their performance. Much of the CSR literature is highly moralistic in nature, reflecting the idealism of scholars who question the profit maximization objective of companies (Wood, 2000). However, Burke and Logsdon (1996) argue that there are sound business reasons for following a strong CSR policy and organizations can expect five strategic outcomes:

- *Enhanced customer loyalty*: Certainly a strong CSR profile can reinforce and enhance brand image (e.g. Body Shop). Customers are increasingly drawn to brands with a strong CSR link and CSR has become an element in the continuous process of trying to differentiate one company from another. In 20 developed countries a survey of 20,000 people showed CSR-related factors collectively accounted for 49% of a company's image, compared to 35% for brand image and just 10% for financial management (Environics International, 2001).
- *Increased future purchases*: Whilst any product must first satisfy the customer's key buying criteria – quality, price etc. – a strong CSR brand can increase sales and customer loyalty by helping to differentiate it. On the other hand a bad CSR image can damage sales quite severely. The same Environics survey showed that 42% of

consumers in North America would punish companies by not buying their product for being socially irresponsible. This fell to 25% in Europe but collapsed to 8% in Asia where CSR issues are seen as less important.

- *Reduced operating costs*: Many environmental initiatives can reduce costs (e.g. reducing waste and recycling, better control of building temperatures or reducing use of agrochemicals). Many social initiatives can increase employee motivation, cut absenteeism and cut staff turnover and an increasing number of graduates take CSR issues into consideration when making employment decisions.
- *Improved new product development*: Focus on CSR issues can lead to new product opportunities. For example, car manufacturers are striving to find alternatives to fossil fuels for their vehicles, whilst developing conventional engines that are more and more economical.
- *Access to new markets*: A strong CSR brand can create its own market niche for an organization. For example, the Co-operative Bank in the UK has a long history of CSR. It has set itself up as an ethical and ecological investor with an investment policy that is the most frequently cited reason why customers choose the bank. It also has been at the forefront of social auditing practices and has produced an independently audited 'Social Report' since 1997 that measures impact and identifies improvements the company could make in social responsibility areas.
- *Productivity gains*: Actions to improve working conditions, lessen environmental impact or increase employee involvement in decision making can improve productivity. For example, actions to improve work conditions in the supply chain have led to decreases in defect rates in merchandise.

Not surprisingly, therefore, strong CSR performance seems to be linked to financial performance. A 2002 study showed that the overall financial performance of the 2001 *Business Ethics* Best Citizen companies in the USA was significantly better than that of the remaining companies in the S&P 500 Index (Verschoor, 2002). There is growing awareness that incorporating CSR into mainstream corporate strategy translates into bottom line performance. In the short term it at least avoids negative consumer or activist publicity, in the medium term it delivers better performance for investors and the community and in the long term, by encouraging consideration of abiding social and environmental interests, it can give management a broader, long-term perspective on the sustainability of the company's performance.

Certainly companies like Body Shop have used CSR as a major plank in their branding since it was set up by Anita Roddick in 1976 – campaigning for many social, moral and environmental issues. But CSR predates Body Shop. In the UK Cadbury, Wilkin & Sons (maker of Tiptree Jams) and the Co-op are all early examples of businesses with a CSR dimension. Today many organizations, like the UK retailers Marks and Spencer (M&S) and John Lewis, and the US company IBM and outdoor-wear manufacturer Timberland, have extensive CSR programmes ranging from community involvement (staff working on community projects in company time) through to ethical sourcing (from humans and animals) and into environmental issues (such as M&S' objective to become completely carbon neutral). M&S' 100 point 'Plan A' is generally seen as a model for today's socially responsible companies.

There is also growing investor pressure to implement CSR. The Environics survey showed that over a quarter of US share owners bought or sold shares because of a company's social performance and a similar pattern emerged in Britain, Canada,

Italy, and France (Environics International, *op. cit.*). There are now stock market indices like the Dow Jones Sustainability Index and the FTSE4Good and, increasingly, mainstream investors see CSR as a strategic business issue and raise it in annual meetings. Activist groups also buy shares in targeted companies to give them access to these annual meetings so that they can raise CSR issues.

CSR can be integrated into the strategic planning process outlined in Figure 10.1. Starting with external considerations in the *strategic analysis*, firms need to be aware of legislation and should compare themselves to competitors (Epstein and Roy, 2001) and find out about the expectations of external stakeholders (Smith, 2003). Similarly companies should investigate the expectations of its internal stakeholders (Smith, *op. cit.*) with a view to assessing the adequacy of its organizational capacity – its resources and processes (De Colle and Gonella, 2002; Epstein and Roy, *op. cit.*). The firm should then be able to assess the fit between the CSR commitments it might aspire to and its central business objectives (Burke and Logsdon, *op. cit.*; Smith, *op. cit.*), which may or may not result in changing the *vision* and mission of the business. CSR *strategy formulation* follows, usually demonstrated as a list of commitments. According to Smith (*op. cit.*), this should reflect 'an understanding of whether (and why) greater attention to CSR is warranted by that particular organisation.' *Strategy implementation* requires concrete actions to be undertaken but also it is important to publicize this to internal and external stakeholders to demonstrate commitment and attainment (Burke and Logsdon, *op. cit.*). These may have to be audited or evaluated (De Colle and Gonella, *op. cit.*).

Sustainability and CSR can therefore be integrated into the strategic planning process. Indeed it should be at the heart of any growth strategy. It encourages the company to take a long-term view and reflects the concerns of the society in which it is embedded. However, it also makes good business sense, providing market and brand opportunities that translate into bottom line profits. CSR is set to become more important in the future and is likely to be an essential element of strategy for all companies.

Case with questions

M&S

M&S has always had an ethical dimension. It started offering staff welfare services that provided pensions, subsidized staff canteens, health and dental services, hairdressing, rest rooms and camping holidays back in the 1930s. In 1999 it published its own code of practice on Global Sourcing as a minimum standard for all suppliers in an effort to improve conditions for workers overseas. Since 2003 M&S has produced a Corporate Social Responsibility Report. In that year it was ranked top retailer and one of the top UK companies in Business and the Communities First Corporate Social Responsibility Index. Stuart Rose has taken this even further and started building it into the M&S brand identity. In 2006 the Look Behind the Label marketing campaign was introduced with the aim of highlighting the range of ethical and environmentally friendly policies M&S had.

➡

These included:

- Fairtrade products – all coffee and tea sold by M&S is Fairtrade and it also offers clothing lines made from Fairtrade Cotton.
- Sustainable fishing – M&S sell only fish from sustainable sources.
- Healthy foods – M&S has removed 90% of its foods containing hydrogenated fats and oils and has cut salt across its food range.
- Support for charities – M&S supports a number of charities. For example at Christmas 2006 it introduced a range of products to support the housing charity Shelter predominantly in the food-to-go range including a range of seasonal Christmas sandwiches.
- Environment friendly – emphasizing the use of environmentally friendly textile dyes and use of environmentally friendly materials for store fit-outs such as flooring made from natural rubber as well as looking to source electricity from environmentally friendly sources.

However, in 2007 M&S went one very significant step further. It launched its 'Plan A', an ambitious 100-point plan to help combat climate change, reduce waste, safeguard natural resources, trade ethically and promote healthier lifestyles. The business-wide action plan will cost £200 million. By 2012, M&S aims to:

- Become carbon neutral – minimizing energy use, maximizing renewables and using offsets as a last resort.
- Send no waste to land fill sites – reducing packaging, recycling and reusing materials.
- Extend sustainable sourcing – using recycled materials, extending free range and organic food products, only selling fish from sustainable supplies.
- Set new standards in ethical trading – leading in labour standards and extending Fairtrade products.
- Help customers and employees live healthier lifestyles – through producing healthier foods and extending health and lifestyle support for employees.

The ambitious plan, which was widely welcomed by environmentalists, will transform the way M&S operates. M&S will set up a Supplier Exchange to share best practice and innovation. The economics of local and ethical sourcing are less straightforward than they might seem. A surprisingly high proportion of a product's vehicle miles come from shoppers driving to their local store. However, the move back to UK sourcing, at least for food, and the emphasis on identifiable, free range, often organic and fair trade produce undoubtedly hits a chord with many middle-class shoppers – M&S target market. And the M&S brand claims influence over 2000 factories, 10,000 farms and 250,000 workers, so if the initiative works its influence will be considerable, albeit tiny on a global scale. Becoming more sustainable is not just about philanthropy, it also make good competitive sense – at least for some businesses. Nevertheless the turnaround of M&S is far from complete.

Visit M&S's website, www.marksandspencer.com, to find out more about their CSR activities.

Questions
1. How embedded within M&S is CSR?
2. What is the role of CSR in the turn around of M&S?
3. Visit M&S's website to assess the progress of Plan A. How successful have they been?

Sustaining growth

Growth is a relative concept. Relative in terms of its measurement – over time – and relative in terms of its temporal context – compared to others in the same industry or sector. Sustaining growth over a prolonged period and compared to competitors is not easy. Many firms try and most flounder, at least at some points along the journey. That is partly because they do not control all the variables that affect them. The terrorist attack in the USA on 11 September 2001 and the recession it precipitated was not predictable and no firms had any plans in place to deal with its effects. However, all too often growth is not sustained because tiredness and complacency set in. Life cycles can be predicted and strategies put in place to counter them, particularly in the context of a portfolio of products or services. But it is people who neglect to do so. It is people that can both sustain and inhibit growth – not the nature of an individual product or service. And people need to be led and managed, but, more than all, motivated to achieve growth.

Beyond this, sustaining capability and distinctiveness is the key to sustaining growth. Using Kay's (1998) three capabilities, outlined in the last chapter, reputation, often communicated in a brand, is probably the easiest to sustain. Strategic assets can be defended over long periods but can disappear overnight – witness the events at Enron. But it is innovation that is probably the most difficult distinctive capability to sustain. And the entrepreneurial architecture needed for this can only endure if all the factors outlined in Chapter 4 are in place and continue to be renewed and re-invigorated through effective leadership, structures, cultures and strategies.

Strategy is just a series of linked, logical actions. There are frameworks to help us develop it and research to underpin our judgement. But strategy is based upon the best judgements, at any one point of time, about imprecise factors and uncertain circumstances – playing the odds. A right decision today can so easily prove to be a wrong decision tomorrow and only a classroom case-study has the benefit of hindsight and 20:20 vision. The best you can expect is to make more right decisions than wrong decisions. And, if you are not making any wrong decisions, you are probably not making any decisions at all. Entrepreneurs keep moving – and not always in a straight line. So too should the entrepreneurial firm. The firm that endorses the status quo is no longer entrepreneurial.

Notwithstanding this, Porter (1991) noted five mistakes that organizations repeatedly make when implementing strategy:

1. *Misunderstanding industry attractiveness* – Attractiveness has little to do with growth, glamour or new technology but more to do with the Five Forces outlined earlier in this chapter.
2. *Not having real competitive advantage* – Organizations need to discover what makes them unique and different, to challenge the status quo and not just copy or incrementally change what competitors do.
3. *Pursuing an unsustainable competitive position* – Organizations need to decide on their core competencies and focus their attempts at exploiting competitive advantage on them rather than strategies that do not play to these strengths and therefore will be difficult to sustain.
4. *Compromising the strategy for growth with short-term goals* – Short-term growth targets can distract the organization from its long-term competitive strategy as it pursues short-term opportunities that are inconsistent with the core strategy.

5. *Failing to communicate strategy internally* – All employees need to know the organization's strategy and what it means for them. All too often they do not.

The entrepreneurial firm will constantly be attempting to develop new products or services and seek out new markets or segments. Judging what combination to pursue these in, at any point of time, is not easy. Pursuing too many at once normally involves extra risk. But pursuing them too late in the face of competition means losing out on what might be lucrative opportunities. This is the classic trade-off between risk and return – and no two people are the same in making this. The frameworks in this and previous chapters can only help with the process of strategizing and inform the decision. They can never make the decision for you.

Case with questions

BAE Systems

BAE Systems is Britain's largest manufacturer, with sales of over £14 billion and some 88,000 staff based in over 100 countries world-wide. It is the largest defence company in Europe, and ranks seventh in the USA. Its size and growth have been largely due to mergers and acquisitions since its very inception.

Today's company began life as British Aerospace in 1977, a nationalized (government-owned) corporation formed from the merger of British Aircraft Corporation, Hawker Siddeley Aviation, Hawker Siddeley Dynamics and Scottish Aviation. The company was privatized (sold off) in 1981. The 1980s saw a string of acquisitions, most with little obvious logic: Royal Ordnance in 1987 (munitions), Rover Group in 1988 (cars) and Arlington Securities in 1989 (financial). By 1992 the strategy of unrelated diversification was discredited and the company was on the verge of collapse. The chairman was forced to resign and the company reappraised its strategies, being forced to sell off Rover to BMW in 1993. Throughout the 1990s the company remained reliant upon a huge weapons contract with Saudi Arabia – a contract that would later prove controversial – but it also started increasingly turning its focus to Europe. This time, rather than acquiring companies, it started forming alliances, doing deals with Dassault, Lagadere, Saab, Daimler Benz Aerospace, Siemens and others. The company also took part in the restructuring of Airbus and took a 20% stake.

However, its most important move was when it merged with GEC's defence business in 1999, giving it a far greater presence in the USA, and greater vertical integration of its activities. From here on the strategy shifted. Mergers and acquisitions were still very important, but the focus for this activity changed. Firstly the company focused very much on the defence business. It took a 33% stake in Eurofighter, a 37.5% stake in MBDA, the world's leading missile systems builder, and a 20% stake in Saab AB, the aircraft manufacturer. In 2006 it sold its stake in Airbus, despite the success of the company.

Secondly, the focus shifted towards restructuring to give greater backward and forward vertical integration. In this way BAE could become one of the very few fully integrated suppliers of weapons for air, land and naval defence needs. It can supply the platform – for example, the ship or plane – and all the electronics, computers or missiles that go in it, which is where the real profit lies. This positions it with fewer direct competitors and providing the sort of turn-key service governments want. Where acquisitions were not possible, strategic partnerships were entered into.

➡

Case with questions continued

BAE Systems

Thirdly the focus shifted very much to the USA, the largest market for defence procurement in the world, and BAE started out on a strategy of buying its way into the US market. In 2000 it sealed its status as defence supplier to the Pentagon by purchasing two electronics businesses from Lockheed Martin. By 2007 it had made 16 acquisitions in the USA at which point it made a $4.1 billion bid for Armor Holdings – the manufacturer of the famous Humvee armoured vehicles. Armor is a prime contractor in the Pentagon (this means taking overall responsibility for complete weapons systems), and its acquisition will seal BAE's status in the US market. However, continuing accusations about bribes being paid to a Saudi prince to obtain the huge contract on which it survived in the 1990s nearly resulted in the acquisition being blocked. Even before the Armor acquisition, the USA accounted for almost 30% of sales, with joint contracts such as the huge F-35 Joint Strike Fighter project. The UK now accounts for only about 25% of sales, with contracts such as the Eurofighter, the Astute-class submarine and Nimrod marine-surveillance aircraft projects.

The final aspect of BAE's strategy was that of attempting to reduce market risk in a cyclical, high-risk market by spreading its customer base across the world. There were also two reasons for wanting to move away from an over-reliance on the British market. Firstly, British defence procurement is now more open to competition than in any other Western country. Secondly, British defence contracts are normally fixed-price, unlike the USA where they are cost-plus with single figure mark-ups for the development of new products, and open competition, fixed-price for the production contracts. The British system has forced BAE to make some expensive write-offs in the past.

Up-to-date information on BAE Systems can be found on their website: www.baesystems.com.

Questions
1. What do you think of BAE's logic for using acquisitions, mergers and strategic partnerships?
2. What are the dangers of using mergers and acquisitions as such a central part of any strategy?

Summary

To achieve growth a company should build on its strengths and core competencies, shore up its weaknesses and develop a marketing strategy for each product/market offering that reflects:

- The appropriate generic marketing strategy;
- The stage the product/market offering is at in its life cycle;
- All placed in the context of its portfolio of product/market offerings.

Research tells us that the strategy with the best chance of generating the highest profits is to differentiate with the aim of dominating that market and to do this effectively and quickly, and continue to innovate based on your differential advantage.

The unique elements of the differentiation strategy are likely to be based on distinctive capabilities that, applied to a relevant market, become a competitive advantage. This will become the firm's core market, the one in which it has a distinct advantage by adding the greatest value for its customers.

Growth through opportunity drives the strategy of an entrepreneurial firm. Ansoff highlighted four growth options:

1. Market penetration
2. Market development
3. Product development
4. Diversification

Any firm wishing to grow must follow a policy of market penetration (option 1) – selling more to existing customers and finding new customers in the market place – until that market is mature. The best way of finding new customers is to understand your existing ones and then try to find more of the same. Marketing mix can be altered to achieve higher sales but this can be difficult in a static or declining market. Returning to the basics of business strategy helped turn around the fortunes of **Standard Chartered Bank**.

Market development is about finding new markets for existing products or services, thus benefiting from economies of scale or capitalizing on the firm's product-knowledge competency. In considering which markets to enter, consideration should be given to Porter's Five Forces and entry and exit barriers. Market development is most successful for companies whose core competencies lie in the efficiency of their existing production methods, for example in the capital goods industries, and are seeking economies of scale, or for firms adept at sales, marketing and developing close customer relationships. This has been a core part of **Royal Bank of Scotland's** strategy.

The classic example of market development is entry into overseas markets, either by opening overseas ventures or by exporting. Many exporters go through an agent who is able to distribute the product for them. Franchising is another approach, particularly for a service or retail business. To succeed there needs to be a symbiotic relationship, based on trust and effective incentives.

Product/service development involves developing new products or services and selling to your existing market. These can be completely new products or incremental changes to existing products. Product development is most successful for those companies whose competencies lie in building good customer relationships, often associated with effective branding. However, of equal importance could be the ability to innovate – both qualities of the entrepreneurial firm. Getting existing customers to buy more is also often very cost-effective.

Related diversification is about staying within the confines of the industry through either backward vertical integration (becoming your own supplier), forward vertical integration (becoming a distributor or retailer), or horizontal integration (moving into related activities). Related diversification is safest for companies who are adept at both innovation and developing close customer relations – key competencies of an entrepreneurial firm. In an entrepreneurial firm the portfolio of core competencies can be combined in various ways to meet opportunities. So it can re-apply and reconfigure what it does best in a way best suited to meet the opportunities in new markets. It therefore has a distinct advantage in related diversification. This is certainly the case in the **eBay** acquisition of **PayPal**, where there were also related marketing synergies.

Unrelated diversification is the riskiest strategy of all and involves developing beyond the firm's present industry, normally because of the claimed benefits of synergy.

Mergers and acquisitions are frequently used as means of achieving rapid expansion, gaining a foothold in new geographical markets or greater backward and forward vertical integration – as with both the **Reliance Group** and the **Ineos Group**. However, the tactic can be time-consuming, expensive and risky. There must be clear strategic reasons for a policy of merger or acquisition. The **Royal Bank of Scotland** has used opportunistic acquisition very successfully to grow the business and gain much needed economies of scale, at all times driving down its costs.

Most mergers and acquisitions fail because of failure of implementation and a clash of cultures. Claimed synergies may not be achieved, perhaps rationalization is insufficiently ruthless, possibly because clear management lines and responsibilities are not laid down.

Sustainability and CSR must be at the heart of any growth strategy. It encourages the long-term view and reflects the concerns of the society in which the company is embedded. It also makes good business sense, providing market and brand opportunities that translate into bottom line profits. **M&S's** 'Plan A' is generally seen as a model for today's socially responsible company.

Research indicates that most successful entrepreneurial firms follow a strategy of incremental, mainly internal, growth. **Standard Chartered** followed this strategy whilst at the same time addressing the realization that many consumer banking services are just commodities and are therefore price-sensitive. Related diversification only works when based on core competencies. The strategy of unrelated diversification is high-risk and only to be adopted after careful consideration. The further the firm moves away from its core competency, the higher the risk. Risk also increases as the firm moves from internal development through alliances to acquisitions.

BAE Systems has refocused on its defence business but has continued to use mergers and acquisitions as a way of gaining forward and backward integration – which is what the market requires of major defence contractors – and entry into its key market of the USA. It has also used it as a way of mitigating geographic market risk.

Essays and discussion topics

1. Penetrating the market is just about selling more. Discuss.
2. Penetrating the market is low-risk and therefore always the most attractive option. Discuss.
3. In what circumstances might product development be a lower-risk strategy than market development, and vice versa?
4. How might a firm go about exporting so as to minimize the risks that it faces?
5. Exporting is expensive and risky. It is therefore not an attractive growth option. Discuss.
6. How do you go about minimizing your exposure to currency fluctuations?
7. Diversification is the 'Wally Box' of the product/market matrix. Discuss.
8. Why might related diversification work best for entrepreneurial companies?
9. Under what circumstances might diversification be an attractive option?

10. Diversified companies underperform 'focused' companies. Discuss.
11. Why might a firm be looking for another to acquire?
12. Under what circumstances might an acquisition or merger be attractive?
13. What is synergy and how might it be achieved?
14. Why do so many mergers or acquisitions fail? Give examples.
15. What advice would you give to a company taking over another?
16. Why might a strategy of internal growth be less risky than one of acquisition?
17. In what circumstances might a strategy of internal growth be more risky than one of acquisition? Compare your answer to that of Question 18. Is there any such thing as an optimal strategy?
18. What are the problems of sustaining growth over a long period of time?
19. What CSR issues are important to you? Rank them in order of importance.
20. How important is CSR to a business and why?
21. Environmental sustainability should be a core requirement for all businesses. Discuss.
22. Why do you think Asian customers are less concerned about CSR issues than those in the USA?
23. CSR is something only big companies are able to address. Discuss.

Exercises and assignments

1. For your own Department in your University or College, use the Product/Market matrix to list the growth options that it faces for the courses on offer.
2. Select a country and find out what help is available in order to export to it.
3. Select a company that has grown rapidly over the last five years. Analyze the strategies it has followed to secure this growth using the frameworks developed in the last two chapters.
4. Select a large, publicly quoted company and, using information from its website, write a report evaluating its CSR strategies.

References

Abell, D. F. (1980) *Defining the Business*, Hemel Hempstead: Prentice Hall.

Ansoff, H. I. (1968) *Corporate Strategy*, Harmondsworth: Penguin.

Bowman, C. and Faulkner, D. (1997) *Competitive and Corporate Strategy*, London: Irwin.

Burke, L. and Logsdon, J.M. (1996) 'How Corporate Social Responsibility Pays off', *Long Range Planning*, 29(4).

Burns, P. (1994) *Winners and Losers in the 1990s*, 3i European Enterprise Centre, Report 12, April.

De Colle, S. and Gonella, C. (2002) 'The Social and Ethical Alchemy: An Integrative Approach to Social and Ethical Accountability', *Business Ethics: A European Review*, 11(1).

Environics International (2001), *Corporate Social Responsibility Monitor 2001: Global Public Opinion on the Changing Role of Companies*, Toronto, Canada: Environics International (now Globescan).

Epstein, M.J. and Roy, M.J. (2001) 'Sustainability in Action: Identifying and Measuring the Key Performance Drivers', *Long Range Planning*, 34.

Johnson, G. and Scholes, K. (2001) *Exploring Corporate Strategy*, Harlow: Financial Times/Prentice Hall.

Kay, J. (1998) *Foundations of Corporate Success*, Oxford: Oxford University Press.

Peters, T. J. and Waterman, R. H. (1982) *In Search of Excellence*, London: Harper & Row.

Porter, M. E. (1985) *Competitive Advantage, Creating and Sustaining Superior Performance*, New York: The Free Press.

Porter, M. E. (1987) 'From Competitive Advantage to Competitive Strategy', *Harvard Business Review*, 65(3).

Porter, M. E. (1991) 'Knowing Your Place – How to Assess the Attractiveness of Your Industry and Your Company's Position in It', *Inc.*, 13(9), September.

Rumelt, R. P. (1974) *Strategy, Structure and Economic Performance*, Boston, Mass: Harvard University Press.

Smith, N.C. (2003) 'Corporate Social Responsibility: Whether or How?', *California Management Review*, 45(4).

Stevenson, H. H. and Gumpert, D. E. (1985) 'The Heart of Entrepreneurship', *Harvard Business Review*, March/April.

Verschoor, C.C. (2002) 'Best Corporate Citizens have Better Financial Performance', *Strategic Finance*, January.

Wernerfelt, B. and Montgomery, C. A. (1986) 'What is an Attractive Industry?, *Management Science*, 32.

Wood, D. (2000) 'Theory and Integrity in Business and Society.' *Business and Society*, 39(4).

Part 4

Encouraging Creativity and Innovation

13 Encouraging Entrepreneurial
    Innovation

14 Encouraging Creativity

15 Encouraging Marketing and
    Product Innovation

13

Encouraging Entrepreneurial Innovation

Contents

- Innovation and invention
- Innovation and entrepreneurship
- Creativity and entrepreneurship
- Innovation and risk
- The process of innovation and risk
- Innovation and size
- Discontinuous innovation
- Strategic innovation
- Successful innovation
- Summary

LEARNING OUTCOMES

By the end of this chapter you should be able to:

- Explain the nature of innovation and why it is so difficult to define;
- Explain the critical role of the entrepreneur in the process of innovation;
- Describe the links between innovation, opportunity and entrepreneurship;
- Assess whether you are an innovative thinker;
- Describe the relationship between innovation and risk and explain how risk can be mitigated or reduced;
- Explain how risk can be managed strategically, in particular by taking a portfolio approach to its management;
- Describe how innovation differs in small and large firms;
- Describe the stimuli for discontinuous innovation;
- Explain why networks can be an important source of knowledge that in turn stimulate innovation and describe the form these networks might take;
- Define the characteristics of successful innovating organizations;
- Explain the link between innovation and marketing strategies and analyze why and how organizations innovate successfully.

Innovation and invention

In *The Competitive Advantage of Nations*, Michael Porter (1990) said: 'Invention and entrepreneurship are at the heart of national advantage.' In saying this he implied two things. Firstly, a relationship between invention and entrepreneurship, which must be correct, since entrepreneurship is the process that brings invention to the market place. Secondly, he implied a direct and important link between invention and national advantage. This is more questionable since invention is not the only source of innovation which can benefit the individual firm and create national advantage. Invention is the extreme and riskiest form of innovation. It is usually associated with the development of a new or better product or process but, arguably, could be associated with different forms of marketing. However, examples abound of inventions that are not commercially successful. Thomas Edison, probably the most successful inventor of all time, was so incompetent at introducing his inventions to the market place that his backers had to remove him from every new business he founded.

On the other hand, innovation is more than just invention and it is not, necessarily, just the product of research. It can be many things, for example the substitution of a cheaper material in an existing product, or a better way of marketing an existing product or service, or even a better way of distributing or supporting an existing product or service. Entrepreneurial firms in particular are often innovative in their approach to marketing, finding more effective, often cheaper, routes to market. Direct Line pioneered car insurance selling – a mature product – to the UK public in a way that was innovative at the time – directly, cutting out insurance brokers. Interestingly they were copying a US firm that had done the same. It looked at the value chain for insurance and concluded that the broker network added substantial cost but little or no value to the customer. Innovation, therefore, is about doing things differently in some way.

Kanter (1983) defines it as 'the generation, acceptance and implementation of new ideas, processes, products and services ... [which] ... involves creative use as well as original invention'. Mellor (2005) defines it simply as either 'creativity + application' or 'invention + application'. I would suggest this 'application' is in fact entrepreneurship.

Schumpeter (1996) described five types of innovation:

1. The introduction of a new or improved good or service.
2. The introduction of a new process.
3. The opening up of a new market.
4. The identification of new sources of supply of raw materials.
5. The creation of new types of industrial organization.

In fact there are considerable problems in interpreting these criteria for innovation. For example, what constitutes a new product or service? When a sofa manufacturer produces a 'new' sofa, is that a new product? Economists would probably argue that it was not (the cross elasticity of demand is unlikely to be zero), but the entrepreneur might disagree. What if the sofa manufacturer starts manufacturing chairs? At what point does the firm start producing genuinely new products? If Schumpeter's description of innovation is inadequate it is because of the myriad forms it can take.

What is more, the central role of the entrepreneurial firm in taking the innovation to the market needs to be explicitly acknowledged in any definition.

Morris and Kuratko (2002) expand on Schumpeter's list and talk about the range or continuum of possibilities shown in Figure 13.1. These relate to either the introduction of new products/services or new processes. New processes can be administrative or service-delivery systems, new production or financing methods, different marketing, sales, distribution or procurement approaches, new information

Product/service development	Process development
New-to-the world products/services	
↑	
New-to-the market products/service	Major new process
↑	
New product/service lines within company	
↑	↑
Additions to the product/service line	Minor new process
↑	
Product/service improvements and revisions	↑
↑	
New applications for existing products/services	Significant revision to existing process
↑	
Repositioning of existing products or services	↑
↑	
Cost reductions for existing products or services	Modest improvement to existing process

Source: Adapted from Morris and Kuratko, *op. cit.*

Figure 13.1 The spectrum of product/service and process development or supply chain management systems. This is a frequent route to innovation for entrepreneurial firms. Dell's fully integrated value chain (B2B2C) is a good example of this. Many of these innovations can be introduced during the life cycle of a product so as to maintain competitive advantage. However, Morris and Kuratko's continuum of possibilities does not include innovations in marketing, a form of innovation that is also used very effectively by entrepreneurial firms – for example when Direct Line introduced direct selling of insurance in the UK, doing away with the traditional insurance broker network. Whether a concept or activity may be described as innovative depends on whether it represents a 'departure from what is currently available' – that is, what is unique or different. This is what makes the concept or activity an innovation.

Mintzberg (1983) defined innovation as 'the means to break away from established patterns', in other words doing things really differently. So, simply introducing a new product or service that has customers willing to buy it, is not necessarily innovation. True innovation has to break the mould of how things are done. New cars are rarely truly innovative, whatever the marketing hype might say. However, the Mini was innovative because it changed the way cars were designed and changed the way people perceived vehicle size.

What constitutes innovation in the context of this continuum may be contentious, but what is true is that the sum of many small, incremental innovations can have an enormous impact on competitive advantage (Bessant, 1999). Often these innovations are introduced during the later stages of the life cycle of a product or service so as to maintain or improve competitive advantage and extend its life. This leads to the idea that the impact of innovation on competitive advantage might be measured on two dimensions – frequency of innovation and scale of innovation. This is shown in Figure 13.2. Frequent small innovations may compensate for the occasional 'big-bang' breakthrough. What is more, frequent small innovations may also be less risky. The entrepreneurial firm, therefore, gains competitive advantage by pushing

Figure 13.2 Frequency and degree of innovation

Table 13.1 Two approaches to problem solving

Adaptor	Innovator
Employs a disciplined, precise, methodical approach	Approaches task from unusual angles
Is concerned with solving, rather than finding, problems	Discovers problems and avenues of solutions
Attempts to refine current practices	Questions basic assumptions related to current practices
Tends to be means-orientated	Has little regard for means; is more interested in ends
Is capable of extended detail work	Has little tolerance for routine work
Is sensitive to group cohesion and co-operation	Has little or no need for consensus; often is insensitive to others

Source: Kirton, M. (1976) 'Adaptors and Innovators: A Description and Measure', *Journal of Applied Psychology*, October.

this envelope of creativity as far as it can, perhaps compartmentalizing and organizing itself in different ways to handle these different sorts of innovation.

Kirton (1976) distinguishes between an innovator and an adaptor in terms of the *approach* each takes to problem solving, rather than the outcome itself. One engages in divergent thinking aimed at innovation; the other engages in convergent thinking aimed at perfection. These are contrasted in Table 13.1.

But entrepreneurial innovation is even more than this. What is needed to make the innovation successful is for it to be linked to customer demand – existing or in the future – a market opportunity. Whilst some entrepreneurs might achieve this link through luck, it is the link between innovation and opportunity in the market place that reduces the risk for the entrepreneurial firm and gives it the competitive advantage it is seeking – and that market linkage needs to be developed and embedded in the processes of the firm. Even process innovation, which may involve no change in the product itself, to be successful, must be linked to customer demand through cost/price, quality lead times and so on. Finding opportunities must become a systematic process for the entrepreneurial firm.

Case insight

Like it or loathe it, **McDonald's**, the ubiquitous hamburger chain, brought true innovation to the food industry. It developed a standardized, high-quality hamburger sandwich, produced using entirely new cooking procedures, delivered with the speed of just-in-time preparation by meticulously trained people, in clean surroundings and at a bargain price. This was something entirely new for customers and it spawned a completely new market called 'the fast-food industry'. In doing this not only did it have first-mover advantage, it also created the rules for a whole new industry. And if you write the rule book, inevitably you have an incredibly competitive advantage. The question today is whether the product has finally come to the end of its life cycle?

Video recorders were invented by an American firm called Ampex in 1954. They were reel-to-reel devices, about the size of a juke box, and were used by television networks to record and then transmit programmes in different time zones. However, the real innovators were the Japanese companies Sony (with its Betamax system) and, to a greater extent, JVC (with its VHS system) who realized that the big market for video recorders would be in the home. They succeeded in producing a small video recorder at an affordable price. Like all the best innovations it did not replace an existing product but created its own market. By 2005 digital computer chip-based recording and CDs/DVDs had all but replaced the analogue video recorders and video cassettes in both sectors of the market because they offered even better quality recording, in a more compact space at an even lower price.

Innovation and entrepreneurship

It is the work of Joseph Schumpeter, an Austrian economist, which most strongly links entrepreneurship to innovation. He was the first economist to challenge classical economics and the way it sought to optimize existing resources within a stable environment and to treat disruptions as a 'god sent' external force. In his primary work, Schumpeter (1934) sets out his overall theory of economic development – an endogenous process within capitalism of wrenching the economy out of its tendency towards one equilibrium position and directing it towards a different one. This fundamental phenomenon entails carrying out new combinations of the means of production – which Schumpeter labels 'enterprise' but we could equally call 'innovation' – by individuals called 'entrepreneurs'. These new combinations 'as a rule … must draw the necessary means of production from some old combinations'.

Schumpeter was arguing against traditional economic theory which presumed that the economy was always tending towards equilibrium and that changes in that equilibrium could only occur through changes in underlying conditions of the economy, such as population growth or changes in savings ratios, or through external shocks such as wars or natural disasters. The former were thought to change only slowly and the latter only unpredictably. Schumpeter sought to explain the process of economic development as a process caused by enterprise – or innovation – and carried out by entrepreneurs.

For Schumpeter a normal healthy economy was one that was continually being 'disrupted' by technological innovation producing the 50-year cycles of economic activity noticed earlier by the Russian economist, Nikolai Kondratieff. Using data on prices, wages and interest rates in France, Britain and the USA, Kondratieff first noticed these 'long waves' of economic activity in 1925. Unfortunately he was executed by Stalin some ten years later because he predicted (accurately as it turned out) that Russian farm collectivization would lead to a decline in agricultural production. It was therefore left to Schumpeter to study these waves in depth.

Schumpeter said that each of these cycles was unique, driven by different clusters of industries. The upswing in a cycle started when new innovations came into general use:

- Water power, textiles and iron in the late 18th century.
- Steam, rail and steel in the mid 19th century.
- Electricity, chemicals and the internal combustion engine in the early 20th century.

These booms eventually petered out as the technologies matured and the market opportunities were fully exploited, only to start again as a new set of innovations changed the way things were done. For the last twenty years of the cycle the growth industries of the last technological wave might be doing exceptionally well. However they are, in fact, just repaying capital that is no longer needed for investment. This situation never lasts longer than twenty years and returns to investors then start to decline with the dwindling number of opportunities. Often this is precipitated by some form of crisis. After the twenty years of stagnation new technologies will emerge and the cycle will start again.

The other factor at work is that innovation – particularly technological innovation – also seems to generate growth that cannot be accounted for by changes in labour and capital. Although the return on investment may decline as more capital is introduced to an economy, any deceleration in growth is more than offset by the leverage effects of innovation. Because of this the rich Western countries have seen their return on investment increasing, whilst the poorer countries have not caught up.

By the time Schumpeter died in 1950 the next cycle of boom was starting based upon oil, electronics, aviation and mass production. Another started in the 1980s based upon digital networks, software and new media. The internet and e-commerce triggered an even shorter boom in the late 1990s. One reason for this shortening cycle may be the more systematic approach entrepreneurs now have towards exploiting innovation.

But innovation does not happen as a random event. Central to the process are the entrepreneurs. It is they who introduce and then exploit the new innovations. For Schumpeter, 'the entrepreneur initiates change and generates new opportunities. Until imitators force prices and costs into conformity, the innovator is able to reap profits and disturb equilibrium'. By way of contrast, early classical economists such as Adam Smith saw entrepreneurs as having a rather minor role in overall economic activity. He thought that they provided real capital, but did not play a leading or direct part in how the pattern of supply and demand was determined.

Pulling together these strands, therefore, real innovation might be defined as a single 'mould-breaking' development in new products or services or how they are produced (the materials used, the process employed or how the firm is organized to deliver them) or how or to whom they are marketed that can be linked to a

Case insight

In 1991 **Trevor Baylis** was watching a TV programme about the Aids epidemic in Africa. It got him thinking about how information about Aids prevention might be broadcast to people in a country where there was no electricity and batteries were prohibitively expensive. He quickly came up with a design for a clockwork radio. Despite being featured on radio and TV he could not convince people that it was a commercially viable product.

It was only when he teamed up with an entrepreneur, **Christopher Staines**, and a company called **Liberty Life** that the radio was produced and marketed. The entrepreneur was able to exploit the innovation in a way the inventor was not able to do. Production began in 1994 and 120,000 radios are now made each month. Without the entrepreneur the invention would not have reached the market place.

commercial opportunity and successfully exploited. However frequent, incremental small-scale 'innovations' may offer similar competitive advantage, with lower associated risk.

Returning to Michael Porter's issue of national advantage, the link in taking invention to the market place is indeed entrepreneurs or entrepreneurial firms but what they are really seeking in doing this is innovation – difference – rather than invention, *per se*. It is innovation and entrepreneurship that are at the heart of success for the individual firm and of national advantage.

Creativity and entrepreneurship

Creativity is also linked to innovation. However, in his review of the literature, Van Grundy (1987) distinguishes between innovation and creativity. Creativity may contribute to innovation, but equally it can be used towards other ends. Indeed, as emphasized by Mellor (*op. cit.*), creativity is only part of the process of innovation, requiring also application – or entrepreneurship – to transform it into innovation.

Bolton and Thompson (2000) have stressed the importance of creativity in this process of invention and innovation. They associated invention closely with creativity but also linked it with entrepreneurship if the invention is to become a commercial opportunity to be exploited. 'Creativity is the starting point whether it is associated with invention or opportunity spotting. This creativity is turned to practical reality (a product, for example) through innovation. Entrepreneurship then sets that innovation in the context of an enterprise (the actual business), which is something of recognised value'. Like Porter, to them creativity and invention need the entrepreneurial context, including the perception of opportunity, to become a business reality. These links between creativity, invention and innovation, opportunity perception and entrepreneurship are represented in Figure 13.3.

Figure 13.3 Invention, opportunity and entrepreneurship

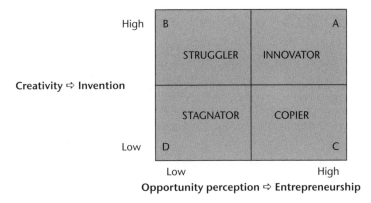

Figure 13.4 Invention and entrepreneurship

Another way of looking at this relationship between invention and entrepreneurship and its real outcomes is shown in Figure 13.4. Only in quadrant A is there a winning combination of invention and entrepreneurship. All other quadrants fail to achieve their full potential. In quadrant B there is a firm struggling with too many wasted ideas. It lacks an entrepreneurial orientation with the ability to both see the commercial application of the idea and to exploit it. In quadrant C there is a firm that lacks invention and creativity but can at least copy and perhaps improve on inventions coming from other firms if they have a commercial application. Firms in quadrant D lack both invention and entrepreneurship, are certain never to grow and indeed their very survival may be questioned.

Case insight

Recently *Time* magazine named **RadioScape** as one of the top 50 technology companies in Europe. The company was set up in 1997 by **Peter Florence**, a serial entrepreneur. Aged only 39 at the time, this was his third technology-based start-up. RadioScape designs and develops enabling wireless communication. The technology developed by the company is part of the dominant digital radio brand and has the potential to be incorporated into every third-generation mobile phone. The company started to develop products on a wide front. Texas Instruments is now using its chip as part of a digital radio package, which means that when the medium takes off the royalty payments could be huge. Said Peter Florence:

'We believed that the world was going digital. We could see that, although the US was ahead of Europe in the use and development of the internet, Europe was way ahead in the use of mobiles and the development of digital technology. Like others, we could also see the potential of digital radio, not least in broadcasting quality sound but in receiving and transmitting raw data that can be used in computers. We went for digital radio as the major players were waiting and it was still at an early stage.'

Peter raised £18 million in venture capital in 2001 against this vision. But timing and credibility are all. Peter's first venture was **Digital Pictures**, a film production house specializing

➡

Case insight continued

in 3D computer graphics. He had identified new technology that worked with the opportunity to generate revenues quickly. Eventually he sold out and moved on to set up **Cambridge Animation**, starting with 3D and expanding into 2D technology. The company grew rapidly, moving to Los Angeles where it worked with studios such as Dreamworks and Warner Bros. He then started looking for the next big technological niche with the help of the technologist behind Cambridge Animation, Gavin Ferris. RadioScape currently has 90 employees and has a turnover of £8 million. Peter continues:

'There was a time if you had good technology in an interesting market and one or two ideas about how it might all end up ok on the night, that was enough. No more. Now you must have proven management, own a pretty solid patent and show that you can generate revenues quickly. Although the UK has been good at inventing technology, we have been poor at marrying the men in white coats with businessmen and entrepreneurs who can make the product work. That is my skill. You need a good chief executive and a good chief technology officer. One without the other is wasted.'

Peter Florence
founder and Chief Executive, **RadioScape**
The Times, 6 July 2002

Innovation and risk

Entrepreneurial firms innovate and innovation is risky. Firms can innovate in the way they produce their product or service so as to be more efficient – important if you are a commodity producer – or the way the product or service is more effective at meeting customer needs – important to improve quality and differentiate the product or service. These are likely to be incremental changes, therefore involving minimal risk. Essentially they improve what the firm is already doing and are a necessary part of long-term development, but they are hardly entrepreneurial.

Ansoff's analysis in the previous chapter gives us a valuable insight into the risks associated with growth through innovation. Bowman and Faulkner (1997) added an extra dimension to Ansoff's analysis by considering core competency and method of implementation. They pointed out that any move into new markets or new products/services becomes riskier, the further the firm strays from its core competencies. Combining these approaches we can see that:

- The lowest-risk strategy of all is market penetration, but in a growth market where gaining market share as quickly as possible is important security might be short-lived. As we shall see in the next section, following a policy of 'no innovation' at all, in the long run, can prove ultimately high-risk because markets are changing so rapidly.
- Innovation through market development is most successful for companies whose core competencies lie in the efficiency of their existing production methods, for example in the capital goods industries, and are seeking economies of scale, or for

firms adept at sales, marketing and developing close customer relationships – the very qualities of our entrepreneurial firm.

● Innovation through product and process development is most successful for those companies whose competencies lie in building good customer relationships, often associated with effective branding. However, of equal importance could be the ability to innovate. Both are qualities of the entrepreneurial firm.

● The highest-risk strategy of all is diversification, with unrelated diversification being extremely high-risk. This can be likened to the introduction of new-to-the-world products. Related diversification is safest for companies who are adept at both innovation and developing close customer relations – which effectively describes our entrepreneurial firms. Thus it was just as well that the Mini – truly a mould breaking innovation in car design – was produced by a car manufacturer.

At the extreme, entrepreneurial innovation is radical and risky, innovating in both product/service and market dimensions at the same time. But whilst this may be risky, the returns can be equally large. As Cannon (1985) points out: 'The ability of the entrepreneurial mould-maker to break free from bureaucratic rigidities, fan the flames of innovation and create new situations has been the basis of the growth of many of today's great corporations. Ford, Durant, Kellogg, Singer, Krupp, Eastman, Courtauld, Daimler, Biro, Siemens and Daussault all built giant enterprises which are virtually synonymous with their industries.' Building on the Ansoff matrix, this is the equivalent of diversification. These developments are represented in Figure 13.5.

With the exception of the 'no innovation' option where risks are minimal in the short term but high in the long term, risk gets progressively higher as the firm moves to the bottom right hand corner of Figure 13.5 in terms of its strategy. This is indicated by the shading. However, risk is not a linear relationship. In the 'twilight

 Figure 13.5 Growth and risk

zone' – marked by the dashed circle at the centre of the matrix – risk can be lowered. This is the zone where continuous, small incremental changes in product and market can greatly expand the product/service offering and its market place and, as we shall see in the next section, this is where risk can be lowest. It is the zone where the entrepreneurial firm may have the greatest competitive advantage and therefore face lower risk than other firms in related diversification or develop new products for slightly different markets because it has the entrepreneurial architecture that allows it to cope with continuous, market-related change.

The riskiest strategy of all is to introduce a new product or service into a completely unknown market – 'new to the world'. This is what happens with a completely new invention, for example when PCs were introduced in the late 1970s. IBM refused to enter the market, partly because market research could not identify a demand for the product. Potential domestic customers could not understand the product, or more particularly, what it would do for them – how it would add value. Existing applications were commercial. Why would they want a machine to 'do sums'? Why was it better than a typewriter? Of course the PC took off when the domestic applications were identified such as games and the internet, and now most homes in the Western world have (at least) one. But investment in the early-stage development of PCs was a leap of faith.

Of course this is not to say that a company should not take risks, but rather that growth involves risks and it is as well to understand the degrees of risk associated with different strategies. Research indicates that successful entrepreneurial firms follow a strategy of incremental, mainly internal, growth (Burns, 1994). They move carefully into new markets with existing products or sell new products to existing customers. Related diversification only works when based on core competencies. The strategy of unrelated diversification – or innovation – is high-risk and only to be adopted after careful consideration. Entrepreneurial firms must consider carefully whether this is really appropriate to their needs.

However, there is another important way that the entrepreneurial firm can mitigate against risk – it can link the innovation to opportunities in the market place. So long as the innovation adds value to the customer, it is likely to find a market place. And here is where a strong linkage to customers, an understanding of who they are and their wants and needs, becomes so important. And this is where the entrepreneurial firm should score again over other firms in the 'twilight zone'.

Another way of mitigating the marketing risk is through joint ventures or strategic alliances, particularly in marketing to overseas markets. Both can be set up relatively quickly. In these circumstances the partner may possess much needed competencies or expertise, such as market knowledge. It even works with product development. This was the basis of the relationship Mercedes had with Swatch when the Smart cars were developed. Swatch offered fashion design. Mercedes offered engineering and production quality. With such relationships the risks can then be compartmentalized and failure will not therefore endanger either core business. What is more, the strategy avoids high set-up costs. And it relies on what an entrepreneurial firm should be good at – building relationships. On the down-side, it does mean that the profits must be shared and control is lost to some extent – which is why firms also consider mergers and acquisitions as a way of diversifying or indeed buying a foothold in a new market. As we saw with Dell, because of their nature, entrepreneurial firms can have some advantage in developing these relationships.

One further important point. For a smaller organization with limited resources, pursuing all four of Ansoff's growth strategies simultaneously within any one time frame is likely to be extremely risky. Assuming market penetration will always continue, it is best advised to follow only one other strategy at a time, perhaps alternating the strategy over time. Making the right choice is an important decision, but one that has to be made by a conscious choice rather than by drift or force of circumstance.

The process of innovation and risk

Risk is not just associated with the introduction of new products/services into new markets. It is also related to the innovation process – how they are introduced. Innovation can be anything from a discrete and infrequent event – a major breakthrough – to a continuous stream of small improvements that often copy the improvements of others. The major breakthrough involves high risk and hopefully generates high returns if followed through successfully. But frequency is also important. So much so that the return from many smaller innovations might exceed the returns from one, infrequent, major breakthrough. What is more, the infrequent major innovation still faces the risk that it might not actually succeed, whilst the odds inevitably mean that at least some of the smaller ones will succeed.

Hamel and Prahalad (1991) liken firms relying on this strategy to baseball players who concentrate on perfecting their swing and always strive to hit a perfect home run, so returning to base to hit again. The result is that they are cautious and hold off until they think they can hit that perfect shot, thus affecting their batting average. The problem is that success is a function of both the ability to bat – your batting average – and the number of times you come to bat. You need to bat more often. So the team that is not striving for perfection may get more of both and win the game.

Risks are better managed by focusing on frequent, lower-risk projects. They are better managed by diversifying the risk into different product/market offerings targeted at different market segments. Entrepreneurs instinctively know this. They engage in lots of experiments, test-markets and trial runs. They learn by doing, learning from their failure, and sharpening their response time by constantly progressing the project. A company relying on a few big projects that it pursues cautiously, always trying to perfect the product/service, is too like the baseball player trying to perfect his swing.

Figure 13.6 shows the risk associated with different approaches to the process of innovation. Dynamic, continuous innovation builds upon existing products/services so that customers understand the nature of the offering, unlike discrete innovation which may address a need but one that has to be explained and accepted by the customer. Continuous innovation is the incremental, step-by-step development of the product/service and market. Finally there is imitation – copying or adapting the innovations of others. Whilst this as an individual activity is low-risk, as an overall strategy, in the long run, it is little better than no innovation at all. As Morris and Kuratko (*op. cit.*) point out: 'the imitative company is apt to miss out on entire market opportunities by the time it is able to respond to an innovative new product or service. When the firm does move, it finds its role to be that of niche player in the market place. It also becomes harder and harder to catch up as innovative

Figure 13.6 Risk and the process of innovation

competitors move from incremental advances in a current technology to a major advance using a new technology. Meanwhile new competitors emerge from other industries to attack the firm's most profitable lines of business with innovative marketing, distribution, and customer services approaches.'

One further dimension to risk and innovation is the time the process takes. If the process takes too long you run the risk that the opportunity may be missed. The longer you delay the launch the higher the risk that a competitor may launch first and the greater the risk of losing first-mover advantage. On the other hand if you launch too early you run the risk of the product/service or marketing strategy being ill-prepared and turning customers against it leaving the market wide open for competitors. Sometimes a product is just 'before its time' and customers need educating about it before it goes into full-scale production. Either way, launching too early can often be even more disastrous that launching too late. Timing is crucial, which leads us to the link between risk and innovation process time shown in Figure 13.7. Entrepreneurial firms should have an advantage here, because of their

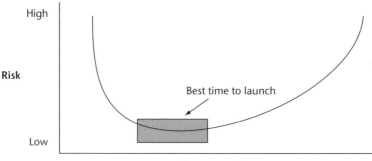

Figure 13.7 Risk and innovation process time

ability to move quickly. Equally, joint ventures and strategic alliances have an important part to play.

One reason for getting the timing wrong arises from whether innovations come through technology-push or market-pull. Market-pull starts with customers and the need for the innovation is derived from them. This innovation is more likely to succeed because the timing, by definition, is right. An innovation based upon technology drive may not yet meet a customer need simply because customers cannot visualize how the new product/service might be used. The PC was one such innovation. When asked, people just could not understand how such an innovation might be of use to them. Technology-driven innovations are also more likely to be large, discrete innovations whereas those driven by the market are more likely to be small, incremental and continuous. Thus technology-driven innovation can be very risky. But once again, entrepreneurial firms should also have an advantage in this because of their market responsiveness and closeness to the customer.

Case with question

Glaxo Smith Kline

Glaxo Smith Kline may be Britain's biggest drug company and may spend £280,000 an hour on research, but its share price reveals a company that is losing its touch at making innovations profitable. The company was formed by the merger of Glaxo and SmithKline Beecham. In their heyday in the 1980s and 1990s such pharmaceutical companies regularly turned in operating margins of 40%. In part, such margins were the norm because the companies were able to extend patents almost at will. A compound could be reformulated with only modest improvements in efficacy but the regulators and courts seemed happy to grant and protect new patents. But things started changing in the 1990s. Glaxo first came up against the change when it failed to protect its ulcer drug Zantac – which had achieved annual sales of over $1 billion. The result was swift and predictable. Generic imitations rapidly appeared on the market and Zantac's sales price and sales volume both tumbled. Pharmaceutical firms started investing heavily in lawyers – Glaxo spends hundreds of thousands of pounds – but at the same time firms producing generic drugs continued challenging patents, realizing that there were high returns to be made if they were successful. And by the turn of 2000 over 85% of such patents were being overturned. In 2002 Glaxo revealed that sales of Augmentin, an antibiotic, fell by 40% in the USA as Geneva Pharmaceuticals launched a cut-price generic version of the drug, having successfully challenged the Glaxo patent. And the politics of drug pricing continues to move against the big pharmaceutical firms with the US government closing a loophole in the law that had allowed companies to extend patents artificially for up to 5 years.

The other side of the problem is that the pharmaceutical firms are finding it increasingly difficult to discover pioneering new drugs at anything like the old rate of invention. The rule of thumb in the industry is that if you spend $1 billion a year on research, you need one new drug approval (by the likes of the US Food and Drug Administration) a year to make an economic return. Glaxo Smith Kline currently spends $4 billion a year but between 1996 and 1999 it averaged just two and in 2000 and 2001 just one. In 2002 there were three, although none were major.

→

Case with question continued

Glaxo Smith Kline

So what is Glaxo Smith Kline doing to address the problem? It has separated its research departments into six semi-autonomous units each with its own budget. The idea is that each unit must manage research using commercial criteria and judge its investment decisions by the commercial return they make.

But perhaps more interestingly Glaxo has observed from its recent history that its profitability can be sustained by its skill in buying drugs from smaller competitors and then using its marketing power and global distribution network to bring the drugs to a global market place quickly. Glaxo employs 42,000 sales and marketing people compared to 15,000 in research and development – a huge investment and a significant competitive advantage. For the time being the company is happy to pursue this twin-track strategy.

Up-to-date information on Glaxo can be found on their website: www.gsk.com

Question
What do you think about Glaxo's policy towards innovation?

Innovation and size

Entrepreneurial firms have not been defined, necessarily, in terms of size. But there are linkages between size and innovation. Few small firms introduce really new products into their product range. Even fewer introduce really new products into the economy as a whole. This role is more likely to be undertaken by larger firms because of the resources they command. However, small firms can, and often do, introduce products or services that are clearly differentiated from those of the 'competition', to the point where one might question whether there is any direct competition. Indeed, this ability to differentiate clearly is a major element in their success. Is this innovation? Perhaps it is, but one would have to stretch Schumpeter's first or even his third criterion (opening up of a new market) to accommodate it.

Small firms are most likely to provide something marginally different to the competition, in terms of the product or service, and thus find a market niche. They are also far more likely to innovate in terms of marketing and customer service (often low-cost options). They often find new routes to market first, for example 'direct' selling, via the phone with the growth of call centres located in low-cost areas or via the internet offering similar advantages through the 'virtual' organization. Small firms are often innovative in their approach to key account management and customer relationships. They find ways of networking with customers and suppliers so as to cut costs and lead times. Which of Schumpeter's categories do these fall into? These are all approaches an entrepreneurial firm – of any size – can adopt.

Many truly successful innovations, particularly product innovations but certainly the ones involving large amounts of capital, originate from large not small companies. There are few Dysons in this world who successfully struggle to bring a genuinely new product to the market themselves, against all the odds. There are just too many problems to sort out – not least of which is finding the finance. Moreover it is easier for a middle-sized or large company to sort out these problems because it has more resources, more experience ... more of everything to throw at a problem.

This is not to decry the importance of small firms in the process of product innovation. Studies suggest that, although they are much less likely to conduct R&D than large firms, they conduct them more efficiently and introduce new products to the marketplace faster than big companies. Studies measuring only R&D expenditure must be treated with caution because of the inability of small firms often to separate out this expenditure. However, a US study (Acs and Aaudretsch, 1990) found that small firms produce 2.4 times as many innovations per employee as large firms. Another UK study (Pavitt *et al.*, 1987) concluded that small firms are more likely to introduce fundamentally new innovations than large firms. In their review of innovation in small firms Deakins and Freel (2006) concluded that 'the innovative contributions of small firms varies across industry sectors and through the industry life cycle, at least with respect to technical innovations. In new industries, where technology is still evolving, small firms have a more significant role to play than in mature industries, where the innovation focus has switched to cost-reducing process innovation and minor product enhancements. However, in mature industries small firms may benefit from innovations in structure, supply or markets.'

What seems clear is that innovative behaviour is not entirely related to firm size. It also relates to business activity, the industry, the nature of the innovation, and the type of company. Large firms outperform small firms where resources are important – because of capital intensity or because of scale of spending on R&D, advertising etc. or simply because of barriers to entry. Rothwell (1989) shows that, where no such prerequisite exists, the share of small firms in innovation is substantial. He concludes that 'innovative advantage is unequivocally associated with neither large nor small firms. The innovatory advantages of large firms are in the main associated with their relatively greater financial and technological resources, i.e. they are material advantages; small firm advantages are those of entrepreneurial dynamism, internal flexibility and responsiveness to changing circumstances, i.e. they are behavioural advantages'. It has also been pointed out that the advantages of large firms are generally the disadvantages of small firms, and vice versa, and therefore collaboration between the two sizes (inside or outside the same corporation) can create powerful synergistic relationships (Vossen, 1998). In other words, the larger entrepreneurial firm should have a distinct advantage in innovation.

This having been said, Christensen (1997) sounded a very loud warning note to large firms facing major innovations due to market changes. He observed that with each generation almost all of the previously successful large firms failed to make the transition effectively and were often squeezed out of the market or into bankruptcy, despite the fact they were often exemplars of good practice – ploughing a high percentage of earnings into R&D; having strong working links with their supply chain; working with lead customers to better understand their needs and develop product innovations; delivering a continuous stream of product and process innovations. The problem they had was their inability to identify and capitalize on the emergence of *new markets* with very different needs and expectations – one aspect of the problem of *market disruption* which we deal with in the next section. Essentially these firms were *too* close to their existing customers, suppliers and technologies. The result was that they failed to see the long-term potential of newly emerging markets.

What might have begun as a fringe business moved into the mainstream and eventually changed the rules under which the mainstream businesses operated so, by the time the mainstream businesses realized this, they had lost their competitive advantage.

Case insight

James Dyson is the inventor of the revolutionary cyclone vacuum cleaner who challenged established large companies in the market to gain a market share in excess of 50%. Inventor of the 'Ballbarrow', a light plastic wheelbarrow with a ball rather than a wheel, the idea for the vacuum cleaner came to him in 1979 because he was finding that traditional cleaners could not clear all the dust he was creating as he converted an old house. Particles clogged the pores of the dust bags and reduced the suction. He had developed a small version of the large industrial cyclone machines, which separate particles from air by using centrifugal force, in order to collect paint particles from his plastic-spraying operation for Ballbarrow. He believed the technology could be adapted for the home vacuum cleaner, generating greater suction and eliminating the need for bags.

Working from home, investing all his own money and borrowing on the security of his home and drawing just £10,000 a year to support himself, his wife and three children, he produced 5000 different prototypes. However, established manufacturers rejected his ideas and venture capitalists declined to invest in the idea. In 1991 he took the product to Japan and won the 1991 International Design Fair prize. He licensed the manufacture of the product in Japan where it became a status symbol selling at $2000 a time. On the back of this and twelve years after the idea first came to him, he was able to obtain finance from Lloyds Bank to manufacture the machine under his own name in the UK.

Early sales were through mail order, then followed a deal with John Lewis and later Comet and Currys. There are now 18 different sorts of Dyson cleaner and the company has captured 38% of the UK market. But the Dual Cyclone was nearly never made due to patent and legal costs. Unlike a songwriter who owns his songs, an inventor must pay substantial fees to renew his patent each year. This nearly bankrupted Dyson in the development years.

Today Dyson products can be purchased in 22 countries and James Dyson is chairman of the Dyson Group, with his personal wealth estimated to be over £700 million. He is in the top 50 richest people in the UK. Dyson's major competitor, Hoover, paid him the ultimate compliment of copying his design with their Vortex range. In 2000 he won his case against them for infringing his patents.

●

Discontinuous innovation

Innovation is not always a continuous process. It can also be triggered by dramatic changes to the status quo (in technology, market, social and regulatory environments) that lead to 'discontinuous innovation' – step changes in products or processes. These are difficult to predict, even if a company is sensitive to the expressed needs of its customers. Famously Henry Ford once said that if he had asked people what they wanted, they'd have said 'faster horses', rather than 'new-fangled' things called cars. Tidd *et al.* (2005) give some examples of these discontinuities:

- *New markets* can emerge unpredicted – one example of disruption that has led to the extinction of many large firms, as highlighted by Christensen (*op. cit.*), is the dot.com bubble.
- *New business models* are established, often by new entrants to a market, who dare to question the 'rules of the game' and end up changing them – another example of the market disruption that large firms are not good at dealing with, such as the emergence of the direct insurance market pioneered in the UK by Direct Line and the success of dot.com businesses like Lastminute and Dangdang.
- *New technologies* can emerge as step changes in product or process technologies (e.g. mobile phones or the internet) or as the result of a single breakthrough (e.g. the LED as a white light source). These can be both in high-technology niches evidenced by pioneering breakthroughs (Utterback and Acee, 2005) or in low-technology niches evidenced by new configurations of existing technologies (Schmidt, 2004), blurring somewhat the distinction between incremental and radical innovation.
- *New political rules* can cause markets to change dramatically, such as the fall of communism.
- *Market exhaustion* for firms in mature industries may lead to exit or radical reorientation of the business.
- *Sea change in market sentiment or behaviour* – for example the move from CDs to music downloads or growth in the organic foods market.
- *Deregulation or shifts in regulatory regimes* can lead to new markets or new market rules – for example the privatization of much of the public sector by Margaret Thatcher in the UK in the 1980s.
- *Fracture along 'fault lines'* can occur when minority opinions gather momentum and cause systems to 'flip' (e.g. opinions over smoking or the environment).
- *Unthinkable events* that cannot be prepared for, like 9/11, and the consequences for business.
- *Shifts in the 'techno-economic paradigm'* are systems-level changes involving the convergence of technology and market changes, for example electricity replacing steam power.
- *Architectural innovations* which rewrite the 'rules of the game' as to how things are done, for example, who you might have to talk to in acquiring knowledge to drive innovation.

A powerful driver of innovation is currently 'sustainability' – environmental responsibility, ethical business practices and other issues often wrapped up in the term 'corporate social responsibility' (CSR). Innovation linked to sustainability often has major systems-level implications, demanding a holistic and integrated approach to innovation management. The commitment of the retailer M&S to be completely carbon-neutral by 2012 requires it to completely re-engineer many of its operations. Berkhout and Green (2003) argue for a systems approach to innovation, linking innovation with sustainable research, policy and management concluding that 'greater awareness and interaction between research and management of innovation, environmental management, corporate social responsibility and innovation and environment will prove fruitful.'

Although the innovations coming from these discontinuities are far from incremental or part of a continuous process of improvement, they can still be managed within established frameworks. This involves dealing with rapidly changing and disparate information – in a wide range of new technologies; in diverse, fragmented and often geographically widespread markets; charting a way through often uncertain political and unstable regulatory environments; facing competitors emerging from unexpected directions. So knowledge can be a powerful source of innovation. In these circumstances effective knowledge management – picking up and making sense of knowledge signals – is vital. And knowledge networks have an important part to play. The issue with discontinuous innovation is that networking too closely with existing customers and suppliers can lead you to become blind to external developments. You need to build networks with new and different partners alongside the more traditional partners. These new networks may be different in nature and weaker.

There is growing evidence of the benefits of networking, in its broadest sense, as a way of stimulating innovation. Chesborough (2003) calls this process 'open innovation' – sourcing ideas from outside the company, where links and connections become more important than ownership of the knowledge. Procter & Gamble use the phrase 'Connect and Develop' (C&D) and see collaborative networks as crucial in helping them keep in touch with the research that they do not undertake themselves. How you operate an innovation network depends heavily on the type of network and the purpose it is set up to achieve. Tidd *et al.* (*op. cit.*) map some of these different networks onto a simple matrix, differentiating between how radical the innovation outcome and how similar the participating organizations. This is shown in Figure 13.8. Zone 1 has similar firms dealing with tactical innovation issues – 'good

Radical innovation	**Zone 2** ● Strategic alliances ● Sector consortia ● New technology development consortia	**Zone 4** ● Multi-company innovation networks in complex product systems ● New product or process
Incremental innovation	**Zone 1** ● Sector fora ● Supply chain learning programmes	**Zone 3** ● Regional clusters ● Best practice clubs ● Topic network
	Similar organizations	Different organizations

Source: Adapted from Tidd *et al.*, *op. cit.*

 Figure 13.8 Innovation networks

practice' fora. Zone 2 has similar firms working together to create new products or processes by challenging existing boundaries, dealing with the issue of knowledge sharing and risk taking through the structures of formal joint ventures and strategic alliances. Zone 3 has different firms bringing key pieces of information, perhaps from a wide range of disciplines, to the network. The risks of disclosure can be high so the ground rules for disclosure need to be set well in advance and any intellectual property rights issues resolved. The stakes are even higher in Zone 4 and third-party gatekeepers such as universities can play an important part as neutral knowledge brokers.

If networks are important in generating information, how that information is generated, disseminated and used within the organization is vital. To be useful information needs to be turned into knowledge. This only happens through learning. Rowley (2000) used the simple model shown in Figure 13.9. Information comes into the organization from a range of sources. It is conceptualized in a way that is consistent with its norms, cognitive frameworks, context and cultures. This is learning, which in turn leads either to tacit knowledge (embedded in minds and activities) or explicit knowledge (stated in verbal communications or documents). This knowledge informs decisions, actions and behaviours and feeds back into the processes creating this knowledge. This brings us back to that aspect of the entrepreneurial architecture that mirrors a learning organization – the emphasis on organizational learning; the ability of the organization to understand the causes of a problem and question 'why'; its emphasis on tacit knowledge. Knowledge-creating companies constantly encourage the process whereby personal knowledge is made available to others to use to extend their own tacit knowledge base. A learning organization should therefore facilitate this whole process.

Rowley (*op. cit.*) agues for greater integration of the learning processes emphasized in the learning organization literature with the systems focus of the knowledge management literature, and coins the phrase 'knowledge entrepreneur' for organizations that can do this. These organizations build bridges between people and systems and this is vital in larger organizations or multinationals where systems are the only practical way to transmit some information. It is also vital in tackling the challenge of sustainability.

Feedback loops

Source: Adapted from Rowley, *op. cit.*

Figure 13.9 From information to knowledge

Case insight

Lastminute.com offers last-minute deals on theatre tickets, flights, holidays and even restaurants. It was set up in 1998 by **Brent Hoberman** (then 30 years old) and **Martha Lane Fox** (then 26), after raising £600,000 in venture capital. In 1999 it had a turnover of £195,000 and did not make a profit. By early 2000 the company was operating in the UK, France, Germany and Sweden, had 162 employees and 800,000 registered subscribers and sales of £30 million. In the same year it was floated on the Stock Market at a valuation of more than £400 million. Lastminute has been one of the dot.com survivors, indeed successes. By 2004 it handled transactions to the value of £990 million and had a turnover of almost £400 million producing operating profits of £7.5 million. In 2005 it was taken over by Sabre Holdings at an offer price valuing the company at £606 million. By 2006 it had expanded its international coverage and boasted 9.8 million registered subscribers to its weekly newsletter.

Back in 2000, apart from the general dot.com frenzy of the time, there were four main reasons for the high float valuation of Lastminute.com, which together led commentators at the time to think the company would be a success – a view that time has proved correct:

1. *Brand*: Lastminute.com claimed early on to be the second most recognised e-retailer in the UK after Amazon. This is partly as a result of a very 'old-media' advertising and promotion campaign. Branding recognition is vital to dot.coms, without it nobody visits their site. Even today its aim is to be the Number 1 independent online travel and leisure group in Europe.

2. *Timing*: It was first in the market place and, in 2000, there were few signs of real competition. Two years later this still proved to be the case. First movers have a distinct advantage in e-commerce – as the success of other dot.coms such as eBay and Amazon has proved. Even by 2005, Lastminute.com, continued to have an aggressive acquisition strategy, taking over potential competition and consolidating its brand across Europe. The acquisition of Med Hotels, First Option, Gemstone and most importantly Lastminute.de in Germany, which created the largest online travel company in Germany, all helped to achieve scale in either a product category or in a relevant geographic market. Lastminute.com recognized early that it had to grow quickly simply to survive. Market share was important, and timing – when the market share was acquired – was vital.

3. *Innovation*: The products/services it offers are tailor made for the internet. Not only are its partners eager to sell off their products at a discount to customers who have forgotten to buy it in the first place, it is also attempting to create a last-minute market place in its own right, when people can leave decisions about holidays etc. until a time that suits them. It is not just selling on cheapness, it is about getting its partners to provide a sufficient supply to make buying at the last minute a viable and reliable option. Hotel chains and airlines were generally receptive to the idea as it was a low-risk venture for them. No investment was required by Lastminute.com, all they had to do was allocate a certain amount of their product. As a result Lastminute.com developed an established supply chain very quickly. By 2004 it could start to expand down its supply chain through strategic acquisitions.

4. *Track record*: Although young, the founders grew the company with determination and a clear vision. Both had worked for Spectrum Strategy, a company that wrote business plans for technology firms, which gave them the opportunity to study the sector and understand what was needed for a successful dot.com start-up. They also recruited a strong, experienced management and directorial team right from the very beginning. At various times, the Board has included Peter Bouw, former chairman and chief executive of KLM,

➡

Bob Colliers, vice president of Intercontinental Hotels, Linda Fayne Levinson, who ran Amex Travel and Allan Leighton, former CEO of Walmart and Chairman of Royal Mail Group. All have enormous experience and credibility with funding institutions. The finance director is David Howell who was formerly at First Choice Holidays. How did they attract such a strong management team? Martha Lane Fox explained:

'We decided not to be greedy about equity but to recruit a highly talented and experienced management team by selling them a dream – a stake in lastminute.com.' (*The Times*, 24 March 2000)

'You try to attract the best person for the job, usually far too qualified for the stage that the company is at, but you hope it will grow to accommodate them. If as founders you think you can do better than everyone else, you are in big trouble, because you never can.' (*Sunday Times*, 28 July 2002)

The success of lastminute.com's business model depends on the number of site 'hits' it receives, how many convert into registrations for regular e-mail newsletters and how many then actually buy something from the newsletters. All of these show a steady growth as the company consolidates its brand awareness, expands its geographic coverage and the number of suppliers it represents.

'We knew that if we had special offers we would get people onto the site, sign up for the e-mail, and forward it to someone who would take up the offer to go to New York for £100. The idea is to convert lookers into bookers. Our customer conversion rate is 19% and we want to get it even higher. Small percentage points have a huge impact on sales. That is critical to the business. It's all about the cost of attracting customers and how much we have to spend to attract them balanced by what they're spending. We still need to build our customer base.'

Up-to-date information on Lastminute.com can be found on their website: www.lastminute.com

Questions
1. Why has the company been successful when most dot.com businesses were not?
2. What is its sustainable competitive advantage?
3. What direction would you take the firm in?

Strategic innovation

For an entrepreneurial firm innovation must be at the core of its strategy. It must permeate everything it does. This involves commitment:

- From top management that innovation is at the core of what the business does;
- That innovation is the responsibility of everyone, not just the R&D department;
- That innovation happens in everything, from developing new products/services to new processes and new approaches to marketing.

Innovation should not happen by chance or in a haphazard, piecemeal or tactical manner, with innovative projects being seen as burdensome additional work to 'business-as-usual'. Innovation must be encouraged, facilitated and just part of that 'business-as-usual'. Strategic innovation involves setting explicit goals and policies for innovation and then following them through, monitoring and evaluating performance and risks and adjusting strategies to reflect shifting realities. This means formulating strategies for the nature of new product/service development. These must reflect the nature of the technology and the realities of the market. They must also reflect an understanding of the needs of customers in different market sectors, so that sub-strategies can be developed to reflect innovation in these different segments.

And we are not just talking about new-to-the-world products. We are talking about the full range of product/service and process innovation reflected in Figure 13.1, plus the important added dimension of marketing. It is important to adopt a portfolio strategy for existing products/services and develop innovation strategies for each one reflecting where it is in its life cycle. The Boston matrix can help with this. Continuous proactive innovation over the product/service life cycle will yield considerable competitive advantage, allowing the company to control the market rather than the other way round. The key is balance across the portfolio, balance between:

• High-risk, high-return innovations and lower-risk, lower-return innovations;
• Discrete, dynamic and continuous innovations;
• Product/service and market innovations;
• Short and long time-to-market innovations;
• Innovations that employ new technology and those that employ existing technology.

Although innovation will be part of the fabric of the organization, the different forms of innovation may well require different organizational structures to encourage their development. For example, as we have seen, the organizational structure required to facilitate continuous process development of a product in the mature stage of its life cycle is quite different from that required to encourage new-to-the-world invention. And strategies need to be developed for sourcing these new ideas. Do they come from internal or external sources, or both, as in the case of Glaxo Smith Kline? Financing also needs to be addressed since the needs of different types of innovation, both in volume and nature (internal vs external and equity vs loan finance) may be quite different. And again as we have seen, a balanced portfolio leads to balance in cash flow.

A portfolio approach to innovation is essential to the understanding and management of risk. By holding a balanced portfolio of stocks and shares you can eliminate all but market risk. Similarly, although the risk associated with a new-to-the-world project may be high, as part of a balanced portfolio of innovations and activities that risk is mitigated by the other, less risky, projects. The role of failure is recognized and accepted as part of the cost of achieving winning innovations and a balanced portfolio. Some innovations will be major and other moderate winners, but some will be failures.

The product/market matrix can be an aid to understanding the risk portfolio. Figure 13.10 shows an example of a portfolio of innovations for an imaginary

Figure 13.10 A specimen risk portfolio

company. It is a snapshot at a point of time or for one operating period that changes over time. Each dot represents an innovative project. The company's highest-risk project is project A, a new-to-the-world innovation that will require careful management and risk assessment. There are only two projects, B and C, that are, on the face of it, in the 'twilight zone' where entrepreneurial firms might operate to greatest competitive advantage and we might seek to question why that is the case. More worrying is the fact that there are so few new market developments. The reasons

Case insight

The skill of diagnosing illness has benefited from many technological advances over the last few decades. However, nothing can replace the role of human beings in actually interpreting the information produced and that can create a bottleneck in the process of diagnosis and lead to delays in essential operations. **Telemedicine Clinic** was the brainchild of **David Bäckström**, a Swedish economist who set up the venture in Barcelona in 2002. Telemedicine offers a distance service in clinical radiology diagnosis using 55 top specialists from seven European countries. The service is currently used by hospitals in England, Norway, Sweden and Spain and it is the largest telemedicine and magnetic resonance diagnostic centre in the European Union. In radiology it offers services in magnetic resonance imaging (MRI), computed tomography (CT) and conventional radiology. Quality of service is vital and that includes double reading of all material, second opinion and support in the implementation of new diagnostic methodologies. The service works like this. The hospital treating the patient simply sends the radiography images to the Telemedicine centre in Barcelona. The instantaneous transfer of information is made possible by a new, secure communication technology called VON. Specialists in Barcelona or elsewhere can then interpret the images and send their diagnosis and other information to the doctor personally responsible for the patient.

for this need to be determined. And why is project G involving no innovation? There might be a good reason, for example that this is a new product and in this period what is required is further market penetration. But the analysis acts as a prompt for the question. For each project a better understanding of the strategic fit with the company's core competencies is central to understanding the risks the firm faces overall. However, for this company the risk portfolio does not appear to be balanced.

Successful innovation

In the real world innovation is not the simple, almost linear process so far implied, coming either out of research ('technology push') or out of the perception of needs or opportunities in the market place ('market pull') where necessity becomes the mother of invention. As highlighted by Van De Ven *et al.* (2000) in their case-study based research programme into widely different innovation types, it can be a complex, nonlinear and uncertain process involving false starts, recycling between stages, dead ends and jumps out of sequence. Coping with this sort of complexity requires the integration of systems in different functional areas, extensive networking to draw in and sift through information and a flexible, customized response to the situation. The word 'flexible' implies that the response is hard to predict or characterize. However, Tidd *et al.* (*op. cit.*) link some characteristics of innovation with the type of product or service being produced, which in turn links to the dominant marketing strategy. This

Table 13.2 Characteristics of innovation and marketing strategy

	Degree of differentiation		
	Low		**High** →
Competitive emphasis placed on ...	Cost reduction	Product/service variation	Functional product performance
Innovation stimulated by ...	Pressure to reduce costs, improve quality	Opportunities created by external technical capability	Information on user needs, technical inputs
Predominant type of innovation	Incremental product and process innovation	Major process innovations required by rising volume	Frequent major changes in product/service
Product line	Mostly undifferentiated standard products	Includes at least one stable or dominant design	Diverse, often including custom designs
Production process	Efficient, often capital intensive and relatively rigid	Becoming more rigid and defined	Flexible and inefficient – aim is to experiment and make frequent changes

Source: Adapted from Tidd *et al.* (*op. cit.*).

is summarized in Table 13.2. The more differentiated the product or service the more fluid are the patterns of innovation.

Quinn (1985) identified six factors in larger corporations that were successful innovators. Many of the factors are recurrent themes in this book – after all the key characteristic of corporate entrepreneurship is its ability to innovate.

- *Atmosphere and vision.* These successful companies had a culture that supported innovation and a clear vision of its importance. The role of leader is crucial. Research by Barrett and Storey (2000) in the UK shows they must be committed, enthusiastic and visionary. The whole organization must be seen to encourage and support constant innovation, research and technological change. They must be future-orientated, protecting creativity, accommodating behaviour outside the norm and willing to condone past failure.
- *Market responsiveness.* These visions were tied into the reality of the market place, where the opportunities originated. Intelligence comes from relationships with customers, but equally, these relationships can be used to convince customers to try the innovations. Storey (*op. cit.*) says they also creatively configure customer relationships to ensure they are long-term and generate knowledge and resources.
- *Small, flat organizations.* Innovative companies had flat organizations and used small project teams. Multidisciplinary project teams help bring a holistic perspective to problem solving and innovation. The team can act as committed champions of the innovation. The firms were people-orientated, encouraging human resource development. Environment can also be important. In Bell Laboratories in the USA, creative individuals are stimulated by office environments of their choice.
- *Skunkworks.* These small teams operate outside traditional lines of authority, eliminating bureaucracy and encouraging speed of response. They have a high level of group identity and loyalty and work very effectively as a team.
- *Multiple approaches.* Several projects were often undertaken simultaneously and in parallel. It is an uncertain world and timing is crucial. Pilots can replace written proposals and cut lead times, learning from the market place and suiting the entrepreneurial style of learning-by-doing. It also encourages the process of try/ test/revise which helps work out flaws.
- *Interactive learning.* In these companies learning and investigation of ideas cut across functional lines. They also are not afraid to adopt best practice and learn from others, anywhere – even competitors.

This effectively describes many aspects of corporate entrepreneurship and the thread that binds it all together is entrepreneurial management. Innovation involves creativity but it *needs* entrepreneurship to be effective. It needs entrepreneurship to link with the market opportunity and to bring it into the market place. In this way the risks associated with innovation are reduced. The dot.com boom of the late 1990s ignored most of these basics with inventions and ideas chasing elusive commercial opportunities that rarely linked to customers willing to part with money. Corporate entrepreneurship involves being creative and innovative, embedding the instinct to do these things in the culture and processes of the organization, but always linked to entrepreneurship.

To get a further perspective on this, Kanter (2004) listed a number of 'rules' for stifling innovation in a firm:

- Regard new ideas with suspicion;
- Enforce cumbersome approval mechanisms, rules, regulations;
- Pit departments and individuals against each other;
- Express criticism, without praise;
- Treat problem identification as a sign of failure;
- Control everything carefully;
- Plan reorganization in secret;
- Keep tight control over information;
- Delegate unpleasant duties to inferiors;
- Assume you (the higher-up) know everything important about the business.

Each of these features inhibits innovative thinking and behaviour. Add them all together and you have an organization that positively discourages innovation.

Case with questions

Dangdang

Peggy Yu studied for an MBA and worked on Wall Street in the USA until she moved back to China in 1997, aged 32. In November 1999, together with her husband Li Guoqing, already in charge of the Science and Culture Book Information Co., she decided to set up her own business and, impressed by the success of Amazon in the USA, she decided to try online bookselling. Today the company she set up, Dangdang.com, is the world's largest online Chinese language shopping retailer selling a wide range of other products such as digital products, cosmetics and domestic appliances with a stated policy of 'lower prices, more choice and greater convenience to the customer'. Peggy Yu is one of China's growing breed of successful private entrepreneurs.

Despite a literacy rate of 86% – compared to 99% in the USA – and a population five times that of the USA, China has only 77,000 bookstores and 10% of these are part of the state owned Xinhua news agency. However, book sales, at some 43 billion yuan, are only one-eighth that of the USA where they topped $40 billion in 2002. Often there is a limited range of titles particularly of foreign books.

Dangdang was based very much on the Amazon model. However, some significant differences were made to the business model to suit China's particular circumstances. For example, Amazon's key asset is its huge database of titles that it licenses from book wholesalers. No such facility was available in China so Dangdang had to build its own over a two-year period. The company has also faced other problems. The internet was slow to take off in China and customers were not used to shopping online. They were also not used to paying in advance for goods that arrive later. Nor were they used to paying for delivery. What is more, the credit card market was in its infancy and even now is still not well developed. All of this meant that some two-thirds of business was 'cash-on-delivery', concentrated in 12 large cities where books are delivered by freelance couriers. The balance of business was based on money orders and credit cards. Only slowly are these things changing.

➡

Initially, to keep its capital spending low, Dangdang owned only one warehouse in Beijing that distributed 15% of its sales. A bricks-and-mortar rival, Xinhua, distributed the other 85% from its warehouses around the country. Dangdang now has a world-wide distribution and collection network, with warehouses in Beijing as well as North and South China.

Dangdang claims to take some 4000 orders a day, generating sales of 35 million yuan in 2002 at a gross margin of 25%. However, this represents less than 0.1% of the market. The book market is gradually being deregulated and sales are growing rapidly but Dangdang faces stiff competition. One of the fastest growing competitors is the 500-store franchise chain of Xi-Shu. And there are online competitors such as Joyo.com and the German-run Bol.com. The question is, when will Amazon enter the Chinese market?

Questions
1. What are the strengths and weaknesses in Dangdang's business model?
2. What are the elements of the company's competitive advantage? Can it be sustained in the face of competition?
3. What are the dangers facing Dangdang?
4. How could it compete against Amazon in the Chinese market?
5. What are the opportunities facing the company?

Summary

Innovation is difficult to define. It is about introducing new products, services or processes, opening up new markets, identifying new sources of supply of raw materials or creating new types of industrial organization. But it is more than that. It is about breaking the mould – doing things differently. That might involve invention or developing an innovative process, as with **McDonald's**. But it must be linked to customer demand.

Innovation is a mould-breaking development in new products or services or how they are produced – the materials used, the process employed or how the firm is organized to deliver them – or how or to whom they are marketed, that can be linked to a commercial opportunity and successfully exploited.

Inventors, like **Trevor Baylis**, cannot necessarily create innovation. They need the help of an entrepreneur or an entrepreneurial organization. Whilst creativity is at the core of invention and innovation, so too is the ability to spot market opportunities – and this is one very important role of the entrepreneur. When these factors come together you get a successful firm like **RadioScape**.

Historically there have been cycles of innovation that disrupted economies, causing rapid growth. These are usually technology-led but facilitated by entrepreneurial activity. Figure 13.1 shows how invention can be successfully exploited in an entrepreneurial environment.

Innovation is risky. Firms can innovate in what they produce (important to improve quality and differentiate the product or service) or the way they produce their product or service (so as to be more efficient). These could be incremental changes, involving minimal risk. Increasing degrees of newness of product and newness of market increase the risk associated with the innovation. Entrepreneurial innovation is likely to be more radical and can be discontinuous, for example when technological change and the advent of the internet created the opportunity to launch **Lastminute**. It can also be triggered by dramatic changes to the status quo. There is growing evidence of the benefits of networking, in its broadest sense, as a way of stimulating this sort of discontinuous innovation. But sometimes, as in the case of **Telemedicine Clinic**, you just have to think outside the square.

Risks are better managed by focusing on frequent, lower-risk projects. They are better managed by diversifying the risk into different product/market offerings targeted at different market segments.

Small firms produce more than their fair share of innovations and seem to do it more efficiently than large firms. However, they tend to do this in sectors where resources, in particular capital, are less important. **Dyson** would seem to be a notable exception. Innovation is not entirely related to firm size. It also relates to business activity, industry, nature of innovation and the type of company. Small and large firms have advantages in producing different types of innovation. **GlaxoSmithKline** recognizes this and is splitting down into small, autonomous research departments and also looking to purchase innovatory drugs from small companies and then using the company's marketing strength to distribute them.

Innovation needs to be managed strategically in the entrepreneurial firm. It should be central to every product/market offering, but each requires a different approach depending on the customers, competitors, the market and the point it is at in its life cycle – as in the case of **Dangdang.com** and **Lastminute.com**.

The innovation process can also be a complex, nonlinear and uncertain process involving false starts, recycling between stages, dead ends and jumps out of sequence. Coping with this sort of complexity requires the integration of systems in different functional areas, extensive networking to draw in and sift through information and a flexible, customized response to the situation. The more differentiated the product or service the more fluid are the patterns of innovation.

A portfolio approach to innovation is essential to the understanding and management of the risks associated with innovation. The key is balance across the portfolio of innovations, balance between:

- High-risk, high-return innovations and lower-risk, lower-return innovations;
- Discrete, dynamically continuous and continuous innovations;
- Product/service and market innovations;
- Short and long time-to-market innovations;
- Innovations that employ new technology and those that employ existing technology.

Organizations that are successful in the process of innovation typically have:

- A supportive culture and vision;
- Market responsiveness;
- Small, flat organizations;
- Skunkworks;
- Multiple approaches;
- Interactive learning.

A powerful driver of innovation is currently 'sustainability' – environmental responsibility, ethical business practices and other issues often wrapped up in the term corporate social responsibility (CSR).

Innovative Thinker Test

Innovation is the prime tool entrepreneurs use to create or exploit opportunity and is one of the two most important distinguishing features of their character. The **Innovative Potential Indicator (IPI)** was developed by Dr Fiona Patterson based upon research on employees in established companies. It is published by Oxford Psychologists Press. It claims to be the only psychometric test able to identify those people who have the potential to become innovative thinkers.

Dr Patterson identifies ten types of people:

1. The **Change Agent**, who thrives on change and is independent. The change agent conjures up the strangest ways to solve problems and does not stick to what he or she was told. This is the innovative thinker who embodies one of the most essential characteristics that differentiate entrepreneurs from owner-managers.
2. The **Consolidator**, whose rigidity and independence militates against innovative thinking but is a safety net because of his or her preference for the status quo.
3. The **Harmoniser**, who likes the challenge but does not disclose good ideas for fear of upsetting people.
4. The **Firefighter**, who flits from one idea to another in an imaginative but unpredictable way.
5. The **Co-operator**, who likes change but 'goes with the flow'.
6. The **Catalyst**, who is good at thinking up ideas but soon loses interest.
7. The **Inhibited Innovator**, whose brainwaves could be valuable but lacks the confidence to push it forward.
8. The **Incremental Innovator**, who dreams up radical ideas but likes to implement them in a step-by-step way which can appear inflexible.
9. The **Spice-of-Life**, whose dominant characteristic is the need to be doing something, anything, new.
10. The **Middle-of-the-Road**, who is good at blending ideas but is ambivalent about them.

The IPI questionnaire asks for agreement/disagreement with 36 statements about how you approach change, how adaptable you are and how you stand up to others. Based upon your answers, it scores you on four main areas of behaviour which Dr Patterson's research shows can be used to establish whether a person has innovative potential. Scores can be between 20 and 80 on each dimension. The dimensions are:

- Motivation to change (MTC).
- Willingness to behave in a challenging way (CB).
- Willingness to adapt and use tried and tested approaches (AD).
- Consistency of working style which indicates efficiency and orderliness (CWS).

Change Agents have high MTC and CB scores, and low AD and CWS scores. So for example, Trevor Baylis, the inventor of the clockwork radio, had a MTC score of 70, a CB score of 60, an AD score of 25 and a CWS score of 35. (*The Times*, 14 March 2000)

Essays and discussion topics

1. Is invention good?
2. Do you agree with Michael Porter that 'invention and entrepreneurship are at the heart of national advantage'?
3. What do you think constitutes innovation? Give examples.
4. At which stages in the product life cycle are the range of innovations in Figure 13.1 best used? Try mapping them onto either a typical product life cycle or the Boston matrix.
5. Can an adaptor also be an innovator?
6. What is the relationship between innovation and change?
7. Why are entrepreneurs interested in innovation?
8. What are the major political, economic, social and technological changes that you expect to see over the next ten years? What are their likely consequences and how might they be exploited commercially?
9. Over the last ten years what was the major commercial opportunity that arose? How was it exploited? Was development technology- or market-led? What were the consequences?
10. Over the next ten years, what are the main commercial opportunities that entrepreneurial firms might be best advised to exploit?
11. What steps would a 'copier' have to take to become an innovator?
12. What steps would a 'struggler' have to take to become an innovator?
13. Do you agree with the comments of Peter Florence in the RadioScape case?
14. How is innovation linked to risk? How can risk be mitigated?
15. If innovation is risky, not exploiting innovation is riskier. Discuss.
16. Why is risk lowest in the 'twilight zone'? Why might an entrepreneurial company have competitive advantage in operating here?
17. Give some examples of new-to-the-world products that have been successful and some that have not. Why have they been successful or unsuccessful?
18. Why is 'time to market' important?
19. What are the advantages and disadvantages of joint ventures and strategic alliances?
20. Why might the entrepreneurial firm have some advantage in developing joint ventures and strategic alliances?
21. List the advantages and disadvantages small firms have over large firms in introducing innovation.
22. What are the main barriers to innovation in large firms?
23. What are the main barriers to innovation in small firms?
24. Large firms are to be more innovative than small firms. Discuss.
25. Why do discontinuous innovations occur? Why might we see more of them in the future?
26. How do networks generate new knowledge that can contribute to the development of innovations?
27. Why do you need to take a portfolio approach to risk management?
28. What relevance is the concept of product life cycle to the specimen company analysis in Figure 13.10?
29. The concept of 'balance' in a portfolio of innovation implies such a diverse range of innovative projects that they cannot be managed in the same organization. Discuss.
30. If you want to make a big return, you need to take big risks – that is what entrepreneurial companies are about. Discuss.

Exercises and assignments

1. Answer the Innovation Potential Indicator questionnaire and assess your innovative potential. You can get more details of how to obtain it from the website of Oxford Psychologists Press on www.opp.co.uk.

2. Research Dyson. How is the company doing today? Does it continue to grow? Does it continue to innovate? How has its strategy changed over the years?
3. Research GlaxoSmithKline. How is the company doing today? What is its current approach to innovation? Is it any more successful?
4. Write up a case study of successful innovation in a large firm. Analyze why it was successful.
5. Write up a case study of successful innovation in a small firm. Analyze why it was successful.
6. Research the reasons for the success of VHS rather than Betamax video format. What are the lessons from this?
7. Research the commercial reasons for the success of the Mini. How important is good marketing to the success of an innovation?
8. Write up a case study of a 'creative' firm. Analyze the factors that contribute to its creativity.
9. Contact the DTI and obtain the most recent reports on innovation.
10. Find out how Britain performs compared to other countries in terms of its ability to innovate.
11. Give examples of likely innovations that would yield commercial advantage to firms following each of Porter's four generic marketing strategies: the outstanding success, the niche player, the commodity supplier and the market trader.
12. Give some real examples of discontinuities and the innovations that have resulted from them.

References

Acs, Z. J. and Aaudretsch, D. B. (1990) *Innovation and Small Firms*, Cambridge, Mass: MIT Press.

Barrett, E. and Storey, J. (2000) 'Managers' Accounts of Innovation Processes in Small and Medium-sized Enterprises', *Journal of Small Business and Enterprise Development*, 7(4).

Berkhout, F. and Green, K. (2003) *International Journal of Innovation Management*, 6(3), Special issue on Managing Innovation for Sustainability.

Bessant, J. (1999) 'Developing Continuous Improvement Capability', *International Journal of Innovation Management*, 2.

Bolton, B. and Thompson, J. (2000) *Entrepreneurs: Talent, Temperament, Technique*, Oxford: Butterworth-Heinemann.

Bowman, C. and Faulkner, D. (1997) *Competitive and Corporate Strategy*, London: Irwin.

Burns, P. (1994) *Winners and Losers in the 1990s*, 3i European Enterprise Centre, Report no. 12.

Cannon, T. (1985) 'Innovation, Creativity and Small Firm Organization', *International Small Business Journal*, 4(1).

Chesborough, H. (2003) *Open Innovation: The New Imperative for Creating and Profiting from Technology*, Boston, Mass: Harvard Business School Press.

Christensen, C. (1997) *The Innovator's Dilemma*, Cambridge, Mass: Harvard Business School Press.

Deakins, D. and Freel, M. (2006) *Entrepreneurship and Small Firms*, 4th edn, London: McGraw Hill.

Hamel, G. and Prahalad, C. E. (1991) 'Corporate Imagination and Expeditionary Marketing', *Harvard Business Review*, 69(4), July/August.

Kanter, R. M. (1983), *The Change Masters: Innovation and Productivity in American Corporations*, New York: Simon & Schuster.

Kanter, R. M. (2004) 'The Middle Manager as Innovator', *Harvard Business Review*, 82(7/8).

Kirton, M. (1976) 'Adaptors and Innovators: A Description and Measure', *Journal of Applied Psychology*, October.

Mellor, R. B. (2005) *Sources and Spread of Innovation in Small e-Commerce Companies*, Skodsborgvej: Forlaget Globe.

Mintzberg, H. (1983) *Structures in Fives: Designing Effective Organizations*, London: Prentice Hall.

Morris, M. H. and Kuratko, D. F. (2002) *Corporate Entrepreneurship: Entrepreneurial Development within Organizations*, Fort Worth: Harcourt College Publishers.

Pavitt, K., Robinson, M. and Townsend, J. (1987) 'The Size Distribution of Innovating Firms in the UK: 1945–1983', *Journal of Industrial Economics*, 45.

Porter, M. E. (1990) *The Competitive Advantage of Nations*, New York: Free Press.

Quinn, J. B. (1985) 'Managing Innovation: Controlled Chaos', *Harvard Business Review*, May/June.

Rothwell, R. (1989) 'Small Firms, Innovation and Industrial Change', *Small Business Economics*, 1, 51–64.

Rowley, J. (2000) 'From Learning Organization to Knowledge Entrepreneur', *Journal of Knowledge Management*, 4(1).

Schmidt, G. M. (2004) 'Low-end and High-end Encroachments for New Products', *International Journal of Innovation Management*, 8(2).

Schumpeter, J. A. (1934) *The Theory of Economic Development: An Inquiry into Profits, Capital, Credit, Interest and the Business Cycle* (trans. by Redvers Opie), Oxford University Press.

Schumpeter, J. A. (1996) *The Theory of Economic Development*, edition copyright 1983, New Jersey: Transaction Publishers.

Tidd, J., Bessant, J. and Pavitt, K. (2005) *Managing Innovation: Integrating Technological, Market and Organizational Change*, 3rd edn, Chichester: Wiley.

Utterback, J. and Acee, H. J. (2005) 'Disruptive Technologies: An Expanded View', *International Journal of Innovation Management*, 9(1).

Van De Ven, A., Angle H. L. and Poole, M. S. (2000) *Research in the Management of Innovation: The Minnesota Studies*, New York: Oxford University Press.

Van Grundy, A. (1987) 'Organizational Creativity and Innovation', in S. G. Isaksen, *Frontiers of Creative Research*, New York: Brearly.

Vossen, R. W. (1998) 'Relative Strengths and Weaknesses of Small Firms in Innovation', *International Small Business Journal*, 16(3), 88–94.

14

Encouraging Creativity

Contents

- Understanding creativity
- The creative process
- Blocks to individual creativity
- Techniques for generating new ideas
- Finding opportunity
- Blocks to organizational creativity
- Encouraging organizational creativity
- Developing national creativity
- Summary

LEARNING OUTCOMES

By the end of this chapter you should be able to:

- Explain what makes individuals creative;

- Describe the creative process;

- Explain how it can be stimulated both in the individual and in the organization;

- Explain a number of techniques for generating new ideas;

- Describe how opportunity seeking can be stimulated in a systematic way;

- Describe the barriers to organizational creativity and explain how they can be overcome;

- Describe some of the factors that contribute to national creativity.

Understanding creativity

Creativity is essential in an entrepreneurial organization. Creativity leads to innovation and entrepreneurship drives the whole process. Creativity is at the very soul of entrepreneurship. It is important in coming up with completely new ways of doing things, rather than looking for adaptive, incremental change. But for entrepreneurs the focus for their creativity is commercial opportunity leading to new products, services, processes or marketing approaches. It has been estimated that for every eleven ideas that enter the new product development process, only one new product will be successfully launched (Page, 1993). So new ideas are at a premium and it is a numbers game: the more you generate, the more are likely to see the light of day, commercially. And remember from Chapter 7 the importance of tacit knowledge (embedded in minds and activities) – which is difficult to share and therefore primarily an individual activity – rather than explicit knowledge (stated in verbal communications or documents). Remember also that the primary focus of the organization should be to stimulate individual creativity and learning – tacit knowledge – and translate this into the products and services that the market values (Grant, 1996). So how do you stimulate individual creativity?

We are now starting to understand how the creative process works on an individual level. The brain has two sides that operate in quite different ways. The left side performs rational, logical functions. It tends to be verbal and analytic, operating in a linked, linear sequence (called logical or vertical thinking). The right side operates intuitive and non-rational modes of thought. It is non-verbal, linking images together to get a holistic perspective (called creative or lateral thinking). A person uses both sides, shifting naturally from one to the other. However, the right side is the creative side. Creative innovation is therefore primarily a right-brain activity whilst adaptive innovation is a left-brain activity.

Left-brain thinkers therefore tend to be rational, logical, analytical and sequential in their approach to problem solving. Right-brain thinkers are more intuitive, value-based and non-linear in their approach. The cognitive styles are also reflected in the preferred work-styles with left-brain thinkers preferring to work alone, learn about things rather than experience them and show the ability or preference to make quick decisions. By way of contrast, the right-brain thinker prefers working in groups, experiencing things (e.g. learning by doing) and generating lots of options in preference to focusing on making a speedy decision. People have a preference for one or other approach, but can and do switch between them for different tasks and in different contexts. There are clear parallels here with the approaches to leadership style outlined in Chapter 5 because it is individuals' cognitive processes that shape their preferred style.

'There are so few new ideas, so few new things that have not been done. But although the safe place to be is copying what others are doing, I think the people who succeed will be those with the boldness to do something in a totally different way. They take an idea and reinvent it. We have seen that in airlines, where people said, It's just a flying bus, why shouldn't tickets cost £29? And there are still plenty of opportunities.'
Rachel Elnaugh, founder of **Red Letter Days**
Sunday Times, 23 May 2004

Left-brain   Right-brain

Logical	Creative
Logical, fact-based, bottom-line orientated	*Intuitive, imaginative, rule-breaking*
Organized, planned, detailed	*Interpersonal, emotional, people-focused*
Seeks answers (often only one) ←→	Seeks questions
Converges ←→	Diverges
Asserts best or right view, follows 'rules' ←→	Explores different views, seeks insights
Uses existing structure ←→	Restructures
Says when an idea will not work ←→	Seeks ways an idea might help
Uses logical steps ←→	Welcomes discontinuous leaps
Concentrates on what is relevant ←→	Welcomes chance intrusions
Closed ←→	Open-ended
Fears making mistakes or looking foolish ←→	Encourages experimentation

Figure 14.1 Dimensions of creative (lateral) vs logical (vertical) thinking

Normally the two halves of the brain complement each other, but many factors, not least our education, tend to encourage development of left-brain activity – logic. Kirby (2003) speculates that this may well explain why so many successful entrepreneurs appear not to have succeeded in the formal education system. He argues that entrepreneurs are right-brain dominant. But he goes even further by speculating that there may be a link between this and dyslexia, observing that so many entrepreneurs are dyslexic, and language skills are left-brain activities. This is an interesting but unproved hypothesis.

However, the point is that most people need to encourage and develop right-brain activity if they wish to be creative. And this is possible, with training. To overcome the habit of logic you need to deliberately set aside this ingrained way of thinking. Creative or lateral thinking is different in a number of dimensions from logical or vertical thinking. It is imaginative, emotional, and often results in more than one solution. Edward de Bono (1971) set out some of the dimensions of difference. Figure 14.1 is based on his work.

One important aspect of high-level creativity is the ability to recognize relationships among objects, processes, cause-and-effect, people and so on that others do not see, searching for different, unorthodox relationships that can be replicated in a different context. These relationships can lead to new ideas, products or services. So, the inconvenience of mixing different drinks to form a cocktail led to the (obvious?) idea of selling them ready-mixed. James Dyson was able to see that a cyclone system for separating paint particles could be used (less obviously?) to develop a better vacuum cleaner. Most creativity skills can be practised and enhanced, but this particular skill is probably the most difficult to encourage. Majaro (1992) believes that, while streotyping is to be avoided, creative types do exhibit some similar characteristics:

Conceptual fluency. They are able to produce many ideas.
Mental flexibility. They are adept at lateral thinking.
Originality. They produce atypical responses to problems.

Suspension of judgement. They do not analyze too quickly.
Impulsive. They act impulsively to an idea, expressing their 'gut-feel'.
Anti-authority. They are always willing to challenge authority.
Tolerance. They have a high tolerance threshold towards the ideas of others.

Mintzberg (1976) makes the interesting suggestion that the very logical activity of planning is essentially a left-brain activity whilst the implementation of the plan, that is the act of management, is a right-brain activity. He bases this claim on the observation that managers split their attention between a number of different tasks, preferring to talk briefly to people rather than to write, reading non-verbal as well as verbal aspects of the interaction, take a holistic view of the situation and rely on intuition. He argues that truly effective managers are those that can harness both sides of the brain.

Case insight

Monorail Corporation is a virtual organization that could provide a glimpse of the future. Like Dell, it sells computers. Unlike Dell, it owns no factories, warehouses or other assets, operating from a single floor in a leased building in Atlanta, USA. Computers are designed by freelance workers. Customers phone a freephone number connected to the logistics service of Federal Express, which forwards the order to a contract assembler that assembles them from parts supplied by other contract manufacturers. FedEx ships the computer to the customer and sends the invoice to SunTrust Bank, Monorail's agent.

●

The creative process

The creative process has four commonly agreed phases, shown in Figure 14.2. There is wide agreement on their general nature and the relationship between them, although they are referred to by a variety of names (de Bono, 1995).

Phase 1: Generating knowledge and awareness

A prerequisite to all creative processes is the generation of awareness of different ideas and ways of doing things through reading and travelling widely, talking with different people with different views about the world. This is, of course, to be placed in the context of the issue being addressed. It is not just about being aware of different approaches or perspectives on the problem, but also about getting the brain to accept that there are different ways of doing things – developing an enquiring mind. Many people have to almost give themselves permission to be creative – to think the unthinkable. Carrying a notebook and recording ideas and information can be useful. So too can developing a small library. Some sources of commercial new ideas are shown in Figure 14.3.

Figure 14.2 The creative process

Phase 2: Incubation process

People need time to mull over the tremendous amounts of information they generate from Phase 1. This incubation period happens when people are engaged in other activities (the best are those instinctive activities that do not require left-brain dominance) and they can let their subconscious mind work on the problem. Interestingly sleep happens when the left brain gets tired or bored and during this time the right brain has dominance. Incubation therefore often needs sleep. It is little wonder that so many people have creative ideas when they are asleep – the problem is trying to remember them. Creativity therefore can take time – enough time to 'sleep on it'.

Phase 3: Generating ideas

Ideas can come up unexpectedly during the incubation period, but often they need encouragement. There are a number of techniques to encourage idea generation. Some of the more widely used ones are explained in the next section.

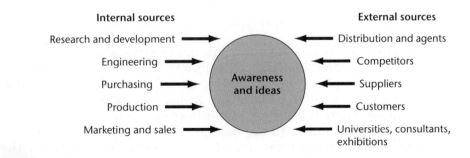

Figure 14.3 Sources of awareness and ideas

Ideas can come from unusual sources. **Great Ormond Street Hospital for Children** took inspiration from watching the McLaren and Ferrari Formula 1 racing teams take six seconds to turn a car around at a pit-stop. Doctors were concerned by the time they took to move patients from the operating theatre to the intensive care unit where they recovered. Delays in emergency handover could cost lives, so they contacted Ferrari to see how it might be improved. They discovered that Ferrari's pit-stop procedure could be drawn on a single diagram, every member of the team knowing exactly what to do and when to do it in a co-ordinated fashion. By way of contrast, they looked at videos of their own handover procedures and were shocked at the lack of structure. Ferrari concluded that, with an ever-changing team and unpredictable demand, the hospital's handover teams needed a formula they could all understand and work to – just like a pit-stop.

Phase 4: Evaluation and implementation

The next stage is to select which ideas are the most promising. This is the convergent stage of the process involving discussion and analysis, possibly voting. Some ideas generated in Phase 3 might be easy to discard because they are unrealistic but others might need to be worked up or modified before they can be properly evaluated. Sometimes a return to Phase 3 is required to do this.

Von Oech (1986) has a slightly different 'take' on this, focusing on the changing role of the individual as the creative process takes its course. He outlines four sequential roles:

1. *The explorer* – searching for new insights and perspectives by sifting through information, being curious, observing other fields, generating ideas, broadening perspective, following unexpected leads, using difficulties and obstacles and constantly writing things down.
2. *The artist* – turning information and resources into new ideas by imagining, adapting, reversing, linking, parodying, evaluating, discarding.
3. *The judge* – evaluating and assessing the merits of a concept and incorporating ideas through objectivity and looking at assumptions, probabilities and timing.
4. *The warrior* – achieving organizational acceptance and implementation of ideas by being bold, courageous and persistent, developing plans, commanding resources, motivating stakeholders to commit themselves to the project.

Some organizations have created environments designed to facilitate these stages of the creative process. The Royal Mail Group has its own 'Creativity Laboratory'. This is made up of a number of open areas – facilitating groups forming, breaking out and coming together again – all with very informal seating arrangements. Standing and walking are encouraged. There is background music as well as toys and drinks and other distractions for the left brain. All the walls are 'white walls' which can be written on with felt-tip pens when ideas are in free flow. Pens are everywhere. There are computer systems that allow ideas to be posted and voted on anonymously. And records are kept of the whole process – even the white walls are photographed – so agreed actions and outcomes can be followed up back in the workplace.

Who invented the World Wide Web (www)?

The first electronic mail transfer took place in July 1970 in the laboratories of consultants Bolt, Baranek and Newman. Building on the work of **Paul Baran** of the RAND Corporation, it was the result of a contract placed by the US Advanced Research Projects Agency (ARPA) to build a distributive network that enabled researchers at one site to log onto and run programs at another. **Roy Tomlinson**, who wrote the program, initiated the use of the symbol '@' to separate the name of the sender from the mailbox ID. He chose it because it was the only symbol that was unlikely to form part of a name or an ID.

Computer networks were also being built elsewhere and ARPA brought researchers from Britain, France, Italy and Sweden to form an international Network Working Group to investigate how the various networks could be connected. In 1973 there was a breakthrough as researchers realized that instead of trying to create a common specification, all they had to do was use dedicated computers as gateways between each network, thus creating a 'network-of-networks'. In 1977 the concept was made a reality as a message was sent on a 94,000-mile round trip from San Francisco to University College, London and back to the University of Southern California. An international network – or 'internet' – was created. The system continued to be used but only by scientists and specialists for many years.

In 1990 an Englishman, **Tim Berners-Lee**, working at CERN, the European Particles Physics Laboratories in Geneva, proposed a solution to the problem they faced of capturing and co-ordinating the work of the scientists and then locating it in such a way that this accumulating knowledge was easily available. He devised a 'hypertext' system that would give access across the internet, allowing users to access the same information from different computer systems and add their own links to information. It also enabled links to be made to live data that kept changing. The system was called the World Wide Web. Shortly after this he devised a 'browser' that linked the resources on the internet in a uniform way. He also devised a protocol to specify the location of the information – the Unique Resource Locator (URL) – and one to specify how information exchanges between computers should be handled – the HyperText Transport Protocol (HTTP). Finally, he invented a uniform way to structure documents, proposing the use of Hypertext Mark-up Language (HTML). In 1992 the browser was made publicly available to anyone with an internet connection to download.

In 1993 a University of Illinois team working at the National Centre for Supercomputer Applications (NCSA), developed the CERN system, which used high powered workstations and the Unix operating system, to operate on PCs and Macintosh. In the same year one of the team, **Marc Andreesen**, posted a message on some specialist Usenet conferences. It read: 'By the power vested in me by nobody in particular, alpha/beta version 0.5 of NCSA's Motif-based networked information systems and World Wide Web browser, X Mosiac, is hereby released. Cheers, Marc.' The World Wide Web, as we know it, had been born.

With the help of Jim Clark, the wealthy founder of Silicon Graphics, Marc Andreesen and others in the team went on to set up **Netscape**. When the company went public it was valued at $3 billion, a valuation that in those days was huge.

Blocks to individual creativity

> We learned the importance of ignoring conventional wisdom ... It's fun to do things that people don't think are possible or likely. It's also exciting to achieve the unexpected.
> **Michael Dell (1999)**
> ➡

People are inherently creative, but most of us stifle it because we find change threatening. We all create rituals and routines that we feel comfortable with and these normally mitigate against questioning the status quo. These routines help us through the day. Being creative often takes people outside their 'comfort-zone'. They are uneasy with it. In that sense encouraging creativity within an organization has many similarities with managing change (Chapter 9). The same skills and approaches are needed. But first blocks and barriers need to be attacked. Some blocks originate with individuals but others can be institutional. Roger von Oech (1998) focuses on the individual blocks and argues that there are ten which are critical to creativity:

1. The fallacy that there is only one correct solution to a problem.
2. The fallacy that logic is important in creativity.
3. The tendency to be practical.
4. The tendency to follow established rules unquestioningly.
5. The tendency to avoid ambiguity in viewing a situation.
6. The tendency to assign blame for failure.
7. The unwillingness to recognize the creative power of play.
8. The tendency to think too narrowly and with too much focus.
9. The unwillingness to think unconventionally because of the fear of appearing foolish.
10. The lack of belief that you can be creative.

Realizing these blocks may exist in yourself can be the first step to dismantling them. It is never easy to change an inherent tendency, but it can be done and the techniques in the next section can help.

Techniques for generating new ideas

There are many techniques designed to help encourage the generation of new ideas. Most are directed at generating a higher quality of idea rather than a greater volume. People with different thinking styles will respond differently to each of them. Here are just a few of the more widely used ones.

Brainstorming

This is one of the most widely-used techniques. It is practised in a group. In the session you do not question or criticize ideas. You suspend disbelief. The aim is to encourage the free flow of ideas – divergent thinking – and as many ideas as possible. Everyone has thousands of good ideas within them just waiting to come out. But people inherently fear making mistakes or looking foolish in front of others. Here making 'mistakes' and putting forward ideas which don't work is not only acceptable, it is also encouraged.

You might start with a problem to be solved or an opportunity to be exploited. You encourage and write ideas down as they come by facilitating all the dimensions of creative thinking in Figure 14.1. There are no 'bad' ideas. All ideas are, at the very least, springboards for other ideas. You allow the right side of the brain full rein and only engage the left brain to analyze the ideas you come up with at a later date. It is often best undertaken with a multidisciplinary team so that the issue can be approached from many different perspectives, encouraging the cross-fertilization of ideas.

How to run a brainstorming session

1   Describe the outcome you are trying to achieve – the problem or opportunity – BUT NOT THE SOLUTION. This could be a broad area of investigation – new ideas and new markets can be discovered if you don't follow conventional paths.

2   Decide how you will run the session and who will take part. You need an impartial facilitator who will introduce things, keep to the rules and watch the time. This person will restate the creative process if it slows down. The group can be anything from 4 to 30. The larger the number the more diverse the inputs but the slower (and more frustrating) the process – so something around 12 is probably ideal.

3   Set out the room in a participative (i.e. circular) and informal style. Comfortable chairs are important. Refreshments should be available continuously. Make certain there are flip charts, coloured pens and so on or, if you want to be high tech, you can use some of the specialist software that is available (e.g. Brainstorming Toolbox). Each person should also have a note pad so he or she can write down ideas.

4   Relax participants as much as possible. The style is informal. The rules of engagement should be posted clearly for all to see and run through so that everybody understands:
     – Quantity counts, not quality – postpone judgement on all ideas;
     – Encourage wild, exaggerated ideas – all ideas are of equal value;
     – Build on ideas rather than demolish them.

5   Open the session by asking for as many ideas as possible. Get people to shout out. Write every one down on the flip chart and post the sheets on the wall. Encourage and engage with people. Close down criticism. Try to create group engagement.

6   When the ideas have dried up – it might take a little time for it finally to do so – close the session, thanking participants and keeping the door open for them should they have any ideas later.

7   Analyze the ideas posted. Brainstorming helps generate ideas, not analyze them. What happens from here is up to you. Sometimes the people who generated the ideas can also help sort them, but remember to separate out the sessions clearly. Perhaps excellent ideas can be implemented immediately, but do not forget to investigate the interesting ones – no matter how 'off-the-wall'.

For more information on the technique visit www.brainstorming.co.uk.

Negative brainstorming – thinking about the negative aspects of problem or situation – can often be used initially to unblock more creative and positive brainstorming. It is particularly useful in getting people to think about what might happen if they do not think more creatively and can be used to help change motivations and behaviour.

A variant on this is called *brainwriting*, whereby ideas are written down anonymously and then communicated to the group (computer technologies can help with this), thus avoiding the influence of dominant individuals. Brainstorming can obviously be used in conjunction with *scenario planning* and *futures thinking* (Chapter 10).

Analogy

This is a product-centred technique that attempts to join together apparently unconnected or unrelated combinations of features of a product or service and benefits to the customer to come up with innovative solutions to problems. Analogies are proposed once the initial problem is stated. The analogies are then related to opportunities in the market place. Operated in a similar way to brainstorming, it is probably best explained with an example. Georges de Mestral noticed that burdock seed heads stuck to his clothing. On closer examination he discovered the seed heads contained tiny hooks. His analogy was to apply this principle to the problem of sticking and unsticking things and to develop what we recognize today as Velcro.

In this way, the first steps to building an analogy are to ask some basic questions:

- What does the situation or problem remind you of?
- What other areas of life or work experience similar situations?
- Who does these similar things and can the principles be adapted?

Often the analogy contains the words '... *is like* ...', so you might ask why something 'is like' another? For example, why is advertising like cooking? The answer is because there is so much preamble to eating. Anticipation from presentation and smell, even the ambience of the restaurant you eat it in, are just as important as the taste and nutritional value of the food itself.

Attribute analysis

This is another product-centred technique designed to evolve product improvements and line extensions – used as the product reaches the mature phase of its life cycle. It uses the basic marketing technique of looking at the features of a product or service which in turn perform a series of functions but, most importantly, deliver benefits to the customers. An existing product or service is stripped down to its component parts and the group then explores how these features might be altered but then focuses on whether those changes might bring valuable benefits to the customer. The 'why? why?' technique can be used to question why the existing product or service is designed in a particular way. Nothing must be taken for granted.

So, for example, you might focus on a domestic lock. This secures a door from opening by an unwelcome intruder. The benefit is security and reduction/elimination of theft from the house. But you can lose keys or forget to lock doors and some locks are difficult or inconvenient to open from the inside. A potential solution is to have doors that sense people approaching from the outside and lock themselves. You could have a reverse sensor on the inside – they unlock the door when someone approaches (which could be activated or deactivated centrally). The exterior sensor could recognize 'friendly' people approaching the door because of sensors they carry in the form of 'credit cards' or they could be over-ridden by a combination lock.

The 'why? why?' technique, explained in the next section, can also be used to question why an existing product or service is designed in a particular way. For example the technique could have been used to question why the domestic lock was designed in a particular way, taking nothing for granted. In this way the technique should uncover the prime attributes that users are seeking. An alternative solution to the problem can then be constructed.

Gap analysis

This is a market-based approach that attempts to produce a 'map' of product/market attributes based on dimensions that are perceived as important to customers, analyzing where competing products might lie and then spotting gaps where there is little or no competition. Because of the complexity involved, the attributes are normally shown in only two dimensions. There are a number of approaches to this task:

Perceptual mapping maps the attributes of a product within specific categories. So for example, the dessert market might be characterized as hot vs cold and sophisticated vs unsophisticated. Various desserts would then be mapped onto these two dimensions. This could be shown graphically (see below). The issue is whether the 'gap' identified is one that customers would value being filled – and means understanding whether they value the dimensions being measured. That is a question for market research to attempt to answer.

Non-metric mapping maps products in groups that customers find similar and then tries to explain why these groupings exist. A classic example would be in the soft drinks market where products might be clustered and then described simply in terms of still vs carbonated and flavoured vs non-flavoured. The key here is also finding the appropriate dimensions that create opportunities for differentiating the product and creating competitive advantage. The mapping of soft drinks on the two dimensions above is unlikely to reveal any gaps in the market.

Repertory grid is a more systematic extension of this technique. Customers are asked to group similar and dissimilar products within a market, normally again in pairs. They are then asked to explain the similarities and dissimilarities. The sequence is repeated for all groups of similar and dissimilar products. The explanations are then used to derive 'constructs' which describe the way in which people relate and evaluate the products. These constructs form a grid that can be used to map the products, using the words used by the customers themselves.

Personal Construct Theory and the Repertory Grid

George Kelly was an American engineer who became a highly respected clinical psychologist, best known for the development in 1955 of his own theory of personality, known as Personal Construct Theory, and a tool to explore people's personalities in terms of the theory, called the Repertory Grid. Kelly believed that the personality theories of the day suffered from three things: an inherent observer bias, a lack of precision and prediction and an over-reliance on the expert.

Kelly believed that we all have our own 'constructs' – views of the world or biases – that help us navigate our way around the world quickly. Certain words will trigger certain preconceptions be they logical or otherwise. When you walk through a door you do so without consciously thinking what you are doing but you are preconditioned to act in a way that has opened a similar door before. The fact that it is locked can often come as quite a sharp surprise. Construct systems influence our expectations and perceptions subconsciously – and introduce bias. This means that one person's constructs are not those of another – and sometimes they can even be internally inconsistent because we never question them.

The Repertory Grid attempts to get rid of this bias. The technique identifies a small set of *elements* (objects, entities) and the user is asked to define some *constructs* (attributes, slots) which characterize those elements. All these terms are identified in terms of the user's own language. So, for example, 'good' can only exist in contrast to the concept of 'bad'. Any construct can reasonably be measured by answering the question 'compared to what?'. Construct values are given for each element on a limited scale between extreme polar points. The process of taking three elements and asking for two of them to be paired in contrast with the third is the most effective way in which the poles of the construct can be discovered and articulated.

It is beyond this book to explain, in detail, how this technique should be deployed. However, one of the most accessible and short books on the topic is by Devi Jankowicz (2003). It really is 'the easy guide to Repertory Grids'.

Finding opportunity

Creativity on its own is not necessarily entrepreneurial. It is only entrepreneurial if it is applied to the process of innovation. Peter Drucker (1985) believes innovation can be practised systematically through a creative analysis of change in the environment and the opportunities this generates. It is not the result of circumstance. Firms that

'Our success is due, in part, to not just an ability but a willingness to look at things differently. I believe opportunity is part instinct and part immersion – in an industry, a subject, or an area of expertise. Dell is proof that people can learn to recognize and take advantage of opportunities that others are convinced don't exist. You don't have to be a genius, or a visionary, or even a college graduate to think unconventionally. You just need a framework and a team … Seeing and seizing opportunities are skills that can be applied universally, if you have the curiosity and commitment.'

Michael Dell

'When I started the Gadget Shop it was from a frustration with the difficulties of finding gifts for family and friends mixed with a love of innovation and gadgets. There are lots of problems in life that could be solved with the right insight leading to a business opportunity; you just have to spot them. Some of the most successful ideas are actually very simple.'
Jonathan Elvidge
founder of **Gadget Shop**
The Times, 6 July 2002

practise innovation systematically search for change then carefully and creatively evaluate its potential for an economic or social return. Change provides the opportunity for innovation and creativity can make this generate an economic return. Drucker said innovation was 'capable of being presented as a discipline, capable of being learned and capable of being practised. Entrepreneurs need to search purposefully for the sources of innovation, the changes and their symptoms that indicate opportunities for successful innovation. And they need to know and to apply the principles of successful innovation.'

Drucker lists seven sources of opportunity for firms in search of creative innovation. Four can be found within the firm itself or from the industry of which it is part and are therefore reasonably easy to spot. They are 'basic symptoms' – highly reliable indicators of changes that have already happened or can be made to happen with little effort. They are:

- *The unexpected* – be it the unexpected success or failure or the unexpected event. Nobody can predict the future but an ability to react quickly to changes is a real commercial advantage, particularly in a rapidly changing environment. Information and knowledge are invaluable.
- *The incongruity* – between what actually happens and what was supposed to happen. Plans go wrong and unexpected outcomes produce opportunities for firms that are able to spot them.
- *The inadequacy in underlying processes* – that are taken for granted but can be improved or changed. This is essentially improving process engineering – especially important if the product is competing primarily on price.
- *The changes in industry or market structure* – that take everyone by surprise. Again, unexpected change, perhaps arising from technology, legislation or other outside events create an opportunity to strategize about how the firm might cope and, as usual, first-mover advantage is usually worth striving for.

Case insight

The iconic **Apple iPod** was developed at a time when MP3 players were well established. The idea was sparked by the launch of Apple's iTunes software. Staff developing this for use with MP3 players formed such a low opinion of the ease of use of MP3s that they decided that they could do better. Team leader Anthony Fadell made models out of foam-core boards, using fishing weights to give his prototype the right feel.

These changes produce sources of opportunity that need to be dissected and the underlying causes of change understood. A learning organization of the sort we have described would understand this. The causes give clues about how innovation can be used to increase value added to the customer and economic return to the firm. An entrepreneurial firm should be adept at this.

The other three factors come from the outside world and you might expect them to be anticipated by regular SLEPT analyses:

- *Demographic changes* – population changes caused by changes in birth rates, wars, medical improvements and so on.
- *Changes in perception, mood and meaning* – that can be brought about by the ups and downs of the economy, culture, fashion etc. In-depth interviews or focus groups can also often give an insight into these changes.
- *New knowledge* – both scientific and non-scientific.

Drucker lists the seven factors in increasing order of difficulty, uncertainty and unreliability, which means that he believes that new knowledge, including scientific knowledge, for all its visibility and glamour, is in fact the most difficult, least reliable and least predictable source of innovation. Paradoxically, this is the area to which

Case insight

The internet is an opportunity that many have struggled to make a profit out of. The dot.com boom and bust underlined the fact that the opportunity created was high risk. eBay, the online auction site, is probably the leading example of a profitable network. But there are others. It all depends on the business model and how revenues are raised.

Yahoo have been bundling services together for customers to subscribe to almost since its inception. For example, Yahoo Mail Plus bundles extra storage space for archived e-mails with a forwarding service for those with more than one e-mail address. With over 2 million fee-paying customers, revenues from fee-based services are now growing at five times the growth of advertising revenue.

NCsoft, a Korean online gaming company, boasts more than 4 million customers of whom some 250,000 pay subscriptions. Customers 'join swords' in 'massively multiplayer' games such as Lineage, a fantasy role-playing game that can involve thousands of people at a time.

Friendsreunited.co.uk, a British website that brings together old friends, started as a hobby working out of a home-based website, now claims 8 million registered users, many of whom pay a £5 annual subscription.

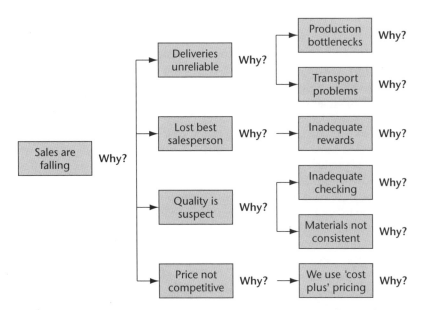

Source: Adapted from Vyakarnham, S. and Leppard, J. (1999) *A Marketing Action Plan for the Growing Business,* second edn, London: Kogan Page.

Figure 14.4   Why? Why? diagram

government, academics and even entrepreneurial firms pay most attention. He argues that innovations arising from the systematic analysis of mundane and unglamorous unexpected successes or failures are far more likely to yield commercial innovations. They have the shortest lead times between start and yielding measurable results and carry fairly low risk and uncertainty.

One technique for getting to the root cause of these 'unexpected events', 'incongruities' or 'inadequacies' is the 'Why? Why?' exercise. This is used to explore options related to the event. Figure 14.4 shows a 'Why? Why?' diagram exploring the reason for a fall in sales (Vyakarnham and Leppard, 1999). From it you can see there are several possible reasons, although the trails have not been taken to completion. The root cause will lie at the end of the 'why?' trail.

Figure 14.4 addresses a problem, but opportunities also spring from other sources. Bolton and Thompson (2000) suggest that three basic approaches to innovation are practised, none of which are mutually exclusive:

1. *Have a problem and seek a solution.*   They cite as an example Edwin Land's invention of the Polaroid camera because his young daughter could not understand why she had to wait to have pictures of herself printed.
2. *Have a solution and seek a problem.*   They cite 3M's Post-it notes as an example of a product with loosely sticking qualities that was applied to the need to mark pages in a manuscript.
3. *Identify a need and develop a solution.*   The example they cite is James Dyson's dual cyclone cleaner that he developed because of his frustration with the inadequate suction provided by his existing vacuum cleaner when he was converting an old property.

Case insight

In 1991 **Phil Cleary**, a former policeman, set up **Smartwater Europe** with his brother Mike. The company developed a water-based product containing 'synthetic DNA'. The idea was that break-ins would trigger a sprinkler system that would drench the burglar in Smartwater, which could not be washed off and could be directly linked to the scene of the crime. Each batch of water was composed differently for each client. Smartwater is now made by the Forensic Science Service, an executive agency of the Home Office and many schools as well as Asda, Marks & Spencer, Morrisons and Thomas Cook have installed it.

Although the first product was well received, the police disliked having to send samples off for laboratory analysis to match the ultra-violet fluorescent marking of stolen goods, crime scenes and suspects' clothing. Consequently the company went on to develop Indsol Tracer, which is painted on to goods. Clients register their unique corporate fingerprint. It is now used by 1200 companies including British Airways, Lloyds TSB and Tarmac. The company has since developed Smartwater Instant, which contains tiny particles and can be identified simply by looking at an item through a microscope. A database available on the internet allows the police to trace the owner immediately. More recently the company's product has been used on Honda motorbikes to give each one a unique fingerprint so as to deter thefts and hence reduce insurance premiums. This can be used on any product to determine whether or not it is original and hence help resolve disputed claims over liability or originality.

●

Firms with a good track record for innovation, therefore, practise it systematically. It does not happen by chance. They look for small changes that can be made to the way they do things. Indeed so systematic can the search for innovation be that some firms have been set up specifically to undertake it. Drucker (*op. cit.*) advocates a five-stage approach to purposeful, systematic innovation:

1. *Start with the analysis of opportunities, inside the firm and its industry and in the external environment.* Information and knowledge are invaluable – from as many sources as possible. Do not innovate for the future, innovate for now. Timing is everything. The right idea at the wrong time is worth nothing.
2. *Innovation is both conceptual and perceptual.* Therefore look at the financial implications but also talk to people, particularly customers, and analyze how to meet the opportunity. Use scenario planning and futures thinking. Information and knowledge help minimize risk in an otherwise risky endeavour and continual strategizing is the key to success.
3. *To be effective, an innovation must be simple and has to be 'focused'.* Keep it as simple as possible. Don't try to be too clever. Don't try to do too many things at once. The slightly wrong-but-can-be-improved idea can always be improved and still earn a fortune.
4. *To be effective, start small.* Don't be grandiose. Take an incremental approach. Minimize the commitment of resources for as long as possible, thus maximizing information and knowledge and minimizing risk. Think 'skunkworks'. Clearly for certain types of innovation this can be problematic.
5. *Aim at leadership and dominate the competition in the particular area of innovation as soon as possible.* Remember the marketing strategies for products at the start of

their life cycle. As we have seen, niche domination is the key to financial success as the product moves through its life cycle, but the investment necessary can drain cash flow.

How innovations, particularly technical innovations, see the light of commercial day is complex. Scientific discoveries do lead to commercial opportunities which entrepreneurial firms can exploit. However, the linkages are not always as you would expect and they involve a labyrinthine series of inter-relationships and feedback networks that underline the importance of a learning organization. William Shockley had to invent a theory of electrons and 'holes' in semiconductors to explain why the transistors that he and his colleagues at Bell Laboratories in the USA had invented in 1948 actually worked. Even then he and his colleagues had to take the transistor idea to Palo Alto in California and start a company that eventually became Intel to get it to see the light of day.

> **Case insight**
>
> **Oxford Asymmetry International** is a British example of a world-class firm that specializes in the systematic development of invention and high technology. When British Petroleum withdrew its financial support for a research project analyzing the small-scale manufacturing of certain chemicals, **Stephen Davies**, an Oxford University professor, secured £500,000 backing from two business angels to continue his work and, in 1992, set up the company with only 4 employees.
>
> The company provides a one-stop shop in chemical discovery and promotes itself as a partner to drug manufacturers who are looking to innovate and are willing to outsource this activity. Successful innovation is the result of an effective partnership, each partner bringing different qualities to the relationship.
>
> Over lunch in 1995 at Oxford University's Innovation Centre, Stephen happened to meet a senior manager from Pfizer and this led to the formation of a joint venture company called Oxford Diversity Pfizer, the company that developed Viagra.
>
> Oxford Asymmetry International now works with companies like Astra, Bayer, Eastman Chemicals, Leukosite, Pfizer, Vanguard Medica and Vertex. It was floated in 1998 with a staff of 200 (40% with PhDs) and a market capitalization of £120 million, a figure that doubled within a year.

Blocks to organizational creativity

Just as individuals have blocks to their creativity, so too organizations can block creativity. Majaro (1992) and Klein (1990) identified five organizational blocks to creativity, many of which will seem familiar:

1. *Lack of organizational slack.* As we have seen, creativity takes time. A lean and fit organization that is constantly going from crisis to crisis is unlikely to have this;
2. *Too much bureaucracy.* Where systems and procedures are designed to ensure a high degree of control, particularly for the purpose of efficiency or productivity, creativity is unlikely to flourish;

3. *Tight financial control.* Just like bureaucracy, overly tight financial control is likely to stifle creativity because it stresses efficiency and effectiveness;
4. *Poor communication.* As we have seen ideas need to be discussed, worked out and made visible;
5. *Not invented here.* Organizations that resist external influences are unlikely to be creative ones, indeed they are likely to resist change of any sort.

Sloane (2003) would add a few more:

- *Too much criticism and punishment of mistakes.* Blame cultures inhibit creativity and discourage anybody from even attempting to do something differently. The only people who will never make mistakes are those who do not take the initiative or try out creative ideas. The important thing is to learn from mistakes and never repeat them.
- *Over-tight planning.* Like tight financial control, this can stifle initiative and opportunity seeking. We have seen how entrepreneurial organizations need to plan.
- *Promoting too many like-minded people from within.* To be creative an organization needs to take on board ideas from outside and one way to do this is to recruit outsiders.
- *Hoarding of problems.* People in blame cultures tend to hoard problems because they know that if they share them they will be criticized. Ideally problems need to be shared and decision making and problem solving pushed down to the lowest level.
- *Insufficient training.* Training can be used as a strategic tool to encourage creativity and innovation.
- *Banning of brainstorming.* We saw just how useful these sessions can be. Using tools like these regularly institutionalizes the process of creativity.

Encouraging organizational creativity

Creativity needs to be encouraged within any organization. That means valuing and rewarding it. It is most likely to flourish with a trusting management that does not overcontrol and has open internal and external channels of communication. The ultimate issue is the degree of *freedom* given to individuals (Sinetar, 1985). Creative people need freedom in the way they work, and slack in the resources they control – and this applies at whatever level they operate.

Encouraging creativity means tolerating the unconventional and encouraging people to challenge the conventional way things are done. It means encouraging curiosity and seeing problems as challenges. It means providing support for creativity – training, resources and all the things 3M provides. It means expecting and tolerating mistakes. It means developing an organizational culture where dreaming is encouraged and being creative is fun. But unfettered creativity can be dangerous. This sort of exciting place to work may all too easily turn out to be anarchic. It may be unprofitable and even fail if the creativity is not anchored in the quest for entrepreneurial opportunity and commercial reality. And that involves not only a disciplined approach to creativity but also a disciplined approach to exploiting the opportunities it generates. But all this describes the essence of corporate entrepreneurship.

Case with questions

Hallmark

Founded in 1910 when Joyce Clyde Hall started selling two shoeboxes of postcards in Kansas City, Hallmark take creativity seriously. You might think they have to because they design about 19,000 new greeting cards every year, and each card costs about £40,000 to produce and is expected to generate some £85,000 in sales. But these days they are not just in the business of cards. They are, according to Paul Baker, senior vice president of creative development, in the business of developing 'emotional content' that can be sold as greeting cards, on the web and through the Hallmark TV channel.

Hallmark's philosophy, work environment and development programmes are designed to encourage creative thinking. Their global headquarters is still in Kansas and their 800 in-house creative staff are based there. They have access to the world's biggest creative library with some 20,000 volumes and 175 current periodicals. They also have a programme of visiting speakers. Recent visitors have been the acclaimed writer Maya Angelou and Dutch nature artist Marjolein Bastin. Their staff development programme is diverse, including, on the one hand, courses on working with Hallmark's colour management process but, on the other hand, including classes on sculpting and even doll-making. They have a 'creative renewal programme' for staff who feel they are losing their edge. Kearney Farm, an old farmhouse set in a 172-acre estate, is their own creativity 'retreat'. It boasts its own art studio and regular creative brainstorming sessions are held there. It also organizes research visits to overseas countries so that staff keep in touch with 'emotions' in different countries. However there is a hard edge and slogans on some office walls remind staff how much a card that does not sell will cost the company.

The company takes trend-spotting seriously and employs staff to constantly scan the environment to monitor new developments. Modern innovations include e-cards that can be sent via Hallmark's own website. You can even create your own card. The site also has a hugely popular 'Say-it-with-music' line where you can send a CD-quality sound card featuring one of more than 100 music artists as well as dialogue and themes from popular movies and TV shows. With over 250 'designs', they feature the original artists and songs and link to the captions and sentiment of the card. The cards even appear on websites such as YouTube, with people lip-synching along to the cards' 45 second music clips.

Launched in 2002, the Hallmark cable TV channel now has global reach, offering 'family friendly' programming. By 2006 it had become the ninth most watched cable TV channel in the USA, generating revenues of £2.1 billion. In that year, buoyed by the success of its cable TV channel, the company launched its own women's magazine.

Up-to-date information on Hallmark can be found on their website: www.hallmark.com

Questions
1. How does Hallmark try to stimulate emotional creativity?
2. How does Hallmark try to stimulate product creativity?

One important message for the management of an entrepreneurial organization is that it needs to recognize that different people have different thinking styles that need to be respected and encouraged. Indeed if these different styles are encouraged so that they generate different ideas, assumptions, approaches, frames of references and even solutions to problems, they will inevitably lead to conflict that has to be managed and resolved (see Chapter 5). What needs to be encouraged, ultimately, is for a whole-brain solution to a problem (or opportunity) to be formulated eventually, perhaps using left and right sides more dominantly at different stages in the process.

Within this process there will, inevitably, be periods of divergence – breaking from the familiar ways of doing things – and convergence when there is some agreement about pursuing a certain course of action (Leonard and Swap, 1999). Without convergence there is anarchy, but equally without divergence there are few new ideas. Both need to be carefully balanced, but the process inevitably leads to conflict. Friction and conflict are inevitable by-products of a creative environment that needs to be channelled in a constructive rather than a destructive way. Different approaches and ideas need to be aired but teams need to be able to air their differences in such a way that they can continue to work together.

Hischberg (1998) talks about developing 'creative abrasion' that facilitates divergence of thinking, supplemented by a leadership style and organizational structures that then seek closure and convergence. This calls for the development of leadership styles 'that focus on first identifying and then incorporating polarized viewpoints. In doing so, the probabilities for unexpected juxtapositions are sharply increased, as are the levels of mutual understanding. The irony is that out of a process keyed on abrasiveness, a corporate culture of heightened sensitivity and harmony is achieved.' This is clearly a delicate task that takes time and patience. It is not about fostering clashes that are personal or built on ego, but rather realizing that there is diversity of viewpoints, ideas and approaches and making the airing of these something that is routine and cannot be avoided.

Creativity is the ability to develop new ideas, concepts and processes. In the business context it is the ability to develop creative, imaginative and original solutions to problems or opportunities that customers face. Encouraging creativity in an organization involves utilizing all the tools we need to encourage entrepreneurship: leadership, structure, culture and strategy. The difference, perhaps, is that there are a number of skills and defined techniques that can help develop the skill of creativity in the individual – because ultimately creativity comes from an individual or group of individuals and an organization can only encourage and facilitate this.

Developing national creativity

Creativity leading to innovation has become a driving force for economic growth and countries are increasingly interested in how it might be encouraged. They see economic growth coming from sectors where value can be added through the creation and application of knowledge. Florida (2002) argues that, rather than people moving to where investment and technology are concentrated, as much of the competitiveness literature assumes, firms increasingly follow the talented, creative

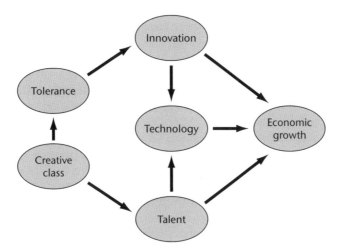

Source: Adapted from Florida and Tinagli (2004).

Figure 14.5 Technology, talent, tolerance and economic growth

people he calls 'the new creative class'. He claims that the ability to compete and prosper in the new global economy 'increasingly turns on the ability of nations to attract, retain and develop creative people.' He argues that this new creative class is drawn to a particular sort of place; 'open, diverse communities where differences are welcome and cultural creativity is easily accessed.' He argues that it is *tolerance* that attracts the 'creative class' and they have the *talent* to develop new *technologies*. New knowledge-based economies thrive in locations and countries that combine these three elements – technology, talent and tolerance – to provide economic growth in the way shown in Figure 14.5.

Florida's work is controversial. The implication of its conclusion is that, as part of the process of encouraging creativity, countries need to foster a culture of openness and tolerance. He claims to have found a strong relationship between openness to gays, Bohemians, and immigrants and the ability of regions to innovate, generate high-technology industry and secure high value-added economic growth (Florida, *op. cit.*). It is not that these groups create the economic growth, rather that their existence is a proxy that indicates something about the culture of a community that encourages growth – one that is open to new people and new ideas. The work also has implications for city planners as they try to mirror the sort of environment these people like – with space for interaction like parks, cafes and small shops and with streets that are safe for these activities to take place.

If this sort of community attracts creative people there is also evidence that this community also helps generate some of those creative ideas – developing a virtuous circle of creativity. Burt (2004) showed that in many business contexts, good ideas do have social origins. He looked at a range of business sectors and measured the number of business ideas that staff came up with. He found that the staff coming up with these ideas spanned 'structural holes' – they looked outwards for their ideas: 'This is not creativity born of genius; it is creativity born out of the import–export business.' Similarly Lakhani (2006) found that it was 'outsiders – those with expertise at the periphery of a problem's field – who were most likely to find answers and do so quickly.' In other words ideas that are commonplace for one group can spark insight for another. It is all about being open to ideas from all and every source and not being inward looking. And this might go some way to explaining why strategic alliances of different organizations might be so useful in stimulating innovation. The other organization exposes them to different ways of doing things, different ideas, and from this there is the spark of creativity.

In a subsequent work Florida and Tinagli (2004) produced indices to measure these three variables – technology, talent and tolerance – for different European countries and looked at the trend over time. The tolerance variable in this study measured attitudes and values rather than concentrations of immigrants, gays, Bohemians and minority groups. The talent index combined data on the proportion of the workforce employed in the creative industries and its trend, with data on the percentage of the population aged 25–64 with a bachelor degree or above and the number of scientists and engineers per thousand workers. The technology index was based on R&D as a percentage of GDP, the number of patent applications per million population and the number of high-technology patents for certain key areas per million population. These indices were combined to produce a creativity index and a creativity trend index. The resulting ranking of countries, with the USA for comparison, is shown below:

	Creativity index	Creativity trend
1	Sweden	Ireland
2	USA	Finland
3	Finland	Portugal
4	Netherlands	Denmark
5	Denmark	Spain
6	Germany	Greece
7	Belgium	Sweden
8	UK	Belgium
9	France	Austria
10	Austria	USA
11	Ireland	Netherlands
12	Spain	Germany
13	Italy	Italy
14	Greece	UK
15	Portugal	France

Florida *et al.* went on to classify countries under four headings, using a combination of their creativity index and creativity trend results. As can be seen in Figure 14.6, the *leaders* were the countries of Finland, Sweden, Denmark, the Netherlands and the USA. All have considerable technological capabilities, continue to invest in developing creative talent and have the values and attributes associated with attracting creative, talented people from anywhere in the world – although, compared to the USA, the European countries still have some way to go on this measure. Sweden outperformed the USA on the creativity index and the improving

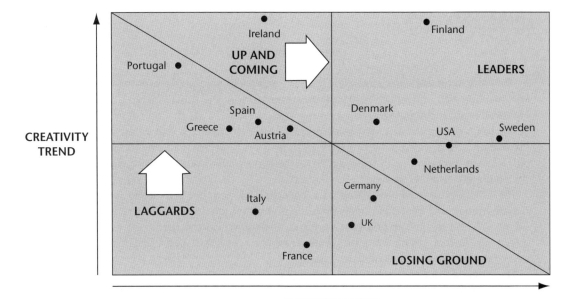

Source: Adapted from Florida and Tinagli (*op. cit.*).

Figure 14.6 The creativity matrix

trend in Finland was second only to Ireland (see *up and coming*). Those countries *losing ground*, albeit from a high creativity base, were France, the UK and Germany. *Up and coming* was Ireland and, to a lesser extent, Portugal. *Laggards* were those countries combining a low creativity index with a worsening trend like Italy. However, Spain, Austria, Portugal and Greece appear to be in a difficult position and France borders on coming into this classification.

An interesting observation on Florida's work is that, if true, the template for stimulating creativity by attracting creative people to 'open, diverse communities' should apply equally to organizations as well as whole nations. However, that does beg the question of the conflict between the cultures in the different communities that individuals inhabit. Florida's work underlines the fact that creativity and innovation are at their heart social processes. People need to spark off other people. At a physical level, we have already noted how certain environments can stimulate creativity and how some organizations have set up Creativity Laboratories. But, equally, at a more general level this realization has implications for the design of the workplace. Being shut away in an office all day does not stimulate creativity. People need to interact in social spaces – at coffee, at water coolers, at the photocopier – and these social spaces can be just as important as the space they inhabit to undertake specific tasks. As Gladwell (2000) puts it: 'Innovation is fundamentally social. Ideas arise as much out of casual conversations as they do out of formal meetings... Innovation comes from the interactions of people at a comfortable distance from each other.'

Case with questions

Nintendo and the Wii

By 2007 the biggest selling games console in the world was not the one with the best graphics, nor the one with the most powerful processor. It was the family-friendly, power-saving Nintendo Wii, a computer games console that shifted the games paradigm rather than compete on computing power with competitors like PlayStation 3. And what is more, whilst PlayStation 3 is expected to be profitable in three years time, Wii is already making profits. So why is Wii so revolutionary and how did Nintendo come to think outside the square and change the nature of computer gaming?

The Wii console is wireless-linked to a hand-held device that can detect and accurately digitize motion and rotation in three dimensions and through 360°. The device can become a sword, a tennis racquet, a golf club or a gun, depending on the game you are playing on screen. Up to four people can participate virtually, in real time and using real movement, depending on what is happening on screen.

The Nintendo development team – which included outside design teams – started out by thinking about the existing market for computer games. The market had stagnated into one for either young males or old males who had retained their youthful interest in gaming and had time to spend on it. The image of the gamer was that of a solitary male in his bedroom, hunched over a TV screen, grasping a controller with both hands, intensely involved in some game – a lonely, exclusive image. Massive as this market was, sales trends showed there was a limit to how often upgrading the hardware would lead to more sales and it was evident that fewer new gamers were entering the market. Pragmatically Nintendo also doubted whether simply increasing the power of its GameCube (the previous flagship console) would cost-effectively produce anything significantly better. This was bold thinking because the whole industry had become technology, rather than consumer, led. Most manufacturers were led by developments in semiconductors and related technologies and what other consumer electronic manufacturers were doing. And all this led towards simply adding in more and more computing power to enable games to become quicker and graphics more life-like and the demand for this seemed to be insatiable. As soon as one upgrade came out, consumers seemed to want more. Nintendo dared to question whether the gains were now worth the extra investment.

So how is Wii so different? The first thing is that the wireless controller is held in only one hand – like a mouse, a TV remote or a mobile phone. This changed the posture of gaming, making it more open and inclusive and encouraging a degree of physicality. The second is that, instead of using technology to ramp up output, the designers used it to power the console down, whilst still maintaining gaming specifications. It is a little known fact that a typical game console running a flight simulator game uses 76% more electricity than a washing machine. So the same technology used in the Wii would use between one-third and one-quarter the electricity of the GameCube. This in turn meant that the Wii could perform other functions. It is designed to be left on continuously as it has several different 'channels' that can, through an integrated web browser, provide a rolling news service with continuous world and local weather reports. It can even be used as a family bulletin board and planner. It can be programmed to switch itself off after a prescribed time and the hard drive features an irreversible memory that catalogues what it has been used for and for how long. Because it is

→

intended for living-room rather than bedroom use, the Wii console is about the size of three DVD cases and is housed in a box that can easily be found a home alongside the AV equipment and TV.

Wii has been described as 'a human-centric, business-technology ecosystem, on a par with the iPod-iTunes-iMac' (Bruce Nussbaum, *Business Week*). It became this icon because, like iPod-iTunes-iMac, its development team dared to think outside the square and to question the status quo. They dared to change the way things were done and the result is a 'low-tech' game that can be more fun, has more functionality and consequently outsells its more powerful rivals.

For more information on how Wii was developed and for interviews with the development team conducted by Satoru Iwata, President of Nintendo, visit wii.nintendo.com/iwataasks.jsp.

Questions
1. Using Drucker's seven sources of opportunity, might you have spotted this opportunity?
2. Using the Why? Why? methodology, might you have spotted this opportunity?
3. What were the key decision points in the development of the Wii that led to it being so different?
4. How easy will it be for competitors to copy Wii?

Summary

Creativity is the soul of entrepreneurship. It underpins innovation and, as such, many business models such as that of **Monorail Corporation**.

The primary focus of the organization should be to stimulate individual creativity and learning – tacit knowledge – and translate this into the products and services that the market value.

Creativity is a right-brain activity that involves lateral as opposed to vertical thinking. It is intuitive, imaginative and rule breaking. It requires interpersonal and emotional skills and is people focused. Creative types do exhibit certain common characteristics and there are tests that purport to detect them.

The creative process involves four steps:

1. Generating knowledge and awareness
2. Incubation
3. Generating ideas
4. Evaluation and implementation

There are techniques, such as brainstorming, analogy, attribute analysis and gap analysis that can help in the process. A key element is the ability to spot relationships and then replicate them in a different context. This is what doctors at **Great Ormond Street Hospital for Children** did when they observed how quickly the F1 team could turn a racing car around at a pit stop. Appropriate facilities and environments can help with the process.

Using new knowledge, including scientific knowledge, is the most difficult form of innovation. Innovation stemming from the systematic analysis of unexpected successes or failures, or the incongruities between what actually happens and what was supposed to happen are far more likely to yield commercially viable innovations. Both **Michael Dell** and **Jonathan Elvidge** believe that opportunities can be spotted, systematically. **Oxford Asymmetry International** and **Nintendo**, the developers of the highly successful **Wii** computer game, prove this to be the case. However, not all opportunities are profitable, as many dot.com businesses have found.

The most important element in encouraging organizational creativity is the freedom given to individuals together with slackness in the resources they control. Clearly there is a balance to be achieved here. And individuals need stimulation and encouragement to 'think outside the box'. Creativity needs 'creative abrasion' which involves friction and conflict that has to be resolved by the manager. There will be periods of divergence and convergence as different ideas and approaches are analyzed, adopted and discarded. This whole process needs to be managed carefully so that the team stays together. **Hallmark** and **Nintendo** prove that companies can organize so as to encourage creativity. There are many similarities with change management, not least the need to 'unblock' individual and organizational barriers.

The thread that binds this all together is the entrepreneurial firm that links ideas to commercial opportunity and, like all the company case studies included in this section, offers an effective business model with good management. Corporate entrepreneurship is about doing just this.

Creativity is a social process and Richard Florida argues that, rather than people moving to where investment and technology are concentrated, firms increasingly follow talented, creative people. This 'new creative class' is itself drawn to particular communities which are open and diverse, where differences are welcome and cultural creativity is easily accessed. This idea has implications for organizations both in terms of the communities they create and the design of the workspace they occupy.

Creativity test

Find out how creative you are by going to www.creax.com/csa and answering the 40 questions in the creativity quiz. It is free and the analysis assesses you on eight dimensions against answers from others with similar backgrounds. The dimensions are:

- **Abstraction** – the ability to apply abstract concepts/ideas.
- **Connection** – the ability to make connections between things that do not appear connected.
- **Perspective** – the ability to shift one's perspective on a situation in terms of space, time and other people.
- **Curiosity** – the desire to change or improve things that others see as normal.
- **Boldness** – the confidence to push boundaries beyond accepted conventions. Also the ability to eliminate the fear of what others might think of you.
- **Paradox** – the ability to simultaneously accept and work with statements that are contradictory.
- **Complexity** – the ability to carry large quantities of information and be able to manipulate and manage the relationships between such information.
- **Persistence** – the ability to force oneself to keep trying to more and stronger solutions even when good ones have already been generated.

> **Creativity Resources**
>
> To find what must be the world's largest resource of creativity and innovation resources go to www.creax.com/portal.aspx. The website contains hyperlinks to around 1000 other sites around the world. These include: authors, articles, books, basic research, creative environments, creative thinking pioneers, design, e-learning and creativity, education, creativity tools, ideas factory, ideas markets, imagination tools, innovation tools, internet assisted creativity, mind mapping, online techniques, ideas management, tests and puzzles and many, many more.
>
> All the techniques discussed here – and more – are covered in more detail somewhere on this website. There are also tools and resources to help you try them.

Essays and discussion topics

1. Creativity is a more difficult skill than entrepreneurship to develop. Discuss.
2. Why is creativity the soul of entrepreneurship?
3. Can you think of an entrepreneur who was not creative?
4. Is creativity the same as opportunity perception? What is the link?
5. Are you a left- or a right-brain person?
6. Are you comfortable being creative?
7. What lessons do you learn from how the World Wide Web has developed?
8. Are there still commercial opportunities on the internet?
9. Why do many people believe the creative process is best handled in small, entrepreneurial firms or units?
10. Looking back to Chapter 5, what might be needed to build a creative team?
11. Do you have an idea for a new product or service? Explain why it might be successful.
12. How might creativity be encouraged?
13. What things discourage creativity?
14. Reflect on the need for freedom and slack to encourage creativity. How does the issue of balance, introduced in Chapter 9, affect this? Is more or less freedom needed to encourage creativity rather than entrepreneurship?
15. Is creativity good in all organizations? Give examples to support your case.

Exercises and assignments

1. Try assessing your creative potential. You can find many tests by undertaking an internet search on 'creativity'. Tests can be found on:

   - www.creax.com/csa
   - www.web-us.com
   - www.angelfire.com/wi/2brains

2. List the barriers that you feel inhibit you from being creative at home and at your college or university. How might they be removed or circumvented?
3. List the sources for awareness and new ideas you have at your disposal. What do you need to do to capitalize on them in a systematic way?
4. Try applying brainstorming to the generation of new ideas. Try thinking of a new product/ service application. Define an area for review, for example by looking at a problem you face in your everyday life and trying to find a solution to it. If you have problems with the technique, go to wwww.brainstorming.co.uk for further explanation.

5. Trying to use analogy in a group to come up with innovative solutions to problems can be more difficult – even with a group of friends. Start with a problem to be solved and find the way similar problems might be solved in a different context. Alternatively find a natural solution to a problem and consider whether it can be applied to a different circumstance.

6. Try using attribute analysis in a group. Again, this can be difficult. Focus the group on an everyday product or service. Select one feature or aspect and ask 'Why does it have to be that way – what benefit does it bring to the customer?' Try it a few times with different product/service features.

7. Try using gap analysis. Select an everyday product or service. Characterize the product or service in two dimensions and use perceptual mapping to plot where competing products lie on these dimensions. Is there a gap in the market? Repeat the exercise for another product/service.

8. Try applying some of the creativity techniques to generate new ideas. Try thinking of a new product/service application. Define an area for review, for example by looking at a problem you face in your everyday life and trying to find a solution to it.

References

Bolton, B. and Thompson, J. (2000) *Entrepreneurs: Talent, Temperament, Technique*, Oxford: Butterworth-Heinemann.

Burt, S.B. (2004) 'Structural Holes and Good Ideas', *American Journal of Sociology,* 110(2), September.

de Bono, E. (1971) *Lateral Thinking for Management*, Harmondsworth: Penguin.

de Bono, E. (1995) 'Serious Creativity', *The Journal for Quality and Participation,* 18(5).

Drucker, P. (1985) *Innovation and Entrepreneurship*, London: Heinemann.

Florida, R. (2002) *The Rise of the Creative Classes: And How It's Transforming Work, Leisure, Community and Everyday Life*, New York: Basic Books.

Florida, R. and Tinagli, I. (2004) *Europe in the Creative Age*, Demos.

Gladwell, M. (2000) 'Designs for Working', *The New Yorker*, December 11.

Grant, R. M. (1996) 'Towards a Knowledge-based Theory of the Firm', *Strategic Management Journal*, 17 (Winter Special Issue).

Hischberg, J. (1998) *The Creative Priority*, New York: Harper Books.

Jankowicz, D. (2003) *The Easy Guide to Repertory Grids*, New York: John Wiley & Sons.

Kirby, D. (2003) *Entrepreneurship*, London: McGraw-Hill.

Klein, A. R. (1990) 'Organizational Barriers to Creativity ... and How to Knock them Down', *Journal of Consumer Marketing*, 7(1).

Lakhani, K. (2006) 'Open Space Science: A New Model for Innovation', *Working Knowledge: Harvard Business School Newsletter*, November 20.

Leonard, D. and Swap, W. (1999) *When Sparks Fly*, Boston: Harvard Business School.

Majaro, S. (1992) 'Managing Ideas for Profit', *Journal of Marketing Management*, 8.

Mintzberg, H. (1976) 'Planning on the Left Side and Managing on the Right', *Harvard Business Review*, 54, July/August.

Page, A. L. (1993) 'Assessing New Product Development Practices and Performance: Establishing Crucial Norms', *Journal of Product Innovation Management*, 10.

Sinetar, M. (1985) 'Entrepreneurs, Chaos and Creativity: Can Creative People Really Survive Large Company Structure?', *Sloan Management Review*, 65(5).

Sloane, P. (2003) *The Leader's Guide to Lateral Thinking Skills: Powerful Problem-Solving Techniques to Ignite Team's Potential*, London: Kogan Page.

von Oech, R. (1986) *A Kick in the Seat of the Pants*, New York: Harper & Row.

von Oech, R. (1998) *A Whack on the Side of the Head*, New York: Warner Books.

Vyakarnham, S. and Leppard, J. (1999) *A Marketing Action Plan for the Growing Business*, second edn, London: Kogan Page.

15

Encouraging Marketing and Product Innovation

Contents

- Relationship marketing
- Value-driven marketing
- Marketing innovation
- Product innovation
- Structures to support product development
- Summary

LEARNING OUTCOMES

By the end of this chapter you should be able to:

- Explain the difference between transactional and relationship marketing;

- Describe what is involved in relationship selling;

- Explain what is meant by value-driven marketing and how this can be used very effectively by an entrepreneurial organization;

- Explain how to go about the process of marketing innovation;

- Explain the entrepreneurial marketing planning process;

- Explain how to go about the process of new product development;

- Describe the structures that might support this process and have a basis for deciding which might be most appropriate;

- Analyze how organizations innovate successfully.

Relationship marketing

As we saw in Chapter 3, one dimension in which entrepreneurial marketing is likely to be different from conventional marketing is its heavy reliance on relationships with customers. In the 1990s this was recognized in the mainstream marketing literature and christened 'relationship marketing' (Christopher *et al.*, 1991). As we noted, supporters of this 'new' approach believe that it can deliver sustainable customer loyalty (Webster, 1992). Where the more traditional 'transaction' marketing approach focuses on the discrete, individual sale – trying to reconcile the conflicting interests of buyer and seller – relationship marketing focuses on developing a strong and lasting relationship in which benefits are shared (Payne, 1994). The former focuses on price whilst the latter shifts the emphasis to non-economic benefits such as service, delivery time, certainty of supply and co-operative working. Relationship marketing, therefore is far more customer-orientated. Relationship- and transaction-marketing approaches were contrasted in Table 3.1, reproduced as Table 15.1.

This approach may not be viable with all products or services – it has been most heavily associated with business-to-business marketing – but it does add yet a further dimension to Porter's generic marketing strategies. Relationship marketing can be mixed with any of the four strategies to create a relationship hybrid that implies a different set of strategic imperatives from those implied by a transaction-marketing approach.

Lambin (2000) catalogues a number of pitfalls in relationship marketing pointing out that often relationships are forced, being based on proprietary technology, patented parts, long-term contracts or high switch costs. He maintains that the firm that builds the relationship usually has some advantage that allows it to charge a premium price but that there are strong incentives for the buyer not to become too dependent upon this supplier. Relationship selling implies that the salesperson is more of an advisor than a salesperson. Lambin (*op. cit.*) believes that there are five phases in relationship selling:

1. *Systematic search for information.* This is a permanent activity of identifying prospects and their needs.
2. *Selecting a target.* This is the process of analyzing why a prospect should become a customer and how the product can meet his or her needs.
3. *Convincing good customers.* This is the phase that culminates in a sale.

Table 15.1 Relationship vs transactional marketing

Relationship marketing	Transactional marketing
• Encourages close, frequent customer contact	• Limited contact
• Encourages repeat sales	• Orientated towards single purchase
• Focus on customer service	• Limited customer service
• Focus on value to the customer	• Focus on product/service benefits
• Focus on quality of total offering	• Focus on quality of product
• Focus on long-term performance	• Focus on short-term performance

4. *Building relationships.* This is the start of building a relationship based on trust – solving problems for the buyer, not just selling product.
5. *Maintaining and reinforcing the relationship.* This involves maintaining close contact with the customer, building up the level of personal service and achieving a better understanding of the customer needs, in this way building customer loyalty and developing switch costs.

Value-driven marketing

Piercy (2001) believes that, as customers become increasingly sophisticated, marketing will move away from relationship to value-driven strategies that reflect customer priorities and needs: 'Achieving customer loyalty with sophisticated customers is the new challenge and we are only just beginning to realize what this means. It will mean transparency. It will mean integrity and trustworthiness. It will mean innovative ways of doing business. It will mean a focus on value in customers' terms, not ours. It will require new types of organization and technology to deliver value.' All these are features of the entrepreneurial organization – so the 'new' marketing paradigm should hold no fears for it. Piercy characterizes marketing strategy and the search for customer loyalty as progress from transactional and brand approaches to relationship and value-based strategies. These are illustrated in Figure 15.1.

Piercy (*op. cit.*) suggests that the sources for this value-driven strategy are:

- *Management vision* – clarity in direction and purpose, effectively communicated.
- *Market sensing and organizational learning* – understanding and responding to the external world.
- *Differentiating capabilities* – using core competencies to build differential advantage.
- *Relationship strategy* – managing the network of relationships needed to achieve superior performance.
- *Re-invented organization* – changing the organization form and process to sustain and renew strategy.

Source: Adapted from Piercy, N. F. (1999) *Tales from the Marketplace: Stories of Revolution, Reinvention and Renewal*, Oxford: Butterworth-Heinemann.

Figure 15.1 From transactions, brands and relationships to value

These are all themes repeated throughout this book. Piercy goes on to call for more strategizing to develop these innovative business models rather than formal planning, and predicts the decline in importance of 'traditional formal marketing functions and systems' to be replaced by process-based approaches. Once more, informality and a focus on process are hallmarks of our entrepreneurial organization. All in all they should be well placed to be exemplars of marketing in the future.

Marketing innovation

So is there such a thing as entrepreneurial marketing that yields innovation? Chaston (2000) argues that truly entrepreneurial firms have a distinctively different approach to marketing which he defines as 'the philosophy of challenging established market conventions during the process of developing new solutions'. The entrepreneurial marketing process is essentially simple, involving understanding conventional competitors and then challenging the approach they adopt. The process of 'rational entrepreneurship' is shown in Figure 15.2. In essence what Chaston is suggesting is that marketing is judged to be entrepreneurial by its degree of innovation. Since this is the essence of entrepreneurship, this is difficult to dispute.

As Chaston points out, even one of the defining features of entrepreneurial marketing – developing customer relationship – can be copied. Here again he encourages the entrepreneurial firm to do things differently. For example, many internet-based businesses can foster relationships with their customers by generating a sense of community on their website. Chaston's approach is deceptively simple as

Source: Chaston, *op. cit.*

Figure 15.2   Entrepreneurial vs non-entrepreneurial planning pathways he points out that there are many conventions that can be challenged. He suggests three categories:

1. *Sectoral conventions* are the strategic rules that guide the marketing operations of the majority of firms in a sector such as efficiency of plants, economies of scale, methods of distribution and so on. So, for example, insurance used to be delivered through insurance brokers until Direct Line came along, challenged the conventional wisdom, and began to sell direct over the telephone.

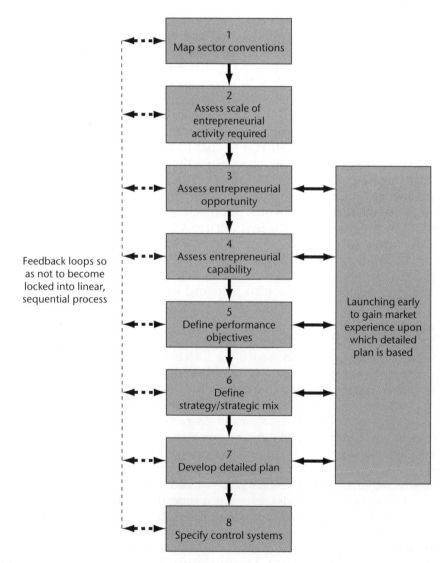

Source: Chaston, *op. cit.*

Figure 15.3 The entrepreneurial marketing planning process

2. *Performance conventions* set by other firms in the sector such as profit, cost of production, quality and so on. In the 1960s Japanese firms ignored Western performance conventions en masse and managed to enter and succeed in these markets.
3. *Customer conventions* which make certain assumptions about what customers want from their purchases, for example price, size, design and so on. Anita Roddick redefined the cosmetic industry's 'feel-good factor' to include environmental factors.

In most sectors there are factors that managers believe are critical to the success of their business. Chaston encourages entrepreneurial organizations to ask 'Why?'. These conventions are all worth questioning and doing things differently is what entrepreneurship is about, but doing things differently is risky and Chaston is the first to say it takes careful research and analysis, matching opportunities to the firm's capabilities. He proposes a somewhat different approach to marketing planning which he calls 'mapping the future' This is an eight-stage process shown in Figure 15.3. Although shown as linear and sequential, the process is interrupted as new market information is discovered and earlier decisions are revisited. The process also includes small-scale market entry and trial to gain further information.

The process starts with the development of a detailed understanding of sector conventions. Stage 2 involves assessing the performance gap between aspirations of future performance and the level of performance currently being delivered. If the size is sufficient to attract an entrepreneurial approach (i.e. an incremental approach is not warranted), then the opportunity is investigated using an innovative approach that questions all current assumptions about delivery. Whatever that approach is, it must next be matched to the firm's ability to deliver. If the firm has the capability then the remaining processes are more straightforward; defining performance objectives, defining strategy, developing a detailed plan and specifying control systems.

Case insight

The Korean car company **Daewoo** entered the UK car market based upon an innovative, mould-breaking marketing strategy – with remarkable success. It decided to sell directly to customers rather than through a franchised distributor network, thus eliminating commission payments. However, to persuade customers to try their offering they had to persuade them that it was safe to buy from them. They also set out to reduce the stress and risks involved in buying a car. Their market research revealed that car buyers disliked dealers on commission, hard-sell, aggressive sales techniques, over-exaggerated promotional campaigns and poor after-sales service.

So Daewoo set up its own dealerships with staff paid a salary rather than commission – trained, helpful sales advisors providing information rather than pressing for sales. Showrooms had crèches and children's play areas and offered coffee. Cars were not serviced at the same location, but rather by the well-known retailer Halfords in their out-of-town service centres. The themes used by Daewoo to further differentiate itself included good value, reliable cars (3-year warranties, AA breakdown cover) with additional safety features (e.g. ABS brakes and side impact protection) and additional features and benefits that would otherwise cost extra

➡

(e.g. power steering, no-fuss guarantees, courtesy cars or pick up and collection for services). The result was that in the first six months Daewoo sold a remarkable number of cars in the UK.

When Daewoo set up its second-hand car operation it had to do the same thing and set about putting together a similarly impressive package of additional benefits to augment the product, offering 12 months comprehensive warranty; 116-point AA-approved inspection; 12 months AA breakdown assistance; independent mileage check; free MOT tests for as long as the car is owned; a free check to ensure the car has not been stolen or written off and has no outstanding hire purchase agreements; 30-day money-back guarantee; direct contact with the previous owner, where possible; 6 months road tax; a free mobile phone; fixed price servicing with a free courtesy car anywhere in mainland UK.

Product innovation

Firms constantly strive to increase efficiency, implement best practice, improve productivity through economies of scale and constant cost reduction. However, there are limits to cost saving. Indeed in a global economy competitors in low-cost countries will ultimately always beat you at this game. It is not a sustainable strategy on its own for success and growth. The best way to create value is to innovate your way ahead of the competition with your marketing or your product. In this way you create a temporary monopoly with yours the only show in town. Product innovation is hard, but it can be very rewarding.

We saw in Chapter 13 how different types of product innovation present different levels of risk. However, generally the failure rate for new products is high, ranging from 60% to 90% depending on the industry and how the product is defined. For example, in the food and drinks industry it is estimated that 80% of new product launches fail ('New Product Failure: A Self-fulfilling Prophecy?', *Marketing Communications*, April 1989). Lack of research, technical problems in design or production and wrong timing can all contribute to failure. And the cost of failure can be high. What is needed is a systematic process that will minimize the risk.

Figure 15.4 shows a seven-stage model of how new products can be developed in a systematic way. It follows on directly from the ideas generation process outlined in the last chapter. It is based upon one of the most recognized activity-stage models, developed by the US consultants Booz, Allen and Hamilton (1968, 1982). Of course products are often not developed in a logical and systematic way but rather the path to market is more haphazard, opportunistic even chaotic. Still, the model gives us a framework within which to work and to analyze the processes sequentially. In the real world with time and resource pressures, some processes may be undertaken concurrently, others ignored completely in the headlong rush to be first to market and gain 'first-mover advantage'. But at each stage the risks of ignoring the systematic, sequential process need to be weighed carefully.

Once beyond the idea generation stage the processes involved are:

Screening. This involves assessing whether the ideas generated match the objectives of the organization, its resources and its core competencies. You must decide whether the firm will actually be able to design, produce and market the product idea

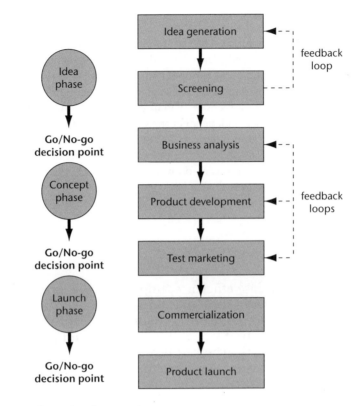

Figure 15.4 The product development process

effectively. At this point the idea may need to be reformulated so as to better match the firm's capabilities or refined so as to enable a more accurate evaluation of its potential.

Business analysis. This is the first major 'go/no-go' point in the decision-making process. More formal analyses of the 'fit' with the company, its core competencies and resources will be made. Estimates of sales, costs and profitability need to be made. Does the firm have the cash to invest? Is the investment worthwhile, given the other opportunities it faces? How robust is the business model? Can it get the product into the market place in a reasonable period of time? Who are the competitors (if any)? What is our competitive advantage, and can it be sustained? What are the risks involved? Inevitably market research information will be needed – consumer surveys, secondary data and so on – so as to enable an estimate of potential sales to be made. If the business analysis does not produce a robust case for taking the product forward its development may be terminated.

Product development. This stage involves deciding whether it is technically feasible to produce the product at costs that allow adequate profits to be made. Normally a prototype is built, although increasingly computer simulations can be used to reduce the number actually produced. For example, cars are increasingly developed using

---

Case insight

As we saw in Chapter 7, strategic alliances can lead to new product development. One example of this is the development of the **Nike+iPod Sports Kit**. This was an acknowledgement of how some people use their iPods to listen to music whilst jogging, often wearing Nike shoes. By connecting one into the other via Bluetooth-type technology, you can listen to music and be interrupted, when you want, with information on your speed, pace, distance covered or time elapsed. It can even urge you to run faster. Linking two well known brands in this development also has obvious marketing advantages.

●

CAD-CAM technology and prototype development is left increasingly to later stages. However, concept cars still represent an important part of product development – an opportunity to test out ideas, not just in terms of mechanical feasibility, but also in terms of market acceptability. And often only by seeing, touching and using the product can the potential consumer make judgements about it.

Test marketing. Often a product is test marketed in a limited geographic area which is chosen to represent the intended target market. The aim is to assess the real response of potential buyers. As such it is not just about trying out a new product, it is a trial product launch. The complete marketing mix needs to be trialled so that weaknesses can be identified and corrected. But market testing takes time and can bring a new product to the attention of competitors. Test marketing may not be economically viable for some products, such as a new car, and it may not be feasible to withdraw some products once introduced. With increasingly shortening life cycles, many firms decide to launch first and test the market as they go along, making modifications rapidly in response to product or marketing deficiencies. The problem is that failure can be expensive. This is another go/no-go point. If the results of the test marketing are not attractive, the project may again be terminated.

Commercialization. This is the stage where plans for full scale manufacture and marketing must be refined and finally decided on. Results from the test marketing need to be incorporated in the final product/market offering. Early adopters need to be identified and a promotion campaign agreed on. The company starts to gear up for the full-scale launch and that means finalizing the complete launch strategy. Budgets need to be set and action plans finalized. At the end of this stage is the final go/no-go decision point. Even at this stage a project might be terminated because the firm realizes that, whilst the product is attractive to the market place, it is not best placed to take it there. In which case it may license or sell off the idea.

In the real world new product development does not evolve in such a neat, orderly fashion. It is neither linear nor smooth. Feedback loops result in multiple iteration of the various stages. Sometimes a project will move backwards in the process as the repeat of the stage in the process creates problems that were not previously apparent. There is often an element of chaos as blocks to progress emerge and ways around them are eventually developed. Since different teams might be working on different stages, information sharing and effective communication are important.

> **Case insight**
>
> The development of **Levi** jeans was certainly neither linear nor orderly. The tailor Levi Strauss started out making hard-wearing work overalls. These were so popular that he ran out of the brown canvas sailcloth from which they were made so he decided to switch to a sturdy twill fabric called serge that was made in Nîme in France. The material was named 'serge de Nîme', but this soon became shortened to denim. It proved very popular. The next development came when a Nevadan tailor called Jacob David suggested to Strauss that he insert metal rivets at points of stress, typically pocket corners and the base of the fly, to make the trousers even sturdier. The pair patented the idea. The final element was added by a rival tailor, H.D. Lee, who introduced a novelty to replace the button fly, called the Whizit. We know this today as the zip or zipper.

The go/no-go decisions at various points in this model – widely referred to as the stage gate process – have been criticized for being particularly rigid and inflexible and taking far too long. Cooper (1994) has proposed that greater creativity within this process can be achieved by permitting progression to the next stage, even though some issues may remain unresolved. In this way the three stages may be viewed as, potentially, happening in parallel. It has been advocated by Takeuchi and Nonaka (1986) that this parallel development process best relies on self-organizing multidisciplinary project teams whose members work together from start to finish such that the process emerges from their constant interaction rather than highly structured stages.

The parallel development process has been characterized by Lambin (*op. cit.*) in terms of Figure 15.5. What drives this view is that firms must find ways of cutting back the lead time on new product development if they are to gain greater competitive advantage. This saving is achieved by undertaking several activities simultaneously and is also due to the more intensive workload facing team members. Indeed in this context any activity that takes too much time needs to be reconsidered very carefully – excessive testing, an over-emphasis on accurate cost estimates etc. – in light of its impact on completion time. Other claimed benefits of this approach include facilitation of cross functional co-ordination and better control of each activity since it directly determines the subsequent activities.

Source: Lambin, *op. cit.*

Figure 15.5 Parallel development of new products

Case with questions

LG Electronics

Design has an important part to play in product innovation. It also allows products to be effectively differentiated. LG Electronics was set up in 1958 in Korea where it broke new ground in that country by hiring an industrial designer and one year later set up a product design department. It now has a turnover in excess of £19 billion and, in 2006, spent some £1.5 billion on R&D in its 25 R&D laboratories around the world. Its strategy of 'global localization' has led it to become the world's leading manufacturer of plasma TVs and number five for mobile phones.

LG has many technological 'firsts' to its credit. It developed the first ever disk player to support both Blu-ray disk and HD DVD content; the most energy efficient side-by-side refrigerator; the industry's first ever steam washer; the ultra-responsive LCD monitor as well as premium mobile phone hand sets, the A Cappella Music Phone and the LG Shine phone.

LG aims to integrate technological developments with design, and design is a key part of LG's culture. In 1999 it defined design as one of its four key skills and in 2006 it announced its 'design management' strategy. Between 2005 an 2007 it won fifty prestigious Red Dot design awards. The company sees design as playing a crucial role in harmonizing the very latest in technological developments with human needs. It strives for design that is at once 'minimalist and seductive'. Designers are encouraged to 'experiment in a playful manner with fresh ideas and unusual combinations ... to predict emerging needs, design new worlds and lifestyle concepts, and hand over their inventions to the public.' Researchers, designers and 'trend scouts' predict the future by examining and identifying consumer needs, observing the public's interest in products, and finally developing design concepts and solutions. In this way LG tries to keep 'one step ahead of the game.'

Kim Jin is in charge of LG's mobile phone design laboratory. She says that the company's design philosophy is to 'appeal to customers' emotions', a concept originally called 'haptic' meaning the feeling of touch but broadened to include all five senses – 'touch, smell the glowing lights, all the emotional things'. LG's products must be technologically advanced and functionally effective, but then most electronic products are. People buy one product rather than another for reasons that involve the intangible elements – and design and brand image have a crucial part to play in this. And whilst the functional elements of any product are usually easy to copy, these less tangible elements are more difficult. LG believes that good design enhances its brand image and this allows it to position its products at the premium end of the market.

Kim Jim encourages designers to do 'town-watching' – visiting the chic streets of Hongdae or Cheongdam-dong to spot new design trends. It was on one of these trips that the trend towards more natural shapes was identified. Eventually that was incorporated into the KG800 mobile phone – the 'Chocolate Phone', which won a Red Dot award. The phone has nothing to do with chocolate, it was just thought that the name was memorable. This was the first mobile phone in the world to have a touch sensitive key pad. Seventeen months after its launch it had sold 10 million units and spawned a limited edition 'White Chocolate' phone with a lavender-scented keypad, which was sold on Valentines Day 2006. The phone model for 2007 was the sophisticated Prada phone.

LG believes it has integrated design into its business thinking. Many innovations are design-led, but responsive to market needs. LG believes it must design its technologies for the way

➡

Case with questions continued

LG Electronics

people actually behave, not the way you would like them to behave. That means designers have to meet people, hear what they have to say and see how they use electronic products. Usability tests are important, and should not be confused with market research or the inherent falsity of focus groups. This research involves collecting conscious and subconscious feedback about design through simulated use of a product prototype. It tries to understand the way users think so as to drive the design process. And it's not just to do with functionality, LG are keen to make their designs 'playful and fun-to-use'.

Up-to-date information on LG can be found on their website: www.lge.com

Questions
1. What is the role of design in product innovation at LG? How important is it?
2. How does LG encourage designers to 'think outside the square'?

Structures to support product development

Product development can be a complex process that involves different teams where information sharing and timing are essential. How this can be facilitated is clearly important, but this depends on the complexity of the task and the nature of the innovation expected. It also depends on the context – both within the organization and its market place.

In the real world, firms are experimenting with a host of different structures to facilitate the product development process. Morris and Kuratko (2002) catalogue ten different approaches (refer back to Chapter 8):

1. *New product division* – a separate, centralized, self-sufficient organization. The advantages of this are that it demonstrates long-term commitment, assures top-management attention and should have adequate resources. However, it may be insular, inflexible and pose co-ordination problems with other divisions.
2. *New product department* – a department within a division. This offers specialist skills and integration of efforts but will have less authority and may have fewer resources than the division.
3. *New product manager* – a single person responsible for development of the product. This is a simple solution but one that runs the risk for the manager of facing isolation, lack of co-operation from others and being overwhelmed by the scale of the task.
4. *Product or brand manager* – new product development is added to the job definition of the product manager. This approach is best for line extensions or minor product modifications. It is unlikely to result in the development of truly innovative products.
5. *New product committee* – a standing committee formed from senior managers from different parts of the organization. This can bring together several

functional areas and, with sufficiently senior managers, have sufficient authority – and resources – to push through new product development, but it runs the risk of diluting responsibility.

6. *Cross-functional project teams* – a team set up for the duration of the project. This diverse team is potentially flexible and fluid, bringing different skills and perspectives to the project but it must have sufficient authority to push things through and may have to compete to get functional, departmental support.

7. *Task force or ad hoc committee* – a temporary matrix approach set up for the duration of the project. Again this brings together a diverse team but members may also face competing demands on their time.

8. *Venture team* – a dedicated, cross-functional team, often teamed with an intrapreneur. This can be extremely effective but it can be expensive and difficult to control.

9. *Outside suppliers* – outside suppliers contracted to develop the product. This uses specialist skills or knowledge that the organization may not possess but it can be expensive and difficult to control and intellectual property rights might not be secure.

10. *Multiple organization forms* – hybrid forms depending on the nature of the project. The form is designed specifically to fit the circumstances but because it is a hybrid it may be difficult to set up, manage and control.

Based upon a survey of companies, Page (1993) reports that more than half the firms were using multiple organization forms to facilitate new product development. He also reported that multidisciplinary teams were by far the most widely used organization structure with over 76% of the sample using them, compared to the next highest score of 30% for new product departments and new product managers. Having said that, these different structures are best suited to a range of different types of innovation. New product divisions and venture teams are most likely to produce disruptive innovations.

Case with questions

LEGO®

LEGO – the well-known children's building system – has been around for a long time and, in an age when new toys come and go with astonishing rapidity and technology-based toys like video games are reaching astonishing heights of sophistication, it might be difficult to understand the enduring market appeal of these basic building blocks. Well the answer is that LEGO has changed with the market and the company, currently owned by the founder's grandson Kjeld Kirk Christiansen, continues to invest large sums around the world to understand changes in children's tastes and to explore new product developments based around its mission 'to inspire children to explore and challenge their own creative potential'.

→

LEGO®

The name 'LEGO' is an abbreviation of two Danish words 'leg godt', meaning 'play well'. The company was founded by Ole Kirk Christiansen in 1932. It is now the world's sixth largest manufacturer of toys, with its head office in Billund, Denmark, branches throughout the world and some 5000 employees. Its products are sold in more than 130 countries. The traditional interlocking LEGO brick has twice been named toy of the century by *Fortune* magazine then by the British Association of Toy Retailers, although in its present form it was launched in 1958. Approximately 17.8 billion LEGO bricks and other components are made every year. However the product range is now far wider than the basic brick with 'classic' products like LEGO DUPLO, LEGO CITY, LEGO TECHNIC being constantly upgraded and augmented with concepts like LEGO MINDSTORMS (robot building sets). There are theme based products like LEGO Harry Potter, Spiderman 2, Bob the Builder and Star Wars, introduced under licence, and there are brand new products like CLIKITS and BIONICLES. BIONICLES allows children to construct action figures like knights and to develop a detailed online world into which they can be placed to play through a story. LEGO has also moved into different market segments. LEGO BELVILLE is aimed at young girls, allowing them to construct scenes from everyday life and, more recently, moving into the world of fairy tale with princesses, fairies and butterflies. These developments have evolved through four 'eras': the first was the developing construction and building as the central elements in play; in the second the LEGO products gained motion through wheels, small motors and gears; role play formed the third era, when LEGO figures were born; and the fourth era introduced intelligence and behaviour. Alongside this LEGO has developed numerous 'play themes' for all their products such as fire stations, police, airport, knights, castles and racing cars. There are also four LEGOLAND theme parks around the world in Denmark, England, Germany and California and a LEGOLAND Discovery Centre opened in Berlin in 2007.

Strategic partnerships have played an important part in recent innovations. In 1984, before digital development really took off, LEGO entered into a partnership with Media Laboratory at Massachusetts Institute of Technology (MIT). By blending physical and virtual worlds into an integrated play universe, the company came up with new products. LEGO TECHNIC Computer Control was the first tangible product of the partnership, launched in 1986. This paved the way for the introduction in 1998 of LEGO MINDSTORMS, integrating robot technology with LEGO constructions systems and enabling children to create and program intelligent LEGO models. LEGO, in partnership with a US non-profit organization called FIRST (For Inspiration and Recognition of Science and Technology), has established FIRST LEGO League, a worldwide tournament in which children compete by designing their own robots and participate in a series of scientific and mathematical or technical projects. The 2006 version, LEGO MINDSTORMS NXT, allows children to build and program a robot that can see, hear, speak, feel and move in just half an hour.

The company's website LEGO.com is more than just a showcase for the company's products, it allows children to play games, enjoy stories and undertake activities. It is important because stories spur children to play games. Over 25% of toy sales are now related to movies or TV series and, since none to date have featured LEGO parts, it is important for the company to be able to inspire children through its own communication medium. In 2006 the website was one of the top 25 'Lifestyles and children's websites' in the USA, building a virtual community of LEGO

➡

enthusiasts. LEGOfactory.com even allows children to build virtual LEGO models, exhibit them in a virtual gallery and then order the parts if they want.

Concept and product development take place primarily in the Concept Centre at the company's headquarters in Billund. This creative core is made up of 120 designers representing about 15 nationalities, most having trained at art school. The company also has what it calls 'listening posts' – otherwise known as Concept Labs – in Munich, Barcelona, Los Angeles and Tokyo. At these Labs children from four very different countries are encouraged to try out different combinations with the same LEGO pieces and create worlds of their own, which the company can incorporate into its 'play themes'. The Labs try to spot trends in children's play, understand the motivations behind them and translate them into what it means for the company and new product development – effectively trying to systematically understand children's' creativity by observing them at play. The Labs also take an active role in the product concept and early development phase of any new product.

Visit the company website on www.lego.com to see some of the features described in this case.

Questions
1. If you were in charge of LEGO what would you want the Concept Centre and its Labs to find out, and how would you set about getting that information?
2. How important are strategic alliances? How do they influence innovation?
3. With whom does the company develop relationships? What role do they serve and how are they developed?

Summary

Relationship marketing focuses on developing strong, lasting relationships with customers, based on customer service and trust, where benefits are shared. It is most frequently associated with business-to-business marketing. Transaction marketing focuses on the discrete, individual sale and is more associated with price decisions. Entrepreneurial firms are good at relationship marketing.

Value-driven marketing is an extension of relationship marketing associated with higher levels of customer sophistication. This new marketing paradigm aligns very closely with the key characteristics and competencies of an entrepreneurial organization.

Innovative marketing involves asking whether the conventional approaches to marketing established products can be questioned and even turned on their heads. All the time you are looking to add value to the customer by doing things differently, as in the case of **Daewoo**.

Product innovation is risky but the risk can be mitigated by adopting a systematic process like the one outlined in Figure 15.4. The drawback with these processes is that they may become linear, sequential and therefore slow when time-to-market is an important determinant of success. One way around this is the parallel development of a new product through the various stage gates that it faces.

Design and designers can have an important part to play in the process of product innovation, as we saw in the case of **LG Electronics**, particularly when designers are encouraged to 'think outside the square'.

Companies are experimenting with many structures to facilitate new product development. In fact most firms use multiple organization forms. The most popular is, however, the multidisciplinary team, whilst new product divisions and venture teams are most likely to produce disruptive innovations. Notwithstanding any of these points, real innovation involves 'thinking outside the square'. It involves inputs from many different sources, but particularly consumers, and, as **LEGO** has demonstrated, it can be systematically built into the business model, even for an international company.

Essays and discussion topics

1. What is relationship marketing? How does it differ from transaction marketing?
2. What is involved in relationship selling? Is it any different from conventional selling?
3. How does transaction marketing differ from relationship marketing?
4. How does relationship marketing differ from value-driven marketing?
5. Are all entrepreneurial firms likely to practise value-driven marketing?
6. What is entrepreneurial marketing? Is there any framework that allows you to systematically 'do things differently'?
7. If doing things differently is important, what is the value of conventional marketing frameworks?
8. What are the problems associated with a structured, systematic product development process? How can they be overcome?
9. What are the advantages and disadvantages of 'parallel processes'?
10. Can an entrepreneurial firm really afford to be so systematic?
11. Systems extinguish the spark of creativity. Discuss.
12. Systems take time and time-to-market as a key source of competitive advantage. Discuss.
13. Why is there no one best structure that facilitates new product development?
14. What are the advantages and disadvantages of venture teams and new product divisions?
15. What is the role of the intrapreneur in the ten structures outlined?

Exercises and assignments

1. Why were Daewoo successful? Was this short-term success sustainable?
2. Why is eBay successful? How might it capitalize further on its success?

References

Booz, Allen and Hamilton (1968) *Management of New Products*, New York: Booz, Allen and Hamilton.

Booz, Allen and Hamilton (1982) *New Products Management for the 1980s*, New York: Booz, Allen and Hamilton.

Chaston, I. (2000) *Entrepreneurial Marketing: Competing by Challenging Convention*, Basingstoke: Palgrave – now Palgrave Macmillan.

Christopher, M., Payne, A. and Ballantyne, D. (1991) *Relationship Marketing*, Oxford: Butterworth-Heinemann.

Cooper, R. G. (1994) 'Third-Generation New Product Processes', *Journal of Product Innovation Management*, 11.

Lambin, J. J. (2000) *Market-Driven Management: Strategic and Operational Marketing*, Basingstoke: Palgrave – now Palgrave Macmillan.

Morris, M. H. and Kuratko, D. F. (2002) *Corporate Entrepreneurship: Entrepreneurial Development within Organizations*, Fort Worth: Harcourt College Publishers.

Page, A. L. (1993) 'Assessing New Product Development Practices and Performance: Establishing Crucial Norms', *Journal of Product Innovation Management*, 10.

Payne, A. (1994) 'Relationship Marketing – Making the Customer Count', *Managing Service Quality*, 4(6).

Piercy, N. F. (2001) 'The Future of Marketing is Strategizing' in S. Dibb, L. Simkin, W. M. Pride and O. C. Ferrell, *Marketing: Concepts and Strategies*, Boston, Mass: Houghton Mifflin

Takeuchi, H. and Nonaka, I. (1986) 'The New Product Development Game', *Harvard Business Review*, 64(1).

Webster, J. E. (1992) 'The Changing Role of Marketing in the Corporation', *Journal of Marketing*, 56, October.

The Profile of an Entrepreneurial Organization

So just what does an entrepreneurial organization look like? Whilst there is no one-size-fits-all blueprint, there are some elements that mean you really will know one when you see one. To start with, it will be creative and innovative, priding itself on its ability to thrive in a competitive, changing environment. Indeed it will see itself as helping to shape that environment. And it will be successful. But there will be other internal, managerial signs.

The organization is likely to be structured more like a grouping of atoms – atoms that may well change and evolve in different situations – rather than a rigid hierarchy. In other words, it will be highly flexible rather than rigid. There will be structures within structures, each with considerable autonomy, that encourage smaller units to develop continually as the organization seeks to replicate itself. Structures within these units will be horizontal and flat – spider-like – rather than vertical and authority will be based on expertise, not role. Spans of control are likely to be broad and controls will be loose, with an emphasis on getting things done. Accountability, however, will be tight. Structures, behaviours, even controls are likely to be more informal than formal. It certainly will not be bureaucratic in any way. There will be an emphasis on team working and open communication. It may already have spun off some of these innovations. There will be mechanisms such as venture teams to encourage the development of innovations. The organization will also be good at developing relationships – inside and out – and networking to share resources and maximize opportunities. The organization is likely to participate in numerous informal networks and relationships. It may have strategic alliances.

The culture within this organization will value these relationships so that they generate a strong sense of group identity. The culture will value and reward the things that entrepreneurship values – creativity, innovation, measured risk taking and continual learning. Indeed there are likely to be intrapreneurs at work within the organization. It will be a culture that sees changes as the norm, certainly not something to fear. It will have confidence in its future. It will be egalitarian but slightly anti-authoritarian – always daring to be different. It will make mistakes, but learn from them. Individuals will be empowered and motivated to make decisions for the good of the organization. Indeed decision making will be delegated down, as far as possible. And information will be shared rather than hoarded. There will be a 'can-do' attitude around that values achievement.

The leadership of this organization will be driven by a strong vision, underpinned by equally strong values. The leaders will be able to communicate this effectively, through many mechanisms, but particularly informal influence. They will lead by example – 'walking the talk'. They will think strategically and build confidence in the organization that it can be managed through the uncertainties it faces. However, they will have a strong sense of reality. They will be adept at reconciling conflict and dealing with ambiguity and uncertainty. They will encourage team working and generate trust through their consistent behaviour and fairness. They will create 'space' for learning, creativity and innovation.

Strategies might be either emergent or deliberate, but characterized by continuous strategizing at all levels in the organization, underpinned by a strong vision and sense of direction. Strategy will therefore come from both the top and the bottom of the organization. Decision making will tend to be incremental and adaptive, so as to maintain maximum flexibility but the organization will be able to respond speedily to opportunities (or threats).

Successful organizations are likely to play to their strengths – particularly their entrepreneurial architecture – emphasizing whatever makes it as unique as possible and delivers as much value to the customers as possible. In this way it will be able to differentiate itself from competitors and it is likely to do so through a strong brand identity.

Growth in the entrepreneurial organization will come primarily from the successful exploitation of market opportunities, requiring good 'environmental monitoring'. This will drive strategy development. For most organizations growth will be internal as new markets and new products or services are developed incrementally. There will also be an emphasis on continual improvement. The organization will be willing to take measured risks, but will identify and monitor them.

It is one thing to describe this 'mythical beast', but quite another to create one. And the most difficult task of all is to turn around an existing organization so as to become one. If entrepreneurs are the super-heroes of the business world, what does that make those who practise corporate entrepreneurship?

Case with questions

3M

3M is often held out as a good example of an organization that practises corporate entrepreneurship. Reread the case in Chapter 4 and review your original analysis.

Questions
1. Does 3M fit the profile you have just read? Be certain to distinguish between areas where the case does not give you the information and those where it does not fit the profile.
2. Compare your conclusions here to your original analysis. What have you learnt?
3. Apply the Corporate Entrepreneurship (CE) Audit tool on page 365 (or use the web-based tool on www.palgrave.com/business/burns) to 3M and map the outcome. Where there is insufficient information in the case to score the question, enter '0' but mark or note the question. When you interpret the results remember that each dimension is measured on a 60-point scale, but if you could not answer any question that scale is reduced by 4 points for each question. So, for example, if two questions could not be scored on one dimension, the maximum score is 52 (60 – 8). The final score must then be interpreted against that benchmark.

Corporate Entrepreneurship Exercise

This exercise is to help assess the entrepreneurial orientation of an organization and the opportunities it faces. It has three parts:

1. A mapping of the frequency (volume) and scale (quality) of innovation within the organization to arrive at an assessment of the extent of innovative activity currently taking place in the organization. This is a subjective assessment but it does get you to think about the degree and nature of the innovation.
2. A review of the strategies the organization is currently employing to achieve its growth objectives and the risks that it faces. This uses the Ansoff matrix as its base.
3. Completion of a Corporate Entrepreneurship Audit (the CE Audit tool online at www.palgrave.com/business/burns). This provides a check on the potential for the organization to be entrepreneurial, as well as the appropriateness of this orientation in terms of the environment.

The CE Audit looks at entrepreneurial characteristics in the four dimensions of architecture outlined in the book: leadership, culture, structure and strategy. However, these must be placed in the context of the environment within which the organization operates. Only if the environment is suitable will an entrepreneurial response be appropriate. These factors are mapped onto a CE Audit Grid that measure both entrepreneurial potential and the appropriateness of corporate entrepreneurship for the competitive environment facing the organization. The environmental footprint, ideally, should map onto the entrepreneurial potential, otherwise there is a mismatch.

This diagnostic tool can be applied to any level of organization – the organization overall, division, department and so on. It provides a means of analyzing potential areas for improvement, rather than a crude pass/fail test. This involves making informed judgements about certain criteria and, as such, is subjective rather than objective. Where benchmark comparisons are required, they should be made against competitor organizations.

When you have completed all three parts of the exercise write up your findings in the form of a report. Be sure to justify your evaluations with evidence and examples.

1 Evaluation of current extent of innovative activity

Locate the organization on the Innovation Grid below by comparing it to the competition in its industry in terms of:

- **Frequency of innovation**: the rate of new product/service innovations, ranging from periodic (low) to continuous (high).
- **Degree of innovation**: the scale of the innovations, ranging from incremental (low) to discontinuous (high).

2   Review of growth strategies

Break down planned sales for next year into the four components of the product/market matrix outlined in Chapter 12.

£ sales   £ sales

Market penetration	Product/service development
Market development	Diversification

Total

Critically analyze how the firm proposes to achieve these sales targets:

- Outline the strategies the firm will use to increase market penetration
- Outline the strategies the organization will use for market development.
- Give details of any new product(s) or service(s) and why existing customers are expected to buy them.
- Give details of and the rationale for any diversification.

Critically evaluate these strategies, the risks associated with them and the safeguards to provide early warning signs and deal with them. Are the strategies coherent and consistent with the firm's vision/mission and its core strengths or competencies? Does it have the resources to undertake them?

If the organization has a number of different product/service offerings, repeat the exercise for each one, bearing in mind where it lies in its product life cycle and the generic marketing strategy being followed. Evaluate its overall portfolio strategy.

Give details of the rationale for any mergers or acquisitions proposed. Explain how the firm will go about achieving the merger or acquisition.

Your evaluation of the firm's strategies should feed into the Strategy section of the CE Audit and form part of your final written report.

3 Corporate entrepreneurship audit

The web-based version is available on www.palgrave.com/business/burns.

Circle the number that best describes your opinion about the characteristic, as it applies to the organization being audited. Jot down evidence and/or examples to justify your scores in the box at the bottom of the page. Use this when you write your report.

Leadership

		Low		Average		High
1	Clarity of vision	0	1	2	3	4
2	Definition of values	0	1	2	3	4
3	Grasp of reality	0	1	2	3	4
4	Effectiveness of communication	0	1	2	3	4
5	Willingness to 'walk the talk'	0	1	2	3	4
6	Level of trust generated	0	1	2	3	4
7	Care and respect shown for individuals	0	1	2	3	4
8	Consistency of behaviour	0	1	2	3	4
9	Ability to influence individuals and outcomes informally	0	1	2	3	4
10	Ability to think strategically	0	1	2	3	4
11	Ability to motivate	0	1	2	3	4
12	Ability to manage change	0	1	2	3	4
13	Ability to resolve or reconcile conflict	0	1	2	3	4
14	Ability to build confidence in the organization	0	1	2	3	4
15	Appropriateness of leadership style	0	1	2	3	4

Total score

Justification for scores

Circle the number that best describes your opinion about the characteristic, as it applies to the organization being audited. Jot down evidence and/or examples to justify your scores in the box at the bottom of the page. Use this when you write your report.

Culture

		Low		Average		High
1	Builds strong relationships	0	1	2	3	4
2	Encourages creativity and innovation	0	1	2	3	4
3	Empowers staff with a 'can-do' attitude	0	1	2	3	4
4	Encourages measured risk taking	0	1	2	3	4
5	Encourages continual learning	0	1	2	3	4
6	Creates a sense of belonging to a group ('ingroup')	0	1	2	3	4
7	Encourages egalitarianism	0	1	2	3	4
8	Encourages achievement	0	1	2	3	4
9	Accepts change as normal	0	1	2	3	4
10	Encourages achievement	0	1	2	3	4
11	Creates a sense of commitment	0	1	2	3	4
12	Creates time or 'space' for learning, creativity or innovation	0	1	2	3	4
13	Encourages team working	0	1	2	3	4
14	Encourages open communication	0	1	2	3	4

Total score

Justification for scores

Circle the number that best describes your opinion about the characteristic, as it applies to the organization being audited. Jot down evidence and/or examples to justify your scores in the box at the bottom of the page. Use this when you write your report.

Size, structure and organization

		Low	Average			High
1	Degree of hierarchy	4	3	2	1	0
2	Degree of bureaucracy	4	3	2	1	0
3	Degree of control	4	3	2	1	0
4	Degree of flexibility	0	1	2	3	4
5	Extent of delegation	0	1	2	3	4
6	Extent of decentralization	0	1	2	3	4
7	Extent that structures are flattened	0	1	2	3	4
8	Typical span of control (broad = high, narrow = low)	0	1	2	3	4
9	Degree to which team working is encouraged	0	1	2	3	4
10	Degree to which smaller units are encouraged to develop	0	1	2	3	4
11	Degree of autonomy of smaller units	0	1	2	3	4
12	Extent of networking with suppliers	0	1	2	3	4
13	Use of intrapreneurs and/or venture teams	0	1	2	3	4
14	Backing and 'space' given to intrapreneurs and/or venture teams	0	1	2	3	4
15	Extent of reward systems that encourage innovation	0	1	2	3	4

Total score

Justification for scores

Circle the number that best describes your opinion about the characteristic, as it applies to the organization being audited. Jot down evidence and/or examples to justify your scores in the box at the bottom of the page. Use this when you write your report.

Strategy

Low　　Average　　High

		Low		Average		High
1	Extent to which strategizing occurs at all levels	0	1	2	3	4
2	Extent to which strategy flexes to meet opportunities/threats	0	1	2	3	4
3	Extent to which strategy is informed by vision and mission	0	1	2	3	4
4	Extent to which strategy is influenced by all in organization	0	1	2	3	4
5	Extent to which there is a strategic vision about the future	0	1	2	3	4
6	Extent to which entrepreneurship and innovation are central to the strategy	0	1	2	3	4
7	Extent to which growth is central to the strategy	0	1	2	3	4
8	Extent to which strategy relies on creating differential advantage	0	1	2	3	4
9	Effectiveness of branding	0	1	2	3	4
10	Consideration and monitoring of risks associated with strategies	0	1	2	3	4
11	Extent of 'environmental monitoring'	0	1	2	3	4
12	Extent of reliance on internal growth	0	1	2	3	4
13	Extent to which the organization pushes the boundaries of new product/new market development	0	1	2	3	4
14	Extent of emphasis on continual improvement	0	1	2	3	4
15	Speed of strategy implementation	0	1	2	3	4

Total score

Justification for scores

Circle the number that best describes your opinion about the environment in which the organization operates. Jot down evidence and/or examples to justify your scores in the box at the bottom of the page. Use this when you write your report.

Environment

		Low	Average			High
1	Change	0	1	2	3	4
2	Degree of turbulence	0	1	2	3	4
3	Degree of instability	0	1	2	3	4
4	Degree of disruptiveness	0	1	2	3	4
5	Degree of uncertainty	0	1	2	3	4
6	Degree of complexity	0	1	2	3	4
7	Importance of innovation	0	1	2	3	4
8	Importance of 'first-mover advantage' (speed of response)	0	1	2	3	4
9	Importance of differentiation	0	1	2	3	4
10	Extent of competition (lack of industry concentration)	0	1	2	3	4
11	Degree of competition (ferocity)	0	1	2	3	4
12	Threat of substitutes	0	1	2	3	4
13	Power of suppliers	0	1	2	3	4
14	Power of customers	0	1	2	3	4
15	Barriers to entry	4	3	2	1	0

Total score

Justification for scores

CE Results

Total the scores for the CE Audit along the four dimensions of leadership (dimension A), culture (dimension B), size, structure and organization (dimension C) and strategy (dimension D) and map them onto the CE Audit Grid. An example of how this might look is shown below. This example shows an organization with strong entrepreneurial leadership and strategies but some work still to be done to bring about an entrepreneurial culture. This would be a consistent pattern for an organization in the process of becoming entrepreneurial, as culture takes time to change.

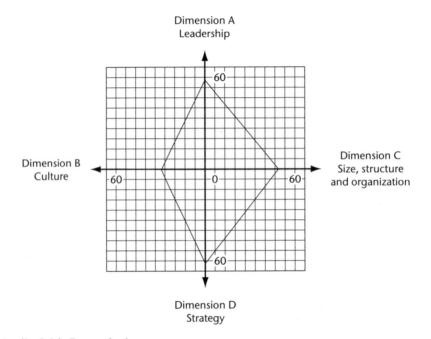

The CE Audit Grid: Example 1

Now total the scores for the Environment and map them onto the grid. The maximum score of 60 should be mapped along each of the four dimensions. An example of how this might look is shown below for the same organization. It is indeed operating in an environment where corporate entrepreneurship should flourish. If the context for this organization is that new entrepreneurial leadership has introduced new strategies and structures but cultures are taking longer to change, then the organization is indeed moving in the right direction.

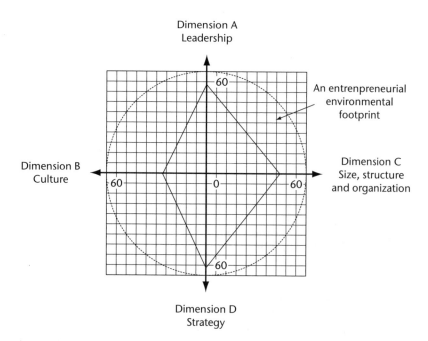

The CE Audit Grid: Example 2

You can map the results for your organization on the grid below.

- What does it tell you about the organization?
- What does the organization need to do to improve its 'fit' with the environment?

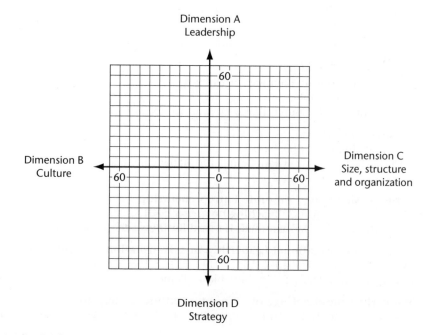

The CE Audit Grid

Learning Resources

Selected case studies

Chapters 2–3: The individuals
Richard Branson/Herb Kelleher – Leaders Extraordinaire.
Case 803–005–1. Teaching note: 803–005–8.
Written by V. Sarvai, under the direction of A. Mukund, ICFA Center for Management Research (ICMR), Hyderabad, India.

Michael Dell – The Man Behind Dell.
Case 402–015–1. Teaching note: 402–015–8.
Written by K Subhadra, under the direction of A. Mukund, ICFA Center for Management Research (ICMR), Hyderabad, India.

Larry Ellison: A Samurai Warrior in Silicon Valley.
Case 402–038–1. No teaching note.
Written by M. Kets de Vries and E. Florent-Treacy, INSEAD, Fontainebleau, France.

Chapters 4–9: Management, leadership, culture and structure
The 3M Company: (A) Building the Entrepreneurial Corporation (1902–1950).
Case 802–001–1. No teaching note.

The 3M Company: (B) Defining Strategy (1950–1990).
Case 802–002–1. No teaching note.

The 3M Company: (C) Dynamic Balance for the 90s.
Case 802–003–1. No teaching note.
Written by M. Ackenhusen, N. Churchill and D. Muzyka, INSEAD, Fontainebleau, France.

3M's Organisational Culture.
Case 403–041–1. Teaching note: 403–041–8.
Written by S. Dutta, K. Subhadra, ICFAI Center for Management Research (ICMR), Hyderabad, India.

3M Optical Systems: Managing Corporate Entrepreneurship.
Case: 9–395–017. Video: 9–395–513. Teaching note: 9–395–017.
Written by C.A. Bartlett and A. Mohammed, Harvard Business School, Boston, USA.

British Petroleum: Transformational Leadership in a Transnational Organisation.
Case: 497–013–1. Interviews: 497–013–4. Video: 497–013–3. Teaching note: 497–013–8.
Written by M. Kets de Vries, INSEAD, Fontainebleau, France.

Branson's Virgin: The Coming of Age of a Counter-Cultural Enterprise.
Case: 495–014–1. Supplement: 495–014–4. Interview: 495–014–5. Video: 495–015–3. Teaching note: 495–014–8.
Written by M. Kets de Vries, INSEAD, Fontainebleau, France.

The House that Branson Built: Virgin's Entry into the New Millenium.
Case 400–002–1. Teaching note: 400–002–8.
Written by M. Kets de Vries, INSEAD, Fontainebleau, France.

Body Shop.
Case 9–392–032. Teaching note: 5–392–038.
Written by C.A. Bartlett, K.W. Eldererkin and K. McQuade, Harvard Business School, Boston, USA.

Dell Online.
Case 5–598–116. Teaching note: 5–598–146.
Written by V.K. Rangan, M. Bell, Harvard Business School, Boston, USA.

Ebay.com – Profitably Managing Growth from Start-up to 2000.
Case: 301–017–1. Teaching note: 301–017–8.
Written by G.J. Stockport, D. Pudney and M. van der Merwe, The Graduate School of Management, University of Western Australia, Australia.

GE and Jack Welch.
Case 402–006–1. Teaching note: 402–006–8.
Written by S. Dutta and D. Sirisha, ICFAI Centre for Management Research (ICMR), Hyderabad, India.

Jaguar comes to Halewood: The story of a Turnaround.
Case 602–013–1. Teaching note: 602–013–8.
Written by L.N. Van Wasssenhove and R. Samii, INSEAD, Fontainebleau, France.

Changing the Culture at DEI Airlines.
Case 402–037–1. Teaching note: 402–037–8
Written by J. Weeks, INSEAD, Fontainebleau, France.

Xerox New Enterprises.
Case 802–071–1. No teaching note.
Written by A. Alyse under the direction of J. Altman, Arthur M. Blank Centre for Entrepreneurship, Babson College, USA.

Body Shop: Social Responsibility or Sustained Greenwashing
Case 707-006-1. Teaching note: 707-006-8.
Written by R. Meenakshisundaram, D. Purkayastha and R. Fernando, ICFAI Centre for Management research.

BBC-Microsoft Tie-up: Strategy for the Next generation Digital Presentation
Case 307-035-1. Teaching note: 307-035-8.
Written by B.A. Rao, I.B. Saravanan and S. Bhaskaran, Institute of Financial Analysts of India Business School, Bangalore.

Chapters 10–12: Strategy
EasyJet: The Web's Favourite Airline.
Case IMD-3-0873. Video: 300–036–3. Teaching note: IMD-3-0873TN.
Written by N. Kumar and B. Rogers, IMD, Lausanne, Switzerland.

Fight over the Internet: The Virtual Battle Between Amazon.com (USA) and Bol.de (Germany).
Case 399–113–1. Teaching note: 399–113–8.
Written by T. Jelassi, Euro-Arab Management School, Granada and A. Enders, Leipzig Graduate School of Management, Germany.

Lego (A).
Case 302–067–1. No teaching note.

Lego (B).
Case 302–068–1. No teaching note.
Written by J. Birkinshaw and L. Birkinshaw, London Business School, London, England.

Method
Case UVA-ENT-0099. This is available as a free case from www.ecch.com/freecase. Teaching note: UVA-ENT-0099TN.
Written by A. Larsen, Virginia Darden School Foundation, Charlottesville, VA, USA.

Virgin in 2006: Managing Brand extensions
Case 506-228-1. Teaching note: 506-228-8.
Written by K. Mukerjee and M. Verma, ICFAI Business School, Bangalore.

Chapters 13–15: Innovation and new product development
Xerox Building a Corporate Focus on Knowledge.
Case 600–015–1. Teaching note: 600–015–8.
Written by S. Dutta and L. Van Wassenhove, INSEAD, Fontainebleau, France.

Domino Printing Sciences (A).
Case 602–031–1. Video: 602–031–3. Teaching note: 602–031–8.

Domino Printing Sciences (B).
Case 602–032–1. Video: 602–031–3. Teaching note: 602–031–8.
Written by K. Goffin, D. Walker and M. Sweeney, Cranfield School of Management, Cranfield, England.

Cirque du Soleil: Attaining 'Extreme Creativity'
Case 407-032-1. No teaching note.
Written by M.F. Kets de Vries, INSEAD.

Cases can be obtained from the European Case Clearing House, England and USA.

North America:	tel: +1 781 239 5884 Fax: +1 781 239 5885
	e-mail: ECCHBabson@aol.com.
Rest of the world:	tel: +44 (0) 1234 750903 Fax: +44 (0)1234 751125
	email: ECCH@cranfield.ac.uk
	web site: www.ecch.cranfield.ac.uk

Selected further reading

Change management
Kanter, R. M. (1983) *The Change Masters*, New York: Simon & Schuster.
Kotter, J. P. (1996) *Leading Change*, Boston: Harvard Business School Press.
Pasmore, W. (1994), *Creating Strategic Change, Designing the Flexible High-Performing Organisation*, New York: John Wiley & Sons.
Yukl, G. (2002) *Leadership in Organisations*, Upper Saddle River, NJ: Prentice Hall Inc.

Corporate entrepreneurship
Morris, M. H., Kuratko, D. F. and Covin, J. G. (2007) *Corporate Entrepreneurship and Innovation*, 2nd edn, Mason, OH: South-Western College.
Sathe, V. (2003) *Corporate Entrepreneurship: Top Managers and New Business Creation*, Cambridge: Cambridge University Press.

Culture

Guirdham, M. (1999) *Communicating across Cultures*, Basingstoke: Macmillan – now Palgrave Macmillan.

Schneider, S. C. and Barsoux, J. L. (1997) *Managing across Cultures*, Hemel Hempstead: Prentice Hall.

Entrepreneurship

Birley, S. and Muzyaka, D. (eds) (2000) *Mastering Entrepreneurship: Your Single Source Guide to Becoming a Master of Entrepreneurship*, Harlow: Pearson Professional Education.

Bolton, B. and Thompson, J. (2000) *Entrepreneurs: Talent, Temperament, Techniques*, Oxford: Butterworth-Heinemann.

Bridge, S., O'Neill, K. and Cromie, S. (2003) *Understanding Enterprise, Entrepreneurship and Small Business*, Basingstoke: Palgrave Macmillan.

Burns, P. (2007) *Entrepreneurship and Small Business*, 2nd edn, Basingstoke: Palgrave Macmillan.

Bygrave, W.D. and Zacharakis, A. (eds) (2003) *The Portable MBA in Entrepreneurship*, 3rd edn, New York: John Wiley.

Deakins, D. and Freel, M. (2006) *Entrepreneurship and Small Firms*, 4th edn., London: McGraw Hill.

Kirby, D. (2003) *Entrepreneurship*, Maidenhead: McGraw-Hill.

Kuratko, D. F. and Hodgetts, R. M. (2001) *Entrepreneurship: An International Perspective*, Orlando: Harcourt College Publishers.

McGrath, R.G. and MacMillan, I. (2000) *The Entrepreneurial Mindset*, Boston, Mass: Harvard University Press.

Timmons, J.A. and Spinelli, S. (2003) *New Venture Creation: Entrepreneurship for the 21st Century*, 6th edn, Singapore: Irwin/McGraw Hill.

Knowledge management

Bukh, P.N., Christensen, K.S. and Mouritsen, J. (2005) *Knowledge Management and Intellectual Capital: Establishing a Field of Practice*, Basingstoke: Palgrave Macmillan.

Nonaka, I. and Takeuchi, H. (1995) *The Knowledge Creating Company*, Oxford: Oxford University Press.

Entrepreneurial marketing

Chaston, I. (2000) *Entrepreneurial Marketing: Competing by Challenging Convention*, Basingstoke: Palgrave – now Palgrave Macmillan.

Innovation

Drucker, P. F. (1985) *Innovation and Entrepreneurship: Practice and Principles*, London: Heinemann.

Peter, T. (1997) *The Circle of Innovation*, New York: Alfred A. Knopf.

Tidd, J., Bassant, J. and Pavitt, K. (2001) *Managing Innovation: Integrating Technological, Market and Organisational Change*, New York: John Wiley & Sons.

Intrapreneurship

Kanter, R.M. (1984) *The Change Masters: Corporate Entrepreneurs at Work*, London: Unwin.

Pinchot III, G. (1985) *Intrapreneuring: Why You Don't Have to Leave the Company to Become an Entrepreneur*, New York: Harper Row.

Learning organisation

Argyris, C. and Schon, D. (1996) *Organisational Learning II*, Reading, Mass.: Addison-Wesley.

Senge, P. (1990) *The Fifth Discipline: The Art and Science of the Learning Organisation*, New York: Currency Doubleday.

Michael Dell

Dell, M. (1999) *Direct from Dell: Strategies that Revolutionized an Industry*, New York: Harper Business.

Organisational form
Aldrich, H. (1999) *Organisations Evolving*, London: Sage Publications.
Pettigrew, A.M. and Fenton, E.M. (eds) (2000) *The Innovating Organization*, London: Sage.

Richard Branson
Branson, R. (1998) *Losing my Virginity*, London: Virgin.
Bower, T. (2001) *Branson*, London: Fourth Estate.

Strategy
Hitt, M.A., Ireland, R.D., Camp, S.M. and Sextion, D.L. (2002) *Strategic Entrepreneurship: Creating a New Mindset*, Oxford: Blackwell.
Johnson, G., Scholes, K. and Whittington, R. (2006) *Exploring Corporate Strategy*, 7th edn, Harlow: Financial Times/Prentice Hall.
Kay, J. (1998) *Foundations of Corporate Success*, Oxford: Oxford University Press.
Lynch, R. (2006) *Corporate Strategy*, 3rd edn, Harlow: Financial Times/Prentice Hall.
Mintzberg, H. (1994) *The Rise and Fall of Strategic Planning*, New York: The Free Press.
Mintzberg, H., Ahlstrand, B. and Lampel, J. (1998) *Strategy Safari*, New York: The Free Press.
Wickham, P.A. (2001) *Strategic Entrepreneurship: A Decision-Making Approach to New Venture Creation and Management*, Harlow: Pearson Education.

Selected journals

There is no single journal dedicated to the topic of corporate entrepreneurship. Articles on entrepreneurship in general can appear in most business and management journals, particularly in the subject areas of strategy and human resources. The easiest way to find academic articles on a topic related to small firms is to use a web-based search engine. Your library will advise you on the most appropriate one to use.

However, entrepreneurship and small business is an academic topic in its own right and, of course, many of the issues facing small firms are interdisciplinary in nature – a feature of corporate entrepreneurship. There are a number of journals that are specifically concerned with entrepreneurship and small business. Here are some of them:

Academy of Entrepreneurship Journal
Enterprise and Innovation Management Studies
Entrepreneurial Executive
Entrepreneurship and Regional Development
Entrepreneurship, Theory and Practice
International Journal of Entrepreneurial Behaviour and Research
International Journal of Entrepreneurship and Innovation
International Journal of Entrepreneurship and Small Business
International Journal of Management and Enterprise Development
International Small Business Journal
Journal of Business and Entrepreneurship
Journal of Business Venturing
Journal of Entrepreneurship
Journal of Research in Marketing and Entrepreneurship
Journal of Small Business and Enterprise Development
Journal of Small Business Management
Journal of Small Business Strategies

Selected journal articles

If you are only going to read a few of the referenced journal articles in this book, here are 25 that I think are the most interesting.

Birkinshaw, J. M. (2003) 'The Paradox of Corporate Entrepreneurship', *Strategy and Business*, 30, Spring.

Burgelman, R. A. (1983) 'A Process Model of Internal Corporate Venturing in the Diversified Major Firm', *Administrative Science Quarterly*, 28.

Christensen, K. S. (2004) 'A Classification of the Corporate Entrepreneurship Umbrella: Labels and Perspectives', *International Journal of Management and Enterprise Development*, 1(4).

Christensen, K.S. and Bang, H.K. (2003) 'Knowledge Management in a Project-orientated Organization: Three Perspectives', *Journal of Knowledge Management*, 7(3).

Covin, D. and Slevin, J. (1990) 'Judging Entrepreneurial Style and Organisational Structure: How to Get Your Act Together', *Sloan Management Review*, 31 (Winter).

Galbraith, J. (1982) 'Designing the Innovating Organisation', *Organisational Dynamics*, Winter.

Garud, R. and Van de Ven, A. (1992) 'An Empirical Evaluation of the Internal Corporate Venturing Process', *Strategic Management Journal*, 13 (special issue).

Greiner, L. (1972) 'Revolution and Evolution as Organisations Grow', *Harvard Business Review*, 50 (July/August).

Guth, W. D. and Ginsberg, A. (1990) 'Corporate Entrepreneurship', *Strategic Management Journal* (Special Issue) 11.

Hamel, G. (1999) 'Bringing Silicon Valley Inside', *Harvard Business Review*, September.

Kanter, R. M. (1982) 'The Middle Manager as Innovator', *Harvard Business Review*, July.

Kim, D. H. (1993) 'The Link between Individual and Organizational Learning', *Sloan Management Review*, Fall.

Klein, A. R. (1990) 'Organisational Barriers to Creativity . . . and How to Knock them Down', *Journal of Consumer Marketing*, 7 (1).

Mintzberg, H. (1976) 'Planning on the Left Side and Managing on the Right', *Harvard Business Review*, 54, July/August.

Mintzberg, H. (1978) 'Patterns in Strategy Formation', *Management Science*.

Morris, M. H., Davies D. L. and Allen, J. W. (1994) 'Fostering Corporate Entrepreneurship: Cross Cultural Comparisons of the Importance of individualism versus Collectivism', *Journal of International Business Studies*, 25(1).

Morris, M. H. and Sexton, D. L. (1996) 'The Concept of Entrepreneurial Intensity', *Journal of Business Research*, 36(1).

Morse, C. W. (1986) 'The Delusion of Intrapreneurship', *Long Range Planning*, 19(2).

Prahalad, C. K. and Hamel, G. (1990) 'The Core Competence of the Corporation', *Harvard Business Review*, 68(3), May/June.

Reich, R. (1987) 'Entrepreneurship Reconsidered: The Team As Hero', *Harvard Business Review*, 65(3), May/June.

Ross, J. E. and Unwella, D. (1986) 'Who is an Intrapreneur?', *Personnel*, 63(12).

Schein, E. H. (1990) 'Organisational Culture', *American Psychologist*, February.

Schein, E. H. (1994) 'Organisational and Managerial Culture as a Facilitator or Inhibitor of Organisational Learning', *MIT Organisational Learning Network Working Paper 10.004*, May.

Senge, P. (1992) 'Mental Models', *Planning Review*, March/April.

Tushman, M. L. and O'Reilly, C. A. (1996) 'Ambidextrous Organizations: Managing Evolutionary and Revolutionary Change', *California Management Review*, 38(4).

Zahra, S. A., Jennings, D. F. and Kuratko, D. F. (1999) 'The Antecedents and Consequences of Firm Level Entrepreneurship: The State of the Field', *Entrepreneurship: Theory and Practice*, 24.

Zahra, S. A. (1991) 'Predictors and Financial Outcomes of Corporate Entrepreneurship: An Exploratory Study', *Journal of Business Venturing*, 6(4), July.

Selected websites

As is the case with journals, there is no single website dedicated to the topic of corporate entrepreneurship. Do a *Google* search on 'entrepreneurship' and you will get over 3 million results. Do one on 'corporate entrepreneurship' and you will get almost 1 million results. Investigating so many sites is virtually impossible. Probably the best place to find resources of any kind related to entrepreneurship or small business is:

The Small Business Portal　　　　　　　　　www.smallbusinessportal.co.uk
This site provides information on academics, books, centres, conferences, government agencies, mega-sites, publications, reviews and has a useful research tools section.

Below are some other sites you might find of interest:

Academy of Management　　　　　　　　　　　www.aomtim.org

Advanced Institute of Management Research　　　www.aimresearch.org

Babson College Centre for Entrepreneurship　　　www3.babson.edu/eship/
This site provides papers and abstracts and details of various initiatives.

British Library Business & IP Centre　　　　　　www.bl.uk/bipc
The website of the British Library provides the most comprehensive business information resource in the UK. Most resources can only be accessed *by personal visit.*

Center for Entrepreneurial Leadership Clearinghouse
on Entrepreneurship Education　　　　　　　　www.celcee.edu
This US Department of Education site has been set up to disseminate information not distributed through normal sources.

Enterweb　　　　　　　　　　　　　　　　　www.enterweb.org
This site provides a wide range of links to other sites around the world.

Imperial College Innovation Studies Centre　　www3.imperial.ac.uk/innovationstudies

Information Centre for Entrepreneurship　　　www.bibl.hj.se/ice/
This site provides a collection of printed material from periodicals to working papers and describes itself as providing 'one of the world's largest collections in the fields of entrepreneurship, innovations and small and medium-sized enterprises'.

Institute for International Economics　　　　　www.iie.com
This website contains numerous resources and links *to trade issues.*

International Association for the Management of Technology (IAMOT)　　www.iamot.org

McMaster University　　　　　　　　　mint.mcmaster.ca/mint/mint.htm
McMaster run an excellent newsletter on innovation.

For anything to do with creativity:　www.creax.com/resources/creax_net.html

WARNING
Information downloaded from websites is easily detected by specialist plagiarism software used by most universities. If you use any information from websites for your coursework assignments ensure that all direct quotes – text copied from the site – are placed in inverted commas and full attribution is given. You may need to seek advice from your tutor on how much material can be used in this way. Failure to follow this advice may lead to your coursework being given a 'fail' mark.

Subject Index

3M   123, 159, 168, 183, 245, 329, 332
7UP   265

A
ABB   138
ABC analysis   243–4
achievement   25–6, 89
acquisitions   246–7, 264–6
Alcoa   138
Ampex   286
analogy   324
Ansoff matrix   *see* product/market matrix
antecedent influences   23, 34–5
AOL Time Warner   130
Apple   168, 168
architecture   15–16, 59, 67–9, 73–5, 204,
    360–1
AT&T   138, 265, 266
attribute analysis   324–5

B
Barclays Bank   222
barriers to
   change   179
   corporate entrepreneurship   175–7
   entry/exit   258
BBC   152
Belbin, Meredith   100–1
Bell Labs   331
benchmarking   206
Benetton   138
Biro   291
BMW   222
Body Shop   93, 130, 206, 222, 259, 262, 268,
    269
Boston Consulting Group   237
Boston matrix   237, 255, 304
   see also product portfolio
BP/British Petroleum   138, 184, 246
brainstorming   322–4, 332
brainwriting   324
brand/branding   222, 345
Branson   24, 222, 255

bring the market inside   13
BT   138, 223

C
Cadbury   114, 259, 265, 269
cash cow   141, 236–7, 238, 239, 240, 243,
    245
cash flow   243
change   5–6, 65, 70, 75, 88–9, 105, 130,
    141–2,
   agent   180
   cube   182
   management   178–182
Cisco   137, 167
Coca Cola   138
cognitive theory   34–5
cognitive processes   112, 114
communication   58, 87, 93, 139
competencies   205, 253, 264, 290–1
competitive advantage   68, 74, 204, 205, 253,
    272, 292
conflict   88–9, 98–9, 104
contingency theory   96
control   58, 87, 113, 183–6
Co-op Bank   222, 269
core competencies   *see* competencies
corporate
   entrepreneurship (definition)   12–14
   social responsibility (CSR)   268–70, 299
   venturing   12–13, 167–7
Courtauld   291
Coutts Bank   222
creative tension   88, 92, 98, 203
creativity   127, 288–9, 316–37
   blocks   322, 331–2
   national   334–7
   organizational   331–3
   resources   341
   test   340
credibility   47
cultural web   120, 126, 128
culture   59, 75, 87–9, 111–32, 176, 208, 221
   Hostede's dimensions   115–19

customer loyalty ladder   223
cycling   188–9

D
Daimler   291
DangDang   152, 292
Daussault   291
decentralization   59, 144
deconstruction   5, 6, 137, 138
decision making   43–4, 57
delegation   58, 59, 105, 139
Dell   4, 24, 74, 91, 138, 167, 206, 284, 292
departmentalization   139
differentiation   221–3, 253, 307
Direct Line   217, 222, 299, 347
diversification   262–3, 265, 291
dominant logic   65
Dom Perignon   222
double loop learning   71
Dupont   167, 246
Dr Pepper   265
Durant   291
Dyson   206, 296, 317, 329

E
early adopters   233, 240
Eastman   291
easyJet   91
economies of scale   206, 212–13, 253, 256
economies of small scale   213, 215
education   34, 47
emergent strategy   45, 202
employment   4, 6, 17
empower/empowerment   70, 92, 125, 127
entrepreneurs   7–10
entrepreneurial
   architecture   see architecture
   character   see personal character traits
   intensity   65–7, 75
   grid   66
   management   14–16
   marketing   346–8
   orientation audit   39
   personality   see personality traits
   school of strategy   202
   spider's web   see spider's web
   transformation   14
environment   74, 75–6, 141–2
environment, audit   269, 362
evaluation (of ideas)   202, 320
experience curve   212
exporting   258–9

F
failure   124
financial analysis   207, 231
financial gearing/leverage   see gearing
fixed costs   6, 43
focus   211, 213, 216, 220–1, 223, 253
Ford   262, 291
Fox TV   137
franchise/franchisee   259
freedom   see slack
futures thinking   209–10, 324

G
gap analysis   325
GDP   4, 17, 336
General Electric   137, 138, 167, 246
General Enterprise Tendancy (GET) test   39
General Electric   246
generic marketing strategies   211–17, 239, 253, 344
Grand Metropolitan   138
growth   253, 272–3
growth cycles   286–7
growth models   52–7, 208
growth strategies   see strategies for growth

H
hierarchical structures   139–41
Honda   138

I
IBM   4, 115, 120, 130, 152, 167, 269, 291
independence   26
in-group   70
innovation   12, 15, 75, 137, 282–308
   continuous v discrete   293–4, 304
   definition   287–8
   discontinuous   298–9
   marketing   344–8
   product   349–55
   size   296–8
innovative character   29–30
Innovative Potential Indicator   311
Intel   152, 167, 168
internal locus of control   26
intrapreneurship   13, 159–62
invention   282–6

J
Jaguar   222
jobs   4–5
John Lewis   111, 269

Johnson and Johnson 138, 167
joint ventures 292, 295
JVC 286

K
Kellogg 291
knowledge 15–16, 59, 67–9
    firm 147, 148–9
    management 179, 300
    networks 300–1
    transfer 148, 168
KongZhong 152
Kodak 246
Kyocera 167

L
laggards 235, 337
Lastminute 292
leaders/leadership 70, 74–5, 85–104
leadership
    skills 103–4
    style 75, 95–9, 113, 127–8, 187–9
learning 15, 301
learning organization 69–73, 87, 92, 125,
    127, 148, 152, 202, 301
Level 3 Communication 66
life cycle 75, 76, 141, 164, 206, 208, 233–6,
    239–47, 284, 331, 351
Lonrho 263

M
machine bureaucracy 141
management 86
    buy-ins/buy-outs 166
    team see team building/working
    style see leadership style
market
    development 254, 256–9, 290
    penetration 254–5, 290, 293
    research 207
marketing strategy see strategy
matrix structures 140–1
M&S 269, 299
McDonald's 206, 222, 235, 236, 256
mental models 72
Mercedes Benz 222, 261, 263, 292
mergers see acquisitions
middle and late majority 233
mission 57, 90–3
Monsanto 167, 168
motivational theory 122, 127–8

N
NCR 265, 266
networks/networking 47–8, 146–8, 300–1
niche markets 216, 221, 239, 240, 331
non-metric mapping 325
norms 112–4, 121
Nucor Steel 66, 75

O
open-book management 184
opportunistic 28–9
opportunity 7–10, 15, 59
    sources 326–8
organic structure 142–4
organization structure 74, 113, 130, 162, 176,
    187–9, 221, 304, 307, 354–5

P, Q
penetration see market penetration
Pepsi 259
perceptual mapping 325
personal construct theory 326
personal character traits 23–36
Polaroid 329
Porter's Five Forces 206, 256–8, 266
portfolio
    analysis 206
    of products 164, 236–9, 244–5, 253, 304
positioning school of strategy 202, 204
proactive 31–2
process school of strategy 202, 204
Proctor & Gamble 66, 75, 246, 300
product
    development 261, 291
    expansion 239, 256, 262
    extension 240, 261, 262
    innovation see innovation, product
    modification 240
    life cycle see life cycle
    portfolio see portfolio
product/market matrix 253–4, 290, 291,
    305

R
R&D department 164, 303
ratio analysis see financial analysis
relationships 15, 47–8, 50, 57, 59, 67–8, 98,
    102, 105, 127, 147
relationship marketing 48, 344–5
repertory grid 326
resource allocation 13

risk   7–10, 15, 43, 127, 162, 213, 262–6, 350
  innovation   282, 284, 290–5
  live with   27–8
  management   189–91
  classification   189–90
  mitigation   240, 292
Rolls Royce   206
Royal Bank of Scotland   45
Royal Mail Group   320

S
scenario planning   210, 324
self-confidence   30–1
self-efficacy   35
self motivation   32–3
shamrock organization   138
Shell   122, 222
Siemens   291
Singer   291
size   74, 130, 137–9
skunkworks   307, 330
slack   185, 331, 332
SLEPT analysis   206, 209–10, 266, 328
small firms, contribution to the economy   4–5
social trends   6
Sony   216, 286
SouFun   152
span of control   137, 139
spider's web   50–1, 68, 139
spin-offs   137, 143, 165–7
strategic
  analysis   203, 204–8
  alliance   151–2, 292, 295, 300–1
  business unit (SBU)   140, 147
  fit   208
  implementation   203–4
  intent   45, 208
  options   44, 204
  planning   203–4
  process   202–3
  partnership   148, 356
  vision   see vision
strategizing   15, 57, 125, 202
strategy   94, 176, 220–1, 235, 238, 246,
    253–73, 303, 306
  formulation/development   43, 44–6, 57,
    203–4, 270, 346–8; see also emergent
    strategy
  misfit   208–9
structure   see organization structure
Sun Microsystems   152
survival   5

sustainable competitive advantage   see
    competitive advantage
Swatch   292
switch costs   256–8
SWOT analysis   203, 204–7
synergy   167, 263, 266

T
tacit knowledge   149, 301, 316
tactics   94
task   96–7, 141–2
team building/working   89, 100–3, 104, 144,
    159–60, 180
technology   6
test marketing   351
Thomas-Kilman conflict modes   98–9
thinking, creative/lateral, logical/vertical
Timberland   262, 269
transactional marketing   344, 345
trust   102, 105, 127, 147

U
uncertainty   see risk
Unilever   122
unitarism   70

V
value chain   206
value-driven marketing   345–6
value drivers   217–9
values   70, 91, 93–5, 111–14
venture teams   163–4, 355
    see also team working
venture division   164
vision   33–4, 45, 58, 59, 87–9, 90–3, 94, 162,
    202, 203, 208, 209, 307, 345
visionary leadership   89, 105
Virgin   222, 246, 255, 261
virtual structure   148

W
walk-the-talk   88, 92, 95, 127, 137
wealth   4
Wendy's   66, 75
wheel of learning   71–2
WH Smith   138
why? why? technique/diagram   325, 329
Wilkin & Sons   269
world wide web   321

X, Y, Z
Xerox   91, 138, 167, 168

Author Index

3i 221

A

Abdesselam, Bonnet and Le Pape 35
Abell 253
Acs and Aaudretsch 297
Adair 98
Adizes 86
Aldrich and Martinez 24
Anderson and Weitz 148
Andersson 8
Andersson, Gabrielsson and Wictor 24
Ansoff 253, 264
Antoncic and Hisrich 160, 162

B

Bagozzi 207
Barret and Storey 307
Bartlett and Ghoshal 90
Baty 24
Belbin 100, 101, 107
Bell, Murray and Madden 24
Bennis and Nanus 15, 93
Bergelman 165
Berkhout and Green 299
Bessant 284
Bettis and Prahalad 65
Bhidé 137
Birch 4
Birkinshaw 13, 184, 185, 186, 187
Birley 221
Birn 207
Blake and Mouton 96
Blanchflower and Meyer 24
Blau 140
Blank 86
Bolton and Thompson 288, 330
Booz, Allen and Hamilton 349
Boston Consulting Group 221
Bowman and Faulkner 112, 264, 290
Brockhaus and Horwitz 24

Brush 24
Bergelman 13
Burke and Logsdon 268, 270
Burns, P. 34, 55, 142, 207, 215, 221, 292,
Burns, P. and Whitehouse 43, 97, 98
Burns, T. and Stalker 140
Busenitz and Barney 30
Buttner and More 24
Buzzell, Heany and Schoeffer 221

C

Caird 24
Cannon 291
Cantillon 9
Case 184
Carter and Cachon 34
Chandler 140
Chaston 346, 347
Chell 100
Chell, Haworth and Brearley 24
Chen, Greene and Crick 35
Chesbrough 13, 300
Chisnall 207
Christensen 13, 162, 297, 299
Christopher, Payne and Ballantyne 344
Churchill and Lewis 54
Clemmer 179
Cohen and Bradford 159
Cooper, A. 73
Cooper, R. 352
Cornwall and Perlman 111, 123
Covin and Slevin 66, 187, 188
Cuba, Decenzo and Anish 24

D

David 164
Davis, Morris and Allen 66
Deakins 24
Deakins and Freel 297
de Bono 24, 317, 318
De Colle and Gonella 270
de Geus 5, 210

Deans, Zeisel and Kroeger   246
Dell   8
Drucker   9, 13, 161, 326, 330
Dubini and Aldrich   147
Dunkelberg, Cooper, Woo and Dennis   221
du Toit   51
Dwyer, Scurr and Oh   152

E
Ely and Hess   9
Emery and Trist   140
Environics International   268, 270
Epstein and Roy   270
Evans and Leighton   34

F
Fenton and Pettigrew   147
Ferreira   75
Florida   334, 335
Florida and Tinagli   336, 337
Foster and Kaplan   13, 183, 203, 211, 246

G
Galbraith   13, 140, 144
Galloway   160
Gardner   92
Garud and Van de Ven   83
Garvin   166
Ghoshal and Bartlett   14, 149
Gladwell   337
Goldhar and Lei   148
Grant   149, 316
Greiner   52, 53, 57, 62, 139, 144
Guiltinan and Paul   242
Guirdham   111
Guth and Ginsberg   12

H
Haige and Aiken   140
Hall   120
Hamel   13, 152, 179
Hamel and Prahalad   208, 209, 210, 220, 293
Handy   138, 148
Harper   35
Harrison and Taylor   5, 221
Hayek   9
Hirsch and Bush   24
Hisrich   162
Hisrich and Peters   10
Hisrichberg   333
Hofstede   111, 115, 116, 117, 118–19, 120,
    121, 122, 123, 124, 127, 128, 133

Hofstede and Bond   117
Hofstede, Neuijen, Ohayv and Sanders   123
Hornsby, Kuratko and Zahra   162
Hornsby, Naffziger, Kuratko and
    Montagno   162

I
Ito   166

J
Jackson and Sculer   179
Jankowicz   326
Johnson   148
Johnson and Scholes   208, 263

K
Kakabadse   178
Kanter   13, 14, 24, 159, 282, 308
Karthik   152
Kay   44, 67, 68, 73, 202, 205, 272
Kets de Vries   26, 51
Kim   71,
Kirby   103, 317
Kirton   285
Kirzner   9, 24
Klein   331
Knight   9
Konstadt   149
Kuratko, Montagno and Hornsby   162

L
Lakhani   335
Lambin   344, 352
Lawrence and Lorsch   140
Leonard and Swap   333
Leonard-Barton   70
Lessem   103, 104
Lewis   148
Lindbolm   45
Lorange and Roos   148

M
MacMillan   167
Macrae   221
Majaro   317, 331
Maletz and Nohria   164
Markoczy   72
Mathewson   45
McCarthy and Leavey   47
McClelland   24
McDougall, Shane and Oviatt   148

McGregor 128
McNulty 210
McQuarrie 207
Mellor 282, 288
Menger 9
Miller, A. 72
Miller, D. 143
Miller, D. and Friesen 66
Miner 73
Mintzberg 16, 45, 181, 182, 202, 284, 318
Morden 122, 128
Morris 176
Morris and Allen 66
Morris and Kuratko 65, 66, 115, 123, 142, 143, 183, 283, 293, 354
Morris and Sexton 66
Morris, Davies and Allen 120, 121
Morse 12

N
Nahapiet and Ghoshal 149
Naisbitt 4, 137
Nanus 90
Nohria 150
Nohria and Joyce 221
Nonaka 95

O
Ohmae 148
Ouchi 127
Oviatt and McDougall 148

P
Page 316, 355
Payne 344
Parkhe 151, 152
Pavitt, Robinson and Townsend 297
Pedler, Burgoyne and Boydell 70
Penrose 9
Perrow 140
Peters 123
Peters and Waterman 14, 66, 253
Pettigrew 138, 150
Pettigrew and Fenton 138, 147
Piercy 345
Pinchot 13, 24, 159, 160, 161, 163
Porras 13
Porter 211, 217, 218, 256, 263, 265, 273, 282
Prahalad and Hamel 205
Pugh and Hickson 140
Pugh, Hickson and Hinings 140

Q
Quinn 204, 307

R
Ray and Hutchinson 98, 221
Reich 163
Rogers 233
Rosa, Hamilton, Carter and Burns, H. 24
Ross 160
Ross and Unwalla 159
Roth and Nigh 149
Rothwell 297
Rowley 301
Rumelt 263

S
Sathe 162
Say 7, 9
Schein 111, 112, 125
Schein, Mueller, Lituchy and Liu 24
Schmidt 299
Schumpeter 9, 24, 282, 286
Schwartz 24, 211
Senge 69, 70, 73, 87, 92
Shapero 9, 24
Shaver and Scott 24
Siegel, R, Siegel, F. and Macmillan 221
Sinetar 332
Sloane 332
Smith 270
Solem and Steiner 221
Stanworth, J., Blythe, Granger and Sanworth, C. 35
Stevenson 253
Stewart 149
Stinchcombe 140
Stopford and Baden-Fuller 159
Storey 34, 35
Storey and Sykes 24
Storey, Keasey, Watson and Wynarczyk 5
Storey, Watson and Wynarczyk 221
Stormer, Kline and Goldberg 39
Symon 72

T
Takeuchi and Nonaka 352
Teece 148
Teece, Pisano and Schuen 70
Tellis, Stremersch and Yin 235
Timmons 5, 70, 87, 123
Thornhill and Amit 144
Tidd, Bessant and Pavitt 299, 300, 301, 306

Torrington   127
Treacy and Wiersema   206, 212, 220
Tull and Hawkins   207
Tushman and O'Reilly   14

U
Utterback and Acee   299

V
Van de Ven   306
Van Grundy   288
Verschoor   269
Vesper   12
Von Oech   320, 322
Vossen   297
Vyakarnham and Leppard   329

W, X
Wack   210
Weber   140

Webster   48, 344
Wernerfelt and Montgomery   263
Whittington, Mayer and Curto   148
Wickham   91
Wilpert   72
Wilson   152
Woodward   140
Wood   269
Wynarczyk, Watson, Storey, Short and
      Keasey   221

Y
Yelle   221
Yukl   180

Z
Zahra   12
Zahra, Jennings and Kuratko   12
Zentner   210